Routledge Revivals

The Medieval Idea of Law

Upon its original publication in 1946, this work represented a new approach to medieval studies, offering indispensable analysis to the historian of legal, political and social ideas. Research into the original sources leads the author through unexplored realms of medieval thought. By contrasting contemporary opinions with those of his central figure, Lucas de Penna, he comprehensively presents the medieval idea of law – then regarded as the concrete manifestation of abstract justice. The intensity of medieval academic life is revealed in the heated controversies, whilst medieval criminology foreshadows modern developments. A significant discovery is the astonishingly great reliance which Continental scholars placed upon English thought. A challenge to certain current misconceptions, this book shows the resourcefulness of medieval thinking and the extent to which modern ideas were foreshadowed in the fourteenth century, a time when the ideas of law and liberty were identical.

THE MEDIEVAL IDEA OF LAW

COMMENTARIA D.

LVCÆ DE PENNA

IVRISCONS CLARISSIMI

DOCTORIS GALLI SVMMI

VTRIVSQVE IVRIS APICES,

IN TRES POSTERIORES

LIB. CODICIS IVSTINIANI.

In quibus amplissimè tractatur de Magistratibus Francorum, & quantùm illi à publicis dignitatibus veteris Romæ differant.

Cum locupletissima rerum quarumcumque insignium suppellectile ac Indice, ordine suo longè melius quàm anteà collocata & disposita & doctissimis aliquot annotationibus illustrata.

Omnia ex antiquissimis exemplaribus maiore ex parte aucta.

LVGDVNI,

EX OFFICINA IVNTARVM,

M. D. XCVII.

Cum priuilegiis summi Pontificis, & Christianiss. Galliarum Regis.

THE TITLE PAGE OF LUCAS'S COMMENTARIES; EDITION LYONS, 1597. TRINITY COLLEGE, CAMBRIDGE

THE MEDIEVAL IDEA OF LAW

AS REPRESENTED BY LUCAS DE PENNA

A STUDY IN FOURTEENTH-CENTURY LEGAL SCHOLARSHIP

by

WALTER ULLMANN

J.U.D.

with an Introduction by

HAROLD DEXTER HAZELTINE

LL.D., LITT.D., F.B.A.

METHUEN & CO. LTD. LONDON

36 Essex Street, Strand, W.C.2

First published in 1946

BOOK PRODUCTION WAR ECONOMY STANDARD

THIS BOOK IS PRODUCED IN COMPLETE CONFORMITY WITH THE AUTHORIZED ECONOMY STANDARDS

PRINTED IN GREAT BRITAIN

CARISSIMAE UXORI SUAE

ACKNOWLEDGEMENTS

IT is a very pleasant duty to express my cordial thanks to Mr. H. M. Adams, the Librarian of Trinity College, Cambridge. The bulk of my material was gathered in Wren's Library, in which, I fear, I often over-taxed the endurance and kindness of the Librarian and his staff. To him and to Professor Z. N. Brooke, F.B.A., former Librarian of Gonville and Caius College, my thanks are due for their permission to reproduce the two facsimiles of Lucas's commentaries. I must, furthermore, express my gratitude to Professor P. W. Duff, of Trinity College, for his kindness in reading some portions of the MS. and for his very helpful suggestions and constructive criticisms. Nor must I omit to thank Professor W. W. Buckland, F.B.A., for much generous counsel during the preparation of the book.

I have to thank the Editors and publishers of the *Law Quarterly Review*, *Juridical Review*, *English Historical Review*, and *Catholic Historical Review*, for their kind permission to reproduce some of the material I had previously published in these periodicals.

I desire to express my gratitude to the publishers for their great understanding and for the spirit in which they have undertaken the production of a work of this kind under very adverse circumstances.

Words can never adequately express my debt to her, to whom this book is dedicated.

W. U.

AUTHOR'S PREFACE

LAW is that expression of civilization which most closely approaches perfection. Nowhere is the spirit of an age better mirrored than in the theory of law. The spirit of the Middle Ages as revealed in theological, political, and social writings has frequently been made the subject of modern inquiries. Yet the medieval theory of law, which is one of the most significant symptoms of medieval civilization, has received but scanty consideration. This book, therefore, attempts to reconstruct the theory of law as it took shape in the mind of one of the most impressive and striking figures of medieval scholarship, whose work has, to all intents and purposes, been forgotten for several centuries. During the fourteenth and fifteenth centuries medieval legal science was in its heyday in the Italian universities, and for at least three centuries was destined to mould the outlook of generations of jurists, and often the law itself. The truly amazing neglect of medieval legal scholarship is indeed difficult to understand. Although our own science of the law was first created by the medieval Italian jurists, and although—if it were only on account of their ancestral character—the knowledge of their theories is bound to contribute to a better understanding of present-day problems, the modern scholar's neglect of his mental forefathers is singularly unjustifiable. Nevertheless, the history of the idea of law and of the evolution of legal thinking is part and parcel of the history of civilization. History of civilization is history of the human mind. The modern idea of law is essentially and substantially the offspring of the medieval idea of law.

The purpose of the present thesis is to reconstruct the main doctrines of the Neapolitan scholar, Lucas de Penna, whose fascinating personality and eminent juristic scholarship will emerge, it is hoped, in the course of the book. His was a mind which harmoniously combined law with philosophy. It is precisely this harmony which makes him so attractive and which enabled him to penetrate into the utmost profundities of the law. It is in this context that the strongly marked English influence emerges in a particularly interesting light and opens up new sidelights on the influence of medieval English philosophic thought. In more than one respect Aristotle and Cicero recede into the background in favour of John of Salisbury. The English philosopher found in the

Neapolitan doctor one of his most ardent and confident adherents, two centuries after he had written his *Policraticus*. John's biting criticisms of existing institutions were readily applied by his Neapolitan admirer to the changed and changing conditions of the mid-fourteenth century; and John's shrewd observations of the perversities, follies, and vices which made twelfth-century scholarship a mockery were eagerly snatched at by his Neapolitan alumnus: like John, he did not mince words in his fierce condemnations of the perversities, follies, and vices which had corroded legal scholarship at *his* time; from John he inherited his aversion to dialectics, in whose network he was never engulfed. It is no exaggeration to assert that, as far as the fundamental principles of social ethics go, Lucas's edifice was largely erected upon the foundations which John set forth in his *Policraticus*. More than that: in the sphere of legal scholarship Lucas's work marks the dawn of the humanistic epoch, and it may well be that it was under John's influence that the first humanistic commentary of law came to be written.

Scholarship owes a debt of gratitude to two Italian writers who have directed our attention to Lucas de Penna in recent years. In 1925 M. M. Wronowski published a lengthy essay entitled *Luca di Penna e sua opera*, giving a survey in very general terms of Lucas's doctrines, whilst the other contribution is written by Professor Francesco Calasso in the *Rivista di Storia del Diritto Italiano*, 1932; this essay is a purely methodological investigation. What has not been attempted is a thorough, systematic investigation of Lucas's theories. An investigation of this kind—which is naturally beyond the scope of the limited space of an essay—necessitates an outline of the legal and philosophic background upon which Lucas worked. In particular, the originality of his modes of legal thinking, together with the uncanny cleverness of his arguments—which resulted from his unparalleled command of the huge bodies of civil and canon law—and the nature of his incomparably rich mental equipment—which he owed to his profound study of the philosophic literature available at his time—merit an exposition for which the length of an essay must necessarily prove insufficient. Above all, the often astonishing grandiosity of his conceptions has entirely escaped notice. Many vitally important theses of Lucas de Penna, often hidden behind the curtain of unassuming phraseologies, have either not been recognized at all in their proper significance, or have been presented in a somewhat perfunctory way. To take only a few obvious instances. Lucas's truly progressive penological ideas, his conceptions of the function of the legislator and of the administrator of the law, his notion of the omnipotence of the Ruler, his social and political conceptions, particularly his ideas of civil liberty and its protection, his thesis of the relationship between secular and ecclesiastical authority in general, and of the relationship between secular and ecclesiastical judge in particular, his criterion, for the first time employed in a fruitful and consistent way, for distinguishing between the temporal and the spiritual—and many other essential theses surely deserve a profounder treatment and investigation than that which they have received so far. It is the comprehensiveness, the logical and material consistency of his doctrines which warrant an examination for which an essay cannot provide sufficient space. In view of Lucas's unusual, not to say unorthodox, argumentation and way of reasoning, which resulted in the often lengthy discussion of apparently unessential topics, it is a very difficult, if not impossible, task to present and reconstruct his theories faithfully within the limits of an essay. But apart from these deficiencies from which the two above named essays suffer, their treatment of the biographical and bibliographical material is in many points inadequate. No mention has been made of Lucas's remarkable influence on jurists of his own time. Nor apparently has it been observed that the high esteem and reputation which he enjoyed in later times spread far beyond the frontiers of his own land, and that sixteenth-century secular and canonistic scholarship held him in great esteem.

The scope of the present work is determined by the consideration that, in a wider sense, the idea of law also embraces its political manifestation; and, in view of the vast output of Lucas, the range is limited to the exposition of the fundamentals of his theory. However much his views resemble modern ideas, and however tempting it is to present his theories as modern rather than medieval, I have taken due care not to yield to this temptation. The present investigation is exclusively historical, and the modernization of medieval ideas would have amounted to a falsification and distortion of them: in all likelihood Lucas himself would have been most surprised to see his theories unrecognizably attired in a modern garb.

Two points deserve special mention. In the first place, with regard to the question of Latin quotations, I have been in a dilemma similar to that of the late C. N. S. Woolf when he wrote his *Bartolus of Sassoferrato* (1913). For several reasons the transcription of the Latin text seemed to me imperative. The comparative inaccessibility of fourteenth-century writings renders it extremely difficult to check the statements made in the course of the book. I believed that the free quotation of the original text might be partial compensation for the difficulty of obtaining access to the sources. In some places quotation of the original Latin appeared to me advisable, in order to establish my points. A mere translation would have destroyed the liveliness, the incisiveness, and the individual flavour of Lucas's statements. " What men say is not the only important thing ; often it is equally important to know, how they have said it ", is a very profound dictum of Woolf (p. xi). It is true that Lucas's Latin suffers from typical medieval corruptions, but it is suffused with an unmistakable personal note. In more than one respect his Latin and his style are that of the humanists of the sixteenth century. Whenever possible, I have transcribed the quotations in the footnotes, which thereby have become very numerous and lengthy.

This brings me to the second point. The copiousness of the footnotes is due not only to the quotations from Lucas's commentaries, but also to those from the writings of his contemporaries. For I have tried to set Lucas's ideas against the background of the scholarship of his time, so that we may be in a better position to evaluate his achievements, his deficiences, and, above all, his independent and detached mind. Our interest is evoked not so much by the man Lucas de Penna, however attractive a figure he may be, as by the ideas which the jurist and scholar Lucas de Penna propounded. For this reason I have always attempted to link up his ideas with those of preceding and contemporary scholarship. My intention was to present a rounded whole of fourteenth-century legal scholarship, Lucas de Penna being the central figure. Some of the prejudices which modernism entertains against medievalism, especially the prejudice against medieval modes of thinking, may be shattered by exposing Lucas's independence of thought. But if, upon all points of doctrine, I had tried to draw comparisons between Lucas and his contemporaries, the book would have grown to an unwieldy size. As a general rule I have therefore selected only points of major importance which, in my opinion, justified such a comparison. But in certain points of minor importance and yet of some interest I have, nevertheless, given the views of his contemporaries in the footnotes. It would be more than presumptuous, however, to claim that justice has been done to all medieval scholars, whose works, set forth in tomes covered with dust and cobwebs, contain sufficient wealth of legal and political material to make them worthy of more systematic and extensive research. This treatise marks a modest beginning and suffers from all those defects which are characteristic of a work primarily concerned with the exploration of untrodden ground.

W. U.

CONTENTS

INTRODUCTION

The Legal and Political Ideas of the Post-Glossators. By Professor H. D. Hazeltine *page* xv

CHAPTER I

INTRODUCTORY

The revival of legal studies—The Glossators—The Post-Glossators—The Post-Glossators and Roman Law—The spiritual background of their researches—Effects of philosophy on legal science—The problems thereby raised—Central thought of their theory of law—Practical achievements—The importance of Italian jurisprudence—Seats of learning—Petrarch on the Neapolitan university *page* 1

CHAPTER II

LUCAS AND HIS WORK

I. Life—Public activities—Teachers—His works—Appreciation in the southern kingdom—In northern Italy—In sixteenth-century France—In sixteenth-century Spain.

II. External characteristics of his main work—His views on legal studies within the framework of academic scholarship—His idea of the function of the academic teacher and of juristic method—His views on dialectics—On gloss and other authorities—The part which is assigned to gloss and authority in his work—Some observations of Lucas on contemporary scholarship.

III. His self-imposed task—Philosophy and Law—Auxiliary sciences—Greek influence—Roman influence—Christian writers—Schoolmen—Illustrative material *page* 7

CHAPTER III

THE FOUNDATIONS AND NATURE OF LAW

I. Justice and law—The derivation of law—The concept of virtue—The divine character of justice—Its substance—Its social implication—Its legal implications—Species of justice—Contemporary views on the idea of justice—Cynus and Baldus in particular.

II. The concept of equity—The idea of natural reason—Implications of equity—Terminology.

III. The notion of law—The idea of the reign of law—Security is the achievement of law—It protects the socially inferior—Divine law—The *jus naturale* and the *jus gentium*—Private property—Natural rights—Human law—The controversy about the legislative authority: people or Ruler?—Contemporary doctrine reviewed—Lucas's theistic standpoint—His arguments against the will of the people as a source of law—The Ruler as the sole legislative authority—The idea of a responsible legislator: individual or collective responsibility?—The binding force of law—The will of the Ruler—The *justa causa principis*—Theoretical limitations of his legislative powers: (1) Moral; (2) Social—Framing of laws—Private and public law: the distinction of no importance in his system—The exercise of rights—The motive of the individual must be the *zelus justitiae*—The 'just' and the 'good'—Purely moral claims. *page* 35

CHAPTER IV

CUSTOMARY LAW

The nature of habit—Lucas's conservative outlook—Lucas and other Post-Glossators—His theory—The binding force of customs—The people's creative part—Reasonableness—Custom and statute—General effects of customs—Scope of validity of customs—Some important customary rules. *page* 62

CHAPTER V

THE APPLICATION OF LAW

I. Positive law and problems connected with it—Special problems—The *jus commune*—Frederick II's constitution—Lucas's dilemma—The practice of the courts—The Lombard laws: *jus commune* ?—A special law only—Characterization of the Lombards—Roman law—The *jus commune* par excellence.

II. Civil and canon law—Actual conditions in the kingdom of Sicily—The universality of the Roman civil law the leading idea—The practical application of this idea—Criterion of application—(*a*) The litigants; (*b*) The cause—The problem of the spiritual cause—Matrimony in particular—Andreas de Isernia's opinion—Lucas's doctrine—Separation of secular and ecclesiastical powers—The social character of matrimony—Its divine character—The inference to be drawn from this twofold aspect—Temporal causes—Applications of the distinction between temporal and spiritual causes—(*a*) Sacred possessions of the Church; (*b*) Temporal possessions of the Church and of the clerics—Further consequences—Civic duties, taxes, and other social burdens of the Church and of the clerics—The legal basis of those duties—Lucas *versus* the canonists—Immunity of the Church? (*c*) Practical examples—Legitimation of illegitimate children in particular—Doubtful paternity of a child—Matrimonial causes as preliminary questions—Conclusion—The common doctrine reviewed—Bartolus's doctrine—Contrasted with Lucas's—Bartolus on legitimation.—The English view (Parliament of Merton, 1235).

III. Territorial scope of law—Are foreign nations subjected to Roman law?—Is the Ruler subjected to law?—The concept of necessity.

IV. Abrogation of law—The test of the secular superiority in temporal matters—A practical example—The chief arguments against the canonistic doctrine—The canonists fail to give the legal basis of their views—The principle of honourable conduct to be applied, not only to be postulated—The ecclesiastical authority has no right to interfere with legislation—Lucas advises the Church to take heed of moral issues—The general principle to be applied to conflicting laws—Natural and civil law—Transfer of property: at once a test case of the *justa causa principis* and of the legislative powers of the Ruler—The approach to full legislative sovereignty—Contemporary doctrine reviewed: Cynus's criticism of the gloss—Jacobus Butrigarius—Bartolus—Baldus—Derogation of divine and natural law by the human legislator: the *non obstante* clause. *page* 71

CHAPTER VI

THE ADMINISTRATION OF LAW

I. The authority of judicial decisions—Judge and legislator compared—The function of the judge—His legal training—Law and judgements—No discretionary powers—The duties of the judge—The unjust decision—No effects—Resistance to the judge—The juristic justification—Automatic and official intervention of the judge in matters relating to the public interest—Miscarriage of justice—Human qualifications of the judge—Technical qualifications—Contemporary views on permissible resistance (Petrus de Bellapertica, Dynus, and Cynus).

II. (1) Interpretation—Its object—Interpreter and legislator compared—Reasonableness of interpretation—Simplicity of conception—The legal text as the basis of interpretation—The meaning of the words—The aim of interpretation—Acceptable subtleties—Sophistry—Analogy—*Casus omissus*—Contemporary doctrine reviewed—Types of interpretation—Authentic—Judicial—Customary and doctrinal interpretation; (2) Evidence—The subject of testimonies—The witness in particular—The basis of his knowledge—Reliability of witnesses—Principles relating to evidence—Presumptions ?—Proof of internal factors (intention, &c.)—Lucas's aversion to torture—Quantity or quality of evidence ?—The conscience of the judge—Accord of conscience and judgement—Discord—Lucas's principle—The common view—Cynus and St. Thomas Aquinas—Lucas refutes their principles because of the hypocrisy of the artificial distinction between a public and private conscience—Lucas's distinction between judgements *secundum* and *contra conscientiam*—His view of the condemnation of Christ—A decision of the Bolognese law faculty—The value of judicial records: distinction between civil and criminal matters.

III. The nature of litigations: *cognitionalia certamina*—Trial—Summons—The right to object to the judge—Judgements—Execution of judgements—The principle of equality to be applied to judicial proceedings—Collegiate tribunals—The liability of the judge for miscarriage of justice; (1) Wilful miscarriage; (2) Negligence—The secular and the ecclesiastical judge: their complete independence—Lucas's opposition to the canonists—The secular judge not bound by a decision of the ecclesiastical judge—Lucas's scepticism towards ecclesiastical decisions—The jurisdictional powers of the secular judge are not inferior to those of the ecclesiastical judge, and are derived from God—No transgression of jurisdictional powers by judges.

IV. Judicial organization in Sicily—*Praeses* and *Judex*—The function of the *Praeses*—The function of the *Judex*. *page* 105

CHAPTER VII

THE IDEA OF CRIME

I. Penal science of the Post-Glossators—Lucas's main idea—Prevention of crimes—Public security—The constitutive element of crime—Crime as a public wrong—The significance of the external act—A test case—The purpose of punishment—'Punitive treatment'—Effects of punishments upon others—Implications of his theory of punishment—The contemporary view contrasted with that of Lucas—Imputable actions (*a*) of a human agent; (*b*) of a free human agent—The concept of responsibility—Flexible according to 'accompanying circumstances'; (*a*) extenuating: provocation—Anger—Superior order combined with threats—Cynus and Petrus de Bellapertica—Drunkenness—Youth; (*b*) aggravating—Time (night and war-time)—The actual perpetration of a crime—The persistent offender—The habitual offender—Exculpating circumstances—Necessity—Self-defence—Defence for others—The right of certain individuals to punish others—Euthanasia—Ignorance—Accessories—Delictal responsibility of corporations ?

II. No (legal) presumptions in criminal proceedings—'Once a criminal, always a criminal'?—Torture: a delicate matter—Should not be used—Requirements of a valid confession of guilt—Indictments—Their official character—The judge who deals with criminal matters. *page* 142

CHAPTER VIII

SOCIAL AND POLITICAL CONCEPTIONS

I. Political science and the Post-Glossators—Lucas and political science—Origin of the human race—Organic structure of human society—Lucas's dependence on John of Salisbury—Implications of the organic view—The State as a living reality—Substantial elements of human society—Faith—Obedience to the Ruler: the idea of a 'social contract'—The co-operative will—Lucas a follower of the organic or social contract theory?—The need for governments—The salutary effect of law: its constraining influence—Monarchy the best form of government—Monarchical power independent of the Pope—Lucas relies on canon law itself to refute other theories—Bartolus on the allegory of the two swords—Lucas's contrary view—Bartholomaeus de Capua—The extreme papal supporters reviewed: Joannes de Lignano—Richardus Malumbra—Oldradus de Ponte—Their views in striking contrast with the theory of Cynus—Coronation—The powers of the Ruler before coronation—Cynus (Jacobus de Arena) and Bartolus—The decree of Louis of Bavaria (*Licet juris utriusque*)—Lucas's theory: the declarative character of coronation—'Realiter assecutus'—Approbation—Effects—Coronation of kings and popes—Cynus (*vice populi*), Lucas (*vice Dei*) and Bartolus contrasted—Sovereign rights—Transfer?—Bartolus's territorial conception of sovereignty—Baldus's view—Prescriptive acquisition?—Civil liberty—Just wages—Revocation of privileges—Compensation for expropriated goods—The Ruler a true guardian and protector of his people—The protection of civil liberty—Tyranny—Justification of tyrannicide—Lucas's dependence on the *Policraticus*—Unauthoritative arrests—Imprisonment for debts?—Transgression of powers by officials—Protection during imprisonment—The 'executive' officials—Resistance to officials.

II. The concept of war—Lucas's distinction—The just war—The legality of war—Warfare—Crimes committed during war—Aim of war—Peace treaties—Internal peace—Reprisals—The basic principle—Lucas *versus* Bartolus. *page* 163

CHAPTER IX

CONCLUSION *page* 199

APPENDIX *page* 207

SOURCES AND AUTHORITIES *page* 208

INDEX *page* 214

INTRODUCTION

by HARODL DEXTER HAZELTINE, LL.D., LITT.D., F.B.A.
of the Inner Temple, Barrister-at-Law ; sometime Downing Professor of the Laws of England in the University of Cambridge

THE LEGAL AND POLITICAL IDEAS OF THE POST-GLOSSATORS

IN this treatise on the medieval idea of law Dr. Ullmann has made a notable contribution to the history of legal and political thought. One of the most valuable features of his book is the comprehensive and lucid exposition of the ideas of Lucas de Penna, the Neapolitan Post-Glossator of the fourteenth century who has long remained for the most part merely a name, nearly forgotten by modern scholars. In the fifteenth century, as Dr. Ullmann has shown us, Lucas's thought had exerted a striking influence on the ideas of Paris de Puteo and other legal scholars in the Sicilian Kingdom, while in the sixteenth century his legal and political ideas had found marked recognition in both Italy and France, where he was ranked as an equal of Bartolus, Baldus, Castrensis, Salicetus, and other eminent Post-Glossators of the fourteenth century. Since the sixteenth century, however, Lucas de Penna's former prestige has suffered from the failure of modern scholars to study his writings. It is true, as we shall see presently, that Savigny was familiar with Lucas's writings, that Gierke dealt briefly with his theory of the corporation, and that Professor Calasso has written a valuable article entitled ' Studi sul commento ai Tres Libri di Luca da Penna ' (1932). But no scholar other than Dr. Ullmann has taken the pains to discover, analyze, and synthesize the social, legal, and political ideas embodied in Lucas de Penna's most important work, his Commentary on the *Tres Libri*—the tenth, eleventh, and twelfth books of Justinian's *Codex*.

Although, largely owing to past neglect, the place of this Neapolitan legist in the history of thought has been overshadowed by the fame of Cynus, Bartolus, Baldus, and certain other Post-Glossators, it is a matter of no little significance to observe that Savigny, the great Romanist of the first half of the nineteenth century, singled out Lucas de Penna from all the Post-Glossators for special praise. While in general severely critical of the methods and attainments of the Post-Glossators, Savigny remarked in his *Geschichte des Römischen Rechts in Mittelalter* that the one work which least displays the faults of the time is this comprehensive and detailed Commentary of Lucas de Penna on the *Tres Libri*. Lucas de Penna is important, Savigny said, because of this work ; and it is a work, he added in a vein of sarcasm directed at the dialectical method of the professorial Post-Glossators, written by a legal scholar who had never taught in a school. Lucas de Penna, declared Savigny, belongs at one and the same time among the least-known and among the most noteworthy of all the legal scholars of the fourteenth century.[1]

In choosing Lucas de Penna as the representative of Post-Glossatorial thought on the nature of law and government, Dr. Ullmann has done much, therefore, to redeem the neglect of past generations of scholars. Although he has devoted special attention to Lucas de Penna, he has not neglected the other Post-Glossators of the fourteenth century: far from it. For several years Dr. Ullmann has made the Post-Glossators the principal object of his historical and juridical studies, as his essays entitled 'Bartolus on Customary Law',[2] 'Baldus's Conception of Law',[3] and some other essays[4] bear witness. His present work is a study of the legal and political ideas of the Post-Glossatorial school of legists as represented by Lucas de Penna. While making this Neapolitan jurist the central figure in his picture, he has nevertheless, throughout his book, compared Lucas's ideas with those of the other Post-Glossators, such as Bellapertica, Cynus, Bartolus, and Baldus. In thus bringing the whole of the Post-Glossatorial school within the compass of his study, Dr. Ullmann has focused attention upon a juristic movement of the highest importance in the history of Western thought respecting law, justice, and government. The ideas of this fourteenth-century group of legists represented late medieval as opposed to ancient developments in law and politics. It was these medieval ideas of the Post-Glossators which left an indelible imprint on the structure of legal and political thought in the fifteenth and sixteenth centuries at the very time when the humanist civilians of the Renaissance were demanding the abandonment of medievalism and a return to the pure Roman Law of the classical jurists.

I

A conception of the true significance of the Post-Glossatorial school of legists in the history of medieval legal and political ideas can be gained only through a knowledge of the state of Romanic legal studies in the thirteenth century. It may be recalled, therefore, that the school of the civilian Post-Glossators, who are known also as the Commentators, had its beginning in the second half of the thirteenth century at a time when Accursius, almost the last and certainly the greatest of the civilian Glossators, was still in his ascendancy. The rise of the school of civilians who glossed the text of Justinian's codification had formed a part of the medieval revival

[1] See Savigny, *Geschichte des Römischen Rechts im Mittelalter*, vol. vi (ed. 2, 1850), pp. 22, 199, 203. Savigny mentions, in addition to the Commentary on the *Tres Libri*, three other works attributed to Lucas de Penna.

[2] (1940) 52 *Juridical Review*, pp. 265–83.

[3] (1942) 58 *Law Quarterly Review*, pp. 386–99.

[4] (1939) 17 *Revue d'Histoire du Droit*, pp. 34–73.

of Latin learning, the so-called 'Lesser Renaissance', which culminated in Dante. The school of the Bolognese Glossators, founded by Irnerius in the last years of the eleventh and the first years of the twelfth century, and later represented by such eminent civilians as Bulgarus, Martinus, Bassianus, and Azo, had been inspired by a double purpose: to discover the exact meaning of the Justinianean texts and to introduce into medieval practice the pure Roman Law contained in those texts. During the progress of the work of the school, however, this original policy was largely displaced by the growth of a vast Glossatorial literature in which the sources of the pure Roman Law of Justinian were increasingly adapted to the current practice of the courts. The Glossators, moreover, gradually included in their writings many medieval elements drawn from the legal development of the centuries that had passed since the time of Justinian. In the wealth of its details respecting Justinianean and medieval law, and even more in the variety of the juristic opinions which it embodied, this accumulated Glossatorial learning of a century and a half became confusing not only to practitioners and judges, but also to teachers and students. What was needed, therefore, was a comprehensive and orderly collection of the glosses in which the whole mass should be clarified by a master's hand. The writing of such a work was the great achievement of Accursius. His Gloss, known as the *Accursiana*, which supplanted in the courts and in the schools alike all the other glosses, was held by the courts to be the law itself: this dominance of the *Accursiana* was expressed by the saying '*Quidquid non agnoscit glossa nec agnoscit curia*'. The *Accursiana* was, in fact, proof that the Glossatorial school, having accomplished its work, was already in process of decline; and it was a clear indication, moreover, that the pure Roman Law had been supplanted by a medieval civil law, which, although based on the Justinianean texts, embodied also other elements derived from medieval legal development.[1]

The rise of the school of Post-Glossators, or Commentators, represented a strong reaction against the authority of the *Accursiana* in the practice and the teaching of law. Originating in France, where during the twelfth and the first half of the thirteenth centuries the exegetical method of the Italian Glossators had been adopted by a certain number of civilians and canonists, the Post-Glossatorial school was founded in the second half of the thirteenth century by

[1] For short historical accounts of the Bolognese school of civilian Glossators, accompanied by bibliographies, see Vinogradoff, *Roman Law in Medieval Europe* (ed. 2, de Zulueta, 1929), chap. ii: 'The Revival of Jurisprudence', and my 'Roman and Canon Law in the Middle Ages' (*Cambridge Medieval History*, vol. v, 1926, pp. 697–764, at pp. 729–38) and 'Glossators' (*Encyclopaedia of the Social Sciences*, vol. vi, 1931, pp. 679–82). Special attention may be drawn to *Studies in the Glossators of the Roman Law: Newly Discovered Writings of the Twelfth Century* (1938), edited and explained by the late Hermann Kantorowicz with the collaboration of Professor W. W. Buckland.

Jacques de Revigny (Jacobus de Ravanis), philosopher and theologian as well as legist, professor at Toulouse and later at Orléans. Jacobus de Ravanis, who was born between 1210 and 1215 and died about 1296, applied to the law the method which St. Thomas Aquinas had used in theology, the dialectics of scholasticism; and he was followed by many disciples, notably Pierre de Belleperche (Petrus de Bellapertica), likewise professor at Toulouse and Orléans, who died in 1308.[1]

When the great reputation of these French jurists had awakened an interest among the civilians of Italy, Cynus de Pistoia (*c.* 1270–*c.* 1337) came to France to study the new method of legal dialectics as taught by Bellapertica: it was Cynus who introduced this method into Italian legal studies. Bartolus of Sassoferrato (1314–57), unquestionably the greatest and most influential of the Italian Post-Glossators, studied under Cynus; Baldus de Ubaldis (1319 or 1327–1400), the pupil of Bartolus, was the most distinguished of his successors. By borrowing the developed scholastic method of deduction from the school of French legists, notably Petrus de Bellapertica, the Italian Post-Glossators, such as Cynus, Bartolus, Baldus, Albericus de Rosate, and Lucas de Penna, were able, therefore, to go beyond the Accursian Gloss and to combine the Roman legal texts with the sources of medieval law as practised in the courts, thus initiating the *usus modernus Pandectarum* as the common law of Italy. In the hands of Cynus and his successors the scholastic method co-ordinated the diverse legal materials, partly Roman and partly non-Roman, under the rule of *ratio iuris*.[2]

The new juristic movement inaugurated by the Post-Glossators, or Commentators, meant a demand for greater independence in legal thought and practice; it was a movement which also called for a new synthesis in order that the law might be developed in harmony with medieval conditions of life. Although they followed a method essentially different from that of their predecessors, the Glossators, the Commentators nevertheless derived much from the accumulated learning to be found not only in the Gloss of Accursius, but also in the writings of the other great Glossators, such as Bulgarus, Martinus, Azo, and Placentinus; and, moreover, the Commentators took fully into account the manifold legal growths of the Middle Ages, such as the Canon Law as expounded by the canonists, Germanic and feudal customs, and imperial and town laws. Following the Glossators, the Commentators based their work on the Justinianean law; they gave, however, a far greater prominence than the Glossators had given to the medieval sources of law. The Commentators aimed at the production of methodical expositions, with divisions and subdivisions: their work was essentially con-

[1] See Savigny, op. cit., vol. v (ed. 2, 1850), pp. 603–14, on Jacobus de Ravanis, and vol. vi (ed. 2, 1850), pp. 26–33, on Petrus de Bellapertica.

[2] See Professor de Zulueta's article on 'Cino da Pistoia' (*Encyclopaedia of the Social Sciences*, vol. iii, 1930, pp. 470–71).

structive, as opposed to the Glossators' main labour of interpretation. The great achievement of the Commentators, the Post-Glossators, was in fact the transformation of the Roman Law into a medieval Italian law. They created a literature on Romano-Italian law which not only possessed authority in Italy itself, but played a rôle of great importance in the legal and political life of Europe as a whole. Thus it was the living Romano-Italian law of the Commentators, and not the pure Roman Law of Justinian, which crossed the Alps into Germany in the age of the Reception.[1]

During the progress of their work of transforming the Roman Law of Justinian into a medieval civil law both the Glossators and the Post-Glossators developed many legal and political theories. Although these theories were in general founded on the *Corpus Iuris Civilis*, they embodied also ideas drawn from Canon Law, Germanic and feudal customary law, and other medieval legal sources. Some of the principal theories of the Post-Glossators were a further elaboration of theories already developed by the civilian Glossators and the canonists before the close of the thirteenth century: included among such theories were those in regard to the nature of law, justice, and equity, the nature and authority of *ius divinum* and *ius naturale*, the nature of the corporation, the source of political authority, and the relations between the ecclesiastical and secular powers.[2]

This marked continuity in the development of legal and political theory may be illustrated by the history of the Romano-canonical theory of the corporation. To the glossatorial theory of the corporation as being the sum or aggregate of its individual members the canonists of the thirteenth century added an institutional element derived from the history of the Church. The canonists, moreover, advancing beyond the doctrine of the Glossators, invested the corporation with a personality of its own. It was this Romano-canonical theory of the corporation as *persona ficta*, the result of the combined studies of the Glossators and canonists during the twelfth and thir-

[1] On the school of the Post-Glossators, or Commentators, see Savigny, op. cit., vol. vi (ed. 2, 1850); Caillemer, 'L'enseignement du droit civil en France vers la fin du XIIIe siècle' (*Nouvelle revue historique de droit français et étranger*, 3rd ser., vol. iii, 1879, pp. 599–618); Flach, *Cujas, les glossateurs et les bartolistes*, 1883; Esmein, *Cours élémentaire d'histoire du droit français* (ed. 15, Génestal, 1925), pp. 723–35; Chénon, *Histoire générale du droit français*, 1926–29, vol. i, pp. 502–13, vol. ii, pp. 329–31; Woolf, *Bartolus of Sassoferrato: His Position in the History of Medieval Political Thought*, 1913. For brief historical accounts of the Post-Glossatorial school of legists, with bibliographies, see my 'Roman and Canon Law in the Middle Ages' (*Cambridge Medieval History*, vol. v, 1926, pp. 697–764, at pp. 738–41; bibliography, pp. 925–26) and 'Commentators' (*Encyclopaedia of the Social Sciences*, vol. iii, 1930, pp. 679–81).

[2] On the history of the legal and political theories of the civilian Glossators and the canonists down to the middle of the thirteenth century, see Carlyle, *History of Mediaeval Political Theory in the West*, vol. ii. On the theories of certain of the Post-Glossators, such as Cynus, Bartolus, and Baldus, and of certain of the later 'Bartolists', notably Bodin, see Carlyle, op. cit., vol. vi, *passim*.

teenth centuries, which was still further developed by the French and Italian Post-Glossators of the late thirteenth and the fourteenth centuries. Bartolus was especially prominent in this development of doctrine respecting the corporation; but the contributions made by other Post-Glossators, including Lucas de Penna, were also of great importance.[1] It was Lucas de Penna who reckoned as the fifty-ninth of the sixty-seven prerogatives of the *princeps* that he, and only he, makes fictions: 'Solus princeps fingit quod in rei veritate non est'. Thus, as Maitland observed in speaking of Lucas's doctrine, '"The Fiction Theory" leads us into "the Concession Theory".'[2] It was these two theories which played so important a rôle in the later history of doctrine, both on the Continent and in England, respecting the nature of the corporation.

Although the legal and political theories of the Glossators and Post-Glossators represent a striking continuity in doctrinal development, it should not be forgotten that in the formulation of their own theories in regard to the nature of law and government the Post-Glossators were under the influence of a current of thought which had not been present in the classical period of the Glossators' school. It is especially important to bear in mind, therefore, that during the second half of the thirteenth century, at the very time when the Post-Glossatorial movement was in the initial stages of its historical development, the legal and political ideas of the schoolmen were beginning to exert a far-reaching influence on Western thought. By the middle of the thirteenth century the doctrines of St. Augustine and the other Church Fathers, as well as the dogmas of the Church itself, had been digested into a compact and intelligible form; and by that time, moreover, the works of Aristotle, which constituted the greatest product of human reason, had been introduced into the West and were before the philosophers of the age. The task of the schoolmen, the most famous of whom was St. Thomas Aquinas (1225 or 1227–74), was to create, as Dunning has observed, 'a single system of ultimate science which should blend, in final harmony, the products of reason and revelation', as represented respectively by Aristotle and St. Augustine. In Dunning's words, the doctrine of St. Thomas Aquinas respecting law, justice, and government 'presents, even more strikingly than many other branches of his system, the characteristic which applies to scholasticism as a whole—the reconciliation of St. Augustine and Aristotle'. The schoolmen, personified by St. Thomas Aquinas and his devoted disciple Ægidius Romanus, known also as Ægidius Colonna, from the name of his family, formed in fact a school of thought aptly described by Pro-

[1] On the history of the Romano–canonical theory of the corporation, see Gierke, *Genossenschaftsrecht*, vol. iii, pp. 186–238 (Glossators), 238–351 (canonists), 351–501 (Post-Glossators).

[2] See Gierke, op. cit., vol. iii, p. 371; Maitland, Introduction to Gierke's *Political Theories of the Middle Age*, p. xxx. Dr. Ullmann has mentioned two or three aspects of Lucas de Penna's theory of the corporation. For additional information, see Gierke, op. cit., vol. iii, pp. 351–501, *passim*.

fessor Roscoe Pound in his *Jurisprudence* as the 'philosophical jurist-theologians'. It was through the wrtings of this school, but notably through those of Aquinas, that politics entered once more into the circle of the sciences by the side of law and theology.[1]

There is one special aspect of St. Thomas Aquinas's thought which deserves at least brief notice here owing to its influence on later thinkers, including the Post-Glossators. It may be observed, therefore, that in the period of the revival of the study of Roman Law in the twelfth and thirteenth-centuries the principle of Germanic law, that the ruler is bound to act according to law, came in contact with the revived ancient Greek idea, which had been given currency in the Byzantine–Roman period, that the State exists for the general welfare, towards which law is but a means, so that the State creates law instead of merely recognizing it. The Germanic concept was that the law, to which the ruler is subject, is a quest for the truth and justice of the Creator, whereas the codification of Justinian, the *Corpus Iuris Civilis*, laid down the doctrine that what the Emperor wills has the force of law. Thus in the period of the medieval legal renaissance there arose a conflict between the Germanic and medieval idea that Law is above the State and the Graeco-Roman idea that the State is above the Law. This conflict of fundamental ideas led scholars of the twelfth and thirteenth centuries to take up once more the distinction between natural law and positive law which had been dormant after the period of the Roman classical jurists. The theory was developed that positive law is the creature of the sovereign, but that all sovereigns are under natural law. St. Thomas Aquinas re-shaped this philosophical theory to bring it into accord with theology: his great achievement was in putting Gratian's identification of natural law with the divine law upon a theological-philosophical basis.[2]

In his *Summa theologica* St. Thomas Aquinas divided the old *ius naturale* into two parts: a *lex aeterna* and a *lex naturalis*. According to Aquinas, the *lex aeterna* is the 'reason of the divine wisdom' governing the whole universe, while the *lex naturalis* is the law of human nature, proceeding ultimately from God, but immediately from human reason, and governing the actions of men only. Man, Aquinas held, being a rational creature, participates in the eternal reason: hence the *must* which *lex aeterna* addresses to the rest of creation is *ought* to him. Thus for Aquinas that part of the eternal law which man's reason reveals is to be called natural law.[3]

[1] On St. Thomas Aquinas and his school, see Dunning, *History of Political Theories: Ancient and Medieval*, chap. viii; McIlwain, *Growth of Political Thought in the West*, chap. vi, *passim*.

[2] See Gierke, *Political Theories of the Middle Age*, pp. 73–8; Pound, 'Theories of Law', (1912–13) 22 *Yale Law Journal*, pp. 114–50, at pp. 116–23, 'The Church in Legal History' (*Jubilee Law Lectures*, School of Law: Catholic University of America, Washington, 1939, pp. 1–97, at pp. 74–9), *The Revival of Natural Law* (reprinted from the *Notre Dame Lawyer*, June 1942), pp. 287–372, at p. 290.

[3] Pound, 'Theories of Law', loc. cit., p. 123, 'The Church in Legal

While this system of thought elaborated by St. Thomas Aquinas made law a body of the enactments of God as the supreme law-giver of the universe, and so properly to be called *lex*, it took from positive law its character of enactment and made it a mere recognition of the *lex naturalis*, which was above all human authority. Thus, as Aquinas himself observed: 'Every law framed by man bears the character of a law exactly to that extent to which it is derived from the law of nature. But if on any point it is in conflict with the law of nature, it at once ceases to be a law: it is a mere perversion of law'.[1] As this natural law, however, was discoverable by reason, the effect of the doctrine was to require all rules of positive law to be tested by reason: in England natural law was itself called the law of reason.[2]

Professor Pound has pointed out that this theological–philosophical theory outlined by St. Thomas Aquinas, which signified a beginning of the movement back to the classical Roman idea of law (*ius*), has been a factor in the development of jurisprudential ideas down to very recent times. Aquinas's theory influenced not only the thought of the Post-Glossators in the late thirteenth and the fourteenth centuries,[3] but also the formulas of practical lawyers, such as Fortescue, down to and after the Reformation. It prepared the way, moreover, for the more liberal notions of the legal humanists in the age of the Renaissance, and also for the return in the seventeenth century to the classical concept of reasonableness as the source of authority in law.[4]

Founded in the second half of the thirteenth century by Jacobus de Ravanis and Petrus de Bellapertica through their application to law of the scholastic method of study already employed by the schoolmen, notably St. Thomas Aquinas, the juristic school of the Post-Glossators continuously drew, throughout the fourteenth century, upon the substantive scholastic learning itself, especially its ideas respecting law, justice, and government. This indebtedness of the Post-Glossators both to the method and to the thought of the schoolmen is a fact of outstanding importance in the juristic

---

History', loc. cit., pp. 78–9. On aspects of Aquinas's theory respecting *lex aeterna* and *lex naturalis*, see also Gierke, op. cit., pp. 172–8, *passim*. For a brief study of Aquinas's theory of law and justice and his four-fold classification of the species of law—namely, eternal, natural, human, and divine—see Dunning, *History of Political Theories: Ancient and Medieval*, pp. 192–7. On the same subject-matter, see also Carlyle, op. cit., vol. v, pp. 36–44, where several passages from Aquinas's *Summa theologica* will be found.

[1] *Summa theologica*, i–ii, q. 95, art. 2 (Rickaby's translation).

[2] See Pound, 'Theories of Law', loc. cit., pp. 123–24, 'The Church in Legal History', loc. cit., p. 79.

[3] For references to the views of Baldus and other legists, see Gierke, op. cit., pp. 174–6, *passim*. From Dr. Ullmann's book it will be seen that the influence of Aquinas's theory may be detected in the ideas of Lucas de Penna respecting the nature of law.

[4] See Pound, 'Theories of Law', loc. cit., pp. 123–4, 'The Church in Legal History', loc. cit., p. 79.

history of the later Middle Ages. It is not surprising to find, therefore, that the legal and political ideas of the Post-Glossators were profoundly influenced not only by St. Augustine and Aristotle, but also by St. Thomas Aquinas and Ægidius Romanus. Through the study of these and other writers, ancient and medieval, by the Post-Glossators, their legal and political thought, although founded on Justinianean and medieval law, was yet coloured by Christian and philosophical concepts. This aspect of Post-Glossatorial thought may be illustrated by Bartolus, as Woolf has shown us,[1] or by Lucas de Penna, as Dr. Ullmann has proved to us in the present work. It is this marked influence of the substantive thought of scholasticism on the ideas of the Post-Glossators which helps us to draw one of the main lines of distinction between their theories of law and government and the corresponding theories of their predecessors, the Glossators.

In any study of the work of the Post-Glossators it must always be borne in mind, moreover, that the fourteenth century, the very period in which this school of legists made their principal contribution to the general stock of legal and political ideas, was an age marked by new tendencies in the political life and thought of the West. The century opened with the age-long controversy as to the respective spheres of the spiritual and the temporal powers absorbing all the thought and energy of both Church and State: it was the period of the bitter struggle between Pope Boniface VIII and Philip the Fair of France. As Dunning has observed: 'So far from the settled and placid progress of Christendom under the principles which the Thomist philosophy had proclaimed as final, the fourteenth century presented, in both theory and practice, a condition of profound and widespread unsettlement. The trend of political speculation in the conflicts of this period was toward the rejection or radical transformation of what was most fundamental in the preceding century.' Thus the fourteenth-century opponents of the Papacy manifested a more confident and aggressive spirit than that found in the earlier supporters of princely independence: the new forces working in the thought of the time were all on the side of the secular authority. All the principal arguments in behalf of temporal rulers against the Papacy included exhaustive discussions of Civil and Canon Law. In the varying phases of the controversy over jurisdiction the civilians, notably the Post-Glossators, were confronted by equally alert and schooled canonists: each body of lawyers strove to demonstrate the supremacy of its own system of authority. With every successful assertion of temporal power the influence of its juristic advisers became more pronounced; and in this way the Post-Glossatorial lawyers and their methods of thought assumed a leading rôle in the consolidation of national monarchies which was just beginning.[2]

[1] See Woolf, *Bartolus of Sassoferrato*, *passim.*

[2] See Dunning, *History of Political Theories: Ancient and Medieval*, pp. 212–24, *passim.*

The main tendencies in the political life and thought of the fourteenth century profoundly influenced the theories of the Post-Glossators not only as to the boundary-line between the spiritual and temporal spheres and the nature of secular government, but also as to the nature of law, justice, and equity: the political and legal ideas of the age were closely interrelated. Various factors contributed, moreover, to the formulation by the several Post-Glossators of many divergent legal and political theories in respect of the very same subject-matters, such as the place of custom in the legal framework and the source of secular authority. Although this absence of complete harmony in the doctrinal teachings of the Post-Glossators was unquestionably caused in part by the general state of political unsettlement in the fourteenth century, it was largely due to the variety of legal and non-legal materials at the disposal of each of these legists. While the *Corpus Iuris Civilis* was the fundamental source of the theories of all the Post-Glossators, each of them was at liberty to derive both legal and political ideas from any one or more of many other sources, such as Canon Law, Germanic Custom, and the writings of the philosophers.

This partial yet marked discordance within the body of Post-Glossatorial doctrine is a subject which has been but little studied by historians of Western thought. It is fortunate, therefore, that Dr. Ullmann has presented us in his book with an illuminating comparative study of the views of the several Post-Glossators on a variety of legal and political topics: by so doing he has shown us that in respect of some matters these legists of the fourteenth century were in general agreement, but that as to others they expressed opinions differing widely one from another. In respect of this matter of concordance and discordance in Post-Glossatorial doctrine Dr. Ullmann has made a substantial contribution to our knowledge of late medieval thought.

Philosophical speculation, inspired by the study of Aristotle, St. Augustine, St. Thomas Aquinas, and other thinkers of ancient and medieval times, gave a new tone to the legal and political theory of the fourteenth century. In a passage where he was speaking of Bartolus, Baldus, and other jurists of the period, Maitland observed that 'political philosophy in its youth is apt to look like a sublimated jurisprudence'.[1] Although this is unquestionably true, it is not to be forgotten, on the other hand, that in the fourteenth century the jurisprudence of the Post-Glossatorial legists assumed in respect of some of its main features the character of a refined philosophy: jurisprudence became in large measure a legal philosophy. This seems particularly true of Lucas de Penna, the Neapolitan Post-Glossator; for, as Dr. Ullmann has shown us so clearly, Lucas's 'legal science is firmly rooted in the philosophy of his time'. In the present work the reader will find an elaboration of this significant

[1] See Maitland, Introduction to Gierke's *Political Theories of the Middle Age*, p. viii.

point in the history of the school of the Post-Glossators—that is, the influence of philosophical ideas on their jurisprudence.

The fourteenth century was the classical period in the history of the Post-Glossatorial legists: it was the century of Cynus of Pistoia, Albericus of Rosate, Bartolus of Sassoferrato, Baldus of the Ubaldi, Bartholomew Salicetus, Lucas de Penna, and other notable jurists of the school. In that century these Italian Post-Glossators, the most famous of whom was Bartolus, had not only made their great contribution to the literature of medieval law and theory, but had risen into a position of dominance both in the practice and in the teaching of law. Their influence spread, moreover, to all parts of Europe. The commentaries of the Post-Glossators, embodying both their adaptation of Roman Law to medieval conditions and their legal and political theories, were transmitted to later ages: these writings of the classical Post-Glossators proved to be a powerful factor in the shaping of the public and private law of many countries. Furthermore, in the fifteenth and sixteenth centuries, and indeed down to the rise of the rationalists of the school of natural law early in the seventeenth century, the work of Bartolus and his contemporaries was continued in Italy, France, and other lands by later Post-Glossators, known everywhere as 'Bartolists'. Even in the age of Renaissance, when the legal humanists, such as Alciat, Cujas, Doneau, and Zasius, were bitterly attacking the Post-Glossators for their barbarization of the pure Roman Law, the Bartolists continued to exercise the controlling influence on practice and theory. The maxim, '*Nemo jurista nisi sit Bartolista*', expressed the professional domination of the Post-Glossatorial school even in the sixteenth century.[1]

Among the last of the Bartolists were three eminent jurists: Charles Du Moulin (1500–66), Jean Bodin (1530–96), and Alberico Gentili (1552–1608). Each of these men worked in a field different from that of the others, but they all belonged to the Bartolist school of thought. Du Moulin, who had been trained in the methods of the legists and canonists, devoted his chief attention to the systematization of the *droit coutumier* of France: within the province of French law he has been described by Esmein as 'the last of the great Bartolists'.[2] Jean Bodin, the famous French political theorist, was also a Bartolist. As Woolf has observed, 'Bodin, in attacking Cujas, tells us that he too, when he only taught, despised the Bartolist tradition, but that he learned to think differently after the experience of practical work': Bodin, Woolf has told us, definitely inscribed himself as a Bartolist. Gentili, the Italian jurist who

[1] On aspects of the history of the humanist and the Bartolist schools of jurists in the age of the Renaissance, see Maitland's *English Law and the Renaissance*, Holdsworth's *History of English Law*, vol. iv (ed. 2, 1937), pp. 1–293, *passim*, and my essay on 'The Renaissance and the Laws of Europe' (*Cambridge Legal Essays*, Cambridge, 1926, pp. 139–71).

[2] See Maitland, op. cit., p. 60.

became Professor of Civil Law at Oxford and the founder of modern International Law, also considered himself to be a Bartolist: he wrote a special work to defend the Bartolists against the 'Novitii'—that is, the legal humanists.[1]

This persistence of Post-Glossatorial influence upon law and theory down into the sixteenth century, the age of Renaissance, Reformation, and Reception, is one of the most notable features of the legal, political, and juristic history of Western Europe. In that century, which was also the age of transition from medieval to modern times, the main creative work of the later Post-Glossators, the Bartolists, lay within the realm of public law and political theory. At a time when the modern territorial states were emerging out of medieval conditions, the writings of both the Glossators and the Post-Glossators provided theorists with many doctrines, based largely on the Roman Law, for strengthening the machinery of secular government and supporting marked tendencies towards absolutism. It was the reception and elaboration of these legal and political doctrines of the later Middle Ages, more particularly the ideas of the Post-Glossators of the time of Bartolus, which gave to the sixteenth century one of its most distinctive traits.[2]

II

Lucas de Penna's contribution to thought must be studied, as Dr. Ullmann has himself proved to us, against the background of this long history of the Post-Glossators from the days of Jacobus de Ravanis and Petrus de Bellapertica through the period of Bartolus and his contemporaries down to the time of Du Moulin, Bodin, and Gentili. In this historical development of the school the classical Post-Glossators of the fourteenth century—scholars such as Cynus, Bartolus, Baldus, and Lucas de Penna—hold a place of supreme importance; for it was they who not only presented a synthesis of the legal and political ideas of the later Middle Ages from the legists' point of view, but also, through their adoption of the ideas of scholastic learning and in other ways, created new trends of thought in respect to the nature of law and government. By providing us with a learned and comprehensive study of the legal and political ideas of these fourteenth-century Commentators, with special reference to the contribution made by Lucas de Penna, Dr. Ullmann has enriched our knowledge of a juristic movement that has exercised a potent influence on thought down to the present day.

Dr. Ullmann has not only assembled all the known facts of Lucas de Penna's career as student, practitioner, judge, and writer, but at

[1] On Bodin and Gentili as Bartolists, see Woolf, op. cit., p. 20, n. 1, 393–4.

[2] For the influence of Bartolus and his school on the legal and political ideas of the sixteenth century, both on the Continent and in England, see Holdsworth, op. cit., vol. iv (ed. 2, 1937), pp. 1–293, *passim*.

the same time he has thrown much light on the history of the Neapolitan law school, where Lucas studied, and of Neapolitan legal thought. He has also given us a clear insight into the nature of the intellectual forces that were moulding the ideas of this fourteenth-century lawyer; and from his detailed account of this matter it will be seen that Lucas de Penna was under the influence of Christian and philosophical as well as legal thought. As legist he was master of the Roman Law embodied in the Justinianean codification; and, like many other medieval legists, he was also familiar with the Canon Law. A thorough knowledge of customary law and of the laws of the Sicilian Kingdom constituted, moreover, a part of his equipment as a practical and theoretical lawyer. From the writings of the civilian Glossators and the canonists Lucas drew many ideas, while at the same time he was intimately acquainted with the doctrines of his legal contemporaries, the other Post-Glossators. A close student of the works of Aristotle, Lucas was also influenced by Cicero and the early Christian writers, notably St. Augustine. Of medieval writings, Dr. Ullmann has told us, it was John of Salisbury's *Polycraticus* which exercised the greatest influence on Lucas's thought; but of scarcely less significance in his studies were the works of the great schoolmen, St. Thomas Aquinas and Ægidius Romanus. All these and many other thinkers of ancient and medieval times, as Dr. Ullmann has pointed out, helped to shape the legal and political ideas of this learned and cultured Neapolitan scholar. Drawing upon this vast storehouse of lore regarding law, philosophy, and politics, as well as upon his practical experience as a lawyer, Lucas de Penna constructed his own system of thought relating to law, justice, and government.

Although Dr. Ullmann has dealt fully with the ideas contained in Lucas de Penna's glosses on the laws of the Sicilian Kingdom, he has drawn special attention to the important point that Lucas's principal work—his Commentary on the *Tres Libri*—is far more than a mere commentary on these last three books of Justinian's *Codex*. In this work, which is in fact an exhaustive exposition of the rules, principles, and ideas of the law as a whole, Lucas incorporated by far the largest part of his general scheme of legal and political thought. By his penetrating and constructive analysis of Lucas's most important work Dr. Ullmann has been able to present us with a systematic and illuminating statement of the main social, legal, and political ideas embodied in it. He has not only traced the many lines of influence which went to the shaping of these ideas, but he has also singled out the elements in Lucas's thought that were original; and he has emphasized, moreover, the breadth of Lucas's juridical and political vision, which embraced the whole of the world order. This recovery of Lucas de Penna's thought, so long concealed from view through the failure of nearly all modern writers to study the works of this Neapolitan Post-Glossator, is an achievement in scholarship deserving of the highest praise.

It is of more than a little interest to observe that in an early part of his book, where he has given us a description of the method which Lucas de Penna followed in the writing of his Commentary on the *Tres Libri*, Dr. Ullmann has absolved this Neapolitan Post-Glossator from the common charge, brought by Cujas and the other legal humanists of the Renaissance period as well as by many modern scholars, that the Post-Glossators were so fully in the fetters of dialectics that they could not give adequate expression to the scientific spirit. Dr. Ullmann tells us that the Commentary written by Lucas is not only completely free from the 'infection' of dialectics, but that he himself strongly condemned the dialectical method. Although some of the other Post-Glossators were infected by the dialectics of scholasticism, none of them, Dr. Ullmann says, concentrated on method at the expense of substance.

This is a new and important point, in connexion with which it should not be forgotten, as Dr. Ullmann has himself shown us, that Lucas de Penna's ideas were profoundly influenced by the substantive thought of three of the greatest of the schoolmen, John of Salisbury, St. Thomas Aquinas, and Ægidius Romanus. After the works of all the Post-Glossators have been re-examined with the same care which Dr. Ullmann has devoted to Lucas's Commentary on the *Tres Libri*, it may well be found that the chief influence of scholasticism upon this school of late medieval legists was its substantive thought rather than its dialectical method of study. Only further scholarly research can provide us with a definitive solution of this important problem in textual criticism.

In an early part of his book Dr. Ullmann has also given us an explanation of Lucas de Penna's ideas as to the nature of legal science and the true function of the academic teacher of law. Here, in the course of his explanation, he has drawn attention to the important point that Lucas, faithful to one of the principal aims of the founders of the Post-Glossatorial school, not only vigorously insisted that in legal science there should be exhibited a critical attitude towards glosses and all other recognized authorities, but that he himself in his own scientific work displayed a marked spirit of independence, refusing to submit to the thraldom of authority without critical scrutiny. It may also be observed that in other parts of the present work the reader will find a statement of Lucas de Penna's conception both of the function of the judge and of the authority of judicial decisions ; and here, too, the reader will discover the main principle underlying Lucas's comparison of the judge and the legislator. Here will be found, moreover, not only the principles of civil and criminal procedure as expounded by Lucas, but also his ideas on the evaluation of evidence. All these above-mentioned features of Dr. Ullmann's treatise are worthy of special notice. For one thing, they enlighten us as to the high ideals which guided Lucas de Penna in the formulation of his thought respecting both the science and the practical application of law.

Dr. Ullmann has achieved a notable success in his presentation of Lucas de Penna's many social, legal, and political ideas as an orderly whole, a system: it is a synthesis wherein all the parts are so intimately related one to another as to form one structure of thought. The unity in Lucas's thought-structure is to be found, as Dr. Ullmann has so clearly shown us, in his vision of God as the ultimate source of law and government alike: it is this theistic concept which dominates his thought. It governs his ideas as to the nature of law, justice, and equity; it is also the basis of his ideas as to the authority of the Pope as the head of the Church and of the temporal Ruler as the head of the State.

In this study of Lucas de Penna's thought Dr. Ullmann has brought under review the Neapolitan Post-Glossator's ideas as to the nature, validity, and applicability of the several systems of law, both divine and human, which prevailed in the fourteenth century. Of fundamental importance in Lucas's system were the law of God and of nature, the Roman civil law, and the canonical law of the Church; but also included in the compass of his study were the various systems of customary law, such as the famous Lombard law and the laws of the Sicilian Kingdom. For Lucas, as Dr. Ullmann has observed, the main divisions of the law as a whole were divine or natural law and human law: since he regarded all human law as the command of the ruler, there was no place in his system of thought for the classical Roman distinction between public and private law. The wide scope of Lucas's inquiry embraced all parts of human law; he devoted, however, special attention to the constitutional law of the secular monarchy, the law of crimes, and the law relating to war and peace. It was upon this broad foundation of law, both divine and human, that Lucas de Penna constructed his whole system of social, legal, and political ideas. His system of thought embraced, moreover, concepts drawn from many non-legal sources, especially the writings of ancient and medieval thinkers ranging all the way from Plato, Aristotle, and Cicero to St. Augustine and the schoolmen, notably John of Salisbury, St. Thomas Aquinas, and Ægidius Romanus.

Of the whole complex of ideas which Dr. Ullmann has discovered in Lucas de Penna's writings attention may be focused for the moment upon three that are of paramount importance: first, the nature of law; secondly, the nature of the relations between the spiritual and the temporal powers; and, thirdly, the nature of secular government. Lucas's ideas in regard to these three subject-matters permeate his whole system of legal and political thought: they form, in fact, its foundation.

In approaching a study of Lucas de Penna's ideas as to the nature of law it is well to remember, as Dr. Ullmann has proved to us, that he postulates the rule of a divine law that is eternal: the law of God, he holds, is the universal and immutable law. Following Gratian and later thinkers, notably St. Thomas Aquinas, Lucas identifies natural law with divine law.[1] Lucas holds the view that the essence of divine law as the creation of the Supreme law-giver is a divinely conceived harmony in the universe; and this to Lucas is pre-eminently nature. Natural law identified with divine law is, therefore, the direct manifestation and expression of the divine will. The divine law, which reveals itself in the harmony of nature as the expression of God's will, is made known to man by the light of natural reason.[2] Human law, Lucas teaches us, must on principle conform to divine or natural law.

It is upon this basis of thought in regard to divine or natural law that Lucas de Penna develops his main idea that law is the realization of justice. Justice is, in fact, as Dr. Ullmann has observed, the fundamental idea round which Lucas's theory of law revolves. Law, he maintains, is the instrument which transforms the metaphysical idea of justice into a workable reality in the affairs of men. For Lucas the Roman civil law, which he regards as the universal human law, presents a true transformation of this metaphysical idea of justice. He holds, moreover, that not only in the province of law, but also in the field of politics, justice is the dominant idea. The idea of justice should be the sole principle of government: the ruler should personify the idea of justice.

From the metaphysical concept of justice, as Dr. Ullmann has explained to us, Lucas de Penna derives the idea of equity. Equity, Lucas maintains, is modified justice and the proximate source of Law. Equity is human justice, while human law is its external form. Equity is a positive instrument for adjusting human relations through the medium of law; an enactment which does not exhibit the characteristics of equity is not law. Equity is, moreover, in Lucas's thought, the criterion of judicial and scientific interpretation. Lucas holds, again, that when the law is silent it is the principle of equity which the judge must apply to cases.

Although these basic ideas of law, justice, and equity are not original with Lucas de Penna, for they pervade the thought of

[1] It was Gratian who, in his *Decretum* (1139–41), first identified the law of nature with the law of God. The relation of natural law to divine law was more fully defined in the next century by St. Thomas Aquinas, who set his stamp on Gratian's doctrine. See Pollock's essay on 'The History of the Law of Nature' (*Essays in the Law*, pp. 31–79, at pp. 40–3).

[2] With respect to the identification of natural law with divine law by Gratian, St. Thomas Aquinas, Lucas de Penna, and other medieval thinkers, compare Grotius, *Prolegomena*, § 11, to the effect that the argument from reason as to natural law 'would still have great weight, even if we were to grant, what we cannot grant without wickedness, that there is no God'. In this Grotius was anticipated by Hemmingius (Hemmingsen), *De lege naturae apodictica methodus* (1562), Q. 9. This passage may be found conveniently also in 2 Kaltenborn, *Die Vorläufer des Hugo Grotius*, 31. The position of Hemmingius as to natural law represents the attempt of the Protestant jurist-theologians to emancipate jurisprudence from theology. See Pound, *Jurisprudence* (ed. 1943), p. 7. Cf. Pollock, *Essays in the Law*, pp. 52 ff.; Dunning, *History of Political Theories: From Luther to Montesquieu*, pp. 153 ff.

antiquity and the Middle Ages, nevertheless this Neapolitan Post-Glossator of the fourteenth century develops and applies them in a way which is all his own. It is the study of these ideas, as expounded by Lucas de Penna, which forms so important a part of Dr. Ullmann's valuable book. Here will be found, moreover, not only an inquiry as to the relation of Lucas's ideas on the nature of law, justice, and equity to the ideas of Aristotle, Cicero, St. Augustine, and St. Thomas Aquinas, but also a comparison of his thought on this subject-matter with the ideas of Placentinus and Azo, the Glossators, and of Cynus and Baldus, the Post-Glossators. By studying Lucas de Penna's ideas upon the background of ancient and medieval thought, Dr. Ullmann has been able to bring the contribution made by this fourteenth-century legist into clear relief.

Lucas de Penna's views in regard to the relations between the spiritual and the temporal powers form a highly important part of his whole system of legal and political thought. It should be observed, however, in this connexion, that although his derivation of both law and government from God represents a marked unity in the general scheme of his ideas, there is nevertheless a dualism in his thought respecting the divine government of the world. In order to appreciate the significance of this dualism in his thought it may be recalled that ever since the eleventh century the central problem of Western Europe had been the true boundary between the respective jurisdictions of *Sacerdotium* and *Imperium* or *Regnum.* By the middle of the fourteenth century, at the very time when Lucas de Penna began to write on law and politics, the fundamental and ultimate issue between the two powers, the Church and the State, had been clearly and definitively stated by the medieval theorists: the arguments of both sides had been carried to their extreme logical conclusion. The issue, as Professor McIlwain has justly observed, was really this: 'Assuming that the government of the world is under divine control, was this government entrusted by God to a single authority empowered to guide and control the affairs of men in this life preparatory to the life to come. If so, the Commonwealth of Christians is in reality a Church and the head of the Church is the ultimate earthly seat of all authority and over all. If, on the other hand, God entrusted the guidance of the world to two separate and distinct authorities instead of to one, then one of these should be spiritual exclusively and the other must be supreme in all temporal matters. The defenders of secular government insisted that the divine government for the world is dualistic, the defenders of the *sacerdotium* held that it is monistic.' [1]

Dr. Ullmann has shown us that Lucas de Penna, repudiating the idea that the Pope possesses both swords, the spiritual and the temporal, takes the position that the divine government for the world is dualistic, not monistic. The government of the world, Lucas

[1] McIlwain, op. cit., pp. 314–15.

declares, is two-fold, *pontificalis* and *regalis*: there is a strict separation of these two powers, the ecclesiastical and the secular. The temporal Ruler, not less than the Pope, receives his mandate from God. The Ruler is the bearer of the plenitude of all temporal power, which is granted to him by God directly and not through the instrumentality of the Pope.

Lucas de Penna aligns himself, therefore, with the defenders of secular government in opposition to those who upheld the claims of the Papacy to dominion in both the spiritual and the temporal spheres. Lucas's doctrine of the two powers, as indeed the theory of all earlier defenders of secular authority, goes back to the older teaching of the Church, based on a dictum of Pope Gelasius I in the last years of the fifth century, that Church and State are two co-ordinate powers, that the two swords are *potestates distinctae*, and that *Sacerdotium* and *Imperium* are two independent spheres instituted by God Himself. This dogma of the two co-ordinate powers became the starting-point in all medieval theorizing on politics. With the rise of the Papacy the theory of the Pope's supremacy in both spiritual and temporal affairs was slowly developed; it was finally given its most emphatic expression in Pope Boniface VIII's famous Bull *Unam Sanctam* (1302), issued in the course of his long struggle with Philip the Fair of France. Throughout century after century the defenders of temporal power, vigorously combatting the claims of the Papacy to supreme power in both spheres, fought for the principle that the *Imperium*, like the *Sacerdotium*, proceeds immediately from God, and therefore depends from God and not from the Church.[1]

Although, therefore, Lucas de Penna's doctrine as to the divine governance of the world by two separate powers, the spiritual and the temporal, was already very ancient teaching, having been expounded by many theorists ever since the days of Pope Gelasius I, nevertheless this Neapolitan legist develops the doctrine by an argumentation of his own which runs counter to the theories of other Post-Glossators of the fourteenth century.[2] Dr. Ullmann's

[1] See Gierke, op. cit., pp. 9–21; Carlyle, op. cit., vol. i, pp. 184–93, 253–7, vol. v, pp. 384–93; Dunning, *History of Political Theories: Ancient and Medieval*, pp. 165–9; McIlwain, op. cit., pp. 164–6, 244–7. For a history of medieval theories of the relation of the temporal and spiritual powers, see Carlyle, op. cit., vols. i–v. Pollock has told us that medieval writers on politics really had no theory of the State: their aim was to maintain the cause of the Papacy or of the Empire, as the case might be. Thus, for example, St. Thomas Aquinas defended the Papal claims, while Dante argued for the independence of the Empire. See Pollock, *History of the Science of Politics* (ed. 1914), pp. 37–41.

[2] It is somewhat surprising that Lucas de Penna seems to have made no reference to the remarkable *Defensor Pacis* of Marsiglio of Padua and John of Jandun, a work which appeared in 1324, a quarter of a century before Lucas began to write his Commentary on the *Tres Libri*. 'The great significance of the *Defensor Pacis*', as Professor McIlwain has observed, 'is the fact that in it for the first time the secular State claims a practical equality

comparison of Lucas's views with those of his contemporaries is not only of great interest, it is also a valuable contribution to our knowledge of the political thought of the Post-Glossatorial legists. Thus he shows us, for example, that while Lucas de Penna's doctrine of two independent and equal powers is remarkably similar to the teaching of the Neapolitan jurist, Bartholomaeus de Capua, it is almost diametrically opposed to the theory of the great Bartolus, who holds, in accordance with the extreme view of Papalism, that temporal rulership has been conferred on the Emperor by the Pope and that the Emperor in both spiritual and temporal matters is completely inferior to the Pope.[1]

Perhaps the most striking illustration of Lucas de Penna's position in regard to the relations of the spiritual and temporal powers is to be found in that part of his system where he discusses the practical application of law by the courts. Here, as Dr. Ullmann has shown us with his accustomed skill in analysis, Lucas is concerned with the jurisdictional problem raised by the co-existence not only of two highly important sets of courts, the secular and the ecclesiastical, but also of two great bodies of law, the Roman civil law and the canonical law of the Church; and here, moreover, in this same context, Lucas is obliged to consider both the difference between secular and ecclesiastical litigants and the distinction between temporal and spiritual causes.

Dr. Ullmann has emphasized the point that the leading idea which governs Lucas de Penna's solution of this problem of jurisdiction is the universality of the Roman civil law as the common law (*ius commune*) of the civilized world: he regards the universality of the Roman law as based on the universal overlordship of the Emperor as Ruler. To Lucas the Roman civil law is the incarnation of culture and reason: it embodies and represents, moreover, the metaphysical idea of justice. The concept of *ius commune*, Lucas maintains with insistence, cannot be applied either to Lombard or to Frankish Law, for they are local and not universal laws. While he fully recognizes both the validity and the applicability of the Canon Law within its own special province, Lucas declares that the universality of the Roman civil law as *ius commune* makes its application imperative in all courts, whether secular or ecclesiastical. The application of the Roman civil law is, however, Lucas explains, absolute in some cases, conditional in others, depending in large measure on the character of the litigants and of the causes; and to this whole matter he devotes special attention. One guiding principle, Lucas maintains, is this: Only when the civil law openly

---

[with the Church] which can be obtained only by a theoretical superiority'. See McIlwain, op. cit., pp. 297–313, at 313. Cf. Woolf, op. cit., p. 72. A comparison of Lucas's theory with that of the *Defensor Pacis* would be instructive.

[1] For the views of Bartolus on the relations of the Empire and the Papacy, see Woolf, op. cit., pp. 53–107.

contradicts the canonical law or infringes the liberty of the Church is it inapplicable to spiritual causes tried before ecclesiastical judges. Of special interest are Lucas's views in regard to the jurisdiction of ecclesiastical and secular courts in causes relating to matrimony and legitimation. Lucas's doctrine of public utility (*publica utilitas*) is of the highest importance, moreover, not only in his solution of the jurisdictional problem, but also in his treatment of other matters connected with the relation between the spiritual and the temporal powers. Dr. Ullmann has rightly stressed the theoretical and historical significance of this doctrine as elaborated by Lucas. Without, however, dwelling further upon the problem of jurisdiction in the present place, it may be remarked merely that the reader will learn from Dr. Ullmann's valuable book the full details of Lucas de Penna's solution of that problem in each of its several aspects. Here, too, the reader will discover the difference between Lucas's views and those of the other Post-Glossators, such as Jacobus de Ravanis, Cynus, and Bartolus.

Without entering into the details of Dr. Ullmann's illuminating exposition of Lucas de Penna's ideas as to the nature of secular government, certain of the main features of his doctrine may nevertheless be mentioned here by way of preface. Thus it should be noticed, for example, that in holding monarchy to be the best form of government, Lucas at the same time develops, following John of Salisbury, an anthropomorphic theory of the body politic. Just as the human body is made up of various constitutive organs, in the same way, Lucas says, the social organism, the *respublica*, is composed of its several constituent parts : he compares the ruler to the head of the human body. Still another point to be observed, for it is highly important, is that Lucas rejects the opinion of those who regard the will of the people as the source of temporal power : [1] he holds the view that the secular monarch, not less than the Pope, derives his power directly from God.[2]

In holding monarchy to be the best form of government Lucas de Penna is in agreement with most medieval political thinkers.[3] In the development of his own doctrine of monarchy, however, as Dr. Ullmann has shown us, he is in advance of other theorists of his age.

Lucas de Penna holds that the Ruler, deriving his authority directly from God, is subject to divine or natural law. The Ruler, be he the Emperor as *dominus mundi* or the King in his domain, is merely the medium through whom God creates the law that is known as human law. Although all human law is the command of the Ruler as God's vicegerent, any particular command of the ruler which contradicts the divine idea of natural justice or the dictates of

[1] On the idea of popular sovereignty, see Gierke, op. cit., pp. 37–61.

[2] In this connexion it may be pointed out that Dr. Ullmann deals at some length with Lucas's position as to the nature and effect of the act of coronation.

[3] See Gierke, op. cit., pp. 30–7.

natural reason is not law. With this limitation, then, that he is subject to divine or natural law, and hence cannot legislate in opposition to it, the Ruler has the power, as God's representative, to issue those commands that are the law. Since in his theory all human laws are the commands of the ruler, Lucas maintains, contrary to views expressed by his contemporaries, notably Bartolus, that even customary law becomes valid and binding only when it is confirmed by the ruler.[1] All the laws of the ruler, Lucas holds, must be based on the ideas of justice and equity; and, since that is so, even the ruler himself is not theoretically excluded from the law, for the conduct of the head of the State should be in harmony with the spirit and content of law the creation of which is his vocational office. Lucas maintains that the ruler should be motivated to observe the law by his innate sense of justice: the famous dictum of the Roman Law, *princeps legibus solutus est*, means, however, that the ruler can never be forced to obey the law. The ruler holds his office as a trustee of God, and he is responsible to no earthly power, but to God alone.

Dr. Ullmann has made it clear, in fact, that one of Lucas de Penna's fundamental ideas is that of the ruler's trusteeship. As the vicegerent of God, the ruler has not only legislative powers, but also administrative duties. It is as their guardian and protector in all temporal matters that God entrusts a people and their property to the ruler.[2] The principle underlying his mode of government should be, therefore, that of equity: his aim should be the preservation of civil liberty, the welfare of his people, and the promotion of the common good. The ruler is overlord of person and property: his overlordship is, however, trusteeship. The ruler is overlord, but he is not the owner of the property of his subjects.[3] Tyranny, Lucas holds, is the misuse of the powers entrusted to the ruler by God; and he maintains, following John of Salisbury, that tyrannicide is not only a justifiable, but even a praiseworthy deed according to both human and divine law.

In approaching Dr. Ullmann's analysis of Lucas de Penna's concept of the nature of monarchy we do well to bear in mind

[1] Dr. Ullmann's exposition of Lucas de Penna's theory of customary law, accompanied by a comparison of his theory with the views of other Post-Glossators, is of great interest.

[2] Lucas de Penna's concept of the ruler as trustee seems to be the Germanic and feudal idea of relation, the idea which stands out so clearly in Magna Carta. See Pound, *Spirit of the Common Law*, pp. 20–31.

[3] On this last point Lucas de Penna held the view which Bulgarus had already expressed on a memorable occasion. An anecdote of the Bolognese schools tells us that when the Emperor Frederick Barbarossa was riding one day with Bulgarus on his right hand and Martinus on the left, he asked these two famous Glossators whether the Emperor was not by right lord (*dominus*) of everything held by his subjects. One of the doctors, Bulgarus, had the courage to answer that he was lord in the political sense, but not in the sense of an owner. See Vinogradoff, *Roman Law in Medieval Europe* (ed. 2, de Zulueta, 1929), p. 62.

that as early as the twelfth century the germ of a doctrine of sovereignty, which in its monarchical form exalted the one and only Ruler to an absolute plenitude of power, had already made its appearance: the idea of monarchical sovereignty remained, however, during the Middle Ages, bound up with the idea of office. The idea of monarchical omnicompetence first appeared in the shape of a *plenitudo potestatis* attributed to the Pope; but, also in the temporal sphere, the idea of monarchy tended to assume an absolute form when in the time of the Hohenstaufen the jurists began to claim for the Emperor the *plenitudo potestatis* of a Roman Caesar, the Emperor's power being treated by the jurists as the very type of all monarchy.[1] In the Middle Ages, however, the monarch's sovereignty was judicial rather than legislative power. Thus for Alvarus Pelagius, the Portuguese Franciscan who wrote his important work—*De Planctu Ecclesiae*—in the fourth decade of the fourteenth century, the King is primarily a judge. This was in general the view of medieval theorists.[2]

For Bodin in the sixteenth century, however, and for almost all theorists since his day, the King is primarily a law-giver, not a judge: the King's sovereignty is a legislative sovereignty. Bodin's idea of sovereignty (*maiestas*) is embodied in his definition of the State: 'Sovereignty is supreme power over citizens and subjects, unrestrained by the laws' (*maiestas est summa in cives ac subditos legibusque soluta potestas*). Sovereignty, declares Bodin, has its chief and characteristic function in the making of laws: from the binding force of these laws the sovereign is free. The sovereign, like the subject, is bound, however, by the law of God and of nature: but his obligation in this respect is to God, by whom it will be enforced. To Bodin every monarchy of the highest type must needs be 'absolute' if it is to effect its great purpose of securing and enforcing peace and justice. An absolute monarchy is one which is founded in law: it is a monarchy, however, in which the 'sovereign' is free from ordinary law, though bound by those fundamental rules which define his authority in the State.[3]

One of the most striking conclusions reached by Dr. Ullmann in his study of Lucas de Penna's political thought is that this fourteenth-century legist developed a doctrine of the Ruler's power which anticipated the theories of absolutism current in the sixteenth century. More particularly, Dr. Ullmann has told us, Lucas's doctrine approached the theory of the monarch's full legislative sovereignty which Bodin systematically elaborated in that century of the Renaissance. Although absolutism is latent in the writings of

[1] See Gierke, op. cit., pp. 30–7.

[2] See McIlwain, op. cit., pp. 280–8, *passim*.

[3] See Dunning, *History of Political Theories: From Luther to Montesquieu*, pp. 96–103; McIlwain, op. cit., pp. 280–8, *passim*, 386. On Bodin's doctrine of political sovereignty and its relation to Hobbes' theory, see Pollock, op. cit., (ed. 1914), pp. 47–56.

other Post-Glossators of the fourteenth century, it was only Lucas de Penna who formulated a theory of the ruler's sovereignty based on political rather than on purely legal grounds; and, moreover, his theory was one of legislative rather than judicial sovereignty.

Mention has already been made of the point that in Lucas de Penna's theory the law as a whole is composed of divine or natural law and human law. Since in his view human law is the command of the Ruler, he has no difficulty in asserting, therefore, that the ruler's enactments against existing human law have full abrogative effect. Although he contends that the ruler is on principle bound by divine or natural law and cannot validly repeal it, he nevertheless envisages a ruler with such absolute legislative power that he can make laws in derogation from that higher and fundamental law, provided only he inserts a *non obstante* clause. If in fact the ruler legislates in disregard of the limitations set by divine or natural law, his enactments are valid and enforceable as against his subjects. If, however, such enactments are issued without just cause, the ruler makes himself responsible to God, from whom he has received his authority as God's vicegerent.

The detailed exposition of Lucas de Penna's theory of the Ruler's legislative sovereignty, accompanied by a comparison of his theory with the ideas of the other Post-Glossators as to the Ruler's powers, forms one of the most instructive features of the book which Dr. Ullmann has presented to us. He has illumined, moreover, the later history of Lucas's theory. He has not only shown us that Lucas in the development of his theory was a precursor of Bodin, but he has also proved to us that this famous French political theorist was familiar with Lucas's principal work and cited it at many places in his own *De Republica*. This close doctrinal connexion between Lucas de Penna, the Neapolitan Post-Glossator of the fourteenth century, and Jean Bodin, one of the last of the sixteenth-century Bartolists, is an aspect of the history of political thought which deserves special notice.

One important point may here be added, as a supplement, to Dr. Ullmann's exposition of Lucas de Penna's theory that the Ruler, be he emperor or king, is primarily a legislator rather than a judge. Now, the older idea of the king as judge primarily rather than as law-maker is the Germanic and medieval idea, the idea which the theorists of the Middle Ages had in general adopted.[1] The idea of the king as law-maker, on the other hand, is the Roman idea, the

[1] In Italy this idea persisted down to the end of the eighteenth century. Thus in Lombardy, for example, the supreme tribunals, called Senates, were referred to as 'potentissimus rex,' to denote that they were but the voice of the King. At the time of the city-states the supreme judicial authority always appertained to the Emperor, being reconcilable with the autonomous character of the free cities. When he sojourned in them, all other courts were closed; in his absence his vicars exercised his rights. See 2 Calisse, *Storia del diritto italiano*, § 222. See also Calisse, *History of Italian Law* (Continental Legal History Series), §§ 30, 45, 94.

idea embodied in Justinian's codification. The significant point is, then, that instead of keeping to the medieval tradition, Lucas de Penna goes back to the texts—that is, the texts of the Roman law in Justinian—and takes the path of the legal humanists, the jurists who insisted on the abandonment of medievalism and a return to the pure Roman law of Justinian. In other words, Lucas de Penna may justly be regarded as a precursor of Alciatus, the founder of the school of legal humanists, and in that way of Bodin.[1]

Closely connected in thought with Lucas de Penna's theory of the ruler's legislative sovereignty is his idea that the ruler derives his powers directly from God, to whom alone he is responsible. Dr. Ullmann has justly claimed that this idea of a divinely empowered Ruler as developed by the Neapolitan legist anticipated the theory of the divine right of kings which became so prominent in the political thought of the sixteenth century.

Dr. Ullmann's researches have revealed several other features of Lucas de Penna's Commentary on the *Tres Libri* which indicate clearly that this fourteenth-century jurist had elaborated ideas that were in advance of the thought of his contemporaries. Thus, for example, as Dr. Ullmann has himself observed, although the Post-Glossators as a school systematically and scientifically investigated the elements constituting the concept of crime and the reasons justifying the punishment of the criminal, it was Lucas de Penna who developed a theory of crime and punishment far ahead of his time. Certain aspects of Lucas's theory show in fact, Dr. Ullmann has told us, a basic resemblance to the penological thought of the twentieth century.

Attention may also be drawn to the point that although the modern concept of International Law was unknown to the Post-Glossators of the fourteenth century, nevertheless Lucas de Penna, the Neapolitan Post-Glossator, dealt at great length with the fundamental principles of war and peace. Since the world of the Post-Glossators was the world of the Western Empire, not the world of modern sovereign and independent States, Lucas de Penna was concerned, therefore, with war and peace as they affected the Empire and the political societies within it. Lucas's chief interest, however, as Dr. Ullmann has explained, was in laying down certain basic principles relating to the notion of war and peace, regardless of time and place.[2] In respect of this matter, therefore, Lucas de Penna may justly be regarded as in some measure a precursor both of Alberico Gentili, one of the last of the sixteenth-century Bartolists, and of Hugo Grotius, the two founders of modern International Law.

By studying the ideas of the Post-Glossators, with special reference to Lucas de Penna, Dr. Ullmann has provided us at the same time

[1] For the point mentioned in the above paragraph I am indebted to Professor Roscoe Pound.

[2] The ideas of Lucas de Penna as to war and peace should be compared with those of Bartolus on the same subject-matter. For the views of Bartolus, see Woolf, op. cit., pp. 198–207.

with a valuable commentary on the principal aims and achievements of a juristic school which long exercised a powerful influence, both reformative and creative, upon the development of legal and political institutions in Western Europe. Thus he has given us abundant opportunity to observe the ways in which this school of legists, originating as a reaction against the domination of the Accursian Gloss in the practice and teaching of law, ultimately achieved its main purpose of contributing to the growth of medieval law and theory by going outside and beyond the *Accursiana*. He has illustrated in a striking manner, moreover, the practical working of that independence of thought which had been claimed by the founders of the Post-Glossatorial school as a prerequisite to the transformation of the ancient Roman Law into a medieval civil law to meet the needs of contemporary society. Independence of thought as practised by the Post-Glossators meant the freedom to derive rules, principles, and concepts not only from the *Corpus Iuris Civilis* and the *Accursiana*, but also from other sources of varied character, such as Canon Law, Germanic Custom, and the literature of ancient and medieval times on law, politics, and philosophy. The studies devoted by the several Post-Glossators to the manifold materials at their disposal gradually resulted, therefore, in the accumulation of a mass of doctrines and theories relating to law, justice, and government many of which were in conflict one with another. The school of the Post-Glossators produced, however, no master-legist, no jurist like Accursius, the great Glossator, to bring all these divergent teachings into an ordered and consistent whole, a synthesis in which the main lines of doctrinal growth should stand out in clear perspective. The work of presenting such a conspectus of the legal and political ideas of the Post-Glossators has been left, therefore, as a task of modern scholarship. By his comparison of the ideas of Lucas de Penna with the corresponding ideas of Bellapertica, Cynus, Bartolus, Baldus, and other notable Post-Glossators of the thirteenth and fourteenth centuries, the learned author of the present work has made an important contribution to the fulfilment of that task. He has in fact brought clearly into the range of our vision, upon the background of the ancient and medieval history of jurisprudence and philosophy, the main traits and trends of Post-Glossatorial thought upon the nature of law and justice, the application and administration of law, the relation of the spiritual and temporal powers, and the nature, source, and function of secular authority. Nor has Dr. Ullmann failed to enlighten us in regard to the later influence of the classical Post-Glossators who developed this body of doctrine concerning law and government. He has not only discovered, but brought into the compass of his present study, fresh proof of the historical fact that the ideas of this renowned school of legists constituted one of the dominant factors in the development of legal and political thought throughout the West both during the fifteenth and sixteenth centuries and in still later times.

CHAPTER I

INTRODUCTORY

THE development of a theory of law by the Italian jurists of the Middle Ages was closely linked up with the general spirit of medieval philosophy. It was in the terms of Christian cosmology that legal theorists attempted to arrive at a rational and scientific explanation of the origin, nature, and scope of law.

The scientific researches of the Glossators of the Roman law pursued aims different from the so-called Post-Glossators or Commentators. The efforts of the former were mainly, if not exclusively, directed towards the restoration of the Roman texts, towards making accessible to school and judiciary alike the newly discovered manuscripts and their contents. The scientific interest of the Glossators was focused on the interpretation of individual legal terms, on the linking up of legal rules dispersed throughout Justinian's law books, and on the reconciliation of contradictory statements and utterances on the part of the Roman jurists. The result was a finely spun web of glosses, which varied in their juridical value and profundity of insight, and which covered the whole codification of Justinian. In modern terminology, the Glossators may be styled analytical jurists: the paramount aim of their legal science was analysis, pure and simple, purporting to explain the Roman law from within itself in purely legalistic terms. Their work was exegetical analysis. It is no disparagement of their great achievements to remark that the overwhelming majority of their analyses resulted in mere literal interpretation. It must be borne in mind, however, that the Glossators were the first to plough the virgin soil of the Roman texts, and that this legal historical fact may account for their tendency to rely on the grammatical, logical, and dialectical method. Nevertheless, the later development of the science of law was based on, and conditioned by, the results obtained by the Glossators.

Fundamentally different was the work of those jurists who were said to be the successors of the Glossators—namely, the Post-Glossators or Commentators. It is only in an external and literal sense that the work initiated by the Glossators was continued by the Commentators, but different style, technique, interpretative conceptions, and originality in the tackling of legal problems resulted in achievements substantially distinct from those of the Glossators. The merely legal interpretation of the Roman texts was completed and concluded by the Glossators. The task which remained, therefore, was the philosophic interpretation of the Roman law, the penetration into the intricate mechanism behind the law, and the exposition of universally valid, general principles. With this aim in view, the Commentators extended the sphere of legal science and studies from the mere interpretation of individual legal rules to the investigation and presentation of the fundamental principles, notions, and sources of the law. The apprehension of the legal problems as a coherent whole, the systematization of the huge body of law, and the conception that the individual jural precept is merely the legal expression and enforceable verification of an idea behind the law, is the great achievement of the Post-Glossators. Only one feature—the legal framework—was common both to the Glossator and Post-Glossator: it was upon Roman law that the scientific research work of both was based. Any doctrine was unacceptable which could not claim, superficially at least, the support of the Roman law. It is especially in the field of jurisprudence proper that those jurists deserve our admiration, since Roman law itself in no way suggested the treatment of the subject in the abstract. It is true that some general notions were taken from the *Corpus juris civilis*, such as those of *justitia* or *natura*, and the like, but in reality they were nothing more than a few resounding phrases—words with little meaning and less substance. The Post-Glossators elaborated those notions and interpretated them with philosophic acumen. In their hands these terms of the Roman law became true concepts of legal philosophy, from which they derived and interrelated subordinate concepts capable of application to all legal rules. One conspicuous example is the notion of justice, which they developed first into a fruitful principle and criterion and finally into an idea manifesting itself in all things legal.

This evolution from the mere literal and grammatical interpretation of legal terms to a synthetic and comprehensive theory of law must be viewed against the background of contemporary philosophy, permeated as it was with the inspiration of the ' new Aristotle '. Little surprise is caused by the comparative sterility of the Glossators in legal philosophy. Medieval legal thought had not yet felt the impact on all branches of learning of the stirring new ideas and their concomitant fertilizing influence.[1] The cessation of the school of the Glossators in the middle of the thirteenth century saw the dawn of a new epoch in all spheres of mental activity. The spirit of the Middle Ages came finally to be shaped by the agency of medieval philosophy as it emerged from the colourful blending of Aristotelian, Stoic, and Christian ideas. The medieval mind was firmly moulded by the attractive and grandiosely conceived designs of that medieval philosophy which, owing to the prevalence of specifically Christian traits therein and owing to its emphasis on the moral aspects of life, may indeed be termed Christian moral philosophy. Its peculiarly many-coloured, but nevertheless harmonious and consistent doctrinal

[1] C. Dawson, *Medieval Religion*, p. 64, very aptly remarks that ' the restoration of contact with the main tradition of Greek thought was one of the most striking achievements of medieval culture . . . it was the conquest of a new world '. On this point see especially De Wulf, *History of Medieval Philosophy*, vol. i, pp. 237–50, 313, and Haskins, *Medieval Science*, pp. 141–54.

content became a welcome and applicable instrument for the jurist in his quest for a solution of far-reaching problems. It affected the workaday world not less than the intellect of the jurists whose indispensable armoury it became. It left an indelible imprint on all their lines of thought, and accounted for their training in the rigid Aristotelian method. Moreover, it greatly aroused the 'pure lawyer's' interest in contemporary and antique philosophy, in religious, ethical, and political discourses. Its spirit fructified and impregnated medieval legal thought and led to the vast expansion of legal scholarship in the fourteenth and fifteenth centuries. The result was a thorough-going application of philosophic arguments to the problems of law, from its origin down to its manifold ramifications.

Christian moral philosophy was not so much a stringent and compact philosophic system as a conception or an explanation of life, its ways and its ends. Several divergent strains of thought constituted this outlook on life, orientating it in its social and individual sphere : Aristotelianism modified and adapted by its enthusiastic exponents and strongly tinged with Christian elements, Augustinian conceptions, platonistic and neo-platonistic ideas, Thomistic doctrines—all converged into one broad stream. Whilst the form was mainly dictated by Aristotle, the Christian element gave the form its main content. The central theme of this conception was the relation of mankind to God. Created and ruled by God—philosophically conceived as the first cause of all Being—mankind was deemed subject to the eternal laws of the Universe. The divine Will and Reason were clearly perceived to be the ever-active powers in the government of the world. Essential to this thought was the idea that the cosmos is one well-ordered, harmonious, and articulated whole, whose parts are at the same time both parts and wholes, and that God is the supreme Ruler of the Universe, its sole source and aim. Human conduct was thought of as purposive and destined to a definitive end. The explanation of jural precepts in this philosophic context was the problem which confronted the scholar jurists. It was their task to assign to law the part which it was to play in the Universe thus conceived. The teleological principle presented itself as an obvious answer. Furthermore, since the relationship of man to his Creator was of an internal character, and therefore of a moral nature, the transplantation of ethical ideas into the sphere of law was an argument which suggested itself as being fundamental to this conceptual framework. This process of reasoning was facilitated by the above-mentioned suggestive Roman notions, which indicated an application of ethical ideas to legal problems. The consultation of Aristotle's *Ethics* and of the Christian teachings was merely an articulate expression of this reasoning, which finally led to an infiltration of ethical content into fundamental legal principles. The self-sufficiency of law was herewith denied. The conception of legal science as a department of ethics was entirely consistent with this line of thought.

> Videndum est, cui parti philosophiae subalternatur scientia nostra? Multa possent dici, tamen Doctores communiter dicunt, quod subalternatur ethicae.[1]

As already indicated, the idea of justice was the central tenet of the medieval theory of law. This was in agreement with Roman law, which stated that the law is based on justice. But there the term did not receive any particular attention, nor was it regarded as a principle either of theoretical value or of practical consequences. Following the lead given by Aristotle, however, the medieval jurists conceived it as an ethical virtue which assumed a supreme function in the edifice of their legal theories. All theoretical interest in the origin, nature, scope, validity of law, all conflict of laws, as well as all practical interpretation and application of law, all ideas concerning rulership, government, State, society, and any other conceivable legal institution, were orientated by this central concept. In short, law was purely the translation of the ethical idea of justice. Law was thought of as one of the strongest moral factors in the individual's social life. Law was considered a guide for human actions towards the goal destined for man as part of the Universe. It was, in fact, the social means that was adapted to the attainment of the recognized end. No wonder that this conception was bound to gravitate towards the maxim: 'Lex injusta non est lex'.

But it was not only in the field of legal philosophy that the Post-Glossators' efforts and results were outstanding. Their practical achievements lay in the adaptation of the Roman texts to the changed social and political conditions of their time. In this scientific activity lies another essential difference between the Glossators and the Post-Glossators. For while the former attempted the explanation of the Roman law as it was presented to them—that is to say, Justinian's law—and were not always particularly anxious to adjust law to fact, the Post-Glossators, on the other hand, harmonized, or attempted to harmonize, law with the social and political realities. It must not be forgotten that more than eight centuries had elapsed since Justinian's codification. Furthermore, since the compilation of the *Corpus* the body of positive law had grown considerably, both by enactment and by custom, two sources of law which received only scanty consideration by the Glossators. The Commentators, however, viewed these sources as parts of the legal order as a whole, and devoted considerable space in their writings to the scientific explanation of municipal statute and gradually developed customs. Lastly, the newly created canon law and the feudal law were adequately treated; in particular the conflict of civil with canon law, overlapping jurisdiction of secular and ecclesiastical judge, the conflict of civil and feudal law, were topics upon which much energy was spent. It was just this many-sided activity of presenta-

[1] Cynus, *Proemium ad lecturam super Digestum vetus*, no. 9.

tion, systematization, interpretation, analysis, and synthesis, which gave their doctrines the profundity of true scholarship.

Thus, for the first time in the history of European jurisprudence, a philosophy of law was created. Cultural conditions not only endowed Italian jurisprudence with an influence destined to survive for generations, but also made it one of the greatest legal movements in the whole history of European law. The thesis that law is a function of civilization, indeed its most symptomatic expression, is nowhere so perfectly illustrated as in the medieval theory of law expounded by the Italian scholars. A systematic study of that theory is indispensable both to the adequate evaluation of the historical development of legal ideas and to the understanding of the idea of law itself. Dogmatic jurisprudence must needs take cognizance of the formative character of those ideological agencies which shaped the principles embodied in positive law. The exposition of the historico-ideological material is essential for the understanding of the principles underlying current legal ideas, which have been gradually annealed by a long historical process. Moreover, investigations into a past theory of law are not only part of legal history, but also of social and cultural history.

The centre of scientific activity rested in the universities of North and South Italy: Bologna, Perugia, Siena, Pavia, and Padua in the north, whilst Naples, as the capital of the Kingdom of Sicily, attracted the scholars of the southern part of the peninsula. The brilliant reputation of the universities in the north may, to some extent, have overshadowed the more reticent research work carried out in the law school of Naples.[1] The gathering in the northern universities of scholars from all parts of Europe is due to accidental circum-

[1] The fourteenth century did not produce any great English writers. 'The activities of the successful lawyers were, as in modern times, taken up by their Inns and by the courts; and their learning is recorded, or perhaps we should say buried, in the Year Books' (Holdsworth, *History of English Law*, vol. ii, p. 566). It was not until the seventeenth century that legal theory proper became established (Holdsworth, vol. v, pp. 16 seq.). The lack of any speculative theory of law in England was due, according to Holdsworth, to the feeling of superiority which the common lawyers entertained towards Roman and canon law. Intense, if narrow patriotism, was created by the Hundred Years War, and the civil law of France was considered inferior. 'Who would wish to study a system which the English lawyers learned to think was the cause of this inferiority?' (vol. ii, p. 288). The complacent attitude of Wyclif is significant (see Holdsworth, ibid., p. 407, Workman, *John Wyclif*, vol. ii, p. 25). Bracton's influence declined, and 'Roman law ceased to influence the development of the common law'. This was a deplorable result, as Holdsworth observes, because 'the common lawyers became wholly ignorant of that fund of legal principles and material for legal speculation which were stored up in the writings of the civilians and canonists, and in the texts upon which they commented' (ibid., p. 287). Moreover, conditions at the universities were not favourable to genuine research work. The medieval English student 'was riotous, lawless, and licentious', often leaving the university without taking a degree, and some students 'roamed the countryside in robber bands' (Trevelyan, *English Social History*, p. 53). See also Coulton, *Medieval Panorama*, p. 401.

stances, and no intrinsic reason can be adduced for assuming that their sister in the south did not attain the same scholastic standard. Founded as early as 1224 by that great benefactor and promoter of arts and culture, Frederick II,[1] the university of Naples produced scholars who can claim equal rank with their colleagues from the north. No lesser authority than Petrarch testifies to the great esteem which this southern university enjoyed in the fourteenth century:

> Fortunata, inquam, et individiosa Neapolis, literarum domus augustissima . . . ubi ingeniorum ac studiorum aequissimus existimator habitat, ad te confugiat quisquis ingenio fidit.[2]

One of the most interesting figures of Neapolitan scholarship is Lucas de Penna. The reconstruction of the theory of law propounded by this alumnus of Naples may be a modest contribution to legal history. His work provides, incidentally, a dramatic refutation of the common charges against the Post-Glossators. Though fallen into oblivion, he is a shining example of medieval scholarship, an attractive figure among the other no less attractive personalities in the Pantheon of Italian jurisprudence.

[1] See Rashdall, *Universities of Europe*, vol. ii, pp. 22 seq., Haskins, *Studies in Medieval Culture*, pp. 124–47. On the attempt of Frederick II to seduce professors and students of Bologna to come to his own university by depriving Bologna of its *studium*, see Prof. Powicke, in Rashdall, vol. i, p. 171.

[2] Petrarch, *Opera Omnia*, 'Epistulae de rebus familiaribus', lib. 1, epistula 1, p. 637.

CHAPTER II

LUCAS AND HIS WORK

I

VERY few details about the life of Lucas de Penna have come down to us. The researches of later scholars have added little new material to the scanty information which we can obtain from Lucas's own writings, which indeed are almost our only source of information. The great work of Diplovatacius [1] is of no avail to us, nor have Panziroli's investigations yielded any appreciable results—'de eius tumulo aut die mortis nihil ad nos pervenit'.[2] He was born in Penna, a small place in the southern part of the Abruzzi near Pescara, about 1320, studied law at the university of Naples, and graduated there in the year 1345.[3] No doubt is permissible about the locality of his birth or place of his studies, although later authorities made him of Gallic origin or located his birthplace at Toulouse: the Paris edition of his Commentaries of 1509 called him 'Doctor Gallicus',[4] and Panziroli [5] styled him 'Doctor Tholosanus'.[6] But the allocation of Lucas's birthplace to France must be considered a mistake in view of the abundant internal evidence—namely, his most detailed knowledge of legal conditions in the Kingdom of Sicily, the personal affection he displays towards Sicilian rulers, such as Frederick II and Robert,[7] the frequent quotations of special laws and constitutions of the Sicilian kings,[8] and the emphasis on their importance for the study and application of the law, certain passages in his work of a type only to be found in the writings of

[1] *Ob.* 1511.

[2] Panziroli, *De Claris Legum Interpretibus*, p. 184. Panziroli seemed to think that Lucas lived in the fifteenth century, because he treated him after Bartholomaeus Capilistius, who died in 1505; Panziroli said: 'In Gallis eodem tempore Lucas de Penna Tholosanus enituit'.

[3] Savigny, *Geschichte des roemischen Rechts*, vol. vi, p. 202, Calasso, 'Studi sul commento ai Tres Libri di Luca da Penna', in *Rivista di storia del Diritto Italiano*, vol. v (1932), p. 403, and Wronowski, *Luca di Penna e sua opera*, p. 16.

[4] Joannes Baptista Caccialupus, Professor in Siena (1472), in his *De Modo Studendo in utroque Jure*, doc. v, p. 348, also called him 'doctor Gallicus'; so did he in his *Succincta Historia Interpretum et Glossatorum Juris*, p. 510. The editions of Lyons, too, styled Lucas 'doctor Gallicus'.

[5] loc. cit., p. 184. See *supra* note 2.

[6] See also the treatise mentioned by Prof. Calasso, loc. cit., p. 403.

[7] Epithets like the following occur frequently: 'Gloriosus et sapientissimus Robertus Rex Siciliae', C. X, 16, 3, no. 4; 'venerandae memoriae Rex Robertus', C. XII, 43, 3, no. 28.

[8] See, e.g., C. XI, 71, 1, no. 3: 'In regno autem est expeditum . . . per capitula regis Caroli II, quod incipit "ab olim";' other examples are in many places. See also the frequent allusions and explicit quotations of Frederick II's decrees.

Neapolitan jurists and which typically refer to the kingdom 'in regno nostro', 'in curia vicariae regni', 'in civitate nostra', and the like, his intimate knowledge of Sicilian public affairs and matters relating to public administration, his constant juxtaposition of Neapolitan law and custom with Italic law and custom, his reminiscences of his activity as a judge in several places in Apulia,[1] and lastly his own reference to his place of birth.[2] If any doubt should remain, it would be dispelled by the fact that Lucas himself wrote glosses on the laws of the Sicilian Kingdom. Numerous glosses were written by him on the laws of King Robert, and there are also some glosses from his pen on Charles II's laws.[3] Furthermore, the contemporary of Lucas, Blasius de Murcone, a judge of the supreme Court of Justice in the kingdom, refers to 'Lucas de civitate Apennae'.[4] Lastly, a citizen of Penna and admirer of Lucas, Mutius Pansa, wrote an inscription on his tomb in which he expressly referred to the 'aemula Gallia' as enrolling Lucas among her sons.[5] The possibility cannot, however, be excluded that Lucas continued his studies at Toulouse and that those designations were merely intended to refer to his place of study, and not to his place of birth. Perhaps the existence of a place called Penne near Toulouse has given rise to the error of styling him 'Doctor Gallicus' and 'Doctor Tholosanus'.[6] It does not seem unlikely, however, that the editions of his commentaries which were printed in France styled him 'Doctor Gallicus' for merely commercial considerations. This

[1] See, e.g., C. X, 69, 2, no. 5, where he recalls his personal experiences in Ruvo near Bari; in C. X, 34, 3, no. 15 he quotes a decision which he made as a judge in Corvara.

[2] In his commentary on C. XI, 53, 1, no. 8 he says: 'Quaeritur hic de questione, quae fuit de facto in civitate, unde mihi origo est'. Cf. also C. XI, 8, 14, no. 1: 'Quidam autem doctor fama gloriosus et regni Siciliae protonotarius', says Lucas referring to a conversation with him, 'ipse praedicta jura dixit se nescire, sed praedictas cautiones ex ritu et inventione curiae regis fore inductas'. Lucas seems to refer to Bartholomaeus de Capua (see C. X, 5, 1, no. 10), when he speaks of judicial customs introduced into the Sicilian Supreme Court through the 'mirabilis vir dominus Barth. de Capua, protonotarius dicti regni'. Most of King Robert's laws end with the phrase: 'Data Neapoli per dominum Barth. de Capua, militem logothetam et protonotarium regni Siciliae' (see *Constitutiones*, pp. 338 seq.).

[3] See, e.g., the gloss on torture in the capitulum *De inquisitionibus, Constitutiones*, p. 323. This important aspect has escaped the attention of Savigny and Calasso. Savigny, loc. cit., p. 207, says that he could not find any glosses written by Lucas, and he thinks that Giustiniani, who also mentioned Lucas's glosses, made a mistake. A glance at the glosses proves that Lucas wrote numerous glosses, particularly on King Robert's laws. We shall have an opportunity to refer to some of them.

[4] In the commentaries on Frederick II's laws, lib. iii, titulus 92, p. 279, col. 2. This notice escaped Savigny, Wronowski, and Calasso. There is no trace of this personality in any authority. It is doubtful whether the remark of Joecher, *Allgemeines Gelehrten Lexicon*, vol. v, col. 204, is correct. He says that Blasius was a jurisconsult and wrote *Singularia*, printed at Francfort, 1596.

[5] See the inscription on his tomb, transcribed in the Appendix.

[6] That is the opinion of Professor Calasso, loc. cit., p. 405.

suspicion is intensified by the fact that the editions of Lyons would have us believe that the commentaries deal exhaustively with ' magistratibus Francorum et quantum illi a publicis dignitatibus veteris Romae differant ' ; indeed, the French legal system, and in particular the French ' magistratus ', do not seem to have aroused Lucas's interest unduly.

No information is available as to his academic activity: we cannot gather from his own writings or from any other source that he was ever officially appointed an academic teacher ; [1] there are, in fact, good reasons to assume that he was never a teacher, although all editions of his main work call him ' utriusque juris professor egregius '. Several passages, however, refer to his activity as a barrister [2] and as a judge,[3] in which latter capacity he sought the advice of Bartolus by personally consulting him.[4] In advanced years he held a high Government office,[5] and shortly before his death was in the service of the Roman Curia.[6] He died, most probably, in 1390,[7] and is buried in his native town.[8]

Two jurists are mentioned by Lucas as his teachers, the one a civilian, the other a canonist. Since he reserves for these two alone the appellation of ' dominus meus ', it may safely be presumed that these were his only teachers : Henricus Acconzaiocus de Ravello, who was professor of civil law at Naples at the time when Lucas pursued his studies there,[9] and Simon de Brussano, who later became archbishop of Milan,[10] and for whom Lucas preserved affectionate

[1] See, for instance, Lucas's utterance in C. XII, 15, 1, no. 19, which, no doubt, betrays a note of sarcasm: 'Ego autem expertus sum veritatis scintillam studio et scriptura facilius reperiri quam disputatione verbali, quae vix potest absque tumultu procedere '.

[2] See *supra*, p. 8, n. 1, and his remarks in C. X, 41, 6, no. 8 : 'Haec quaestio fuit de facto in civitate nostra . . . pro parte accusatoris allegabam ista jura '.

[3] C. X, 69, 2, no. 5 : 'Constat judici, ut mihi de facto quadam vice accidit ' ; C. X, 19, 5, no 3 : ' Et sic determinatum fuit per me . . .'

[4] C. X, 13, 1, no. 21 : 'Nam cum ista quaestio verteretur coram me et coram alio . . . ego pro nepote sentirem, communi deliberatione quaesivimus super eo doctores, inter quos profundioris scientiae domini Joannes de Laudo et Bartolus de saxoferrato in meam sententiam inclinaverunt '.

[5] If the information of the famous Neapolitan professor of laws, Paris de Puteo, is correct. He says in his treatise 'De re militari' in *Tractatus*, tom. xvi, fol. 394, no. 3, that Lucas was protonotarius and that he was ' regio consilio praefectus ', in which capacity he ' abundantius consuluit '.

[6] See Calasso, loc. cit., p. 403.

[7] See Calasso, loc. cit., and in the *Enciclopedia Italiana*, s.v. Luca da Penna.

[8] Giustiniani, *Memorie Istoriche degli Scrittori Legali del Regno di Napoli*, vol. iii, p. 41. See also the inscription on his tomb in the Appendix.

[9] C. XII, 58, 6, no. 18 : 'Hanc opinionem tenebat subtilis ingenii dominus meus Henricus Acconzaiocus de Ravello '. Henricus was also member of the Supreme Court in the Kingdom. Blasius de Murcone refers to one of Henricus's decisions (see Blasius's commentaries in *Constitutiones*, p. 389, col. 1).

[10] C. XI, 57, 3, no. 14 : 'Super hoc dominus meus doctor excellens Simon de Brussano, nunc Mediolanensis archiepiscopus, sic distinguit . . .'

feelings of friendship.[1] In his juristic thought he was often guided by two other Neapolitan jurists—namely, Andreas de Isernia and Bartholomaeus de Capua.

Lucas de Penna's main work is a commentary on the 'Tres Libri Codicis' (C. X–XII), a voluminous book of some 1050 folio pages, dedicated to a Cardinal Petrus Sanctae Mariae Novae.[2] The preface relates how this commentary came to be written. The learned librarian of the royal library of King Robert of Naples, Paulus Perusinus—'ingenuus et magnae potentiae vir', as Lucas calls him—drew his attention to the neglected study of the three books and himself expressed a wish to comment on them. After the death of Paulus in the plague of 1348, Lucas remembered that conversation when he himself was laid up with some grave illness. Brooding over it in his sick bed, he imagined that he would not recover unless he engaged his mind in some absorbing activity: 'Cognovi, quod in me corporis vires non poterant restaurari, nisi aliqualiter efficeretur animus meus gaudens'. He resolved to utilize his enforced idleness by studying the three books of the Codex.[3] There is no indication as to when exactly the work was begun or was finished. Certain parts at least must have been written after 1358, because Raynerius de Forlivio died in that year, and he is referred to as 'dominus mirabilis memoriae'—a reference only possible after his death. Lucas frankly admits that his commentaries caused him much toil and sweat—'ecce pro intelligendis legibus ultimorum librorum Codicis longo tempore desudavi'.[4] Other writings of Lucas are extant in manuscript only, such as a treatise *De juris interpretatione*,[5] and an essay *De praesumptionibus juris*, preserved in the Biblioteca Angelica at Rome.[6]

According to Caccialupus, Simon de 'Bursiano' wrote commentaries on the *Clementines*, loc. cit., p. 510. This scholar was probably Simon de Bursano, archbishop of Milan, one of the Italian cardinals who took part in the historic election of Urban VI (see Hefele, *Conciliengeschichte*, vol. vi, p. 728). He was created a cardinal by Gregory XI in 1375 (see Baluzius, *Vitae Paparum Avenionensium*, tom. i, col. 433). Although voting for Urban VI, Simon maintained later in a declaration (1380) that the cardinals elected Urban 'solum timore mortis, ut mortis periculum possent evitare et si tempore prolationis fuissent in loco secuto, nullatenus elegissent ipsum' (see Baluzius, op cit., tom. ii, col. 935 seq.). On his death-bed Simon solemnly declared on 26.8.1381 that the election was a farce, see Bulaeus, *Historia Universitatis Parisiensis*, tom. IV, p. 586. He possessed the archdiaconry of Wells and a prebend of Salisbury, see Perroy, *L'Angleterre et le Grand Schisme de l'Occident*, p. 59.

[1] See Calasso, loc. cit., p. 404, and Wronowski, loc. cit., p. 24.

[2] For a possible explanation of this personality, see Girard, 'Les preliminaires de la renaissance du droit romain', in *Revue Historique du Droit Français et Etranger*, 4th series, vol. i, 1922, pp. 41 f.

[3] '. . . ideo tres libros codicis legere destinavi, ubi multa sunt incognita et per antiquos doctores neglecta', Preface.

[4] Preface no. 1.

[5] Giustiniani, loc. cit., vol. iii, p. 42, reports that this manuscript is in Bologna.

[6] Prof. Calasso, loc. cit., p. 403. The sixteenth-century jurist Rolandus

Lucas is never weary of modestly pointing out that his commentaries are not written for the public, that they are not meant to rank with the works of other jurists of great name, and that they are not intended to be a contribution to legal scholarship. He simply writes, as he says, for his own delight and for his own benefit.[1] Nevertheless, it can easily be verified that his commentaries on the *Codex* acquired great authority with Neapolitan jurists. The glosses on the Sicilian laws contain numerous references to his main work, which one Glossator recommends to students of law for exhaustive perusal because of the clearness of its author's thought.[2] In another gloss the reader is simply referred to Lucas: 'Vide omnino in hac materia unam auream quaestionem, quam ponit Lucas de Penna'.[3] A third gloss mentions Lucas's viewpoints and adds the terse advice: 'quem semper videas'.[4] Similar examples from the gloss could be multiplied.[5] Yet, in spite of the low estimate of his own abilities, Lucas's voice had great weight with the supreme Court of Justice in the Kingdom, as is testified by the report of Blasius de Murcone, who, in his capacity as a judge of the Court, personally consulted him.[6] Evidence of the greatness of Lucas's influence and prestige can be found in the writings of the fifteenth-century Neapolitan jurist, Paris de Puteo, professor of laws at the university of Naples; his writings abound in references and quotations from Lucas.[7] Paris de Puteo may well be taken as the last

---

a Valle in his treatise 'De confectione inventarii' in *Tractatus*, tom. viii. pars 2, fol. 168, reports of a tract written by Lucas and entitled *De privilegio fisci*. But I could not find any other mention of a treatise of this title composed by Lucas, except a reference by Jean Bodin, *De Republica*, lib. i, cap. 10 (p. 269, note (c)), where Bodin speaks of a tract *De fisco* written by Lucas, who is, however, qualified as 'Parmensis'.

Paris de Puteo refers to a commentary of Lucas on the *Digestum vetus* (see Paris in his tract 'De sindicatu' in *Tractatus*, tom. vii, fol. 227). But none of the modern authorities refers to either of these works. On the tract of Lucas *In Valerium Maximum, Quem Librum Dedicat Gregorio P.P.*, see Girard, loc. cit., p. 42. The manuscript of this tract is in the Library of Leiden (see Savigny, loc. cit.).

[1] A typical remark is this which is not in the preface, but in the commentaries: C. X, 59, 1, no. 26: 'Scripsi quippe quam plurima in hoc opusculo sint, sed per me mihi saepius recensenda'.

[2] 'Quia pulchre loquitur', gloss on Charles I's laws, *Constitutiones*, p. 305.

[3] Gloss on Charles II's laws, loc. cit., p. 314.

[4] Gloss, loc. cit., p. 316, col. 2.

[5] The commentator of the Sicilian laws, Diomedes Mariconda (born 1470, died 1511, see Giustiniani, loc. cit., vol. ii, p. 224) refers to Lucas frequently and with great reverence, see *Constitutiones*, pp. 205, 232, 242, 330. Diomedes reports of cases occurred in 1496, 1499, and 1505, in which Lucas's doctrine was followed. Another commentator who signs himself V.M.A., whose identity could not be established, also frequently refers to Lucas (see pp. 299, 309, 316, 408, &c.).

[6] See the long report of Blasius de Murcone in his commentaries, loc. cit., p. 279, col. 1, where he says also: 'Lucas de Penna a me interrogatus sic de verbo ad verbum respondit . . .' No mention of this report is made by Giustiniani, Wronowski, Calasso, or Savigny.

[7] See his treatise 'De sindicatu' in *Tractatus*, tom. vii, fol. 215 seq.

great representative of the Neapolitan law school. He is a striking example of the vast influence which Lucas's views obtained in fifteenth-century Neapolitan legal thought. When consulted in actual cases, Paris not only gave the views of Lucas as his answer,[1] but also reported that Lucas's theories were to be preferred to those of Bartolus [2] and to those of Cynus and Baldus.[3] Moreover, the great confidence that Paris had in Lucas's doctrines is apparent in his advice to legal scholars to take Lucas's disquisitions into account: 'vide late dominum Lucam'; [4] and Paris was not sparing in his praise of his fellow-countryman when he said: 'dixit notabiliter dominus Lucas de Penna'.[5] In particular, Paris de Puteo closely adhered to Lucas's views on the aim of interpretation, on the value of the evidence taken in Court, and on the role which the conscience of the judge has to play in judicial decisions; Paris followed Lucas's sceptical attitude towards confessions obtained by torture and his theory of resistance to the orders of officials, which theory of Lucas Paris termed 'unique'; [6] he also accepted Lucas's idea of rulership, of the significance of the Ruler's coronation, of tyranny, and the justification of tyrannicide,[7] and Lucas's theory of crime and punishment was fully adopted by Paris. These are only instances which go to show how much Lucas's thought influenced fifteenth-century legal science in the Neapolitan seat of learning.

It is certainly true that outside the Sicilian Kingdom the appreciation of Lucas's legal and political thought became noticeable only at the beginning of the sixteenth century. That Lucas was not appreciated before then is clearly due to the comparatively late publication of his Commentaries—the first edition dates from 1509—and to his having no opportunity of making his views publicly known, since he was no academic teacher. Both facts account for the late recognition—admittedly at a time when, at all events, Italian jurisprudence had passed its zenith and the jurists were no longer imbued with the same genuine spirit of research that marked the work of their predecessors in the fourteenth and fifteenth centuries. Nevertheless, the sixteenth century saw Lucas ranked equally with Bartolus, Baldus, Castrensis, and Salicetus. This growth of Lucas's reputation and prestige is certainly not only attributable to the outstanding intrinsic value of his doctrines, however much they were esteemed by sixteenth-century writers—it was by Lucas's views on war and peace that the jurisconsult Nicolai Moroni was stimulated

[1] loc. cit., fol. 259, verso, no. 6.
[2] loc. cit., fol. 263 verso, no. 2.
[3] loc. cit., fol. 275.
[4] Fol. 267 verso, no. 2.
[5] loc. cit., fol. 269, no. 3.
[6] loc. cit., fol. 303, no. 6.
[7] See, e.g., fols. 216, 217, 237, 244, 259 verso, 263 verso, 275, 301 verso, 305 verso, 314, 315 verso, 317, 319, and *passim*. See also the tract 'De re militari' in *Tractatus*, tom. xvi, fol. 411 verso, 412, 419, 422, &c.

to write a special treatise,[1] whilst the famous jurist Octavio Simoncelli designated Lucas's mode of thought as 'egregie',[2] and the Veronese scholar Augustinus Dulcetus dealt with Lucas's theories as if they were the truth [3]—but also to a mere external circumstance. The French professor of laws, Andreas Tiraquellus, propounded the view, which became current in the sixteenth century, that Bartolus's commentaries on the last three books of the *Codex* were not from Bartolus's own pen.[4] Jacobus Menochius, professor of laws at Pavia University at the end of the sixteenth century, bears witness that Tiraquellus's views had gained rapid currency.[5] Thus Lucas's most detailed commentaries on the *Tres Libri* assumed ever greater importance and reputation. As a matter of fact, the great jurists had never devoted much attention to this part of the *Codex*—the complaint of Paulus Perusinus remained true throughout the whole period of Italian jurisprudence—and it was therefore only natural that eventually Lucas's commentaries came rightly to be considered as the sole source of authoritative information in respect of the three books. Hence, whenever circumstances necessitated the interpretation of a legal enactment contained in the three books, serious legal scholarship had to resort to Lucas. Furthermore, Lucas's views resembled political thought fashionable in the sixteenth century so much that the political writers of the sixteenth century constantly referred to Lucas for confirmation. The already mentioned Jacobus Menochius may be taken as a typical example of late sixteenth-century legal thought; he constantly referred to Lucas whenever an item of the three books required elucidation.[6] Another example is Rolandus a Valle, whose *Consilia* and tracts are also full of quotations from Lucas, not only on special matters relating to the enactments of the three books, but also on general legal and political questions.[7] Nicolas Boer, Julius Clarus, and Stephanus Aufrerius

[1] 'De treuga et pace' in *Tractatus*, tom. xi; the preface relates that Moroni was stimulated by Lucas's views, fol. 418. He argues at great length on Lucas's viewpoints, see, e.g., quaestio vi, viii, ix, xvii, xviii, lii, lvi, lix, lx, lxviii, lxxv, lxxix, cii, cv, cvii, cxiii, cxx, cxxviii, cxxix, cxxxv, cxxxviii, cxlvii, clviii, clix, clxxvi, clxxxvi, clxxxvii, &c.

[2] In his tract 'De decretis' in *Tractatus*, tom. vi, pars 2, inspectio iv, no. 36, fol. 321.

[3] See his tract 'De sindicatu', loc. cit., tom. vii, fol. 361, no. 27.

[4] Tiraquellus (Tiraqueau) in his treatise 'De legibus connubialibus et jure maritali' in *Opera Omnia*—the treatise was written in 1524, see preface —lib. i, no. 35: 'Sed illud te hic scire oportet, lector', he says, 'multi addubitant, alii constanter affirmant eos commentarios, qui nomine Bartoli circumferuntur . . . non esse Bartoli, sed cuiuspiam Contis'. In no. 36 he says: 'Certum est, multum interesse inter Bartolum maximae auctoritatis virum et illum Contem nullius propemodum, uti semper inter artifices longa est differentia'.

[5] Jacobus Menochius in his book *De recuperanda possessione commentaria*, p. 306, no. 6.

[6] loc. cit., *passim*. See also his book *De praesumptionibus*, pp. 318, 357, 651, &c.

[7] *Consilia*, see vol. i, cons. 81; vol. ii, cons. 48, 83, 90; vol. iii, cons. 52,

must not be omitted as a further instance of the greatness of Lucas's reputation in the sixteenth century.[1]

The very fact that Lucas's work on the *Tres Libri* was printed six times in France alone illustrates the great demand for his work in French legal and political circles during the sixteenth century.[2] Indeed, the French jurists most frequently refer to Lucas. The works of the already mentioned Tiraquellus,[3] the writings of the professor of constitutional law, Jean Montaigne,[4] the commentaries of the professor of canon law, 'the celebrated jurist'[5] Petrus Rebuffus,[6] and the famous *De Republica* of Jean Bodin,[7] are merely a few obvious examples that bear convincing testimony to the high esteem which those eminent scholars had for Lucas.[8]

His reputation was also well established among the scholars of sixteenth-century Spain. The noted jurist, Antonio Gomez, who, through his systematic treatment of legal problems, exercised great influence on both Spanish scholarship and judiciary, constantly resorts to Lucas, especially in criminal and political matters.[9] Another Spanish jurist of the sixteenth century is Franciscus Vargas, who occupied high political offices and wrote a treatise on the political

---

&c. See also his tract 'De inventarii confectione' in *Tractatus*, tom. viii, pars. 2, fol. 166, 168 verso, 177, &c.; and the tract 'De dote' (written in autumn 1551) in *Tractatus*, tom. ix, fol. 352 verso, &c.

Alciatus too refers to Lucas, especially in political matters, see, e.g., C. I, 2, 5, no. 11, col. 27, &c.

[1] Nicolaus Boer, 'De Custodia Clavium' in *Tractatus*, tom. xvi, fol. 282 seq. Julius Clarus, 'der Kriminalist des 16. Jahrhunderts', as E. Moeller calls him—*Opera Omnia*, lib. v, §, fin., quaestio VII, no. 11, pp. 119, &c. Stephanus Aufrerius, 'De Potestate Ecclesiae super Laicis', in *Tractatus*, tom. xvi, fols. 297 seq.

[2] The following editions were printed in France: Paris, 1509, Lyons, 1557, 1582, 1586, 1593, 1597. The last-named edition is rarely known; there are no references to it in Giustiniani or Savigny or Girard, nor does Professor Calasso mention it. This edition is in the Library of Trinity College, Cambridge. Italian editions: Venice, 1512, Mantua, 1529, 1538.

[3] See, e.g., his treatise 'De jure primigenitorum' in *Opera Omnia*, quaestio 31, 35, 40, &c. References to Lucas can be found throughout Tiraquellus's books.

[4] See his treatise 'De parlamentis' in *Tractatus*, tom. xvi, fol. 273 seq.

[5] See McIlwain, *The Growth of Political Thought in the West*, p. 381.

[6] *Tractatus varii*, pp. 86, 144, 220, 472, 473, 484, 494, 568, 572, 577, 599, 601, 603, 605.

[7] Bodin's *De Republica*, Francofurti, 1609, lib. i, cap. 10 (pp. 260, 267, 271), lib. iii, cap. 3 (p. 435), cap. 8 (pp. 547, 553, 557, 560), lib. vi, cap. 2 (p. 1033), cap. 5 (p. 1165), &c.

[8] The fact that Lucas's commentaries ran through so many editions in France alone within a relatively short period is of course not accidental. His views resemble, in many points, those of the partisans of the divine right of kings, but the presentation of this resemblance merits a study of its own and cannot be undertaken in the framework of the present thesis. That he was quoted by some French political writers more often than Bartolus deserves special attention.

[9] See his *Commentariorum Variarumque Resolutionum juris civilis, communis et regii tomi tres*, tom. iii, cap. 3, p. 471, no. 5, with verbal quotations, and his tract *De Tortura Reorum*, p. 559, no. 8, p. 576, no. 37, &c., &c.

aspects of ecclesiastical power; he is also well versed in Lucas's writings, as his numerous references to the latter's commentaries prove.[1]

II

The significance of Lucas's main work is inversely proportionate to its somewhat unassuming title. It is not a simple commentary on the *Tres Libri*, as the title misleadingly suggests; it is rather a complete exposition of the fundamental legal principles and juristic rules relating to all departments and ramifications of the law.

Each commentary is introduced by a practical case which illustrates the content of the enactment he is to comment on. Then follows the commentary proper in which he employs a typical scheme of his own device containing two parts. The first deals with the grammatical and philological analysis of the terms which are used in the particular law. This philological explanation, in which he extensively draws on the dictionary of the medieval grammarian Papias,[2] aims at a linguistic clarification of the terms. The collection of equivalents is followed by a rejection of those meanings which have no bearing on the juristic import of the term or of the whole passage. Sometimes he resorts to an analysis of the component grammatical elements when, in his opinion, the juristic elucidation of the term may benefit from this purely grammatical investigation.[3] The second and far more important part of his scheme is the legal analysis proper. Here he tries to show the origin of a particular concept, its theoretical and practical meaning, its value for the application and interpretation of the law, its different connotations in other passages of the *Corpus*—in short, Lucas here proceeds to a systematization of jurisprudential concepts and to an investigation into the general principles behind the particular law. Yet the *Corpus juris civilis* is not the only basis of his research work. Whenever a legal concept or idea is treated by both civil and canon law, he consults canon law and canonistic research extensively. His perusal of both bodies of law reveals his most detailed knowledge of their enactments and testifies to his desire to interpret the individual law in terms of the whole—the legal order, which in its turn is an integral part of a larger whole—the world order.

[1] See his treatise 'De auctoritate Pontificis' in *Tractatus*, tom. xiii, fol. 113 verso, no. 2, &c.

[2] See on the importance of this dictionary in the Middle Ages, Sandys, *History of Classical Scholarship*, vol. i, p. 521, and Kantorowicz, *Studies in the Glossators* (in collaboration with Prof. W. W. Buckland), p. 60.

[3] The following example may suffice to show his philological analysis: C. X, 31, 65 Rubrica: 'Excelsas'—excelsus dicitur valde celsus, elatus, immensus, altus, eminens, secundum Papiam; 'relaxatione'—liberatione; 'dispositiones'—constitutiones; 'promulgata'—pronuntiata, prolata, patefacta; 'regulas'—dicitur regula, quod recte ducit . . . An example of a grammatical analysis: C. X, 16, 3, no. 1: 'ascribuntur—adscribo componitur cum "a" et "scribo" et proprie est alicui qualitatem scribere'.

A brief discussion of Lucas's views on legal science may appropriately precede the exposition of his theory of law and enable us to gain a more proportionate view of his whole system. Legal science is conceived by him as simply a species of science in general whose task is the discovery and comprehension of the immutable truth.[1] Science, he says, assumes the character of an 'assidua et sagax retractio cognitionis, aliquid involutum explicare nitens vel scrutans penetrare secretum'.[2] 'Scientia' as contrasted with 'sapientia' is concerned with human things only.[3] Its aim is the perception of first causes—'fontes rerum videre'[4]—and of those principles which are eternal in the government of the world.[5] Its immediate object, he avows, borrowing the words of John of Salisbury, is to instil into the mind of human creatures that 'homo subjectus sit legi Dei'.[6]

He outlines the subject-matter of legal science upon the basis of a fixed world order and the conception of a divine contrivance comprehending all Being. From the metaphysical point of view, he assures us, law is derived from divine authority and should be taken in a far wider sense than the term usually suggests. For, he argues, behind all worldly phenomena there is a regularity of working and a harmony of activity which can only result from some irresistible directive force. It is this very force which he considers as being imparted to all worldly mechanisms and as the foundation of all Life and Being. In the true medieval fashion Lucas identifies this determinative force with Reason immanent in the working of Nature: 'Lex est ratio summa insita in natura'. It is an intelligent force regulating all activity and directing all action to a definitive, preconceived end. Stripped of its concrete accompaniments, this power appears as the manifestation of an all-embracing and all-powerful law (*lex*). The divine origin of that (metaphysical) *lex* is an unquestionable premise. Law, in this sense, is the unchangeable order of the Universe.[7]

That metaphysical tenet is projected by Lucas on to the plane of human life and social activity. Indeed, the juristic *lex* is the offspring of the metaphysical *lex* and has substantially the same function—namely, that of a directing force, an unfailing and unerring guide of human actions in the social field: 'Lex est lux et

[1] 'Scientia est rerum, quae sunt comprehensio veritatis, immutabilium', C. XI, 18, 1, no. 10.

[2] loc. cit., no. 25.

[3] 'Scientia intelligitur quoad humana, sapientia quoad divina', loc. cit.

[4] loc. cit., no. 21.

[5] 'Aeternum quidem, quod universum mundum regeret', loc. cit., no. 12.

[6] He refers to the *Policraticus*, lib. VII, cap. 11, and says: 'Omnis doctrina illuc tendit, ut homo sit subjectus legi Dei'. The wording of Lucas agrees with that of John. On the latter's great influence see *infra*, sect. III.

[7] On this Augustinian conception of the universal law see also *infra*, ch. III.

via vitae '.[1] The juristic law is merely a subordinate species of the generic concept. It is the very agency through which divine power motivates human beings and directs their life in society. Thus law is ' perfecta ratio ', ' summa ratio '. Originating in divine contrivance, law manifests itself as the principle which orientates and orders harmoniously all human social activity. Its precepts are identical with the dictates of reason : ' Lex est summa ratio . . . i.e., scientia vel sententia, firmitas et immutabilitas Dei. Et hoc modo dicitur lex perfecta ratio a Dei scientia sententiave procedens '. Accordingly, the juristic idea of law presents itself as a moral force which directs human social life towards the definitive, preconceived end of man. It is not therefore surprising to find that our jurist—in common with contemporaries—asserts that the law is ' donum Dei ' or is ' divinae voluntatis imago '.[2] In other words, law in this sense is conceived by Lucas as a rule of human action. Conceiving human conduct as purposive, he is necessarily led to expound a notion of law that is at once normative and teleological.

His claim that legal science is sacred science, to a no less extent sacred than theology itself,[3] and that jurists are, properly speaking, ' sacerdotes ' is a corollary of his speculative view of law. Still less surprising is the further claim that, since legal science is concerned with the exposition and elaboration of the precepts inherent in the law, it is raised to the sublime level of a sacred art—' ars est habitus quidam cum ratione vera factivus ; ars est collectio praeceptorum et hoc modo scientia legalis dicitur ars '.[4] The central theme of this science—namely, the idea of justice—renders it useful : ' Illa sola utilis et laudabilis est scientia, quam commendat comes justitia '.[5]

The discussion of the merits of legal science induces Lucas to expose the pretensions of medical science : a curious parallel, reminiscent of modern disputes, becomes apparent in this controversy. Though not directly bearing on our subject, a sketch of this dispute should not be omitted. The medical scholars, in whom we may recognize the precursors of modern natural science scholars, denied legal science all scientific character, although, as Lucas indignantly remarks, it is the science *par excellence* and can be compared with philosophy only.[6] He thinks that this arrogant attitude on the part of medical science is the result of certain privileges granted to medical scholars and refused to the doctors of law.[7] On account

[1] C. X, 5, 2, no. 9, where he refers to *Proverbs*, vi, 23.

[2] C. XI, 18, 1, no. 12, referring to the *Policraticus*, lib. IV, cap. 1, lib. VI, cap. 25. This expression, attributed to Demosthenes, was usually derived from Martianus, see Bartolus on D. 1, 3, 2.

[3] loc. cit., no. 10. See also C. X, 52, Rubrica, no. 3.

[4] C. X, 54, 1, no. 1.

[5] C. XI, 18, 1, no. 33.

[6] ' Scientia juris et legum dicitur profundior et philosophiae comparatur . . . quod est contra medicos asserentes hanc scientiam non habere subjectum nec procedendi modum ', loc. cit., no. 19.

[7] ' Professor medicinae, sive Romae sive in patria, profiteatur, habet

of its profundity, its usefulness to mankind, its sacredness, and its subject, the scientific character of legal science is beyond dispute. Unlike medical science, its scope and aim are not limited to questionable remedies for physical maladies; [1] for, he asserts with great vigour, the aim of legal science is loftier. It attempts to lay bare the immaterial forces constituting the essence of social life. But a deeper investigation into the real differences between medical and legal science convinces him that the conception of life held by the 'professores medicinae' is essentially different from that held by the 'Doctores legum'. He argues that the medical attitude is determined by too great a reverence for 'nature', entailing a conception of creator and creation and of notions, such as soul, virtue, and the like, totally at variance with the conceptions presented by the Faith: 'aliter quam fides habeat'. It is in this different conception of, and attitude to, the fundamentals of life that he sees a substantial difference between the two sciences.[2] He speaks of medical science in rather sarcastic terms and maintains that it focuses its main attention on merely physical aspects of life and on matter, whereas legal science deals with spiritual elements and forces and is, therefore, 'quanto nobilior et honorabilior medicinali'.[3]

The character of Lucas's commentaries necessitates an outline of the suggested functions of academic teachers, and the proposed lines of research, he holds, should be acted upon in all fields of academic studies. The supreme task of the academic teachers, the 'Doctores legum', he avows, is the discovery and dissemination of

excusationem a muneribus . . . item a patrimonialibus . . . quod non invenitur in legum doctore', C. X, 52, Rubrica no. 1.

[1] 'Haec adversus medicos scientiae legalis aemulos et veritatis justitiae inimicos perstrinxisse sufficiat . . . solus enim Deus et non medici liberant ab omni malo, neque herba neque malagma . . . ideo medici grandes morbos naturae relinquunt'. In order to express his feelings forcibly he exclaims 'Tuus, domine, sermo, qui sanat omnia. Tu es, qui vitae et mortis habes potestatem et deducis ad portas mortis,' loc. cit., no. 3.

[2] The extraordinary resemblance of John of Salisbury's views to those of Lucas becomes increasingly apparent when we compare the latter's assertion of the supremacy of the mind over matter with the former's insistence on the superiority 'of the ideal over the material' (R. L. Poole, *Illustrations of the History of Medieval Thought and Learning*, p. 190).

[3] loc. cit., no. 2. The unabridged quotation of the relevant passage is advisable because of the illuminating sidelight it throws upon scientific activities in the Middle Ages:

> Physici, dum naturae nimium auctoritatis attribuunt, in auctorem naturae adversando fidei plerumque impingunt, non enim omnes erroris arguo, licet plurimos audiverim de anima, de virtutibus et operibus eius, de augmento corporis et diminutione, de resurrectione eiusdem et creatione rerum, aliter quam fides habeat, disputantes. De ipso quoque Deo ita loquuntur, ac si terrigenae tentarent astra gigantes et inani conatu cum Encelando, ut eis Ethnae onus ignifluum imponatur cupiant promereri, sed in his facile possunt labi, qui quanticumque ingenii vires circa profunditatem difficultatis, quae in his vertitur, substituunt: ubi vero deficit intellectus fidei ratione deducta, quae media est, restat sola opinio.

truth. They can be equal to their high responsibility only when they become aware of the ulterior motive of all research work: it is not to be undertaken for its own sake, but is to be pursued to praise God. He declares that legal science 'non ad delectationem hominum, sed ad Dei laudem praedicanda est'.[1] This ulterior motive not only bestows truly scientific character upon the science of law, but also dignifies it and, above all, guarantees the pursuit of truth. Similarly, the teacher's motive for scientific investigation should not be the desire for flattering praises and tawdry distinctions, but for the discovery and communication of the truth.[2] In Lucas's conviction, the suggested attitude of the teacher presupposes that the teacher is imbued with the spirit of the Christian Faith, because it is precisely this spiritual element which safeguards the search for truth.[3] All science, he says, serves one purpose only—namely, to know God in His eternal wisdom, because God 'cuncta praevidet et cuncta dijudicat'. He is the beginning and the end, the cause of all Being: 'Deus est alpha et omega, principium et finis, cui saecula nec accesserunt nec coaeterna sunt' (C. XII, 46, 1, no. 2). True happiness, Lucas declares, can only come through the acceptance of the ideas contained in the Christian revelation: 'Vera autem beatitudo est revelatio gloriae magni Dei et salvatoris nostri Jesu Christi'. At the same time he significantly declares that in these matters there can never be the certainty established by scientific inquiries, but only belief: 'De hac autem non potest esse certitudo scientiae, sed credulitas tantum'.

Lucas attacks with particular venom those teachers whose motives are personal vanity, ostentation, or other reprehensible desires; they do not deserve the name of a 'Doctor legum', and should be removed from the chair.[4] Simplicity of style and speech[5] and the adaptation of material to the intellectual level of the audience are indispensable both for the imparting of knowledge and for its adequate apprehension by the audience: 'Quid prodest integritas eloquentis, quam non sequitur intellectus audientis?' he asks pertinently.[6] He advises the teacher to refrain from profound dis-

[1] C. XII, 15, 1, no. 17.

[2] 'In docendo quoque delectetur non aviditate consequendae laudis, sed charitate seminandae veritatis', ibid. He thinks it apposite to remind scholars that they have to renounce all their worldly gains and that they must not expect any profitable pursuit from their studies: C. XI, 18, 1, no. 29.

[3] 'Nulli dubium, quod fides foret sibi integraliter adhibenda', C. XII, 15, 1, no. 27.

[4] He says that they teach 'non ad eorum (scil. auditorum) utilitatem, sed suam ostentationem . . . et hi amovendi sunt ab ostentatione vulgari', C. XII, 15, 1, no. 27. A few lines before this passage he says: 'Doctores quidem sine veritate scientiae quantum ad formam et habitum sunt doctores, inanes autem quoad effectum et falsi', loc. cit., no. 25.

[5] 'Bonus doctor vulgi more loquitur, ut ambiguitates obscuritatesque vitet, non sic dicat, ut a doctis, sed ab indoctis dici solet', loc. cit., no. 17.

[6] loc. cit., no. 17.

courses before an audience incapable of appreciating the value of scientific research, because they 'despiciunt doctrinam eloquii tui'. His use of the metaphor is appropriate: 'Hoc est etiam mittere margaritas ante porcos'.[1] Lucas cannot discover any scientific zeal in those scholars who are desirous of finding difficulties where none are and who thereby obscure simple issues.[2] He writes scornfully that it is precisely they themselves 'qui grandi aut torto naso sese plus quam necesse est exercentes ex nimia subtilitate falluntur'.[3]

The proposed lines of research deal with method and the value and importance of the gloss and other authorities in the field of legal studies. It is well known that the age of our jurist was the heyday of scholastic philosophy which was characterized by the over-luxuriant, formalistic use of equally formalistic schemes—dialectics. To a slight degree the dialectical method infected some Post-Glossators, but none of them concentrated on method at the expense of substance. Lucas, the Post-Glossator, is not only completely free from this 'infection', but strongly condemns the dialectical method. Incidentally, his work furnishes impressive evidence against the common charge of modern scholarship that the Post-Glossators were in the fetters of dialectics which, it is said, thwarted all their scientific efforts and precluded the display of any scientific spirit.[4]

[1] He continues: 'Beatus homo, qui loquitur in aurem audientium . . . sicut enim abominatio est peccatoris Dei cultus, sic et abominatio est ignorantis doctrina sapientis'.

[2] loc. cit., no. 17: 'Sunt nonulli, qui in legibus nihil obscuritatem habentibus ingerunt quaestiones ex studio et ad suam intentionem obscuritatem introducunt'.

[3] loc. cit., no. 11.

[4] The contempt with which modern scholarship treats Italian jurisprudence goes back to certain humanistic jurists, such as Cujas—it was he who coined the cheap phrase that the Post-Glossators were 'verbosi in re facili, in difficili muti, in angusta diffusi'—and has received fresh life from Savigny of our own time. It was Savigny who justified the neglect of the Post-Glossators, and his attacks on them have been reproduced since with varying degrees of ingenuity. See Savigny, loc. cit., vol. vi, pp. 9, 14, and *passim*; Calisse, *Storia del diritto italiano*, vol. i, partly translated in *Continental Legal History Series*, ed. by J. H. Wigmore, vol. i, pp. 87 seq. Of recent date are the derogatory remarks of Rashdall, *Universities of Europe*, vol. i, pp. 255 seq., and of Mr. J. W. Jones, *Historical Introduction to the Theory of Law*, pp. 15 seq. But for the permanent contributions of the Post-Glossators see, on the other hand, Professor Pound, *Introduction to the Philosophy of Law*, p. 37, P. Vinogradoff, *Roman Law in Medieval Europe*, *passim*, Professor de Zulueta, 'The Science of Law' in *The Legacy of Rome*, p. 178, Professor Meynial, 'Roman Law' in *The Legacy of the Middle Ages*, pp. 371 seq., Professor Hazeltine, 'Roman and Canon Law' in *Cambridge Medieval History*, vol. v, p. 739, and Professor McIlwain, loc. cit., pp. 344 seq.

The late Sir W. Holdsworth, loc. cit., vol. iv, p. 224, very aptly draws attention to the similarities which existed between the writings of the Italian scholars and the English Year Books. The prolixity of statements characterizing the formers' commentaries is also to be found in the Year Books. 'Their method of scholastic dialectics with its divisions and

Logic, he affirms, cannot be called a science by itself, but only a 'modus sciendi'.[1] His line of thought and argumentation reveals, as it so often does, his deeply religious mind. He reminds his readers that God's kingdom rests on the simplicity of Faith, not on certain sophisticated arguments.[2] In pursuance of this thought he expresses his disapproval of the dialectical method. The relevant passage is couched in sarcastic terms and strikingly proves how unfounded the indictment of modern scholarship is: 'Dialectorum namque tendicula sunt quaedam phantasmata et umbrae, quae cito resolvuntur . . . et qui dialectica arte diebus noctibusque torquuntur, in obscuritate mentis gradiuntur'.[3] In his opinion, the dialectical method leads to a distortion of the legal text and to an ambiguity of doctrine as well as to a disregard of the important maxim: 'Leges sub ambage tradendae non sunt'. The tendency of certain scholars to dally superficially with words instead of recognizing them as mere vehicles of expression is fostered by the dialectical method.[4] Though it may gratify the taste of a rude and uncritical mind, Lucas scornfully writes that the effort to interpret the law solely by finding dictionary equivalents for the words used by the legislator, is unworthy of a scholar.[5] It is the thought and the idea behind the word that the true scholar must lay bare.

Lucas also treats of the part which gloss and authority in general should play in the pursuit of legal studies. Here, too, modern scholarship charges the Post-Glossators with slavish dependence on the gloss and the worship of authorities. To both charges Lucas, the Post-Glossator, furnishes us with the appropriate reply. The criterion for the juristic value of glosses is their conformity to the legal text. Glosses which at the outset are at variance with the law may be disregarded, for 'glossae cuiuscumque facultatis sic debet textui convenire'.[6] He says that only those glosses are fruitful and of scientific value by which the proper meaning of the words or the construction of the passage 'vel ipsa lex aut con-

---

distinctions, its rules and exceptions, its amplifications and additions, its declarations and repetitions, was used by our English lawyers in arguing upon the many analogous cases which were suggested by the ingenuity of the bar or bench as the debate in court proceeded', ibid. See also Coke's utterance, ibid., note 5.

[1] 'Scientia quidem logicalis non est scientia, sed quidam modus sciendi', C. XI, 18, 1 no. 6, referring to the *Policraticus*, lib. vii, cap. 12.

[2] 'Non in dialectica placuit Deus pater filio suo, quia regnum in simplicitate fidei est, non in contentione sermonis', loc. cit., no. 7.

[3] loc. cit., no. 7, alluding to *Decretum, dist.* xxxvii, c. 3.

[4] 'Plerumque enim, dum proprietas verborum attenditur, sensus veritatis amittitur . . . mens namque potior est quam vox', C. XII, 15, 1, no. 9.

[5] 'In lectura vel in scriptis id idem, quod continetur in textu vel glossa apponere quamquam per diversa verba, inde esset occupare membranas, et si rudibus forte placeat, non tamen puto viris intelligentibus', C. X, 7 Rubrica.

[6] Preface no. 9.

stitutio quasi grammaticaliter ad literam vel intelligibilius exponuntur, nec intellectus earum per glossantem depravatur '.[1] The tendency of certain contemporary scholars to rely too much on the gloss is stigmatized by Lucas in these words: 'Multi autem non advertentes legum rationes . . . adhaerent simpliciter glossae dictae legis '.[2]

He counsels a similar independence in regard to other recognized authorities, the criterion being again the truthful exposition and accurate interpretation of the legal concepts: 'Magno doctori non est necesse credi', he warns, 'nisi dictum suum probet auctoritate vel authentica scriptura '.[3] The guiding principle should be this: however great the fame of the authority may be, his reputation does not exempt the genuine scholar from testing the truth and scientific value of the doctrine concerned: 'Non refert, quis doceat, sed qualia doceat', is his motto.[4] Nobody is compelled to 'stare verbis magistri', once he arrives at conclusions which he thinks come nearer to the truth than his master's. The glittering renown enjoyed by some scholars may be deceptive, because 'non omne, quod rubet, est aurum '.[5] He is bold enough to pass the judgement probably arrived at in the course of his own scientific experience that 'plerumque plus premit quam docet auctoritas '.[6]

The question may not inconveniently be asked in this context, whether Lucas himself observed his counsels, particularly the last two mentioned.[7] What part is assigned to gloss and authority in his own work? All his analyses reveal that independence of thought which, in his opinion, is the desirable hall-mark of all scientific study. He considers the gloss as of no greater value than the writing of any other authority. The scientific character of the gloss as a

[1] C. XII, 1, 2, no. 4.

[2] C. XII, 19, 14, no. 12.

[3] C. X, 31, 33, no. 54.

[4] C. XII, 15, 1, no. 3. Cf. also C. X, Proemium no. 4: 'Non doctorum auctoritas, sed rationis veritas semper investiganda est. Non tam auctoris in disputando quam rationis munimenta quaerenda sunt.'

[5] C. XII, 15, 1, no. 10.

[6] Preface no. 7. Prof. Powicke somewhat mitigates Rashdall's general indictment against the Post-Glossators, loc. cit., vol. i, p. 258. In spite of his general appreciation of the work of the Post-Glossators Holdsworth reproduces the well-worn charge against them—i.e., that with them 'truth was the child of authority', ii, 131. Lucas and nearly all his contemporaries furnish excellent proof of the inaccuracy of this indictment. Another palpably wrong indictment is that 'in the Middle Ages all departments of thought were conceived as subordinate to theology in such a way that the methods of theology fettered and strangled free development in science, or art or literature . . . theology had attempted unreasonably to dominate politics, and had committed men to an unphilosophical basis and uncritical method', Figgis, *Divine Right of Kings*, p. 259. It is strange to hear this prejudice voiced by a historian of the late Dr. Figgis' standing. The case of Lucas illustrates how little the Post-Glossator was influenced by theology.

[7] The following pages will prove sufficiently that the counsels were not empty addresses to other jurists. His researches go to show the strict observance of all the rules he desired to see applied by other scholars.

whole is not disputed by Lucas, but the juristic value of individual glosses undergoes rigorous examination in his commentaries. Whenever he is unable to agree with the doctrine of the gloss, he never fails to give his reasons for rejecting it. And when he agrees with the gloss, the acceptance is likewise based on rational considerations. As a rule he quotes the substance of the gloss—' de jure civili glossa determinat . . .'—into whose juristic merits he carefully inquires, which scrutiny is followed, in case of agreement, by ' dic secundum glossam ', or, in case of rejection, by ' licet glossa contrarium teneat '. Phrases such as ' sed certe quicquid in hoc glossa dicat ' are a frequent feature in his work.

The same independence of thought is displayed by Lucas in regard to other authorities. True to his dictum that ' non moveat dicentis auctoritas, non quis, sed quid dicat, attendas ',[1] he critically scrutinizes the contents of the doctrine and is unperturbed by the name and fame of its author, so that, not infrequently, he stands alone against the herd of ' communis opinio ', as, for instance, the following phrases testify : ' In contrarium est communis positio theologorum, canonistarum et legistarum . . . puto posse melius non sine ratione distingui '.[2] Indeed, he attaches very little weight to prestige and authority : ' Dixerunt quidam doctores clarae dignitatis et auctoritatis . . . puto verius '.[3] In another commentary we read that ' communis tamen doctorum opinio est, quod . . .', but he has good reason to say ' puto melius distingui '.[4] Those are only typical, ever-recurring phrases in his commentaries. He examines the doctrines of contemporary eminent jurists carefully and critically. His attitude towards the doctrines of Bartolus provides a striking example of his independent and detached mind : whilst not concealing his admiration for Bartolus, he in no way bows down before him. The tremendous prestige and the titanic figure of Bartolus are no impediments to an uncompromising rejection of some of his doctrines when our jurist disagrees with them : ' Videtur, quod sic . . . et hoc tenuit Bartolus de saxoferrato et quidam alii sequentes eum. Ego autem reputo hanc maximam falsitatem '.[5] Although, on account of its penetrating analyses, he calls Bartolus's political treatise *De repressaliis* ' perutilis ', he is unable to follow some of the doctrines set out in it : ' Scripsit dominus Bartolus . . . puto melius distingui '.[6] In another place Lucas disagrees with Bartolus

[1] C. XI, 18, 1, no. 21.
[2] C. X, 69, 2, no. 5.
[3] C. X, 48, 2, no. 2. Other similar phrases occur frequently, such as : ' Sed quicquid alii dicant, mihi videtur, quod . . .', C. XII, 49, 4, no. 1 ; or ' Per plures doctores scripta diversa reperiuntur, verius tamen credo . . .', C. XII, 57, 6, no. 18.
[4] C. XII, 29, 3, no. 11.
[5] C. XII, 1, 2, no. 19.
[6] C. XI, 56, 1, no. 2. In C. XI, 8, 14, no. 1, Lucas reproaches Bartolus with lack of legal knowledge : ' In hoc etiam deficit dominus Bartolus, qui scripsit hic . . . contrarium patet per jura praedicta. . . .'

and cannot be influenced or even moved by the latter's prestige; he adheres to his own view 'licet dominus Bartolus oppositum dicat'.[1] With much sarcasm Lucas remarks in yet another commentary:[2] 'De hoc satis notat Bartolus ff. de verb. obl., l. inter stipulantem, para. 1. Contrarium videtur verius, ut patet subtiliter intelligenti.' Nevertheless, Lucas has the highest esteem for this urist who overshadowed all his contemporaries for centuries to come. Other authorities are treated from the same independent point of view.[3] None of their doctrines is accepted because of the fame of its author, but because on rational grounds they appear acceptable, whilst the rejection, in its turn, is always based on punctilious consideration.[4] The critical discussion of contemporary doctrines sometimes induces him to make caustic remarks about the scientific devotion of certain contemporaries to their teachers,[5] sometimes expresses the acid contempt of the thinker who scorns the ill-contrived attempts of the bungler.[6]

III

Lucas's independence of thought and his critical attitude towards scholars of whatever rank emanate from his breadth of mind and are a consequence of the vast erudition which he had acquired by intensive study of antique and contemporary philosophic writings. His profound knowledge of all branches of learning enables him to abandon the traditional landmarks of jurisprudence, to throw light upon legal problems from the philosophic angle, and to deal with them under the perspectives of a fixed and stable world order. It is material to his conceptual framework that adequate understanding of the social function of the law and of the complex mechanism behind the law presupposes its deduction from extra-legal premisses, since the juristic law is but a manifestation of an extra-legal principle.[7] That idea emerges as the main thesis of the unusually long preface. He complains in it of the unsatisfactory results attained by jurists, which, to his mind, are due to their endeavour to solve legal problems by purely legalistic arguments and by the accustomed modes of legal thinking. He emphatically opposes this narrow conception by

[1] C. XII, 45, 1, no. 35.

[2] C. XI, 1, 1, no. 7.

[3] See, e.g., his remarks in C. XII, 50, 3, no. 16. He investigates a distinction made by Dynus and says: 'Haec distinctio, licet in se bona sit, non tamen dirimit quaestionem'. Another typical example is provided in his commentary on C. X, 41, 1, no. 2: 'Milites extraordinaria non subeunt . . . secundum Odofredum, quod per legem ipsam assumere nequeo'.

[4] See, e.g., the long dispute he has with Raynerius de Forlivio in C. XII, 1, 17, no. 35, which dispute he concludes: 'Sed quicquid dicatur, aliud videtur'.

[5] 'Cynus tenuit cum Petro (i.e., Petrus de Bellapertica), quem ibi sequitur pro evangelio . . .', C. XI, 47, 14, no. 17.

[6] 'Hanc quaestionem disputavit Jacobus de Belvisio arguens more suo pro et contra.'

[7] See *supra*, section II.

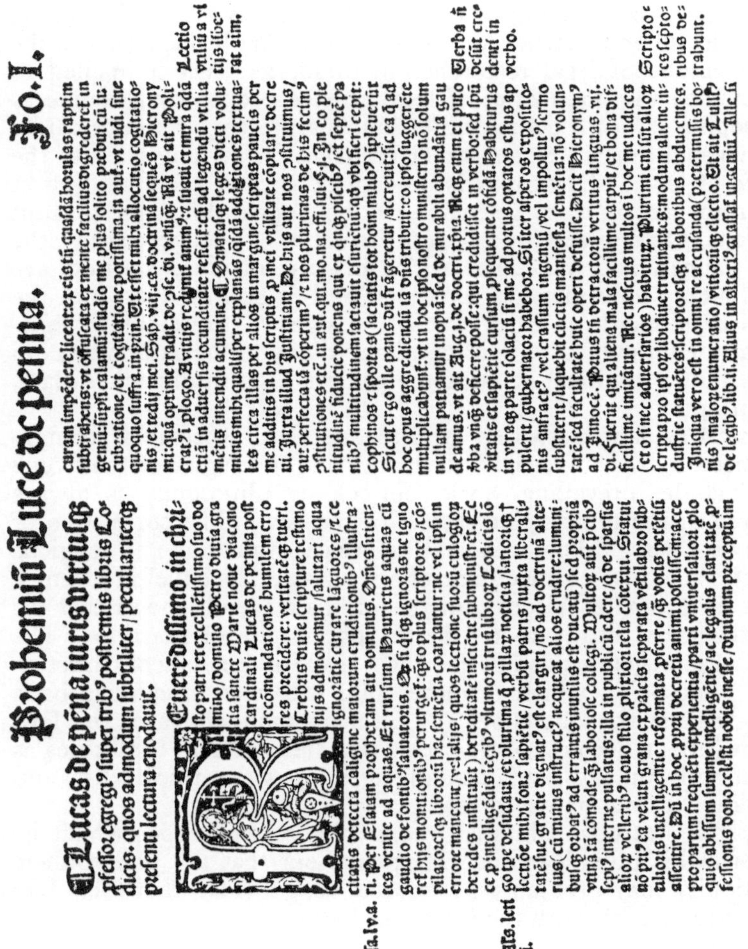

The first part of the preface; first edition, Paris, 1509. Gonville and Caius College, Cambridge declaring that his own scientific interest centres not so much in the 'verba legis' as in the 'vis ac potestas legis' [1]—that is, in the basis from which the individual jural precept secures its authority—in the effects of legal rules within the various branches of the law, and in the conditions of the validity and the binding force of laws. He sets himself the task of laying bare the roots of the law and of bringing to light its inner substance and significance. With this task and the barren results of legal researches in mind, he feels compelled to step outside the boundaries of legal science proper by recourse to philosophy—'rerum divinarum et humanarum cognitio cum studio bene vivendi juncta' [2]—and other branches of learning alien to the science of law: 'Ex scripturis quidem peregrinis a legibus, sed et ex earum sororibus et germanis, in hoc opusculo congesta sunt quaedam ultra praeterque legum materias'.[3] Appreciating the many dangers and difficulties which his task involves, he implores the Almighty to render him assistance and to bestow upon him the necessary strength to carry out his designs: 'Omnipotens desiderium meum audiat . . . in eo plenitudinem fiduciae ponens, qui ex quinque piscibus et septem panibus multitudinem satiavit esurientium'.[4]

It is an evident truth that legal theorists are necessarily strongly influenced by the philosophic doctrines and ideologies of their time and that the prevailing world outlook or philosophy is always mirrored in the philosophic system of the law. The correlation of law to its ideological environment, to ethical evaluation and religious convictions, is also characteristic of our jurist. His belief in ultimate Truth, in ultimate Wisdom, in the ultimate Good, shows that his legal science is firmly rooted in the philosophy of his time. His theory of law is embedded in the whole circle of the ideas of Christian moral philosophy, which furnishes him with the speculative basis for systematic thought about the ultimate foundations of the law. It is mainly on account of this basis that he conceives legal rules as emanating from, and fundamentally agreeing with, ethical rules, and accordingly as normative in essence.

Yet it is not only Christian moral philosophy proper which he applies to his investigations. He points out that the philosophers of antiquity may profitably be resorted to, provided that their lore is not incompatible with the Christian Faith:

> Si philosophi antiqui aliqua forte vera fidei nostrae dixerunt accomoda, non solum rejicienda non sunt, sed ab eis tamquam ab injustis possessoribus in usum nostrum vindicanda sunt.[5]

[1] 'In ipsarum quidem legum expositione vidi quosdam perfunctorie transivisse posito quidem casu collectisque notabilibus, plurima verba seu rerum officiorumque vocabula inexposita dimisisse . . . ad nova praeter ordinem festinantes. Ego autem, inquantum potui, huiusmodi inusitata, quin et alia exponere et explanare curavi, eo quod scire leges non est earum verba tenere, sed vim ac potestatem, ff. de legibus, l. scire,' Preface no. 6.

[2] C. X, 53, 8, no. 2.

[3] Preface no. 12.

[4] Preface no. 2.

[5] loc. cit., no. 11.

He attaches great value to the study of ancient writings in the original, and warns the student against the dangers and errors hidden in the current translations. His exact quotations and precise references seem to imply an acquaintance with Greek, although no direct evidence is available that he knew Greek. Since he views law as a consistent and harmonious whole, he takes into account canon law,[1] feudal law, and municipal statutes. In one of his commentaries he epitomizes his own method in these words: 'Mihi autem, qui scripturam sacram cum utroque jure ac philosophicis rationibus libenti corde compenso, videtur, quod . . .'[2] With particular satisfaction he discloses that the doctrines of 'canonum professores illustres' are presented in his work as 'prius legistis incognita'.[3] On account of their illustration of the good and evil character of human actions, the consultation of historical and poetical works appears to him imperative. He announces, in somewhat apologetic terms, this intention:

> Si etiam describantur inferius alia secundum Isidorum aliosque doctores . . . vel quid forte poeticum nullus ea tamquam puerilia teneat vel subsannet insidiator, cuius proprium est in malum convertere et in electis ponere maculam.[4]

However extraordinary this procedure may appear to the average jurist, the frequent quotations of the Old and New Testaments are warranted by their authoritative character: 'Si pro uberiore expositione auctoritates insertae sunt novi et veteris testamenti, legista nullus irrideat'.[5] It is his conviction that it is only this proposed latitude of jurisprudence which will further the cause of truth and which may reveal the principles underlying the social aspects of human volitions. That is the keynote of the concluding passage of his preface which ends in these words:

> Cessat igitur arguta correptio, et ut verius loquar, execranda detractio, solumque assistat fovendae veritati indago. Fugiendum quippe, quod malum est, quod vero est . . . undique melius inquirendum et inveniendum est.

[1] He announces this intention in the preface: 'Fit autem aperta remissio ad decretales et canones, ubi dicta ipsa doctores ibidem utiliter glossaverunt', no. 12. That is indeed a very rare occurrence in medieval legal scholarship. The legists, as a rule, did not take much notice of what the canonists said. See Lucas's attacks against the legists who neglect the canonists, in particular against Jacobus Butrigarius, who 'satis habuit odio jura canonica' (C. XII, 1, 17, no. 36). Nor did the canonists take account of the legists, see Kantorowicz, loc. cit., p. 91, and my remarks in *Revue d'Histoire du Droit*, vol. xvii (1939), p. 31.

[2] C. XII, 43, 3, no. 29.

[3] 'Adjectumque est, ut cum per dominum Innocentem et alios canonum professores illustres quam plurima tacta determinataque sint voluminibus eorum sparsa diversis, prius legistis incognita, hic ubi materia exactionem praebuit, velut in singula vasa illorum scripta confecta, sed discussa parata sunt', preface no. 12.

[4] Preface no. 9.

[5] loc. cit., no. 7.

It would be a fascinating study of its own to trace the influences of the diverse philosophic conceptions and to show which of them was most determinative in its influence on Lucas's trains of thought. The temptation, however, must be resisted. A mere enumeration of the *principal* authorities and works to which he frequently refers should suffice to show the wealth of extra-legal material which our jurist skilfully handles, and employs for the expansion of juristic thought.

Resuscitated Greek philosophy supplies Lucas with his basic philosophic equipment. The revived Aristotle not only moulded Lucas's modes of thought by the rigid instruments of logic, but the doctrinal contents of his theories are also strongly influenced by the 'princeps philosophiae'. In particular, Lucas's conception of philosophy as a universal science, his idea of the individual's being essentially a member of society, his views on fundamental ethical tenets, such as virtue and justice, faithfully reflect the strong influence exerted by Aristotle's *Ethics* [1] and *Politics*.[2] But these two works are not the only sources from which Aristotelian influence emanates: the *Metaphysics* [3] and *Rhetoric* [4] are other fountains of Aristotelian thought. Attention must, furthermore, be directed to the perusal of Aristotle's letters to Alexander [5] in the commentaries of Lucas. Another source of indirect Aristotelian influence is that intermediary between the ancient world and the Middle Ages—namely, Boethius. Lucas frequently refers to his *Consolatio philosophiae*,[6] and in some places also to his *Scholastica Disciplina*.[7] Plato, on the other hand, seems to have exerted a very small influence on Lucas. The quotations from Plato are far less frequent than those from Aristotle. Moreover, they lack the precision which he displays with regard to Aristotelian writings: he merely refers to Plato without indicating the source of his authority. But, apart from this consideration, there are scarcely any internal traces of *original* Platonic thought, though there are certainly modified Platonic ideas in Lucas's work which he may have derived from Plato's medieval adherents and interpreters. This is particularly obvious when Lucas's close dependence on the 'Christian Plato' [8] is seen in its

[1] This and the references to quotations of authors and works in the following footnotes are by no means exhaustive. The *Ethics* is referred to, e.g., in C. X, 19, 2, no. 9; 47, 14, no. 6; 72, 4 pr; XI, 22, 1, no. 4; 26, 1, no. 8; XII, 1, 12, no. 12; 40, 7, no. 73, &c.

[2] Quoted, e.g., in C. X, 48, 3, no. 1; 70, 4, no. 6; XI, 47, 15, Rubrica; XII, 1, 12, no. 16; 60, 2, no. 4. It should be noted that Lucas never omits to indicate the book of Aristotle's works.

[3] e.g., C. XI, 19, 1, no. 6 and in many other places.

[4] Cf. C. X, 19, 7, no. 5; XII, 1, 2, no. 18, &c.

[5] e.g., C. XII, 43, 3, no. 14; 59, 8, no. 3.

[6] See, e.g., C. X, 16, 3, no. 3; 65 Rubrica, no. 5; XI, 19, 1, no. 26; XII, 1, 12, no. 14; XII, 15, 1, no. 1, &c. Here too Lucas's quotations refer minutely to the part of the book of the *Consolatio*.

[7] C. XI, 18, 1, no. 35; XII, 15, 1, no. 18.

[8] J. Maritain's description of St. Augustine, see his essay 'St. Augustine

true proportions. Finally, mention must be made of other sources of Greek moral philosophic thought, though, to judge by the arguments, their influence does not go beyond mere quotations from their works. These are the peripatetic Andronicus,[1] the neo-platonist Macrobius,[2] and lastly Plutarch.[3]

First place among the Roman thinkers is taken by Cicero. Lucas refers to him simply as 'Tullius'; he is honoured with the epithets 'secundus philosophus', or 'excellentissimus philosophus et jurisconsultus'[4]; in one place he styles him 'magister eloquentiae'.[5] His accurate quotations leave no room for doubt that Lucas is extremely well versed in Cicero's main works. Moreover, among the ancient thinkers, Cicero's influence on Lucas is second only to that of Aristotle. Lucas's idea of a life in harmony with nature, his emphatic insistence on the pre-eminence of justice in all walks of life, his views on a vaguely conceived brotherhood of man, the prominence assigned to reason in the government of the world—typical Romanized versions and transformations of Greek thought—unmistakably reveal Ciceronian trains of thought. In particular, Lucas draws extensively on the *De Officiis*,[6] *De Legibus*,[7] *De Republica*,[8] *De Oratore*,[9] as prototypes of Roman thought and culture, whilst the contents of the *Tusculan Disputations*,[10] the *Philippics*[11] and the *De Amicitia*,[12] to mention only a few examples, serve to provide illustrations. Far less marked is the influence of the other Roman figure upon whom Lucas relies, namely Seneca. References to him testify to Lucas's study of the *De Clementia*,[13] *De Providentia Dei*,[14] *De Ira*,[15] and the *Naturales Quaestiones*[16] and also the Epistles.[17] Lucas ascribes the *De Quatuor Virtutibus* to Seneca.[18]

---

and St. Thomas Aquinas' in *A Monument to St. Augustine*, p. 203. Prof. Powicke maintains that Plotinus had greater influence on St. Augustine than Plato, loc. cit., vol. i, p. 38, note 2.

[1] C. XI, 22, 1, no. 6.

[2] His *Saturnalia* referred to, e.g., in C. X, 53 Rubrica, no. 2; 54, 1, no. 5; XI, 18, 1, no. 32; 47, 1, no. 5; XII, 9, 1, no. 3. His *Somnium Scipionis* is mentioned in C. XI, 22, 1, no. 6; XII, 15, 1, no. 20, &c.

[3] C. X, 19, 2, no. 7; XII, 55, 2, no. 1.

[4] C. XII, 1, 3, no. 5 and *passim*.

[5] C. XII, 5 Rubrica no. 5.

[6] Referred to in C. X, 72, 4, no. 1; 69, 2, no. 13; XI, 70, 5, no. 15; XII, 60, 2, no. 4; 63, 1, no. 7.

[7] See, e.g., C. X, 31, 33, no. 38; 37, 1, no. 4; 72, 4, no. 1; XI, 19, 1, no. 6, &c.

[8] C. XI, 21, 1, no. 1; 46, 1, no. 10, &c.

[9] C. XI, 18, 1, no. 21; 26, 1, no. 8; 36, 1, no. 1.

[10] C. X, 19, 2, no. 4 and in numerous other places.

[11] C. X, 19, 7, no. 5; XI, 36, 1, no. 2; 48 Rubrica, no. 10; XII, 15, 1, no. 17.

[12] C. XII, 63, 1, no. 12.

[13] C. X, 31, 33, no. 62; 37, 1, no. 6; 38, 1, no. 6; 53, Rubrica no. 2.

[14] C. XI, 70, 5, no. 15; XII, 63, 1, no. 17.

[15] C. XII, 35, 11, no. 8.

[16] C. X, 19, 7, no. 5; XII, 63, 1, no. 11.

[17] C. XII, 19, 2, no. 4.

[18] In C. XI, 18, 1, no. 21. Sandys, loc. cit., p. 615, draws attention to the fact that Dante, too, declared this a work of Seneca.

The Roman spirit of Quintilian's *De Oratoria Institutione* [1] seems to have attracted the literary taste of Lucas. Valerius Maximus is referred to in several places.[2]

The early Christian writers are represented in Lucas's commentaries by Lactantius, Cassiodorus, Cyprian, Chrysostom, Jerome, Ambrose, Orosius, and, above all, Augustine. His thorough knowledge of their writings—books, treatises, and letters—can be deduced with certainty from the exact quotations of their works. He consults them in all things which bear upon Christian interpretation and conceptions of the fundamentals—the *Homiliae super Mattheum* of St. Chrysostom,[3] the collection of Cassiodorus's *Variarum Epistulae*,[4] the writings of Lactantius[5] and St. Cyprian,[6] and numerous letters of St. Jerome,[7] whose vigorous style seems to have attracted Lucas, are frequently referred to, whilst the letters of Orosius [8] and St. Ambrose's *De Officio* [9] are not less often quoted in support of arguments. But in St. Augustine Lucas sees ' senex et episcopus pluriumque annorum, sol sapientiae in ecclesia Dei ',[10] and his safest guide in the solution of all legal problems with ethical aspects. The *Civitas Dei* is his favourite source of information,[11] and the quotations from the *De Doctrine Christiana* [12] and the *De Libero Arbitrio* [13] testify to their exhaustive perusal by our jurist. Besides these he also mentions Augustine's *Retractationes*.[14] Almost

[1] Mentioned in C. XI, 18, 1, no. 35. See also C. XII, 35, 11, no. 8; 63, 1, no. 15.

[2] Lucas omits to mention the title of the work he refers to, but simply quotes the book. It seems certain that he refers to the *Facta et Dicta Memorabilia* of Valerius Maximus. See, e.g., C. X, 16, 3, no. 3; 19, 2, no. 4; 39, 9, no. 17; XII, 8, 1, no. 1.

[3] C. X, 19, 2, no. 6; XI, 47, 15, no. 3; XII, 63, 1, no. 10. Lucas also mentions St. Chrysostom's *Tractatus de Symbolo* in C. XII, 43, 3, no. 25.

[4] C. X, 16, 3, no. 3; 48, 3, no. 4; XI, 70, 5, no. 15; XII, 19, 12, no. 30; 40, 7, no. 73.

[5] Cf. C. X, 31, 33, no. 34; 72, 4, no. 4.

[6] C. XII, 19, 12, no. 31; 63, 1, no. 10.

[7] Lucas's detailed knowledge of the great variety of letters of Jerome is astounding. They are referred to in many places, see, e.g., C. X, 19, 2, no. 9 (*Ad Augustinum*); X, 54, 1, no. 4 (*Ad Honestum, Ad Celantiam, Ad Amandum*); XII, 15, 1, no. 12 (*Ad Damasum*), no. 18 (*Ad Heliodorum*); 19, 4, no. 6 (*Ad Demetriadem*), and some other twenty letters in his commentaries.

[8] *Ad Augustinum*, C. X, 16, 3, no. 3; XI, 71, 1, no. 14; XII, 35, 14, no. 6; 40, 7, no. 31, &c.

[9] C. X, 1, 5, no. 13; 19, 12, no. 4; 69, 2, no. 11; XII, 59, 7, no. 1.

[10] C. X, 31, 33, no. 36.

[11] Always quoting book and work: C. X, 52, 6, no. 7; XI, 19, 1, no. 10; XI, 70, 5, no. 35; XII, 46, 1, no. 3; 63, 1, no. 9, and in many other places.

[12] Preface nos. 2, 6; XII, 15, 1, nos. 16, 18, &c.

[13] C. X, 5, 2, no. 9; XI, 19, 1, no. 16, &c. On the immense influence of the *City of God* in the Middle Ages, see Professor E. Barker in his introduction to the *City of God*, transl. by J. Healy, 1934, especially pp. lv seq.
Although Lucas is profoundly influenced by St. Augustine, he is never a slavish follower: this, we will see, is particularly true as regards his political conceptions, of the relations between Emperor and Pope, and the absence of any doctrine of the ' sinful origin of the state '.

[14] In C. X, 43, 3, no. 1.

equal influence is exercised by Gregory the Great—' Beatus Gregorius '[1]—on whose *Registrum Epistularum*[2] he confidently relies and whose *Moralia*[3] he also quotes. From Isidore's *Origines*[4] Lucas gathers much encyclopaedic knowledge. It is not difficult to perceive that the doctrines transmitted to Lucas through the media of those authorities constituted a colourful compound of heterogeneous elements all of which received their orientation from the Christian Faith: Platonism and Stoic ideas in particular were merged with Aristotelian and Ciceronian conceptions, were adopted and finally transformed in the light of, and impregnated with, the Christian view of the world.

Scholarship nearer to his own time was naturally bound to exert considerable influence on Lucas. The man who ranks first in the list of medieval schoolman who affected Lucas's thought is the Englishman John of Salisbury. However surprising this sway of an English scholar over a Neapolitan may appear, a glance at the commentaries will verify the assertion that John of Salisbury's *Policraticus* must be regarded as the most conspicuous influence of medieval scholarship on our jurist. It is especially in problems touching upon social-ethical issues and concerning public administration that the *Policraticus* enjoys absolute authority and becomes Lucas's trusted adviser. Yet the name of its author never appears in the commentaries, and all his numerous quotations refer simply to the Polycraticus without ever mentioning the author. In fact, Lucas substitutes the title of the treatise for the name of its author, as may be seen from this passage: ' De tyrannicida ipse Polycraticus multa scripsit nimium memoriae infigenda '.[5] In another passage

[1] C. XII, 46, 1, no. 1.

[2] With exact statement of book and chapter: C. X, 16, 6, no. 3; 19, 2, no. 17; 48, 3, no. 1 and no. 6; XI, 18, 1, no. 23; XII, 19, 4, no. 4; 60, 2, no. 11, &c.

[3] In C. XII, 1, 2, no. 18. Quotations of other works include: *Pastoralia*, C. X, 10, 1, no. 2; 54, 1, no. 5; XII, 43, 3, no. 14, &c.; *Homiliae super Evangelio*, C. XII, 15, 1, no. 21, and *Homiliae super Ezechiel*, C. XI, 18, 1, no. 34.

[4] Mentioned in C. X, 31, Rubrica no. 1; XI, 36, 2, no. 1; 46, 1, no. 4; 71, 1, no. 1, &c. C. Dawson's statement in *Medieval Religion*, p. 99, that the *Etymologies* were the encyclopedia of the Dark Ages is misleading. Isidore's work enjoyed a very high reputation down to the sixteenth century.

[5] C. X, 31, 42, no. 2. He always speaks of the *Policraticus* as if it were the author, see also the preface: ' Nam ut ait Polycraticus in prologo . . .' It is superfluous to give any detailed references to the quotations, because the treatise is mentioned in almost every other commentary. Lucas always quotes book and chapter of the *Policraticus*. A check of the references confirmed the exactness of Lucas's citations.

It should be noted that Lucas is not the only scholar who knows the *Policraticus*. A contemporary of his, the Bolognese professor, Guilielmus de Pastrengo, also knows John's *Policraticus*, but not the author, see his *De Originibus Rerum Libellus authore Guil. Pastregico*, Venetiis, 1547, folio 36. John seems to have had particular attractions for jurists, though it has been assumed that his influence did not extend beyond the shores of his own land, see, for instance, Professor Hazeltine's remarks in his the same personifications occurs: 'His addamus Polycratici verba, qui sic de his scripsit libro secundo, capitulo ultimo'.[1] That the immense influence of John of Salisbury on Italian jurisprudence should have escaped the attention of historians and lawyers alike is all the more remarkable.[2] The deep humanistic spirit which pervades John's *Policraticus* is faithfully reflected in Lucas's work. The spirit, outlook, detachment from contemporary affairs, the timeless character of ideas and theories, the preponderance of 'the positive ethical element',[3] the classical erudition, the fondness for quotations and illustrations of statements, are typical features of the Englishman's book and, to no less a degree, characteristic of the Neapolitan's commentaries. Like John's theory, Lucas's conception is idealistic and 'bears almost an ironical complexion'[4] if compared with the realities of medieval life;[5] like John, Lucas stands aloof from the turmoil of the workaday world and tries to be an impartial, disinterested onlooker, whose only interest is the discovery of fundamental premisses. Another great theologian to be mentioned in this context is St. Anselm of Canterbury, to whom Lucas also refers, but who has no apparent influence upon him.[6] One of John of Salisbury's pupils, Pierre du Blois, is also mentioned by Lucas.[7] French medieval thought is transmitted through St. Bernard of Clairvaux,[8] Hugh[9] and Richard[10] of St. Victor, Alanus (Alain de Lille),[11] and, above all, Aegidius Colonna, whose treatise *De Regimine*

---

preface to S. B. Chrimes, *Sir John Fortescue*, pp. xvi, xlv. The fifteenth-century Neapolitan Professor, Paris de Puteo, referred to the *Policraticus* frequently, see his tract 'De sindicatu' in *Tractatus*, tom. vii, fol. 217 seq., with accurate quotations. The sixteenth-century French scholar, Petrus Rebuffus, in his *Tractatus varii*, p. 603, col. 1, shows knowledge of the *Policraticus*, though he, too, does not know its author.

[1] C. X, 51, Rubrica no. 2.

[2] Miss Waddell, 'John of Salisbury', in *Essays and Studies*, vol. xiii, p. 30, reports that the *Policraticus* was known to Benvenuto da Imola, Dante's commentator. The only place she quotes—i.e., vol. iii, p. 235—does not contain any reference, though there is one brief reference—namely, 'ut ait Polycraticus' in vol. iii, p. 523. The commentator gives no quotation or references from the *Policraticus* in the only passage where he mentions the work. Our author, however, constantly and correctly quotes book and chapter of the *Policraticus*.

[3] R. L. Poole, loc. cit., p. 190.

[4] R. L. Poole, loc. cit., p. 205.

[5] On this point see also Dr. Coulton, *Studies in Medieval Thought*, p. 95.

[6] C. XII, 23 Rubrica no. 2 and in other places.

[7] See, e.g., C. X, 11, 6, no. 6; XII, 45, 1, no. 61. Lucas refers to the letters of Petrus Blesensis. Other jurists also knew Pierre du Blois—for instance Baldus in his tract 'De Exemptionibus' in *Tractatus*, tom. xii, fol. 195: 'Commendat Petrus Blescensis, qui fuit Anglicus in suis epistolis'.

[8] His considerations *Ad Eugenium Papam* referred to, e.g., in C. XI. 18, 1, no. 33; XII, 59, 7, no. 1; XII, 42, 1, no. 9: 'Sanctissimae religionis et obedientiae beatus Bernardus'.

[9] C. X, 54, 1, no. 6; XI, 47, 15 Rubrica; XII, 1, 2, no. 18, &c.

[10] C. XII, 3, 3, no. 3.

[11] Also called Alanus ab Insulis, see C. XII, 19, 1, no. 18.

Principum Lucas consults frequently; he refers to Aegidius as 'frater Aegidius'.[1] The consultation of St. Thomas Aquinas's *Summa* in many places will cause no surprise, in view of Lucas's spiritual environment, the Neapolitan seat of learning; it is always with great reverence that Lucas refers to the 'sanctus Thomas'.[2] Lucas discloses his familiarity with contemporary scholarship by references to relatively unknown authors of his own time, for instance, Gerardus de Senis, an Augustinian monk who lived in the middle of the fourteenth century.[3]

Finally, attention must be drawn to the wealth of material that Lucas uses for illustrative purposes. In the first place there are the historians and prose-writers: Hippocrates,[4] Herodotus,[5] Livy,[6] Sallust,[7] Apuleius,[8] Hegesippus (Josephus Flavius),[9] Suetonius,[10] Pliny,[11] Solinus[12]—to mention only a few of the many writers. Secondly come the poets: Virgil,[13] Horace,[14] Terence,[15] Ovid,[16] Plautus,[17] Tertullian,[18] Sidonius,[19] whilst the poet of his time, 'dominus Petrarca laureatus', [20] did not fail to attract Lucas. The quotation of the *Trismegistus*,[21] a collection of ancient Greek and Latin writings of a religious and philosophic nature, ascribed to Hermes Trismegistus, should also be noted.

[1] With exact quotations of book: C. XI, 26, 1, no. 9; 47, 15 Rubrica; XII, 43, 3, no. 14.

[2] He calls him also 'sanctus doctor': C. X, 69, 2, no. 5. Lucas quotes accurately part, question, and article of the *Summa*, see, e.g., C. X, 19, 3, no. 2; 72, 4, no. 2; XI, 41, 1, no. 21; 9, 3, no. 2; 47, 1, no. 5, &c.

[3] See C. XI, 32, 2, no. 1: 'Has quaestiones' (Lucas deals with problems arising out of usury) 'plenius et potissime theologice examinatas per fratrem Gerardum de Senis ordinis Eremitarum . . .' He apparently refers to the monk's treatise *De usuris*.

[4] C. X, 12, 2, no. 3.

[5] C. XII, 44, 3, no. 12.

[6] *De Bello Macedonico:* C. XI, 19, 1, no. 14; 71, 1, no. 14; XII, 63, 1, no. 12. *De Bello Punico:* C. X, 16, 3, no. 6; XI, 36, 1, no. 1; 71, 1, no. 17; XII, 50, 16, no. 1, &c.

[7] *Bellum Catilinae:* C. X, 30, 3, no. 6; XI, 36, 1, no. 1; 71, 1, no. 17; XII, 1, 2, no. 18. *Bellum Jugurthinum:* C. X, 19, 7, no. 5; 37, 1, no. 6; XII, 46, 1, no. 10.

[8] His *Metamorphoses*, book 10: C. XII, 15, 1, no. 19.

[9] *De Bello Judaico:* C. XII, 19, 2, no. 6; 50, 23, no. 1; 59, 7, no. 2; 63, 1, no. 24, &c.

[10] C. X, 18, 1, no. 5.

[11] C. X, 53, Rubrica no. 2.

[12] Preface no. 12, *De Memorabilibus Mundi*.

[13] C. XI, 8, 4, no. 4; 36, 1, no. 1; XII, 28, 1, no. 3.

[14] C. X, 1, Rubrica no. 1; XI, 48, 1, no. 10.

[15] C. XI, 36, 1, no. 1; XII, 1, 2, no. 12; 63, 1, no. 26.

[16] C. XII, 15, 1, no. 3; 64, 1, no. 2.

[17] C. X, 65 Rubrica no. 33.

[18] C. XII, 35, 11, no. 8.

[19] C. X, 53, Rubrica no. 2.

[20] C. XII, 43, 3, no. 2; also in C. X, 18, 1, nos. 5, 8. Correspondence between Lucas and Petrarch in 1374 is referred to by the latter, loc. cit., lib. xv, ep. 1, pp. 1046 seq.

[21] C. X, 72, 4, no. 4. This collection was written about A.D 270. The doctrinal content is derived from Greek philosophy and is influenced by Egyptian thought, see W. Scott, *Hermetica*, 1936, vol. i, p. 11.

The employment of that vast material, however, must not evoke the impression that Lucas is less a jurist than a philosopher of the medieval type. Nothing would be farther from the truth. That material has auxiliary value only in the purview of his legal studies. The extraordinary length of some of his commentaries—often true systematic monographs in themselves—is due precisely to the extensive discussions of the doctrines of past and contemporary legal scholars, legists and canonists alike. The glosses of Accursius as well as the doctrines of individual Glossators, such as Hugo and Martinus, Placentinus, Azo, &c., are fully considered in his commentaries, whilst even the lesser-known jurists of his time receive adequate attention, e.g., Joannes de Laudo; [1] the Bolognese jurists Joannes de Lignano [2] and Oldradus de Ponte,[3] then Andreas de Barulo [4] and Petrus Piccolus de Monteforte [5] are referred to. The extent of his investigations necessitated the careful scrutiny of his other famous countrymen, Andreas de Isernia [6] and Bartholomaeus de Capua.[7] Lucas is fully conversant with the main works of all his eminent contemporaries, and often reveals astonishingly detailed knowledge of recently written tracts and *Consilia* given in special cases. At the same time the canonistic doctrines are taken into consideration: the canon law itself as the basis of canonistic research and the theories of the 'Archidiaconus'—that is, Guido de Baysio, Hostiensis, Joannes Andreae, and Innocent IV, to mention only a few of the often-quoted authorities. If one jurist particularly commanded Lucas's respect it was Cynus, whose sagacious distinctions and classifications seem to have attracted our jurist, though he never adopts Cynus's views without examination and scrutiny. Cynus is referred to by Lucas as 'summae auctoritatis et scientiae doctor et compilator egregius dominus Cynus Pistoriensis'.[8]

[1] No traces of this scholar could be found, see also Savigny, loc. cit., vol. vi, p. 201; nor does Panziroli contain any information. A Glossator of the Sicilian laws who signs himself 'M.' refers also to Joannes de Laudo and to a tract of his *De fisco*, see *Constitutiones*, p. 314, col. 2.

[2] 'Doctor modernus et praecipuus dominus Joannes de Linguario Bononiae', C. XII, 40, 7, no. 2. It appears that the printer made a mistake and wrote 'Linguario' instead of 'Lignano', who was a contemporary of Lucas and died in 1383, see Savigny, loc. cit., vol. iii, p. 190, note 122. Lucas apparently refers to Joannes's treatise *De Bello, repressaliis et duello*, which was written, according to Panziroli, loc. cit., p. 344, about 1365. He also wrote two tracts maintaining the validity of Urban VI's election, see Raynaldus, *Annales Ecclesiastici*, tom. vii, pp. 321–5, 631–57.

[3] Oldradus died in 1335.

[4] Died in 1292.

[5] Petrus Piccolus de Monteforte wrote very many glosses on the Sicilian laws. He lived about 1340, was professor of law and later a judge in the Supreme Court, see Giustiniani, loc. cit., vol. iii, p. 62. He is referred to by Lucas in several places, e.g., C. XI, 22, 1, no. 3: 'profundae intelligentiae dominus Petrus de Monteforte'; see also C. X, 31, 14, no. 3.

[6] Andreas died in 1316. He is referred to very frequently by Lucas.

[7] Died in 1328 according to Savigny, loc. cit., vol. v, p. 391.

[8] C. XI, 53, 1, no. 41. See also Chiapelli, *Nuove ricerche su Cino da Pistoja*, p. 5, and Monti, *Cino da Pistoja*, p. 190. Both authors point out the great esteem Cynus enjoyed in the Neapolitan university.

CHAPTER III

THE FOUNDATIONS AND NATURE OF LAW

I

LUCAS, in agreement with all medieval legal philosophers, derives the notion of law from an extra-legal premiss—that is, from justice. It is true that this derivation was already to be found in the Roman texts, in which, however, it was a figurative phrase rather than a workable principle. Neither the Roman jurists nor the Glossators dwelt on the significance of this idea to any appreciable extent. Lucas, the Post-Glossator, deals with this conception theoretically, examines the idea in all its legal aspects, and demonstrates its practical application and its effects on the various branches of law. Indeed, the derivation of law from justice becomes an intrinsically fruitful principle and the foundation upon which his jurisprudential system is erected.

According to Lucas, law is but the translation and realization of the ethical virtue of justice. The ordinances of justice are made enforceable by transplanting them from the moral sphere into the legal domain. Law is articulated justice and is its practical execution: 'Jus est justitiae executivum'.[1] The idea of law, therefore, is identical with the idea of justice: it is the eternal idea of right which unfolds itself in all legal rules and institutions. These are but manifestations of the unchangeable idea of right. The understanding of the substance of law, consequently, presupposes the understanding of the substance of justice:

> Cum scientia totius utriusque juris quamvis particulariter vertatur circa justitiae notitiam, eo quod jus est objectum justitiae . . . et a justitia appellatum est . . . et justitiae executivum, non est incongruum, hic de tam excellenti et saluberrima virtute quaedam memorari.[2]

The generic concept of virtue, he states, signifies a quality of the will which, being directed essentially towards the good, impels man to morally good conduct in life, whether social or individual. Through virtue, divine power becomes operative within man, although without his participation.[3] Virtue is infused into man as a rational and moral creature. Claiming the support of St. Thomas Aquinas,[4] Lucas professes that, among the cardinal virtues,

[1] C. X, 70, 4 proemium. That this theme is the central theme of medieval jurisprudence is emphasized throughout the great work of Dr. A. J. Carlyle, *History of Medieval Political Theory in the West*.

[2] loc. cit., no. 1.

[3] 'Virtus est bona qualitas mentis, qua recte vivitur, qua nemo male utitur, qua Deus in nobis sine nobis operatur', C. XI, 21, 1, no. 4.

[4] 'Quarta virtus magis tamen et prima inter cardinales est justitia, quamvis a plerisque prudentia ponatur prior; hoc tamen tenet pro veriori sanctus Thomas in secunda secundae, quaestione 58, articulo ultimo. Ad quod Proverbia 15', loc. cit., no. 6.

justice ranks first, and even excels prudence. He feels justified in his deviation from the common theory by declaring that, in the point of mutual relations between the various virtues, prudence cannot be possessed without justice, whereas the latter can certainly exist without prudence.[1] Justice is 'the queen of all virtues', and comprises all other virtues.[2] In Lucas's opinion, the eminent social and ethical significance of justice is best illustrated by Cicero's famous dictum that the force of justice is so great that not even those who live by ill-doing or crime can manage to exist without some share of justice.[3] At the same time he recalls with approval the eulogistic words of Lactantius, that 'nobody is poor, unless he stands in need of justice'.[4]

After these preliminary remarks Lucas proceeds to investigate the origin of justice and to hammer out its meaning, availing himself at the outset of the established Christian teaching. Divine authority is the effective principle and immediate cause of justice: 'Justitia nihil aliud est quam Dei motus'; it is a 'divinus fructus'.[5] In another passage he declares that 'Dei spiritus' is properly speaking 'justitiae lumen'.[6] Following St. Chrysostom, he corroborates this thesis with the argument that God is justice itself, and that justice indeed constitutes 'cingulum lumborum Christi'. The true perception of God presupposes that man acts in accordance with the injunctions of justice.[7] In substantiation of his view of the divine character of justice he refers to the following passage of the Old Testament: 'The path of the just, as a shining light, goeth forward and increaseth to perfect day'.[8] Life, which is to conform with the divine will, should render justice the basis of human conduct: 'In semita justitiae vita, iter autem devium ducit ad mortem. Justum deducit dominus per vias rectas'.[9]

His disquisitions on the substance of justice begin with a brief review of the philosophic conceptions of the term. Aristotle, he says, defined it as a state of mind ('habitus') which becomes operative through the choice of the just.[10] Cicero, in Lucas's opinion, lays stress on this constant element inherent in justice, whereas

[1] C. X, 70, 4, no. 5.

[2] loc. cit. Cf. also no. 1: 'In justitia quidem simul omnis virtus est'.

[3] 'Tanta enim est vis justitiae, ut nec illi, qui maleficio et scelere pascuntur, sine ulla eius particula vivere possint. Nam et princeps latronum, nisi aliqualiter praedam dispartiat, aut interficietur a sociis aut relinquetur, dicit Tullius, I de Off.,' loc. cit., no. 5.

[4] loc. cit., no. 4.

[5] loc. cit., no. 4.

[6] C. XII, 45, 1, no. 28.

[7] 'Deus enim justitia est, ergo quid eripuit se a malis et fecerit bona, secundum hoc Deum videt', C. X, 70, 4, no. 5.

[8] 'Unde Proverbia 4: Justorum semita quasi lux splendens procedit et crescit usque ad perfectam diem. Via impiorum tenebrosa, nesciunt, ubi corruant,' loc. cit., no. 5.

[9] loc. cit., no. 8.

[10] 'Justitia est habitus secundum quem aliquis dicitur esse operativus secundum electionem justi', loc. cit., no. 1.

St. Augustine appears to him to have emphasized the element of volition. He cannot establish any substantial differences between the three definitions fully quoted by him. Nevertheless, they have in common the idea that justice confers rights upon everyone: 'Perfectissima virtus, quae jura nobis distribuit'.[1] However much the individual definitions may differ, Lucas declares, the assignation of rights is the focal point of the idea of justice. Ulpian, too, stresses this central theme in his formula which, as Lucas remarks, meets with the approval of St. Thomas Aquinas. Lucas, however, is not entirely satisfied with Ulpian's diction, because his formula substitutes the individual will-act for the essential element of constancy, which is inherent in the individual's temper.[2] Thomas Aquinas's version, according to Lucas's conception, which amends Ulpian's deficient formula,[3] is wholeheartedly accepted by our jurist:

> Reducit (scil. Thomas) autem ad perfectam definitionem justitiae, hoc modo: justitia est habitus, secundum quem aliquis constante et perpetua voluntate jus suum unicuique tribuit.

Justice, by bestowing rights, adjusts human relations and harmonizes the interplay of social forces. The relations between man and his fellow-men should be determined by the maxim which epitomizes the injunctions of justice in the adage: 'Quod tibi fieri non vis, aliis non feceris'.[4] He conceives all injustice as a disregard and infringement of this maxim.[5] In almost exhilarating terms [6] Lucas stresses the supreme value and importance of justice

[1] loc. cit., no. 2.

[2] Earlier jurists were accustomed to stress the volitional character of justice. See, e.g., Placentinus, *Instit.* I, 1, where he said: 'Omnis justitia est voluntas . . . tolle voluntatem, omnis actus est indifferens, quippe affectio tua votum imponit operi tuo'.

Others, again, distinguished between divine and human justice, so, for instance, Azo, *Instit.* I, 1, no. 1: 'Definitio potest intelligi duobus modis: uno prout est in creatore, id est, in Deo . . . justitia est Dei dispositio, quae in omnibus rebus recte consistit et juste disponit . . . altero in creatura'. But he, too, emphasized the volitional element of justice: 'Voluntas dicitur justitia, et dicitur voluntas tribuere jus suum, non quantum ad actum, sed quantum ad affectionem'.

The early Glossators, on the other hand, stressed the element of constancy. See the definition of Irnerius as transcribed by Kantorowicz, *Studies in the Glossators*, p. 240: 'Habitus est voluntas difficile mobilis et in vita permanens . . . justitia est habitus mentis bene constitutae . . .' Kantorowicz thinks that Irnerius derived his formula from Papias, p. 60.

[3] On Thomas's view of Ulpian see also A. J. Carlyle, loc. cit., vol. v, pp. 41 seq.

[4] loc. cit., no. 9.

[5] 'Omnia tamen possunt ad unius praecepti violationem reduci', loc. cit., no. 9. This idea is clearly derived from *Tobias*, iv, 16: 'See thou never do to another what thou wouldst hate to have done to thee by another'. John of Salisbury, too, referred to *Tobias* in *Policraticus*, lib. IV, cap. 7. A similar thought is in the gloss to D. 2, 2, 1, and in *Decretales*, i, 2, 6. On this point see Schulz, 'Bracton on Kingship', *E.H.R.*, vol. lx (1945), p. 167.

[6] 'Haec est virtutum praeclarissima, et neque hesperus neque lucifer ita admirabilis', loc. cit., no. 1.

in all walks of life and in all branches of law, private and public alike. He succinctly draws attention to the pre-eminence of justice as the bond of citizenship within states and as the principle governing the relations between states. Embodying the idea of right conduct, it affects all human actions. Indeed, there is no field of human activity wherein justice is not an ingredient and constitutive part. Even those spheres of human activity which are excluded from human legislation or which cannot, by their very nature, be made the direct object of law, he considers subject to the injunctions derived from the idea. Religion, as the true worship of God establishing the relation of man to his creator, loyalty, patriotism, piety, liberality, benignity, and a score of other ideological values are conceived by Lucas as falling within the province of justice.[1] These virtues are annexed to justice [2] and inculcate upon men a corresponding duty. All the duties originating in justice and bearing upon man's relations to others constitute the proper precepts of justice. They are a combination of the ten commandments with Ulpian's famous 'praecepta juris', to which Lucas adds the duty of restitution.[3] It may easily be perceived that justice so widely understood virtually extends to all aspects of human activity.

His system of legal thought reveals the execution of his fundamental idea—namely, that not only is the notion of law based theoretically upon justice, but also that every individual law, whatever issues it may touch, hypostatizes the idea of justice. Law can be an enforceable rule of action only when its ordinances realize the idea of right. The *raison d'être* and the intrinsic authority of law are derived from justice. Moreover, the idea of justice is apprehended by our jurist as the principle upon which rests all application of law, particularly in the domain of jurisdiction. For, according to Lucas, judgement proper is that judicial decision the content of which is directly derived from the idea of justice.

[1] He declares that it would be an arduous task to enumerate all the virtues comprised by justice. After the full quotation of Aristotle's, Cicero's, Andronicus's, and Macrobius's relevant passages, he concludes with this statement: 'Infinitae sunt species partesque justitiae, quas non modo stylo persequi, sed cogitatione etiam capere difficillimum est, quas omnes una brevisque sententia comprehendit, videlicet, omnia quaecumque vultis, ut faciant homines, haec et facite illis', C. XI, 22, 1, no. 6.

[2] The advance in jurisprudential thinking may be properly evaluated when we consider the views on the same topic of one of the great jurists of the thirteenth century, Azo. He did not conceive justice as an all-embracing idea, and he came to derive purely ethical values from the *jus gentium*. See his *Summa Institutionum*, lib. I, no. 4: 'Hoc autem jus gentium solis hominibus commune est: veluti erga Deum religio, ut parentibus et patriae pareamus, ut vim atque injuriam propulsemus'. Even self-defence followed from it: 'Nam hoc jure evenit, ut quodquisque ob tutelam sui corporis fecerit, jure fecisse existimetur'. The *jus gentium*, as we shall soon see, plays a very inferior part in Lucas's system.

[3] 'Praecepta justitiae vero sunt decem praecepta decalogi, alieni restitutio, ac honeste vivere, alterum non laedere, jus suum cuique tribuere', C. XI, 22, 1, no. 6.

Through the pronouncement of justice, embodied in the decision and applied to the particular case, judgements acquire validity and authority.[1] But the province of law, in the strict sense of the word, is not the only sphere wherein the idea of justice constitutes an all-permeating principle. In the political field also, the idea of justice should be the sole principle of government and the criterion of a civilized community. The Ruler should personify the idea of justice—'justitiam debet in se habere'[2]—and he is the legitimate Ruler only as long as his government conforms to the requirements of justice.[3] The State, too, as an institution of a civilized society, derives its existence from the idea of justice. Internal peace and security within the State can be maintained only by applying the maxims of justice,[4] disregard of which would reduce civilized communities to mere bands of robbers.[5] In short, justice is the fundamental idea around which his theory of law revolves.

The abstract idea is divided by our jurist into two main species—i.e., into a general and a particular justice. In the former sense justice deals with human actions in so far as they are directed towards the common good; this justice may also be called legal justice. It is this kind of justice which induces man to give society its due. Particular justice, on the other hand, comprises human actions which concern the dues between man and man.[6] The corresponding Aristotelian notions of distributive and commutative justice are employed to show that crimes are simply violations of justice in either of these senses; the right to punish is based on

[1] See *infra*, ch. VI, sect. I.

[2] C. XI, 58, 9, no. 2.

[3] 'Princeps quidem justitiam in se debet habere, alias non rex, sed tyrannus rationabiliter diceretur . . . at illa est vera justitia, quae suum cuique jus tribuit, nulli tollit', loc. cit., no. 2.

[4] 'Sine justitia vero impossibile est civitatibus pacem dare . . . opus justitiae pax', C. X, 70, 4, no. 4; in C. X, 31, 33, no. 33 he says: 'Infundendus est animis hominum justitiae amor, sine qua non solum res publica, sed nec exiguus hominum coetus nec domus quidem parva constabit'. See also C. XII, 63, 1, no. 15: 'Sed quantum ad effectum et custodiam pacis magis est necessarium aliud praeceptum negativum . . . videliciet quod tibi fieri non. . . .'

[5] 'Sublata namque justitia et regna, res publicae urbium singularum nihil aliud sunt quam latrocinia', C. XI, 22, 1, no. 1, with a reference to the *Civitas Dei*, lib. IV, cap. 4. Lucas seems to have laboured under the same misapprehension as modern authorities with regard to this famous passage of St. Augustine. See C. Dawson, 'St. Augustine and his Age', in *A Monument to St. Augustine*, pp. 63 seq.

[6] 'Justitia alia generalis, alia particularis. Generalis dicitur . . . ordinat hominem ad bonum commune, haec eadem dicitur legalis justitia . . . particularis est, quae ordinat hominem circa ea, quae sunt ad alterum vel ad singularem personam', C. X, 70, 4, no. 3.

This classification was by no means generally accepted. To quote a contemporary of Lucas, Angelus de Ubaldis, a brother of Baldus; Angelus distinguished between a natural and a positive justice. D. 1, 1, 10, no. 2: 'Accipio naturalem illam, quae habet naturalem rationem urgentem; est positiva, quae procedit ex mera voluntate jus statuentis'. See also Azo's definition.

the supposed violation of justice.[1] This is a material rather than a formal conception of crime.[2]

At this point it may not be inappropriate briefly to view Lucas's theory of justice against the background of preceding and contemporary scholarship, in which connexion the already quoted passages of Placentinus and Azo become of especial interest. A study of the various works justifies the emphasis that is to be laid on the fact that neither contemporary jurisprudence nor scholarship before the fourteenth century devoted much energy to the philosophic elucidation of the concept of justice, to a theoretical clarification of the relations between justice and law, or to an examination of the practical implications of justice as an agency penetrating all legal departments. This last aspect, in fact, received very scanty treatment from medieval legal scholarship; the former aspects were not, as a rule, sufficiently separated. Following the lead given by the gloss, early Italian jurisprudence dealt with this subject in a somewhat figurative way: 'Est autem jus a justitia sicut a matre sua, ergo prius fuit justitia quam jus'.[3] This descriptive derivation was later given greater profundity when 'mater' was interpreted as 'materia', though this alteration was almost invariably accompanied by prolific disquisitions purporting to prove the ethical identity of justice and law. Odofredus may serve as a typical example.[4] The end of the thirteenth century saw a gradual change of outlook. The metaphorical relationship came to be replaced by abstract characterizations. Jacobus de Arena taught that justice and law 'differunt auctore et substantia': the author of justice is God and that of law is man, whilst the substance of justice is 'anima non formata in jus' and that of law is justice 'in praeceptis juris redacta'. Cynus's way of reasoning, probably stimulated by his great teacher, Dynus,[5] suggests that this abstract characterization had become familiar in the first half of the fourteenth century. Cynus viewed the relationship of justice and law as that of 'producens et productum'.[6] Lucas's theory and Baldus's analytical treatment[7] marked a complete break with the old metaphorical

[1] C. X, 11, 5, nos. 29–34. He gives here a very detailed description of crimes. [2] For further details see *infra*, ch. VII.

[3] Gloss on *Digestum vetus*, De justitia et jure, lex: operi dat.

[4] Odofredus, D. I, 1, 1, no. 7: 'Jus appellatur a justitia ut a matre vel a materia . . . sicut se habent mater et filius, ita justitia et jus. . . .'

For a particularly attractive way of a figurative treatment of justice see the passage of the *Quaestiones de juris subtilitatibus*, para. 5—erroneously ascribed to Irnerius by Fitting and, following him, by Carlyle, loc. cit., vol. ii, p. 11, vol. v, p. 466, see Kantorowicz, loc. cit., pp. 35, 181—in the latter's work, p. 184.

[5] Cynus said in his lecture on D. 1, 1, 10, no. 2: 'Doctor meus Dynus de Mugellano sicut ab eo percepi. . . .'

[6] 'Justitia et jus se habent ut producens et productum . . . juris auctor et expressor et executor et deductor materiae est homo, productor Deus', loc. cit.

[7] See the essay 'Baldus's Conception of Law', in *L.Q.R.*, 1942, pp. 389 seq.

lore. The advance in jurisprudential thought, which had been effected within less than a hundred years, is not difficult to perceive. The deep penetration into the meaning of justice and the exposition of its significance for all legal topics and of its practical implications, particularly by Lucas—in short, his fundamental view that justice is a generic concept from which all things legal are derived—is an integration of the theory of justice. This integration was facilitated, if not conditioned, by a thorough-going application of philosophic axioms, and it was characterized by a harmonious combination of legal with extra-legal arguments, leading eventually to a complete system of legal thought.

II

The concept derived from the idea of justice in its abstract meaning is equity, which is characterized by its peculiar structure. The conception of equity serves as the proximate cause of law and has also to fulfil other vital functions in the legal sphere. Lucas takes great pains to clarify this concept. He follows Aristotle in his methodological setting by declaring that equity (*epieikeia*) is an epiphenomenon of justice. He submits that justice, the highest moral virtue, is an ethical ideal whose full realization is impeded by the multifold conditions of real life. In its purely idealistic sense it involves absoluteness of principle and rigidity of application. These implications diminish, he maintains, the practical value of justice as an idea for the ordering the interplay of the manifold and fluid social forces. The rigidity of justice must be tempered, he declares, so that it becomes an elastic and flexible instrument. He says: 'Justitiam debet temperare moderatio, quod quidem verbum habet operari diminutionem, non augmentum'.[1] If applied rigidly and blindly, justice disturbs rather than harmonizes human relations. The result is the very opposite of that which is justice's purported aim: the idea of justice defeats itself. He advances the argument that the aim of justice can, nevertheless, be realized, in actual life, when the emotional element of charity is brought to bear upon justice. Charity transforms justice into equity: 'Aequitas est justitia dulcore misericordiae temperata'.[2] By its assuaging influence charity deprives justice of its absoluteness and rigidity, while leaving its aim unimpaired.

His further analysis brings to the fore the function of natural reason, which is conceived as the fountainhead of all human conduct. He avails himself of the view, propounded by contemporary philosophic thought, that man acts in accordance with the dictates of natural reason. Man, he holds, is endowed with natural reason, which, being divinely infused, prompts him to act in conformity

[1] C. XII, 42, 1, no. 15. [2] C. XII, 19, 12, no. 31.

with the divine will.[1] It is nature which, through the potency of reason, brings about social co-existence: ' Natura vi rationis hominem conciliat homini '. It is nature itself that strives after ' vitae societatem '.[2] Actions springing from natural reason, therefore, are essentially reasonable and cannot contradict nature or be at variance with divine will. Equity, then, is modified justice—that is, a mode of conduct which is born of natural reason—' ipsa aequitas ex naturali ratione procedit ' [3]—and which aims at rendering everyone what is rightfully his. In other words, the emotional attitude of charity is called into action by natural reason, which is the source of direct, universal, understanding of human situations. Equity is thought of by Lucas, not as a metaphysical concept nor as an ethical ideal, but as a practical proposition. Equity is a positive instrument for adjusting human relations reasonably through the medium of law. In short, this modified justice is human justice or natural or substantial justice.[4]

The concept has far-reaching jurisprudential implications. Firstly, equity is the immediate source of law: ' Lex est super aequitate fundanda '.[5] It is of such importance ' quod ad esse legis expresse requiritur '.[6] Law which does not exhibit the traits of equity is no law at all, and any such idea of law is untenable to Lucas: ' Jus nisi aequum, jus non est, nec est opus sanae mentis '.[7] Law is merely the external form, the manifestation of the idea of equity—' (lex) est aequitatis forma ' [8]—and therefore its interpreter: ' Lex vero eius interpres est '.[9] Law rationalizes the idea of benevolence inherent in equity,[10] which becomes a directing force for the legis-

[1] See also *infra*, p. 95. [2] C. X, 5, 2, no. 8.

[3] loc. cit., no. 7. Contemporary science did not, as far as could be ascertained, derive the concept of equity from natural reason, but used synonymous expressions. See Baldus, *Super Decretalibus*, II, 12, 5, no. 12: ' Naturalis justitia et aequitas idem sunt '. Angelus de Ubaldis, *Consilium* 345, no. 5: ' Est enim naturalis ratio idem quod justitia naturalis praevalens rationibus conjecturalibus '. The sixteenth-century jurist, Phil. Decius, maintained the same view, see his *De Regulis Juris*, regula 90.

[4] It is interesting to observe that early jurisprudence conceived of the relationship between justice and equity differently. The jurists of the preceding century thought of equity as the primary concept, whence justice is derived. See the passages of the *Summa Trecensis* (according to Kantorowicz, loc. cit., pp. 35, 146, its author is Rogerius) and of the *Fragmentum Pragense* (about its origin see Kantorowicz, loc. cit., p. 50) transcribed by Carlyle, loc. cit., vol. ii, pp. 8, 9: ' Nihil aliud est aequitas quam Deus '. Carlyle, vol. ii, p. 7, says: ' When this temper (i.e., equity) is fixed in a man's soul and will, it is called justitia ', see also vol. v, p. 459. But fourteenth-century scholarship conceived of the relationship in reverse terms. Not only Lucas, but also all Post-Glossators, regarded justice as the primary concept. See also the quotations in my paper ' Baldus's Conception of Law ', loc. cit., p. 390. [5] loc. cit., no. 7.

[6] C. XII, 1, 2, no. 18 and C. X, 5, 2, no. 2.

[7] C. XII, 19, 12, no. 31.

[8] C. XI, 18, 1, no. 12. [9] loc. cit., no. 12.

[10] ' Dicas, quod proprie aequitas est quid benignum, jus vero proprie est quid rationabile ', loc. cit., no. 12.

lator: 'Aequitas', he says, 'est virtus dirigens ad positionem bonarum legum'.[1] In plain language law is identical with equity: 'Jus simpliciter sumptum est aequitas'.[2] Indeed, equity as the proximate source of law implies equality of rights to be conferred upon individuals: 'Aequitas . . . *in omnes aequalis* unicuique tribuens quod est suum; lex vero eius interpres est'.[3] Moreover, the law whose root idea is that of equality is the only adequate instrument whereby social unity and harmony of diverging interests can be achieved: 'Lex quidem est super aequitate fundanda, quia *aequalitas est affectus unitatis*'.[4]

Akin to this function of equity is the further implication that the judge has to apply the principle of equity to the decision of cases concerning which the law is silent (*casus omissi*). Equity, then, becomes the deciding element in cases which are not covered by any positive law or dealt with by any legal rule.[5] Here the practical meaning of equity is 'rerum convenientia, quae cuncta aequiparat ratione et in paribus rebus paria jura desiderat'.[6]

Thirdly, equity is the criterion of judicial and scientific interpretation. It is a safeguard against the mechanical, literal, interpretation of law, which frequently results in the paradox 'summum jus, summa injuria'.[7] He holds that the tendency to a sophisticated interpretation is born of a petrified, soulless conception of justice and that this tendency can be neutralized by the animated and vigorous spirit of equity.[8] Equity deprives 'strict law' of its rigidity. He advises the interpreter to prefer the 'ratio aequitatis' to the 'ratio stricti juris'.[9]

It now becomes necessary to touch briefly upon Lucas's terminology. The notions 'jus' and 'lex' are overlapping conceptions. 'Jus' and 'lex' refer, in his system, to the whole body of legal rules (*Recht*, *Droit*), but both notions comprise also restricted mean-

[1] C. XI, 22, 1, no. 6. [2] C. X, 5, 2, no. 7.

[3] C. XII, 19, 12, no 31. The idea of a 'quasi aequalitas' was expressed by Placentinus, *Institutiones*, lib. I, p. 1: 'Dicitur quoque aequitas quasi aequalitas, et vertitur in rebus, id est, in dictis et factis hominum'. The same idea is to be found in Azo, loc. cit., no. 7. Equity did not assume that wide theoretical meaning, in jurisprudence, either before or during the fourteenth century. The jurists, as a rule, were satisfied to give a definition in more or less lucid language, without, however, investigating the various implications of the concept or examining its structure. See also Baldus, loc. cit., p. 391.

[4] C. X, 5, 2, no. 7.

[5] 'In casibus quidem, in quibus jus non invenitur expressum, procedendum est aequitate servata', loc. cit., no. 7.

[6] He refers to the *Policraticus*, lib. IV, cap. 2, which contains this statement. John of Salisbury does not say where he derived this formula, but simply refers to the 'jurisperiti'; he has in mind Cicero's *Topica*, 23, where the formula occurs. Early Italian jurisprudence knew this formula well, see Carlyle, loc. cit., vol. ii, p. 7 and vol. v, p. 459.

[7] C. XII, 42, 1, no. 15, and in many places quoted as a deterrent example.

[8] For further details see *infra*, pp. 113 seq.

[9] C. X, 5, 2, no. 5: 'Rursus in legibus praeferenda est ratio aequitatis stricti juris rationi'.

ings distinct from each other. 'Lex', in Lucas's system, denotes also the individual law (*Gesetz*, *Loi*), whilst 'jus' signifies the right proceeding therefrom.[1] The terms are not interchangeable within their restricted meanings. The term 'jus' furthermore denotes the just act [2]—that is to say, the term refers to that mode of conduct which conforms to the jural precept.

III

Notionally and substantially Lucas conceives law as a reasonable command addressed to everyone, issued by the competent authority and regulating social life by injunctions and prohibitions. His theory of law is distinguished by the employment of the teleological principle, a sequel to his axiom that human life is purposive, transcendental, and destined to a definitive, preconceived end. His notion of law, consequently, is normative.

In agreement with Roman law he declares: 'Lex est commune praeceptum'.[3] In order to fulfil its regulating function, law necessarily imposes restrictions on the free play of human activity.[4] It provides the mightiest protection for the socially inferior who thereby obtain equality and may effectively pursue their rights.[5] The laws are 'certissima humanae vitae solatia', form the strongest defence of the weak against arbitrary encroachments by more powerful members of society, and appropriately check the latter's activities.[6] Security, he is anxious to point out, is the achievement of the reign of law: 'Unde securitas venit et conscientia proficit'.[7] As a command, law embodies an authoritative 'ought' and prescribes 'id, quod fieri debet'.[8] It is a feasible rule of action, promotes social stability, and is a conservative factor in social relations. Thus 'justae leges', Lucas recognizes, 'factivae sunt et conservativae humanae felicitatis'.[9] Based on equity (natural justice), it comprises the idea of right conduct dictated by reason in the most perfect form: 'Lex est recta ratio imperandi et pro-

[1] 'Jus idem est quod potestas', C. X, 1 Rubrica, no. 1; 'iste habet jus, i.e., pro se justitiam, a qua dicitur jus', loc. cit., no. 1. On the great importance of these passages see *infra*, sect. III.

[2] 'Jus dicitur id, quod actum est, ut sit justum . . . dicitur jus rectum vel justum', loc. cit., no. 1.

[3] C. X, 52, 6, no. 8.

[4] 'Juste constringit hominum vitas', loc. cit. In another passage he says: 'Leges quoque factae sunt, ut humana coercetur audacia et tuta sit innocentia', C. XI, 18, 1, no. 14.

[5] 'Officium autem legis . . . ut ait Polycraticus, libro IV, cap. secundo, illis, qui nimium possunt, plurimum prodest et illis, qui nocere desiderant, plurimum adversatur. Nam qui minores sunt, semper quaerunt justum et aequale, prae-eminentes autem nihil curant,' C. X, 70, 4, no. 6.

[6] 'Infirmorum auxilia, potentium frena', C. X, 31, 33, no. 33.

[7] loc. cit., no. 33.

[8] C. X, 1 Rubrica, no. 1.

[9] C. XI, 47, 21, no. 1.

hibendi '.[1] It is 'summa ratio '.[2] Reason, therefore, is at once the substance of law and determines the character of the action prescribed: 'Ratio est fundamentum legis ' [3] declaring what is just and right action. Inasmuch as they touch upon the social relations of man, the dictates of right or natural reason should be substantiated in law—' quod rationabile est, debet in jus perfectum deduci ' [4]—which commands reasonable rules of action, prescribing the path along which man may attain his end. Law, therefore, can appeal to man only on account of his endowment with reason which, Lucas states in the true medieval fashion, is the distinguishing mark between man and the brute.[5] Reason itself is presented as the unifying bond between man and man: ' Summum humanae societatis vinculum est ratio ', which 'conciliat inter se homines '.[6] Nevertheless, in view of his marked tendency to disregard the dictates of right reason, and in recognition of his proneness to senseless passion, whereby he avails himself of reason for wrongful purposes,[7] man is in need of a guiding force. Without this guiding force man would become 'pessimum omnium animalium '. Law functions as that guiding force.[8] It effectively directs man to reasonable actions, and is viewed by Lucas as the strongest social factor in man's life—' lex est lux et via vitae '. Law effectively checks the individual's selfish desires, which endanger the peaceful continuance of society. Laws are made, Lucas declares, 'ut appetitus noxius sub juris regulis limitetur '.[9] They provide a balance of interests and, by their sanctions, restrain man from activity harmful to society. Lucas rightly recognizes the negative aspect of the laws when he says that they can check mischief, but cannot compel individuals to ethically valuable actions, which should be the outcome of the individual's free choice: ' Licet etiam per leges homines malefacere compescantur, per eas tamen benefacere non coguntur; hoc enim non nisi per electionem fieri potest '.[10]

Manifesting the idea of conduct which is right, because reasonable, it serves as the safest guide to the attainment of man's destined end, since it is the reflection of the divine will,[11] and submission and obedience to law mean ' exclusio et exterminatio vitiorum '.[12]

[1] C. XI, 18, 1, no. 12.
[2] C. X, 5, 2, no. 9.
[3] C. XI, 18, 1, no. 16.
[4] C. X, 5, 2, no. 9.
[5] C. XII, 1, 12, no. 14.
[6] C. XII, 19, 2, no. 4. Contemporary English thought on this topic is perhaps best expressed in Y. B. 15, Ed. III (R.S.), 126: ' Law ought to be in accordance with reason and to take away mischief ', quoted after Holdsworth, vol. ii, p. 602.
[7] Cf. C. XII, 59, 7, no. 2: ' Genus hominum praeceps ad avaritiam et paratum ad versutiam, nihil tam atrox, quod refugiat, nihil tam turpe, quod erubescit '.
[8] ' Sicut perfectum animalium omnium homo est, sic et separatum a lege et justitia pessimum est omnium ', C. XII, 1, 12, no. 16.
[9] C. XI, 9 Rubrica.
[10] loc. cit.
[11] ' Lex est divinae voluntatis imago ', C. XI, 18, 1, no. 12.
[12] loc. cit., no. 12.

Law would contradict itself if it forced unreasonable action on man and hence induced him to a mode of living at variance with that of reason or nature. Reasonableness is the pre-eminent criterion of law, indeed the common feature of all law, validly conferring rights and imposing duties.

Reasonableness is a self-evident constituent of the divine law which is, he holds in agreement with contemporary doctrine, a set of rules derived directly from the divine Being and consisting of authoritative, unchangeable principles. Being the creation of the Supreme law-giver, not the work of man—' nec hominum ingeniis excogitata '—the divine law is eternal—' aeternum quiddam '—and reigns over ' universum mundum '.[1] It is the emanation of the ' cogentis et vetantis Dei '.[2] Its essence is a divinely conceived harmony in the Universe which, to Lucas's mind, is pre-eminently nature : ' Lex est multiplex, videlicet divina, quae natura constat '.[3] The principles of the divine law are implanted in the heart of every human creature. Thus the divine law is a ' lex privata ', which can also be termed the ' lex spiritus sancti ', because it is the Holy Ghost which infuses God's law into the human heart. ' Item ', says Lucas, in the same passage, with reference to the divine law, ' lex privata seu lex spiritus sancti cordi inscribitur '. A corollary of his view that God is nature itself—' Deus est summa natura ' [4]—is the identification of divine law with natural law : ' Jus divinum, id est, jus naturale ', he declares.[5] The divine law reveals itself in the order and harmony of nature, itself the expression of God's will : ' Natura idem est, quod Dei voluntas ',[6] and is made known to man by the light of natural reason. Natural law identified with divine law, therefore, is the direct expression and manifestation of the divine will.[7] In some places Lucas posits the *jus gentium* as an equivalent to the *jus naturale*, but he does not attach any distinct importance to the former concept. He holds that the *jus gentium* consists of fundamental principles of conduct based on natural justice. This mode of conduct is common to all mankind, and he designates this law in fact as ' jus commune '.[8] It has been created at the same time as the human race itself.[9]

[1] loc. cit., no. 12. [2] loc. cit., no. 12.

[3] Ciceronian and Augustinian trends of thought can clearly be discerned in Lucas's conception of the divine law as the universal law. Particularly Augustine's idea of a universal, reasonable order which governs all worldly events—i.e., ' like the stars in their courses and the rise and fall of kingdoms ', C. Dawson, loc. cit., p. 64, is pre-eminent in Lucas's mind ; see *Civitas Dei*, lib. v, cap. 9.

[4] C. XII, 60, 3, no. 8. [5] C. X, 1 Rubrica, no. 4.

[6] C. X, 5, 2, no. 4, referring to the *Policraticus*, lib. II, cap. 2.

[7] It is interesting to observe that, as a Glossator of one of Bracton's MSS. said, ' in Anglia minus curatur de jure naturali quam in aliqua regione de mundo ', quoted after Holdsworth, vol. ii, appendix II, p. 602.

[8] C. X, 1, Rubrica, no. 4.

[9] C. XI, 71, 1 pr. : ' Jus gentium cum ipso genere humano proditum est '.

In this context the opinion of Lucas about private property is noteworthy. Property, he holds, should be distributed according to the idea of natural law embodied in the *jus gentium*. But the existing order concerning private property, Lucas points out, is not based on natural justice. The craving appetite of man for wealth has produced the actual distribution of private property. Therefore this distribution does not rest on the idea of natural justice, but on that of injustice. 'Nota', says our author, 'quod haec duo pronomina "meum" et "tuum" non ex justitia, sed ex iniquitate mortalium processerunt, quod exponit glossa, id est, per consuetudinem juris gentium aequitati contrariam naturali'.[1] This passage leaves no room for doubt as to the real opinion of Lucas. He thinks that private property ought to be distributed according to the principles of natural equity (equality ?). But he does not say whether the institution of private property originates in natural law. Nevertheless, property, in its actual distribution, is protected by positive law.[2]

Being part of universal nature, man is God's creature—'opus quippe Dei homo est'[3]—and is therefore endowed by God with natural—that is, inborn—indestructible rights which he possesses regardless of human legislation, such as his right to just wages,[4] or which he can exercise even against legitimately instituted laws, such as his right of disobedience against unjust demands of officials.[5] Every human creature has the right of freedom which is acquired by birth—'ad libertatem nati sumus'.[6] That Lucas regards slavery as an institution against natural law cannot cause much surprise—'servitus autem est contra jus naturae' is his verdict on this institution—since the author of liberty is God Himself: 'Libertatis ipse Deus est auctor'.[7] The right of defence in all its aspects is another example of an unimpeachable and indestructible natural right.[8] The observance of contractual stipulations is yet another instance of natural law.[9] The criminal must suffer punishment on

[1] C. X, 70, 4, no. 10. Lucas does not refer to any specific gloss, but we may be justified in assuming that he has in mind a gloss by Irnerius on D. 1, 1, 6. This gloss of Irnerius is transcribed by Carlyle, loc. cit., vol. ii, p. 43. Odofredus, too, referred to Irnerius's gloss, and said: 'Dicit glossa interlinearis: additur vel detrahitur juri communi, tum nova materia, ut tutela . . . tum iniquitas, ut dominium', Odofredus on D. 1, 1, 6. But I could not find anywhere else an allusion to this gloss, which, if Lucas meant the Irnerian gloss to which Odofredus referred, was by no means so outspoken as Lucas presents it.

[2] C. X, 31, 33, no. 19.

[3] C. XII, 63, 1, no. 14.

[4] Further details, *infra*, p. 184.

[5] See *infra*, p. 110.

[6] On this inheritance of the principle of freedom by the M.A. and the modern world, see Carlyle, loc. cit., vol. v, pp. 442–449.

[7] C. XII, 63, 1, no. 73. Though Lucas does not say so, he has obviously in mind Lactantius's *Div. Inst.*, Carlyle, loc. cit., vol. v, pp. 15, 16.

[8] See *infra*, p. 132, n. 7.

[9] C. XI, 47, 23, no. 8: 'Observantia pacti est de jure naturae . . . quod est immutabile'.

the basis of natural law.[1] It need hardly be said that Lucas's natural law doctrine is not identical with that of contemporary jurists, who still adhered to Ulpian's conceptions.[2] Based as it is on the identification of natural law with divine law, Lucas's idea of natural rights is grounded on his view that men are equal in the eyes of God and are, accordingly, equipped with basic natural rights. It is no exaggeration to assert that this conception contains the germ of the natural law theory which was to be treated systematically centuries later.[3]

The essential difference between the divine and the human law, in Lucas's opinion, lies solely in the law-creating authority. The divine or natural law is a direct emanation of divine power, whereas human law, although it, too, rests ultimately on divine providence, is issued by the human authority entrusted with its creation. But here arose a problem of profound significance: what human power has the right to make laws? The controversy as to whether the creation of laws was the function exclusively of the people or of the Ruler stood very much in the foreground at Lucas's time. The *Lex Regia* provided the legal basis for the attempted solution of the problem. In a narrower sense the question concerned the validity of the *Lex Regia*.[4] The minority view was that of Jacobus Butrigarius and Martinus Sullimanus. They maintained that the *Lex Regia* was a revocable law and that the people had voluntarily transferred their legislative power to the Ruler; since their grant was revocable, they still had the power to make law.[5] The overwhelm-

[1] 'Delinquens naturaliter obligatur', C. XII, 45, 1, no. 37. See also C. X, 58, 1, no. 1: 'Est ab ipsa natura, ut maleficium non transeat impunitum'. Further details see *infra*, ch. VII.

[2] See 'Baldus's Conception of Law' in *L.Q.R.*, loc. cit., p. 393. I could not find any passage in Lucas's commentaries which would suggest any view resembling the old Roman conceptions of natural law. But whilst Baldus still accepted Ulpian's conceptions, Cynus, on the other hand, showed signs of dissatisfaction with Ulpian's view, but did not pursue the idea sufficiently far to reach the conclusions at which Lucas arrived. Cynus said in his commentaries, D. 1, 1, 1, no. 9: 'Homo est creatus in duabus materiis: una, scil. quam communem habet cum caeteris animalibus, puta alimentationem vel sensualitatem, et secundum hanc naturam describitur jus naturale in legibus; altera vero, quam communem habet cum angelis, scil. rationabilitatem, secundum quam jus naturale diffinitur in canone . . . jus naturale est quoddam jus animae sensibili in eius productione a nativitate insertum, prout vero homini tantum'. But in no. 12 of the same lecture he fell back on Ulpian's procreation and alimentation as well as on matrimony as issues of natural law.

[3] On the development of the later natural law doctrine see in particular Gierke–Barker, *Natural Law and the Theory of Society*, vol. i, pp. 96 seq.

[4] On the whole question of the *Lex Regia*, particularly as far as the literature of the medieval publicists is concerned, see the account given by Gierke–Maitland, *Political Theories of the Middle Age*, pp. 39 seq. Cf. also Carlyle, loc. cit., vol. v, pp. 48 seq.; vol. vi, pp. 13 seq.

[5] The first, to my knowledge, to have clearly formulated this view was the French jurist, Petrus de Bellapertica. In his lecture on C. I, 14, 12, he said that, in his opinion, the people has 'jus imperii vel jus eligendi imperatorem'.

ing majority, however, expressed the opinion that the *Lex Regia* was absolutely valid and, therefore, that the people had no legislative authority. But this extreme view, which was in fact older than its counterpart,[1] soon became modified, particularly through the influence of Odofredus, Cynus, and Bartolus: the jurists availed themselves of the concept of an independent community (city, &c.) to which had been conceded the faculty of making law as a result of the 'consensus populi'. The power to give law to the whole Empire was considered as the exclusive prerogative of the Emperor.[2]

Lucas, on the other hand, leaves all legalistic arguments on one side and approaches the whole problem from the theistic point of view. He argues that the people had not been, and could not be, given any authority to create law, because the 'will of the people' is subject to so many influences and, consequently, is so unstable that the thesis of the law, being based on justice, would be difficult to uphold and would become highly fictitious. It is well worth quoting the main parts of the rather long passages in which he denies the people all right to legislate, not only because of the arresting arguments he puts forward, but also because they reveal strikingly, and in somewhat forceful language, the mentality of our jurist.

> Si populorum jussis [he says], si sententiis judicum jura constituerentur, jus esset adulterare, jus lactrocinari, jus falsa testamenta supponere, si ex suffragiis aut scitis multitudinis probarentur[3] . . . vanae voces populi non sunt audiendae . . . electio seu postulatio

---

He strongly insisted on the right of the people to withdraw their mandate from the Ruler: 'Sicut est in judice delegante quod jurisdictionem suam a se non abdicat, populus Romanus concessit imperatori potestatem imperii, sed a se non abdicavit . . . ecce ratio, quae me movet. Credo, si imperator male egerit, posset populus eum revocare . . . item sic fecit alius populus Romanus; dedit potestatem decem viris; illi viri male se habuerunt, opprimebant subjectos, voluit populus, quod resignarent—et resignaverunt . . . item esto, quod si populus voluisset a se abdicare non potuit, nam potestatem vel jurisdictionem sibi commissam non potest abdicare quis a se, nisi in manu superioris . . . et *populus non habet superiorem*; verum est, quod imperator est superior quolibet de populo, sed non est superior populo.' He adds that 'hodie non est populus Romanus, sed translatum (scil. jus imperii) in Germanos'.

[1] Already Placentinus taught it: 'Populus in principem transferrendo communem potestatem nullam sibi reservavit, ergo potestatem leges scriptas condendi . . .', *Inst.* lib. i, p. 2. See also his remarks in C. VIII, 53, 2: 'Hoc arguo: in principem per regiam legem populus Romanus omne jus transtulit, ergo jus condendi jura et abrogandi'. Irnerius and Rogerius had similar views, see Carlyle, loc. cit., vol. ii, pp. 58 seq.

[2] Odofredus, D. 1, 1, 9, no. 1: 'Solus princeps potest facere legem generalem, quae ligat omnes cives subjectos Romano imperio, sed civitas potest facere legem, quae ligat tantum cives suos'. See also on the whole question, C. N. S. Woolf, *Bartolus of Sassoferrato*, p. 35, and my remarks in 'Bartolus on Customary Law', in *Juridical Review*, 1940, p. 271.

[3] C. XI, 19, 1, no. 17. His contemptuous attitude towards the people may have been influenced by the *Policraticus*, VII, 9, although no direct reference is made to John.

> facta vocibus popularibus et confirmatio inde secuta nulla sunt. Multitudo namque libenter consentit in vitio . . . et ob tumultum cito a vero deviat pergitque in indirectum. In malum quoque pronus est populus . . . plebs enim saepe clamoribus aut gratia vel praetio forsitan agitata seu excitata moveri solet. Multitudinis vero imperitae consilium et quae (quod ?) populare consilium sequitur, nec fructus boni nec jucunditatem nec memoriam habet . . . nihil tam facile quam vilem plebiculam et indoctam conditione et linguae volubilitate decipere; quae quicquid non intelligit, plus miratur, populum namque decipiunt, qui beatificunt eum . . . mihi nihil unquam populare placuit eamque optimam rem publicam esse dico, quae sit in potestate optimorum . . . nam quanto major est populus, tanto ab intellectu est remotior.[1]

This passage presents a curious resemblance to Bodin's derisive views on the capabilities of the people.[2] Lucas feels, however, the necessity of adding that customary law obtains its efficacy and binding force from its confirmation by the Ruler: 'Praemissa tamen', he declares at the end of the quoted passage, 'non urgent in casu nostrae quaestionis, nam consuetudo ipsa et aliae sunt regis privilegio confirmatae'.

The only competent authority, then, is the Ruler—the Emperor as the 'dominus mundi' and the King in his domain.[3] The Ruler is God's temporal representative on earth, His vice-gerent, and is vested with virtually unlimited powers which he derives immediately from God: 'Est enim rex in terra sicut Deus in coelo . . . generaliter autem amplissima est potestas eius'.[4] More than that: 'Imago divinitatis est princeps'.[5] The Ruler's overlordship rests solely on divine authority.[6] Indeed, this language might have been used by

[1] C. X, 36, 1, nos. 25–26.

[2] See A. W. Dunning, *History of Political Theories*, vol. ii, p. 102.

[3] Our present purpose does not necessitate a distinction between the Emperor, King, and Princes, since our problem in this context concerns the fundamental position of every legitimate ruler. Lucas, too, employs the terms Imperator, Rex, Princeps, without distinguishing between them.

It should be borne in mind that when a fourteenth-century writer uses these terms he simply indicates the secular authority anywhere; see the remarks of Professor J. W. Allen, 'Politics', in *Medieval Contributions to Modern Civilization*, ed. by Prof. F. J. C. Hearnshaw, p. 259.

[4] C. XII, 35, 14, no. 6.

[5] C. X, 31, 42, no. 3. It is therefore inaccurate to assume that this conception of the Ruler as the image of God was first elaborated in the fifteenth century. This assumption is made by Prof. J. W. Allen, *History of Political Thought in the Sixteenth Century*, p. 282. Lucas is perfectly familiar with the 'conception of a Prince ruling absolutely as the representative of God', p. 281. On Bracton's views, see Schulz, loc. cit., pp. 139, 147.

[6] C. XI, 71, 1, no. 11. See also *infra*, p. 170. We venture to doubt the correctness of Dr. Carlyle's general statement, loc. cit., vol. vi, p. 25, as regards the jurists of the fourteenth century. Dr. Carlyle's statement cannot be applied to Lucas. Carlyle says that it will be evident that the jurists 'can hardly be said to express any very clear judgements upon the

the sixteenth-century partisans of the divine right of kings.[1] According to Lucas, every Ruler is instituted for the sake of the community whose leadership is his prerogative. By divine ordinance he is entrusted with the protection of his subjects, and is responsible for the promotion of their prosperity and that of the public weal in general: 'Principes terrarum a Deo instituti sunt, ut communem populi utilitatem procurent'.[2] The Ruler holds his office as a trustee of God, and is responsible, accordingly, to no earthly power, but to God alone: 'Cor regis est in manu Dei' [3] and the Ruler 'soli Deo habet de peccato reddere rationem'.[4] Lucas bases his view of the all-powerful position of the Ruler on the Gospel and on the theories which were propounded by the Church and the theologians, particularly on the doctrines of St. Augustine and Orosius.[5] Apart from the considerations expounded by these authorities, there is one more which is determinative for Lucas's point of view and which will be pointed out in its proper context.

This trusteeship of the Ruler is truly personal, indivisible, inalienable, and non-transferable. The Ruler cannot delegate his authority to his wife and transfer to her the mandate which he alone received from God: 'Princeps licet det Augustae suae privilegia, quae ipse habet . . . non potest Augusta condere leges et huiusmodi praecipua imperialis dignitatis exercere'.[6]

A corollary of his trusteeship and the main function of the Ruler is legislation by establishing rules of action which are binding on all his subjects. The Ruler alone has received the divine mandate

---

general question of legislative power'. Nor can that statement be applied to Bartolus.

On the other hand, the truth of the statement by W. A. Dunning, loc. cit., vol. i, p. 192, may well be doubted in view of the achievements of secular jurisprudence. He says: 'St. Thomas's theory of law and justice is the channel through which the doctrines of Aristotle, the Stoics, Cicero, the Roman Imperial jurists and St. Augustine, blended into a rounded whole, were transmitted to modern times'. Lucas's theory of law—like that of most of the Post-Glossators—is the result not only of speculative thought, but also of practical experience gained in Court and at the bench. That Lucas was no less versed with ancient philosophy and jurisprudence than St. Thomas cannot seriously be doubted.

[1] The tendency to absolutism is also clearly recognizable in Baldus, who in his lecture on C. VII, 50, 3, no. 2, says that 'princeps enim legitime electus est in terris Deus'.

[2] C. X, 18, 1, no. 9, and in many other places.

[3] C. XI, 70, 5, no. 18. The phrase occurs in *Proverbs*, xxi, 1.

[4] C. XII, 35, 14, no. 1.

[5] Although Bartolus does not mention any writers, he adheres to the same opinion. Cf. D. 49, 15, 24: 'Si quis diceret dominum Imperatorem non esse dominum et monarcham totius orbis, esset hereticus. Quia diceret contra determinationem ecclesiae, contra textum sancti Evangelii, dum dicit "exivit edictum a Caesare Augusto, ut describeret universus orbis", ut habes Lucam II. Ita etiam recognovit Christus Imperatorem ut dominum.' See also Woolf, loc. cit., p. 27. For further details see *infra*, ch. VIII. On the inconsistency of Bartolus see *infra*, pp. 90–91.

[6] See C. XI, 29, 2, no. 4.

to create law: 'Per Imperatores quippe Romanos Deus humano generi leges distribuit'.[1] That statement, in conjunction with the often-repeated expression 'jus civile divinitus est per ora principum promulgatum',[2] makes it abundantly clear that the Ruler is merely the medium through which God creates the law which is known as human law. It attains binding force, not because it emanates from the Ruler by virtue of his supreme power, but because it emanates from him by virtue of his divine mandate: 'Imperator a Deo condendae legis potestatem accepit', from which premis Lucas deduces 'et sic dici potest divina sanctio omnis lex'.[3] The obligatory character of law rests on divine will as the ultimate source of all law. The 'divinum lumen', with which only the Ruler is endowed,[4] imparts binding force to his laws alone: 'Nam sanciuntur bene et juste ex illuminatione divina'.[5] Consequently, the constitutive element of the obligatory character is, not the Ruler's will *per se*, but God's will, for 'non est homo, qui ligat, sed Deus, qui dignos facit homines tanti honoris'.[6] The basis of the binding force of law is both moral and religious; therefore, the bond between man and God, in the sphere of law, is established by the Ruler.[7] Law is hallowed ordinance—'sanctio sancta jubens honesta, prohibens contraria',[8] because it descends from the holder of the divine office of legislation: 'Deus enim Imperatori sanciendi leges potestatem dedit'.[9]

The idea which underlies his doctrine of the exclusive legislative authority of the Ruler can be no other than that of individual responsibility. The notion of the legislator includes the conception of the legislator's responsibility before God, the source of all power. The idea that the people, taken as a whole, could be called upon to answer for any legislative measures which they introduced is wholly inconceivable to him. God could not have handed over powers to an indefinable and amorphous aggregate of individuals. Since he does not recognize any collective responsibility, he is necessarily led to deny to the people all political and legislative powers. It is the individual alone who can be made responsible. Consequently, 'a saecularibus autem principibus et ab ecclesiasticis praelatis gravis ratio a Deo exigitur', and it is very significant that imme-

[1] C. X, 71, 1, no. 15, with a reference to St. Augustine. Bracton's dicta on kingship are now conveniently transcribed by Schulz, loc. cit., pp. 137–9.

[2] C. X, 18, 1, no. 8, and in numerous other places.

[3] C. XI, 18, 1, no. 3.

[4] 'Nam dicitur habere divinum lumen', loc. cit., no. 3.

[5] C. X, 18, 1, no. 8, repeated in C. X, 70, 4, no. 2.

[6] C. XI, 70, 5, no. 42.

[7] Professor d'Entrèves, *The Medieval Contribution to Political Thought*, pp. 8, 9, from the political point of view, makes the same observation when he says that 'the problem of authority and obligation was felt by the medieval mind primarily to involve a religious issue, and urgently to require an answer which should be in accordance with the principles of the Christian Faith . . . authority has assumed a sacred character'.

[8] C. XI, 18, 1, no. 3.

[9] C. X, 18, 1, no. 8.

diately after this statement the following appears: 'Imperator, quod secundum leges imperium a Deo custodiendum accepit'.[1] It is the individual legislator alone who concentrates all power in his hands through the divine appointment. And God can make him accountable for any misuse of his authority.[2]

The Ruler's function as the earthly representative of God designates his will alone as the source of the authoritative commands indirectly expressing God's will: inasmuch as it bears upon the social relations of men, the Ruler's will is law itself. Indeed, the Ruler is 'lex animata'. He excogitates his laws on the strength of the 'coeleste arbitrium' which he possesses by virtue of his trusteeship: 'Princeps ista (scil. jura) pro motu suo disponit, sola quidem voluntas principis est lex . . . tamen talis motus justus sit juxta coeleste arbitrium'.[3] In all worldly matters the divine judgement imposes upon the Ruler as the legislator the duty to follow God as his example—'rex habet coeleste arbitrium, ut praedictum est, ex quo nedum potest, sed etiam debet imitari Deum' [4]—which duty is considered by Lucas as an effective barrier against the creation of laws in conflict with natural law or natural justice.[5] The concept of 'justus motus' implies that the law proceeding from it conforms with natural law and justice. In short, divine judgement manifests itself in the will of the Ruler. Lucas draws our attention to the fundamental similarity which he perceives between human law and Holy Writ, for both are expressions of the supreme will: the former of the Ruler's will, the latter of God's will.[6]

The Ruler's duty to follow God as his example, both in government and legislation, entails the obligation that he should not create law without a reasonable cause ('causa'). For God never intervenes in worldly affairs without a legitimate cause, and thus God's earthly representative and vice-gerent, the Ruler, should also refrain from creating law without a legitimate cause, although he

[1] C. X, 5, 2, no. 11.

[2] It is interesting to observe that sixteenth-century political thought had ideas not unlike those of Lucas. See Prof. J. W. Allen, *History*, &c., p. 385: 'The very root of the theory (scil. of the divine right of kings) is the idea that authority to command, implying obligation to obey, cannot possibly be created by man'.

[3] C. X, 26, 4, no. 1, repeated in many places, see, e.g., C. X, 59, 1, no. 20. Albericus de Rosciate claimed a 'coeleste arbitrium' for the pope, but not for the Emperor, see his commentaries on C. VII, 37, 3, no. 21, whilst, not unlike Lucas, Cynus maintained that 'imperator divinus est et coelestis semper', see his lecture on D. 1, 4, 3, no. 1.

In contemporary England the principle was 'quod paribus placuit' rather than 'quod principi placuit', Holdsworth, vol. ii, p. 196.

[4] C. XI, 70, 5, no. 18.

[5] 'Talis motus sit justus juxta coeleste arbitrium . . . non contra jus naturale aut naturalem aequitatem vel divinam . . . sed pro communi utilitate procedat', C. X, 26, 4, no. 1.

[6] C. XI, 19, 1, no. 19: 'Leges scriptae . . . sicut scriptura sacra nihil aliud est quam voluntas omnipotens Dei ad creaturam suam, secundum Gregorium in registro, lib. 3, cap. 83'.

is not bound to state the cause in his legal enactment. Since nothing in the world happens without cause, the presumption that law emerges from a just cause is, in Lucas's opinion, justified.[1] We shall see that this conception has far-reaching consequences.

Yet it would be hasty to conclude that the Ruler has complete liberty in the discharge of his legislative powers. It is precisely his function as the divinely appointed Ruler and the purposive idea inherent in human life which set limits to his powers. For the moral as well as the social aspects of law impose limitations on the exercise of his legislative will. The former aspects involve obligations towards his divine superior, the fulfilment of which Lucas considers as an indispensable condition for the validity of all human law; whilst the latter aspects concern the requirements of law as a social force, which the legislator is bound to fulfil by virtue of his function as the divinely appointed leader of his people. The validity of law depends on its conformity with divine or natural law—'humanae leges eatenus valent, quatenus non discrepant a divinis'[2] which should serve as the guiding model for human law.[3] The duty incumbent upon the Ruler is to avoid the issue of law whose content is opposed to the divine ideas of the government of the world or to the principles of nature, because law of this kind would inevitably impinge upon the harmony in the Universe. The sanction for the neglect of his duty is the invalidity of his laws. The Ruler cannot claim the validity of, and demand obedience to, his command, when it contradicts the counsels and ideas expressed in the Holy Scriptures which have 'vicem legis' and must, accordingly, be obeyed by the Ruler.[4] Contradiction to them entails the invalidity of his law: 'Oportet autem leges sacras regulas sequi', our author says, 'quia vicem legis obtinent'. Moreover, 'si ab eis discrepant, nullae sunt'.[5] Furthermore, any command of the Ruler which contradicts the divine idea of natural justice or the dictates of natural reason fails to constitute law.[6] The binding character of law is in abeyance when the Ruler's will is not a true

[1] 'Non teneatur causam exprimere, sine ipsa tamen quid statuere non debet. Nam Deus, quem princeps sequi tenetur, nihil agit sine causa in terra, ut dicitur Job., cap. 5, et Polycraticus, lib. 2, cap. 1. Nihil enim est vel fit, cuius ortum legitima causa et ratio non praecedat, inde dicitur jus aequum praesumptione legis', C. X, 26, 4, no. 2.

[2] C. X, 48, 2, no. 5.

[3] Cf. C. XI, 18, 1, no. 14: 'Omnium legum inanis est censura, si non divinae legis imaginem gerant'. On this tenet of John of Salisbury, see also R. L. Poole, loc. cit., p. 206.

[4] C. X, 26, 4, no. 2.

[5] With a reference to the *Policraticus*, lib. IV, c. 8.

[6] It is the principle of the 'moral purpose and function of the State' (Carlyle, loc. cit., vol. v, p. 449, see also Prof. Powicke, 'Reflections on the Medieval State' in *Transactions of the Royal Historical Society*, 4th ser., vol. xix (1936), p. 10) which lies behind such conceptions. This conception was not uncommon in medieval lore, particularly amongst the profound thinkers. Thomas Aquinas held a similar view, see Prof. d'Entrèves,

expression of the ' coeleste arbitrium ' ; lacking ' divina illuminatio ', his command establishes no valid law : ' Manifestum est, quod cum voluntas principis ab aequitate, justitia et ratione deviet, non est lex '.[1] A logical sequel, therefore, of Lucas's view of the moral and religious basis of the binding force of law is the thesis that the command of the Ruler is theoretically to be divested of its binding force when it flatly opposes divine or natural law. The moral obligation of law must be ' salubris '. If it fails to produce this effect the command of the Ruler is then styled a ' bad law '. A law of this kind should rather be disobeyed : ' Malae leges servandae non sunt '.[2] But Lucas does not appear to concede active resistance to the law, though he grants active resistance to officials. Since law ' jubet ea, quae facienda sunt, prohibet ea, quae contraria sunt ',[3] he emphasizes that its precepts must be of a content which is ' pia et Deo placens '.[4] The same train of thought is revealed in his thesis that all validity has to be withheld from laws which restrict the freedom of the Church : ' Mundanis legibus sancta mater ecclesia non constringitur '.[5] The freedom of the Church would be restricted, Lucas thinks, if the legislator encroached upon privileges granted to the Church by Emperor or Pope, and deprived her of the effects of those privileges.[6]

Viewing the social implications of law, Lucas posits the consideration of the common good as the supreme principle in the creation of law. By virtue of his office, the legislator is bound to promote the common good of his subjects. Law is the instrument whereby he can most effectively enhance the common weal. From every action which is deemed useful from the point of view of society should be derived an enforceable rule : ' Praeses facere debet quicquid omnino est publico et civitatibus utile . . . publica enim utilitas privatae praefertur '.[7] Lucas admits, however, that the

---

loc. cit., p. 39, who summarizes Thomas's theory in these words : ' The *voluntas principis* has *vigorem legis* only inasmuch as it is *ratione regulata*. According to Thomas it was the natural and rational order of justice which limits the sovereignty of the particular state '. But it must be kept in mind that Thomas's conceptions were always dictated by an over-emphasis of the divine and natural law. See Prof. d'Entrèves, p. 34, who says that the limits of the Ruler's authority are necessarily ' fixed by the correspondence of human authority with divine and natural law '. See also Carlyle, loc. cit., vol. v, p. 91. Social realities play, with Lucas, a role equally important as divine (natural) law.

[1] C. X, 26, 4, no. 5.

[2] C. X, 31, 33, no. 23, and C. X, 1, 4, no. 17.

[3] C. XI, 18, 1, no. 12.

[4] C. X, 5, 2, no. 4.

[5] C. XI, 18, 1, no. 14.

[6] See C. XI, 3, 2, no. 5 : ' Illa dicuntur contra libertatem ecclesiae statui quae sunt privilegia concessa clericis et ecclesiis a Papa vel a principe '. That was general opinion, see Cynus, C. I, 1, 2, Authentica *Cassa et Irrita*, no. 5 : ' Omnia illa, quae sunt contra privilegia concessa universali ecclesiae, sive a Deo sive a Dei vicario sive ab Imperatoribus '. Cynus reports that this was the theory of Innocent IV.

[7] C. XI, 41, 1, no. 11.

desirable effect cannot always be achieved for all the members of society, but he declares that it is sufficient when law fulfils this criterion with respect to the majority of the people: 'Si forte non omnibus utile est . . . sufficit tamen, si majori parti; nulla enim lex omnibus satis commoda est', he declares. It must suffice, if the law 'in summa prodest'.[1] He stresses the necessity of creating law for the sake of the common good and lays a corresponding duty on the part of the legislator. Probably with contemporary conditions in mind, he considers it advisable to state that legislation is an office out of which no private advantage must be derived: 'Lex enim nullo privato statuentis commodo, sed pro communi bono ponenda est'.[2] But provided that a law is useful to the whole or to the majority of the community, he recommends, in order to deprive law of any private effects that 'lex ubique debet extendere virtutem suam'; therefore he holds that 'constitutio personalis habenda est pro generali'.[3]

Another indispensable requirement of law—considered from the social aspects—is its conformity with nature: 'Subjungo, quod lex a natura deviare non debet'.[4] He hastens to add that the concept 'nature', as used in this context, has the meaning of human nature, not of divine nature: 'Intellige naturam humanam potius quam divinam'. In other words, he postulates conformity with what is usual or normal. This is made clear by the stress he lays on the necessity of considering legislative precedents, because only a gradually progressive development should take place in the sphere of legislation. Only if he takes into account the existing social conditions and prevalent ideas, will the legislator succeed in creating laws which will prove beneficial to his people and which will serve as a *feasible* rule of action.[5] That is the meaning of the otherwise misleading passage:

> Leges nulla alia causa nos tenent quam quod judicio populi sunt receptae . . . nam et lex debet anterioribus exemplis submitti . . . id enim, quod usitatum non est, fieri non potest.[6]

[1] C. X, 5, 2, no. 4. It is interesting to note that the same phrase occurs in Bodin's *De Republica*, lib. IV, cap. 4, p. 689.

[2] C. XII, 37, 15, no. 8, repeated in many places, see, e.g., C. XI, 70, 5, no. 4.

[3] C. X, 28, 1, no. 4. Cf. also no. 2 of the same passage, where he speaks of laws made in favour of certain officials of the Crown: 'Lex quidem scripta uni officiali potest universo orbi conveniens esse'.

[4] C. X, 5, 2, no. 4, reasserted in many places, e.g., C. X, 36, 1, no. 21, X, 61, 1, no. 8, &c.

[5] Cf. C. X, 26, 4, no. 5: 'Lex justa et *possibilis* debet esse'.

[6] C. X, 28, 1, no. 5. When law is considered from this aspect alone, the dictum of Dr. Carlyle, loc. cit., vol. v, p. 457, may appropriately be applied to Lucas, namely, that law is 'the expression of that which the community acknowledges as just, law . . . is the expression of the life of the community'. See, however, vol. vi, p. 3, where Dr. Carlyle says that law is 'the expression not merely of the will of the ruler, but of the life of the community'. The addition is very significant.

Moreover, the legislator is advised to issue penal laws whose sanctions are not too harsh. Lucas also recommends him to take into account human nature as it is, not as it should be ('naturae humanae conditionem').[1] It is due precisely to the differences of social conditions and development that law varies in time and place: 'Leges humanae secundum dispositionem terrarum variantur et secundum varietates temporum . . . et sic diversae diversis temporibus emanarunt'.[2] In short, the legislator has to take cognizance of the actual conditions in a given society. Social and political diversities account for diversity of law.

It can readily be perceived that all these foregoing considerations represent severe limitations of the Ruler's legislative powers. They are curtailed—at least theoretically—by his subjection to higher laws. Yet, in spite of this theoretical foundation, the idea can already be clearly discerned in Lucas's system that the Ruler has the power to issue laws which, at least to a certain extent, disregard the contents and precepts of those higher laws. The concept of an absolute legislative authority emerges in Lucas's system, though probably unnoticed by himself. We shall return to this interesting point when we discuss the validity of certain legal enactments which were understood to have been issued against natural law and without a just cause, and when we consider the validity of laws which derogate divine and natural law.

Lucas considers the external shape of the laws as of no less importance than their contents. The principle in framing laws should be this: simplicity and lucidity of style, brevity of language, employment of unambiguous terms, and avoidance of superfluous expressions.[3] Legislative technique based on these principles will not only greatly enhance the efficacy of laws, but also facilitate their interpretation by scholarship and judiciary. He bitterly deplores the use of empty phrases in laws, because they are apt to obscure their object and purpose. Moreover, it is the office of the legislator to speak in unmistakable language and, if need be, in 'verba vulgaria',[4] so that his law becomes an efficient and applicable instrument in the ordering of human relations. Laws whose meaning has become obscure should be abolished and their place taken by laws which give a clear ruling and are incapable of being interpreted and applied in different ways.[5] At the same time the legislator should proceed cautiously—'debet futura caute consti-

[1] C. XII, 45, 1, no. 47: 'Leges enim non vehementer durae constituendae sunt, sed mediocres juxta naturae humanae conditionem'.

[2] C. XI, 19, 1, no. 16.

[3] 'Magis placet in legibus simplicitas quam difficultas (referring to the *Policraticus*, lib. VII, cap. 12) . . . lex debet esse clara . . . nam clare et lucide verba legis scribenda sunt . . . lex nullam ambagem continere debet, imo veteres ambages rumpere', C. X, 47, 14, no. 4. Cf. also C. X, 75 Rubrica, no. 11: 'Inutilia lex refugiat . . . in legibus nullum verbum, nisi necessarium, est ponendum'.

[4] C. X, 47, 14, no. 4.

[5] loc. cit., no. 4.

tuere '[1]—and should leave a margin for liberal interpretation. Lucas does not conceal his contempt for those legislators who, for the sake only of exercising their legislative powers, issue laws which lack stringency and clearness of conception, for these violate a fundamental principle—' non enim in vanum debet occupare membranas '.[2] The idea of equality, he thinks, should find expression in the indifferent language of laws: ' Nec est eis amare vel odisse, sed cum omnibus una semper eadem voce loquuntur '.[3]

The topic of the present chapter necessitates a reference to the division into public and private law. Lucas conscientiously refers to the definitions given in the Roman texts, but he omits to elaborate the import and implications of the Roman concepts. In fact, his whole system shows the little value he attaches to the Roman classification. Nowhere in his commentaries can be found any theory which is based on the traditional distinction between public and private law, for natural (divine) law and human law are the divisions upon which he works. As to human law, it may be correct to assume that he conceives all human law as public law. In some places he contrasts public law issued by the proper authority with private law, which is, for him, only another name for moral law or, as he calls it, the ' lex conscientiae ' or ' lex spiritus sancti '.[4] He seems to feel that no room is left within the conception of law as a command of the Ruler for the classical distinction between public and private law.[5]

This chapter may fittingly be concluded by representing Lucas's thoughts on the exercise of rights. According to him, the pursuance of rights against other individuals is an effluence of the individual's *potestas* derived from the law. This power of the individual is termed by our jurist ' virtuosa potestas '.[6] At first sight this expression may appear to lack intrinsic meaning, but a close study of his system of legal thought shows that the term is full of significance. Its meaning is this. The bearer of a right—which is granted by the law—is not in all circumstances entitled (or empowered, as Lucas would say) to the action which is the content of the right.

[1] loc. cit., no. 4.

[2] loc. cit., no. 4. Cf. also C. X, 32, 33, no. 40: ' In legibus enim nihil debet esse vacuum seu frustra '.

[3] C. X, 48, 2, no. 10.

[4] See, e.g., C. X, 69, 2, no. 5: ' Est lex publica, quae scil. statuta est ab eo, qui legis condendae habet publicam potestatem, et privata, i.e., lex conscientiae . . . lex spiritus sancti '.

See also C. X, 43, 2, no. 7, where he says that public law derives its name from public order—' quod non privatae personae, sed forte ordini . . . concessum fuerat '.

[5] Mr. J. W. Jones, loc. cit., p. 146, discussing the nature of this distinction from the modern point of view, very succinctly points to the idea of subordination (public law) and co-ordination (private law) inherent in this distinction. For Lucas, who perceives all law as a command of the Ruler, there is indeed no place for this distinction.

[6] C. X, 1, Rubrica no. 1.

He is entitled to the pursuance of the right under one condition only—namely, that his motive for exercising his right does not deviate from the motive of the legislator when he established the right in question. In other words, the pursuance of a right keeps within the ambit of permissible actions—that is to say, is lawful—when its bearer is motivated by the same reasons which prompted the legislator to grant the right. The bearer of a right is conceived by Lucas as an individual who has the power to make use of his right, provided that his purpose of exercising the right is in harmony with that of the legislator when he laid down the right. The individual is, so to speak, the executor of the legislative will. He is entitled to certain actions against other individuals when his motive coincides with that of the legislator. He acts on behalf of the legislator and is backed by his power. The position of a person upon whom a right is bestowed, particularly those rights which permit inroads upon the legal sphere of other individuals, makes it imperative that he acts in the spirit, and with the intention, of the legislator. For—we may assume that this consideration is at the back of Lucas's mind—how can the law-giver be expected to support, if need be with force, the exercise of a right when its bearer is impelled by motives opposed to, or at least deviating from, those which caused the legislator to grant the right? It appears repugnant to Lucas's moral sense to call an action rightful merely because a legal basis can be found for it. In order to make an action 'right' ('justum'), the individual who performs it must also have the 'right' intention. In Lucas's opinion the exercise of rights should not be a cloak for evil intentions. The idea of law would become a travesty altogether if the exercise of rights was not pervaded with the spirit underlying the law wherefrom the right is derived. That is why he who has a right is said to have 'pro se justitiam',[1] and why Lucas so strongly insists on the 'rectum vel justum' of any action based upon a right: 'Dicitur jus id, quod actum est, *ut sit justum*: habendo respectum ad *id, quod fieri debet*'.[2] Thus, if its agent had not the intention which the legislator presupposes, the character of an action may be unlawful, although this action is derived from positive law. No one is entitled to claim the support of the law unless his intention is in accord with that of the legislator.

This thesis is contained in Lucas's important statement that, in spite of a legal right conceded to an individual, liability is incurred when he pursued it with an evil intention. The presumption, however, is that he had no such intention, but if it were proved that he had, he was then not entitled to his action, which must be considered unlawful: the individual is exposed to the *actio* applicable to the case in question.

> Is, qui publico jure utitur, si aliquid faciat, quod est ad gravamen alterius, non tenetur injuria, quia non praesumitur causa injuriae id

[1] loc. cit., no. 1.

[2] loc. cit., no. 1.

facere . . . tamen si constat, quod ex dolo ad id processerit, tenetur actione in factum.[1]

A practical application of his principle is his view of the exercise of property rights. They should be pursued without detriment to other individuals. It would be against the idea and purpose of the institution of property if it were allowed to make use of one's property to the detriment of others. The rights of ownership preclude such exercise of them whereby another individual is wronged: 'Ipsius rei dominus in re propria nihil agere potest, quod alteri noceat'.[2]

Lucas carries his principle to its logical conclusion. His theory of criminal demeanour furnishes a test case. In the realm of crime his conception of the exercise of rights becomes of crucial importance and a fruitful principle. He says that parents and teachers have the right to punish children only when they proceed 'ex causa correctionis'; if they are prompted by some other motive, their action would not be within the ambit granted to them purely for one specific purpose; their action would be unlawful.[3] Another example is his view of the legality of killing a 'bannitus'—that is, a person who is outlawed as a consequence of some crime. According to the view regarded hitherto as indisputable, everyone had the right to kill the 'bannitus'. But Lucas does not concede this right without further examination of the killer's motive: if moved by the desire of vengeance or hatred of the 'bannitus', he cannot claim this right. Thus Lucas advances this general statement: 'Si non zelo justitiae, sed ex propriae iniquitatis libidine id faciat, meritum legis et justitiae rationabiliter perdit'.[4] Accusations against criminals should proceed, he is wont to stress, 'ex zelo justitiae', otherwise they are 'damnabiles'.[5] We may in anticipation add here that it is through this fundamental view that he arrives at a theory of crime at once unique and cogent, and which fulfils the requirements of justice.

To sum up: the exercise of rights which are onerous for others is lawful only if the pursuance of the right springs from an intention identical with that of the legislator. Lucas's main idea is that law cannot serve as a means to cover unjust, evil intentions. Rights are granted only for a specific purpose, and the bearer of a right cannot plead the cause of law and right when his intentions are in opposition to those of the legislator.

This fundamental thesis reveals a mind which is permeated with the spirit of morality rarely—if ever—to be found amongst jurists. The hypocritical idea of an 'objective nature' of law, a slogan of

[1] C. XII, 53, 1, no. 62.

[2] C. X, 47, 4, no. 34. It is interesting to note that Lucas refers to D. 8, 5, 8, 5 as the legal confirmation of his view. But this passage deals only with the exercise of the rights of servitudes, a typical example of a generalization of special point, so common amongst the Post-Glossators.

[3] C. XII, 52, 1, no. 4. Further details *infra*, pp. 145, 155–6.

[4] C. XII, 53, 1, no. 62.

[5] C. XII, 45, 1, no. 36.

modern jurisprudence, is plainly rejected. Lucas would certainly not have justified the coinage of the trite dictum 'Juristen sind böse Christen'. Nor would Shylock have found any support from our jurist.

Nevertheless, Lucas is fully aware of the difference between the 'legally right' or the 'just' and the 'good'. The 'bonum', he says, can properly be applied only to the quality of an internal substance, whilst the 'justum' refers to an external act: law establishes rules of action, and thus lays down a relationship between individuals. Consequently, the term 'justum' can only refer to actions between individuals, which relationship is not constitutive of the latter concept: 'Est differentia inter bonum et justum, nam bonum est in essentia vel natura, justum vero actum respicit'.[1] Furthermore, moral claims do not constitute rights in the meaning of the law: purely moral obligations are not actionable. Actionable claims must be based upon the 'necessitas justitiae'—that is to say, rights must proceed from that justice which has found concrete expression in the law. Only those rights are enforceable through the power of the Ruler as the legislator. The 'sola moralis aequitas', according to Lucas, is no basis 'sufficiens ad agendum'.[2] Nor would a purely natural obligation—'naturalis obligatio'—constitute an adequate basis for an action. Unless such moral or natural claims are supported by the 'communis utilitas', they are not actionable. Such claims cannot appeal to the law, because this presupposes the 'necessitas justitiae', but to moral reasons only, such as 'reverentia, beneficium, eleemosyna'. These moral reasons alone cannot, therefore, justify an actionable claim, he says, 'nisi necessitas ex alia parte praeponderet, vel alia causa seu ratio, puta communis utilitas'.[3] Although the distinction between morals and law dawns on him, and although he recognizes the coercive nature of human law, he omits to draw the inevitable conclusion and fails to recognize the essential similarity of the precepts of morals to those other precepts which are alleged to have the character of law.[4] The chasm between the jural precepts and the other normative injunctions had yet to be clearly recognized.

[1] C. X, 1, 5, no. 2.

[2] C. XI, 24, 2, no. 11.

[3] loc. cit., no. 11.

[4] If the interpretation of Prof. d'Entreves, loc. cit., pp. 59–65, is correct, Marsiglio seems to have drawn this inevitable conclusion. But, as far as could be ascertained with reasonable certainty, the legists did not enter into profound discussions on this topic.

CHAPTER IV

CUSTOMARY LAW

IN Lucas's opinion, the legal philosopher has to take cognizance of the habitual performance of certain rules which constitute an essential feature of individual and social life alike. The customary observance of those rules, he asserts, leads to the conclusion that habits, once they have become ingrained in man's personality, may be envisaged as innate tendencies or propensities of the personality itself: 'Quod consuetum est, est velut innatum'.[1] It is, he maintains, man's second nature which makes him perform certain actions habitually—'consuetudo est altera natura'—and any deep-seated habit resembles a natural human disposition: 'Similis est consuetudo naturae'.[2] Lucas fully realizes the great sway habits hold over both man and society—'gravissimum est imperium consuetudinis'[3]—recognizing, at the same time, that they diminish the volitional character of the action performed and its ethical value. He epitomizes this recognition in the dictum: 'Omnia vim suam a consuetudine perdunt'.[4] On the other hand, he holds, the fact must not be lost sight of that the habitual performance of ethically valuable actions tends to become part of the agent's nature and raises in this way the ethical value of his character correspondingly: 'Generaliter autem magna est virtus consuetudinis, nam consuetudo bene agendi vertitur in naturam'.[5]

His conservative outlook is illustrated by his intense distrust of all novelties and 'modern' innovations because, to his mind, they breed only discontent and discord amongst members of society: 'Discordiam pariunt novitates'.[6] He views old customs from a conservative standpoint as the pillars of society whose overthrow would inevitably disturb the ordered harmony of existence as he perceives it. It must be borne in mind, he strongly emphasizes, that only extraordinary conditions can justify a disregard of long-established social habits. There should be no deviation from traditional custom without urgent reason. His great reverence for the established social order, with its manifold customs, and the distrust he obviously feels for the changes effected by innovations are expressed in these words:

> Minime sunt mutanda, sic et prisca debent pro sua reverentia instituta manere, quae, ubi nulla rerum vel temporum urget angustia, regulariter convenit custodire.[7]

[1] C. X, 19, 7, no. 5. [2] loc. cit., no. 6. [3] loc. cit., no. 6.
[4] loc. cit., no. 6. [5] loc. cit., no. 6.
[6] C. XII, 37, 16, no. 5. [7] loc. cit., no. 5.

His theory of the exclusive sovereignty and the legislative monopoly of the Ruler makes him relegate custom, as a source of law, to a subordinate and inferior position. Statutory enactments are 'longe majoris auctoritatis' than customary law,[1] Lucas declares, herewith stating his opposition to the generally prevailing view, particularly to that of his great contemporary, Bartolus, who maintained the equal authority of both written and unwritten law. Nevertheless, Lucas's thesis by no means implies that, in so far as it was recognized as valid, customary law had not the same force as statute law. His view is not only based on his conception of the legislative authority, but also motivated by his prejudice against all things 'popular', hence the lesser 'authority' of customary law. The other Post-Glossators held that, owing to its origin, customary law represented the same authority as written law. They elaborated an exhaustive theory about customary law, once again failing to find any comprehensive principles in the Roman texts.[2] Almost without any exceptions, the medieval jurists based the binding force of customary rules on the tacit consent of the people. They conceived the difference between written statute law and unwritten customary law to lie in the manner in which the popular consent was expressed: the former proceeds from the 'expressus consensus populi'—within the limits of their legislative powers [3]—the latter originates in the 'tacitus consensus populi'.[4] Since the people was considered as the sole creator of customary law, whose binding force consequently was independent of any additional act of a higher authority, it became necessary to lay down certain fundamental conditions that had to be fulfilled by the creating agency, the people, if their customs were directly to display binding force.[5] The Post-Glossators viewed custom as the will of the people expressed in acts, and compared it with another institution where the will was an equally essential feature—that is, a contract: 'Con-

[1] C. X, 71, 1, no. 7.

[2] It is interesting to note that jurists as early as Azo complained of the lack of principles in Roman law. When commenting on C. VIII, 53, 2 he wrote in no. 2: 'Quae sit longa consuetudo? Et ita licet contineatur in rubrica, tamen leges sub ea positae obscure quaestionem istam prosequantur'.

[3] See *supra*, ch. III.

[4] To quote only a few typical examples. Cynus, C. VIII, 53, 2, no. 23: 'Consuetudo sicut statutum introducitur ex consensu populi'; in no. 5 he says: 'Differunt ergo statutum et consuetudo inter se sicut expressum et tacitum'. On Bartolus see my paper 'Bartolus on Customary Law' in *Juridical Review*, 1940, p. 271. Angelus de Ubaldis, D. 1, 3, 32, no. 3: 'Lex populi et consuetudo populi conveniunt in paritate potentiae causae, sive loquamur de causa efficiente, quae est populus, sive de causa materiali, quae est consensus'. Albericus de Rosciate, ibid., pr.: 'Causa enim juris scripti est consensus expressus populi, consuetudinis vero est consensus populi tacitus. Sed hi duo consensus sunt pares'.

[5] So, for instance, the conditions relating to the lapse of time, the frequency of acts, &c. The problem of judge-made law, too, was investigated in this connexion; for details see *Juridical Review*, loc. cit., p. 276.

suetudo aequiparatur pacto; ratio, quia utrumque procedit ex consensu '.[1] Hence they transplanted all the important principles of the doctrine of contracts to the theory of customary law, in particular the rules concerning mistake, coercion, ability to express the will, and the like. In short, their theory was concerned with the presuppositions of valid customary law, which derived its binding force solely from the tacit consent of the people.

Once again, Lucas follows his own line of thought, unperturbed by contemporary fashionable views. We shall search in vain in his writings for an elaboration of the general conditions and principles of valid customary laws, such as we find in other writers of the same period. Indeed, it would have been inconsistent with his general train of thought, if he had gone the way his contemporaries went and had attributed the binding force of customary rules to any other authority than to that of the Ruler. Consequently, Lucas perceives the customary observance of certain rules of conduct merely as factual phenomena, being essentially extra-legal and non-obligatory. Those rules constitute usage in the strict meaning of the term, and they obtain no binding character unless their practice had been consented to by the Ruler. The Ruler's approbation, therefore, is the constitutive element of the law character of social habits. Moreover, Lucas holds, the tacit toleration of customs by the Ruler would not be sufficient: by his explicit consent he has to take an active part, as it were, in the creation of customary law: 'Ad esse consuetudinis et roborationem inter alia requiritur, quod de conscientia principis sit inducta, non ex sola tolerantia '.[2] Law, being essentially the command of the only authority entrusted with its creation, cannot be established without that authority's participation; where the content of a rule has hitherto been followed, it becomes necessary for the Ruler to express his explicit approval in order to ensure its obligatory character.[3] The willed participation of the Ruler is, according to Lucas, an indispensable condition for the validity of customary law.[4] When doubt arises as to the knowledge of the Ruler the judge should refer the matter to him; the actual observance is a question of fact, and has therefore to be

[1] On Bartolus's definition, see loc. cit., p. 269.

[2] C. X, 46, Rubrica no. 10. Here again the close resemblance of Lucas's views to those held in the sixteenth century is too obvious to be overlooked. Absolutist sixteenth-century theories held, in consistency with their basic tenets, that 'mere customary law can derive authority only from the Sovereign's sanction' (Prof. J. W. Allen, *History of Political Thought in the Sixteenth Century*, p. 412, dealing with Bodin's theories). That is, of course, the only tenable idea in sixteenth-century conceptions. In England, too, customary law was 'only law so long as he (the sovereign) suffered it to exist' (Holdsworth, iv, 196). Hobbes even went so far as to declare that no custom 'of its own nature can amount to the authority of a law' (Holdsworth, v, 481, note 3).

[3] loc. cit., no. 9: 'Cum praesumatur scire princeps et consentire . . . alias non valet'.

[4] loc. cit., no. 9.

decided by the judge himself.[1] It is self-evident that Lucas postulates uniform and continuous practice which is of long standing and frequently observed.[2]

A further consideration here enters Lucas's investigations: a consideration that follows from the very nature of this species of law. Customary law notionally presupposes the creative participation of the whole, or of certain sections of the people, in bringing it about. For it is the citizenhood who set the conditions for the willed participation of the Ruler. Seen from this angle, customary law is for Lucas—as for all other Post-Glossators—the willed observance of unwritten rules and precepts. That observance is also perceived by him as the expression of the will of the people. But, for reasons already explained, he cannot resort to the antithetic scheme of 'expressus' and 'tacitus consensus populi', nor, indeed, is that will of the people conceived by him as a 'tacitus consensus', nor, above all, does the will of the people constitute any enforceable rule of action, unless sanctioned by the explicit approval of the Ruler. Considering the people's creative function in establishing customary rules of action, Lucas, quite in consistence with the will theory, unhesitatingly accepts the idea unanimously agreed upon by contemporary scholarship—namely, that, from the legal point of view, the customary observance by a plurality of individuals is a juristic act that closely resembles the conclusion of a contract by two individuals: both custom and contract presuppose the exertion of the will by the individuals concerned; and just as the latter cannot encroach upon the legal status of others, in the same way a custom—even supposing it has obligatory character—has no effect upon those who did not partake in its creation: 'Consuetudo', Lucas declares, 'stringit illos, inter quos est mos et consuetudo, non inter alios, sicut nec pactum nec aliud actum inter alios'. Thus Lucas, in the province of customary law, conceives two agencies are to be at work: the will of the people in creating and observing certain rules, and the will of the Ruler in approving them. Having been entrusted with the care of his subjects, it is the function of the latter to give his approval to rules which affect social life. In this idea of trusteeship we may once again discern the intrinsic and material reason for Lucas's insistence on the Ruler's approval, whereas the conception of law as a command seems to have furnished our jurist with the formalistic justification for the Ruler's participation.

Reasonableness of custom is an element necessary for its validity. Lucas regards that custom as reasonable which is neither in its contents nor in its effects opposed to the 'canonicis institutis'—that is

[1] '. . . negotium (judex) referat principi, qui est lex animata in terris', C. XII, 49, 2, no. 9. 'Judices abstinere debent a referrendo principi ea, quae in facto consistunt . . . nam sunt plura, quae magis potest scire quam princeps', C. X, 19, 7, no. 10.

[2] C. XII, 59, 8, no. 7.

to say, to the foundations of the established order which constitutes the social and political organism. Expressed in positive language, the idea to be realized by custom, in order that it should become a valid, enforceable rule of action, can be no other than the idea of all law. That idea should be identical with that underlying the conception of law in general. Accordingly, those customs are not valid which prove disruptive to the established political order or, as he expresses it, by which the 'status rei publicae deformaretur '.[1] Unreasonable custom would upset the smooth working of the social organism : 'Illa dicitur rationalis, quae non obviat canonicis institutis vel quam jus sustinet etiam contra leges vel rationes. Irrationabilis autem est, quae improbatur a jure '.[2] Furthermore, custom which 'ratione caret ' is considered to have no effects.[3] Lucas goes even so far as to declare that the observance of unreasonable customs exposes the observer to the *actio injuriarum*: 'Irrationabilis consuetudo enim non est fovenda, imo exstirpenda, unde ille, qui illa utitur, tenetur actione injuriarum '.[4]

It is in this setting that Lucas examines the relationship between customary law and statute law. Somewhat deviating from the commonly taught doctrine, he maintains that a distinction has to be drawn between customs concerning juristic acts which are, and those which are not, practised within the framework of statute law. The latter comprise all those juristic acts which are not dealt with by statute law and, therefore, fall outside the scope of statutory enactments and provisions altogether. Since it relates to juristic acts not contained in any statute, custom of this kind is bound to create as yet unknown categories of juristic acts. He attributes to it equal force with written law.[5] The former case, however, necessitates a further distinction—namely, that of whether the statute to which the juristic act refers expressly favours the application of customary rules—'aut expresse assistit consuetudini '—or is expressly opposed to them—'aut expresse resistit '—or simply is silent about them : 'aut est casus relictus extra expressam assistentiam vel resistentiam juris scripti '.[6] The first two alternatives do not present any difficulties, for a custom specially referred to, and approved of, by the statute in question is of necessity valid, whereas the unreasonableness of the second case, because contradictory to the express declaration of the statute, precludes its validity. Lucas follows the canonist Hostiensis in his statement that the judge has to decide into which category the custom falls.[7]

In cases falling into the third alternative which seem to afford the most frequent subjects for customary rules, our jurist avails himself of that classification, usually propounded by the Glossators

[1] C. XII, 43, 3, no. 32.
[2] C. X, 28, 1, no. 9.
[3] loc. cit., no. 9.
[4] loc. cit., no. 10.
[5] 'Aut consuetudo est de negotiis vel actibus, quibus non utimur jure scripto, et tunc pro lege servatur ', loc. cit., no. 8.
[6] loc. cit., no. 9.
[7] loc. cit., no. 9.

and adopted by all Post-Glossators, with some minor modifications. Whenever statute law makes no explicit declaration as to customs, they may be classified, in the main, into three categories—namely, those which were developed in accord with the law (' consuetudo secundum jus '), above the law (' consuetudo supra jus '), and against the law (' consuetudo contra jus '). In the strict meaning of the term the first species does not constitute new law, but contains rules which consolidate the power of written law; those customary rules concern actions which are undertaken in the spirit of all law. Custom of this kind is valid, enhances the application of statute law, and functions as a solidifying element: ' Consuetudo est secundum jus . . . valet et jus corroborat '.[1] The second species is characterized by its interpretative function, whereby it supplements law and makes it specific, and necessarily relates to a definitive statute: ' Quando est supra legem, interpretatur illam '.[2] Its validity is beyond doubt, as this kind of customary law also strengthens the cause of law. The problems arising out of the third category vary according to the kind of law against which this custom is directed.

(1) If the custom is only contrary to the formalities connected with the realization of divine commands, it acquires legal validity. Custom which contradicts the substantial content of the divine injunctions and prohibitions is, for understandable reasons, proclaimed by Lucas as invalid. He says: ' Aut illud divinum est morale consistens in praeceptis vel prohibitionibus, et tunc non valet (scil. consuetudo) . . . aut est ceremoniale vel sacramentale et contra literam illius juris, valet consuetudo '. As an example Lucas quotes the effect of customs on matrimony. In his opinion customary rules may validly affect the external form of the marriage ceremony or other ' accessoria ', such as dowry, but they can never introduce something that is contrary to the essence of matrimony.[3]

(2) Unless a special cause can be adduced for its observance, and unless the public weal is affected by it, custom opposed to the *jus gentium* is held to be invalid: ' Quando contra jus gentium, dicunt doctores, quod non valet, nisi cum causa et in ea publica versatur utilitas '.[4] Lucas's lack of interest in the *jus gentium* is shown by the terseness of this statement, which merely refers to the opinion of other jurists.

(3) If it is generally observed, Lucas attributes abrogative effect to custom that is directed against positive law, provided that the legislator has knowledge of the custom and approved of it. Local customs have that effect only within the boundaries of the locality wherein they are observed: ' Si vero sequitur legem, aut est generalis,

[1] loc. cit., no. 9. [2] loc. cit., no. 10.

[3] ' Illud est sciendum, quod consuetudo impedit et suspendit usum matrimonii et fortius impedit contrahendum . . . quoad accessoria matrimonii, puta circa dotem, potest aliqua inducere consuetudo, sed quoad substantialia nihil ', loc. cit., no. 12. [4] loc. cit., no. 10.

qua utitur legis conditor, et tunc arrogat . . . aut est particularis, et tunc valet in illo loco '.[1] But apart from the explicit consent of the legislator, the condition of validity of any custom against the law is the deliberateness associated with its observance : 'Ex certa scientia contra legem consuetudinem introducere '.[2] As a rule, subsequent legislation destroys the authority of customs,[3] but Lucas follows the canonist Joannes Andreae and holds with him that, unless the new statutory enactment makes specific reference to those customs and deprives them of any further effects, even a general law has no invalidating effect upon local customs.[4] 'Dic latius secundum Joannem Andream, quod lex, quae sequitur consuetudinem specialem locorum vel personarum, illam non tollit, nisi id exprimat, dummodo illa sit rationabilis '.[5]

In virtue of the Ruler's consent to its observance, valid custom generally displays the same legal force as written law. Disregard of valid customs entails sanctions identical with those ensuing from a disregard of statute law : 'Obligat consuetudo sicut jus scriptum '.[6] Consequently, rights which are based merely on the customary observance of rules may be effectively asserted and successfully brought before the judge. The question, 'an possit ex consuetudine agi, ut peto hoc, quia consuetum est ? ' is therefore answered in the affirmative by our jurist.[7] Apart from this general effect of social habits which have reached the form of customary law, Lucas, somewhat differing from contemporary doctrine,[8] holds that they can also establish the right of jurisdiction, be it contentious or voluntary.[9] But he concedes this right of customary jurisdiction only to those

[1] loc. cit., no. 10.

[2] C. X, 46 Rubrica, no. 9.

[3] From his point of view, Lucas had no need to enquire into the reasons for the invalidating effect of customs on preceding local enactments. But it may not be without interest to see how the other jurists justified this abrogation. The standpoint of Albericus de Rosciate is typical. The thesis, he says, that written law can never in any circumstances be abrogated may well have reasons which he, however, does not share : 'Opponitur, quod lex per consuetudinem non tollatur, quia lex est inventio et donum Dei . . . et eius praecepta concordant cum divinis . . . ergo consuetudo legi contraria erit iniqua et injusta contra praecepta divina et contra rationem et per consequens invalida nec poterit tollere legem '. The solution which Albericus puts forward throws an interesting light on the ways of thinking in the fourteenth-century jurisprudence : 'Solutio : omnia concedo omnibus in eodem statu manentibus, sed quia nihil adeo est stabile vel immobile inter homines . . . propter novas causas occurrentes potest esse consuetudo bona et justa et lex, quae ab initio fuit justa, modo erit injusta '.

[4] Lucas obviously has in mind juristic persons who have acquired legal status. The details are of no interest in this context.

[5] C. X, 28, 1, no. 10.

[6] C. X, 1, 9, no. 4.

[7] C. XII, 37, 16, no. 6.

[8] See Bartolus, loc. cit., p. 277.

[9] 'Consuetudo dat jurisdictionem contentiosam ', C. XII, 59, 8, no. 3 ; 'item consuetudo jurisdictionem tribuit voluntariam ', C. X, 19, 7, no. 4.

communities which already possess jurisdictional powers. We may, therefore, safely assume that he has an extension and specification of an already existing jurisdiction in mind, rather than its original establishment: 'Dic plenius, quod universitas, quae jurisdictione caret, nullam consuetudinem introducere potest, per quam detur jurisdictio '.[1] Being included in the 'regalia', jurisdiction cannot consequently be acquired by private citizens, because otherwise 'disrumperetur nervus publicae disciplinae'. Only 'publicae personae'—that is, those corporations which already have jurisdictional powers 'ex auctoritate principis'—can extend their powers by customary observance.[2]

As regards the scope of the validity of customs, Lucas applies the principle of contracts—'de juris efficacia illi tantum debent stringi consuetudine, inter quos est inducta' [3]—that the customs of one State have no effects on the legal status of another State, because the State, being an organized entity, has the 'jus terrendi et distringendi' only over its own citizens and, accordingly, has no right of interference with those of another State.[4] Nevertheless, he recommends the observance of customary rules of a neighbouring State, when they are reasonable, not 'contra jus', and when the statute law contains no regulation relating to the particular item:

> Sed si inveniret, licet perraro, quod consuetudo sit praeter, non contra jus, et rationabilis, de re, de qua vel circa quam nihil est statutum vel sui simile . . . non absurde diceretur consuetudinem vicinorum servandam.[5]

Apparently an exception to the restricted scope of valid customs is the subjection of ecclesiastical persons to the customs which have been observed by the laity only. Furthermore, the ecclesiastical judge is bound, if the necessity arises, to base his decision on those customs: 'Consuetudo laicorum ligat clericos et est etiam in foro ecclesiastico observanda'.[6] The general opinion, however, adhered to the logical application of the principle of contracts—that is, strict separation of lay and clerical customs.[7]

[1] C. XII, 59, 8, no. 3.

[2] C. XII, 59, 8, no. 3.

[3] C. XI, 20, 1, no. 3.

[4] 'Sed una civitas alii non imponeret legem, sed sibi et suis civibus tantum, quia inter eos tantum habet jus terrendi et distringendi . . . ergo nec consuetudinem', loc. cit., no: 2.

[5] loc. cit., no. 4.

[6] C. XI, 71, 1, no. 7. Our jurist refers to canon law itself and quotes *Decretales*, i, 41, 8, and ii, 15, 3, and ii, 27, 8. He believes that he finds corroboration in these passages.

[7] This idea of separation is perhaps best brought out by Cynus, C. VIII, 52, 3, no. 26: 'Quaeritur, numquid consuetudo populi liget clericos. Et dicimus, quod non, duabus rationibus: una, quia duo sunt populi, quod patet, quia duo sunt judices, ergo, &c. . . . alia, quia clerici sunt majores respectu laicorum, sed statuta minorum non ligant majores.' This last-mentioned principle also applies to customs which have no effect upon clerics, 'nisi voluerint'.

Customs, Lucas states, are a very suitable instrument for the interpretation of a contract whose content is controversial: 'Semper in contractibus, si non appareat, quid actum est, sequimur consuetudinem regionis'.[1] In the opinion of Lucas, the immense influence of customs upon social life may be seen from the wide range of topics which they affect. For it is not infrequently, for example, a matter of customary regulation that the magistrates keep their office for a period extending the stipulated year, that minors are granted full majority in certain circumstances, that persons otherwise ineligible for certain official positions are admitted 'ex consuetudine', that easements, such as the right to use water and the like, are specifically regulated and modified, that even the admission into the profession of the medical doctors is conceded to those who 'ex consuetudine' have 'curandi peritiam'.[2] Moreover, for reasons of social stability, the officials who represent the Ruler are strongly urged by our jurist to observe in their official capacity the special customs of the population with which they are in contact. Lucas mentions some of the customs which may have been developed and are to be observed by the officials:

> Nota, quod officiales debent servare consuetudinem regionis, in qua gerere debent officia . . . servanda est consuetudo in tributis exigendis . . . in muneribus subeundis . . . in judiciis et causis decidendis . . . in ultimus voluntatibus . . . in instituendis vectigalibus . . . in rebus publicis distrehendis.[3]

Lastly, customs are not without effects within the ambit of procedure proper. According to Lucas, customs not only determine the content of legal issues, but also the form to which the plaint containing the claim must conform, for 'et forma consuetudinis est servanda'. It is the 'mos judiciorum' that certain formalities must be adhered to in the plaint, otherwise it is not valid.[4]

[1] C. XI, 47, 1, no. 4.
[2] C. X, 19, 7, no. 4.
[3] loc. cit., no. 3.
[4] C. X, 3, 4, no. 12.

CHAPTER V

THE APPLICATION OF LAW

I

THE medieval system of positive law cannot be conceived as a homogeneous and unified body of legal rules. Three distinct systems of statutory enactments can clearly be discerned: Roman law, as transmitted through Justinian's compilation and modified subsequently by additional legislation of the Emperors; canon law, as represented in the various collections; and thirdly, the Germanic Lombard law.[1] To these must be added the numerous statutes of the municipalities and independent States, around which enactments there cluster many customary formations of law, mostly of a supplementary and interpretative character. This complex mosaic of legal systems naturally presented many difficulties to the application of the abstract legal rule to the given set of concrete circumstances. The problem was to find the abstract rule appropriate to the particular case. It is not therefore surprising to find that this heterogeneous legal system gave rise to many problems, discussions, and controversies, the solution of which eventually became a question of applying fundamental principles. The solution of problems emerging from this complex structure of positive law presupposed the theoretical recognition of the fundamental principles which underlay the idea of all law and from which could be deduced special theses capable of direct application. This theoretical recognition was the distinctive task of the scholar jurists. Their scientific discussions of the problems connected with the application of law give us an insight into many domestic conditions, throw light upon the spiritual and temporal claims of the ruling (and often rival) powers, and lastly allow us to see the clash of ecclesiastical and secular jurisdiction with the eyes of the disinterested, pure lawyer, who anxiously strove to obtain an equitable solution of problems vitally affecting the smooth working of the social organism. These scientific discussions on the part of the medieval jurists show their zeal to lay down a clear line of demarcation between the various bodies of law and to attempt a delimitation of jurisdictional powers, from the standpoint of the body politic based on Christian principles. In this field the investigations of our jurist carry particular weight and are especially interesting, because he has at his disposal not only the necessary theoretical equipment for dealing with these

[1] On the importance of Lombard law in the Middle Ages, see Vinogradoff, *Roman Law in Medieval Europe*, 2nd ed., by Prof. de Zulueta, pp. 47 seq., Engelmann, *Die Wiedergeburt der Rechtskultur*, pp. 97 seq., and Prof. Hazeltine, 'Roman and Canon Law' in *Cambridge Medieval History*, vol. v, p. 730.

problems, but also the appropriate practical experience gained by him in his capacity as a judge and as an advocate. His commentaries leave no room for doubt as to the magnitude of the various difficulties and problems which confronted him in his official capacity in all their uncompromising reality. Moreover, his investigations are based on the peculiar conditions of the southern Kingdom, and never lose touch with its prevailing political and social conditions, which, in many respects, were unlike those in other parts of the Empire.

The social and political structure of the Kingdom of Sicily, also comprising Apulia and Capua, was moulded by the legislations of the Emperor Frederick II and the Kings Charles I and II and Robert. Their legislative activity had far-reaching effects on the state of legal affairs in this Kingdom. It was not only of the greatest practical importance,[1] but also of particular theoretical interest. Only in this latter aspect does Frederick's legislation enter into the scope of this essay. The problem that was considered as of crucial importance by medieval scholarship concerned the notion of the 'jus commune'. In a statute which deals with the oath to be taken by the judge, Frederick II laid down that the 'jura communia' have to be resorted to when neither his own constitutions nor customs were applicable to the individual case.[2] Because the wording of the statute became a point of major importance, we may profitably refer to the testimony of our jurist and quote the relevant passage:

> Per constitutionem Frederici Imperatoris et Siciliae regis judices judicare debeant primo secundum ipsas constitutiones et consuetudines approbatas, quibus deficientibus secundum jura communia, Langobarda videlicet et Romana.[3]

Thus the 'jura communia' which Frederick mentioned by name were, in the order of citation, rank, and importance, firstly, Lombard law and, secondly, Roman law. In this manner, not only was Lombard law made 'jus commune', but it was also given the preference over Roman law. With this statute Frederick created a problem that did not exist in this form in any other part of the Empire. For outside the Sicilian Kingdom Lombard law was not only not regarded as 'jus commune', but, above all, had long ceased

[1] See Michelangelo Schipa, 'Italy and Sicily under Frederick II', in *Cambridge Medieval History*, vol. vi, pp. 148 seq.

[2] This statute is contained in *Constitutiones regni utriusque Siciliae*, lib. I, tit. 63, incip. 'Puritatem'. On alleged interpolations see Savigny, loc. cit., vol. vii, p. 67. This statute lays down that the judges have to take an oath to the effect that 'pure et sine fraude, non amore, non odio, non praece, non pretio, nec timore, omnibus conquerentibus absque personarum exceptione, prompto zelo justitiam ministrare curabunt secundum constitutiones nostras et in defectu earum consuetudines approbatas, ac demum secundum jura communia, Langobarda videlicet et Romana', p. 84 of the *Constitutiones*. A similar idea is expressed in the *Rubrica* to the constitution lib. I, tit. 47, but Lucas does not refer to it.

[3] C. XI, 71, 1, no. 13.

to be of any practical value.[1] What theoretical explanation does Lucas offer for this paradoxical idea of a co-existence of two bodies of law, both of which were expressly declared to be 'jus commune'? Could any scientific justification be given for the prevalence of Lombard law over Roman law?

It may be safely assumed that neither Frederick's own constitutions nor particular customs covered the majority of cases brought before the judge and that, consequently, the resort to the 'jus commune', envisaged by his legislation as exceptional, became more or less the rule. The problem which the theoretical jurist had to face was this: which law is universally valid and generally applicable, the Lombard law or the Roman law? For both systems cannot be 'jus commune' at the same time. By Frederick's legislation and unmistakable preference for Lombard law the importance of Roman law was diminished, if not practically lost, and it is with good reason that Lucas asks the pertinent question whether in the Kingdom 'Romanae leges omnino servandae sunt'. If Frederick's law is taken at its face value, the question must be answered in a negative sense: 'Videtur, quod non', for 'Langobardae leges Romanis legibus veniunt praeferendae', and hardly any room would be left for applying Roman law. He reports that this is indeed the opinion of some experienced jurists in the Kingdom who maintain that 'nedum constitutiones, sed etiam jus Langobardorum Romano juri praeferendum est in regno'. They argued that the wording of that statute leaves no room for doubt as to the inferior position of Roman law.[2] Lucas, as we may well expect, is by no means satisfied with this literal acceptance of Frederick's law. The idea that Roman law should have to give way to Lombard law to which he denied even the character of law—'Langobardae non merentur leges dici, sed foeces'[3]—appears to him truly preposterous. But, on the other hand, his dissatisfaction entails opposition to the explicit declaration of the very authority to which he himself concedes legislative omnipotence, and obedience to whose laws he considers as the primary duty of every citizen. The reconciliation of Lucas's antagonism to that legal enactment with his own theory was considerably facilitated by the practice constantly observed by the Courts for well over a hundred years. Their interpretation

[1] Odofredus, C. V, Authentica *Dos data*, says in his characteristically theatrical way: 'Sed signori . . . langobarda non est lex nec ratio, sed est quoddam jus, quod faciebant reges per se, et vocantur longobardi, i.e., Apuli, quia primo venerunt de Germania in Sardiniam et postea in Apuliam'. Baldus adheres to the same opinion, see C. V, 4, 11 and *Decret.* I de constitut. c. 3. That was the general opinion.

[2] Though Lucas does not say so, he seems to have in mind Andreas de Isernia and Bartholomaeus de Capua. Indeed, in his gloss on the constitution, the former was not perturbed by the elevation of the Lombard law to the level of a *jus commune*, p. 84. The same opinion was held by Bartholomaeus in his gloss on the constitution, lib. I, tit. 47, p. 71.

[3] loc. cit., no. 2.

stood only in need of a scientific justification, as it were, and this was to be furnished by Lucas.

The practice of the Courts was to make an interpretation which complied with the letter, but perhaps not with the spirit, of the law. Ironically enough, they actually succeeded in increasing the prestige of Roman law by this practice. For in cases in which its observance was the custom they declared that Roman law must be given preference to Lombard law, this being tantamount to a victory for Roman law. The Courts, in fact, combined the second with the third proviso of the statute. Thus Lucas is able to introduce his 'Solutio' of the problem with the laconic statement that Roman law has to be given preference to Lombard law. With apparent satisfaction he notes the fact that the Royal Curia adhered to the same opinion and that the practice of the Courts was approved by that highest Court of Justice in the Kingdom:

> Verius est, quod jus Langobardorum Romanis legibus non sit praeferendum, nisi eatenus, quatenus et in illis locis, in quibus et inter illas personas, inter quas consuetudo illud admittit . . . et haec sententia plene matureque digesta semper observata fuit in curia vicariae regni.

Lucas does not conceal his doubts about the legality of Frederick's statute on the oath of the judges. Setting out from the rules clearly expressed in C. XI, 71, 1, where it is laid down that everyone has to adhere to the 'leges', Lucas writes: 'Ex statuto illius, qui potestatem habuit condendae legis in ipso regno, ab hac lege et similibus videtur esse recessum'.[1] But beyond the expression of doubt Lucas does not go.

The concept of 'jus commune' cannot be materially applied to Lombard law, Lucas holds with great emphasis. By its very name that law is only a special law relating to the Lombards. It has no more significance than the law of any other German tribe, as, for instance, the 'jus Francorum': 'Patet esse singulare seu speciale, sicut jus Francorum'.[2] Moreover, Lombard law and, say, Frankish law differ in their treatment of one and the same topic and, surely, Lucas holds, the identity of the topic should entail identity of legal regulation. He concludes that Lombard and Frankish law merely constitute special laws and the term 'jus commune' can rightly be applied solely to Roman law, the implication being that not even the legislative act of the proper authority can change the character of a 'jus speciale' into a 'jus commune'. The denotation of a law common to the whole of the civilized world can be attributed to Roman law only. This idea leads our jurist to a consideration of the intrinsic difference between Roman and Lombard law. He arrives at the conclusion that Roman law was authentic in origin, and that it fulfils all the requirements of validly-promulgated law—'divinitus fuit per ora principum promulgatum'.[3]

[1] loc. cit., no. 13. [2] loc. cit., no. 13. [3] loc. cit., no. 13.

This essential requirement the Lombard laws fail to meet, for, in Lucas's opinion, they were made by barbarians, a people who lacked all culture and had seized power in Italian lands 'more praedonum'.[1] With withering contempt our jurist speaks of the Lombard people, whom he calls a 'gens effera, id est, feralis', extolling 'libidinem et superbiam'. They are far too remote from a 'cultus justitiae' for one to suppose they could have made laws which conform to the standard set by civilized races. It is small wonder that Lucas urges the disregard of their laws because of the unbridled barbarity of their makers. He recalls with approval the dictum of Orosius that on no account should any one 'parere legibus (scil. Langobardorum) propter effrenatam ipsorum barbariem'.[2] Their nature—which he characterizes as 'proxima belluis natura'—has enraged them and kept them out of the comity of societies held together by the standards of a humane law.[3] In short, the Lombards are barbarians who live like 'insensata animalia et ferino (more ?) degentes Dei cultum ignorant'.

Roman law, on the other hand, is the incarnation of culture to Lucas. Roman law is also the incarnation of reason, whilst the Lombard law 'regulariter asininum dicitur, licet sit tempore posterius'.[4] For, apart from the essential fact that Roman law was given to mankind by the only authority entrusted with the creation of law, it embodies precisely that spirit of culture which no other law can claim to have achieved, least of all Lombard law. The Roman Emperors have been the Rulers of 'universus orbis', a fact that is borne out by the testimony of the Holy Scriptures.[5] It was by Christ's own order, Lucas declares, that Rome was raised to that position which she has ever since occupied.[6] The Roman city, therefore, is 'sacerdotalis et regia, principatus omnium nationum et origo sanctitatis'. Considering Roman law with this reverence, Lucas strongly insists on its impregnable position[7]: to accept any objection to Roman law appears to him not only foolhardy, but also

[1] loc. cit., no. 13. [2] loc. cit., no. 13.

[3] 'Quos procul omnis juris humani societate submotos proxima belluis natura efferavit', loc. cit.

[4] loc. cit., no. 15.

[5] 'Romani principes universum orbem tenuerunt, ut patet ipsius divinae scripturae testimonio Luc. 2', loc. cit., no. 13.

[6] He continues: 'Dominus noster Jesus Christus hanc urbem scil. Romanam nutu suo auctam et defensam in hunc rerum apicem pervexerit'. The superior character of the Romans over all other nations, particularly the Lombards, is borne out by the fact that they have deserved their Empire on account of their virtues. Hannibal, the mortal foe of Rome, testifies to the greatness of the Romans: 'Romani quippe imperium virtutibus meruerunt secundum Hieronymum . . . et Augustinum 5 de civitate Dei cap. 12. Nulla quoque gens neque rex Romanis par fuit, dicit Hannibal hostis maximus Romanorum Antiocho regi, ut refert Titus Livius, de bello Macedonico, lib. 3,' loc. cit., no. 14.

[7] 'Nemo igitur contra statuta Romanorum principum obiiciat aliquid', loc. cit.

dangerous.[1] Roman law presents a true transformation of the metaphysical idea of justice into a workable reality. It was created ' in orbis capite ', is law common to all mankind and civil law *par excellence.* His conclusion is set forth in these words :

> Sic ergo rationabiliter solum jus Romanum dicitur jus commune, quod absque alia adjectione prolatum simpliciter per excellentiam dicitur jus civile . . . quod juste constringit hominum vitas et sanctissimum est et ab omnibus debet sciri . . . per Imperatores quippe Romanos Deus humano generi leges distribuit, ut dicit beatus Augustinus.

These are the considerations on the basis of which Lucas not only disposes of the special problem created by Frederick II's legislation, but also constructs his fundamental axiom that Roman law is the universally valid and generally applicable law, is simply the law common to the whole of mankind. Viewing the Roman Emperor as ' dominus mundi ', the law that results from his legislative activity must necessarily be the law of the whole world—' quo omne genus hominum detinetur '.[2] Roman law is the creation of the Roman Emperors and the instrument by which they rule the world. The universality of the Roman civil law is based on the universal overlordship of the Ruler (Emperor). The term Roman law refers to the whole body of law that is contained in Justinian's compilation and added to by the subsequent Imperial legislation. The idea of the universality of Roman law is to prove both a cornerstone and a fruitful principle in his theory of law, and has far-reaching consequences. All his further investigations are orientated by the idea of the universality inherent in Roman law.

II

Lucas applies this idea of universality of Roman civil law in his investigations, in which he attempts to clarify the relationship between civil and canon law. But before we proceed to a detailed discussion of this topic, it will be advisable to glance very briefly at the actual conditions in the Kingdom of Naples, which, at the time of Lucas, was dependent on the Church. This fact deserves our particular attention because of the influence, importance, and prestige that were attributed to the law of the Church. The Southern Kingdom came rightly to be considered as a fief of the papal Curia. Lucas states that ' Sicilia est ecclesiae et praecipuum eius patrimonium '.[3] As a consequence of this close relationship, canon law

[1] ' Nam quicquid contra illorum definitionem, in quibus spiritum sanctum locutum fuisse credendum est, dictum fuerit recipere non solum temerarium, sed etiam periculosum esse non dubium est.'

[2] loc. cit.

[3] C. XI, 71, 1, no. 13. On the struggle between Empire and Papacy concerning Sicily, see Dr. Carlyle, loc. cit., vol. v, pp. 187–317.

naturally gained far greater prominence here than in other parts of the Empire. It is, therefore, understandable that this peculiar political structure should be followed by claims—more persistent and far-reaching than in other territories—for a wider range of canon law application, thus inevitably resulting in a displacement of the authority of civil law. This state of affairs actually ensued: canon law did in fact come into conflict with civil law upon more points than it did elsewhere. Thus a clear line of demarcation became necessary in order to show when each particular law should be applied. This also necessitated an attempted delimitation of the jurisdictional powers of the secular and ecclesiastical judge—another point which had especial interest in Sicily owing to Frederick's reformation of the judicial organization. In order to secure an efficient administration of law and the harmonious working of the State organism, the solution of these intricate and delicate problems became an urgent and pressing practical necessity.

Lucas avows that the idea of universality inherent in Roman law calls for its widest possible application; it is the actual scope of application of Roman law with which he is mainly concerned. He handles this difficult subject in several places, in all of which he concentrates upon the leading idea of the universality of Roman law. In his commentaries he tries to forestall possible objections to his theory, and conscientiously endeavours to establish principles of application which should prove beneficial to the practical administrator of the law—an endeavour which is not surprising in view of his own practical experience.

As his fundamental thesis he lays down the dictum that the universality of Roman civil law makes its application imperative before all Courts, whether secular or ecclesiastical: regardless of the deciding Court, its application is absolute in all temporal causes of secular litigants; it is conditional in all spiritual causes of secular litigants and in those temporal causes tried before the ecclesiastical Court which involve ecclesiastical litigants only. In the latter case the conditions which Lucas attaches to the application of Roman law are: that civil law must not be in open contradiction to canon law, and that it must not be directed against the liberty of the Church. In the strict meaning of the term, however, this last-mentioned condition does not concern the application, but the validity, of civil law. For any law that is directed against the liberty of the Church is invalid from the very start, and the problem of its application does not therefore arise. The former condition is a true condition of application, and does not affect the validity of civil law; it will be dealt with later in its proper context.

Whether civil (Roman) law is to be applied absolutely or conditionally, depends (1) on the character of the litigants involved, whether secular or ecclesiastical, and (2) on the character of the cause, whether temporal or spiritual. These criteria have now to be discussed in greater detail.

(1) That civil law is to be applied to the causes of secular litigants is a fact that is in no need of further explanation. But Lucas investigates the problem, which, indeed, was of profound significance at his time and under the conditions prevailing in Sicily—namely, the problem of whether clerical litigants are to be subjected to secular law in cases in which the ecclesiastical judge tries their cause. Lucas's answer is in the affirmative. The omnipotence, as it were, of the Roman civil law is primarily based on his axiom that 'leges divinitus sunt per ora principum promulgatae et ideo judices ecclesiastici secundum divinam et humanam legem judicare debent'.[1] Some canonists, however, would like to deny the truth contained in this dictum. Our jurist advises those canonists to eradicate the papal decrees in which that dictum is expressly adhered to. On this point Lucas says:

> Canonistae autem, qui contradicunt, deleant ex volumine decretorum papale decretum, xvi, qu. 3, 'nemo', quod dicit venerandae Romanae leges divinitus sunt per ora principum promulgatae, et xxv, qu. 1, 'satagendum', ubi Papa se legibus subditum profitetur.[2]

It is precisely the divine mandate of the Ruler which subjects the Church to civil law: 'Scriptae leges . . . divinitus promulgatae, patet apertius, quod ecclesia, quae Dei est, eas implere teneretur', he says in another passage when discussing the Church's duty to undertake public services for the State.[3] In pursuance of this argument he develops his thesis—namely, that when even the ecclesiastical causes of the Church, taken as a juristic person and as an entity, have to be decided on the basis of the secular civil law, there is all the more reason for the subjection of the clerics as individuals to civil law: 'Expressum est, quod causa ecclesiastica est Romanis legibus decidenda . . . fortius causa clericorum, quae potest esse de re temporali, quae ecclesiam non contingit'.[4] Moreover, when even secular customs have binding force on clerics, why, he asks, should not written law, whose authority is greater than that of customary law, be applied to ecclesiastical persons: 'Consuetudo laudabilis laicorum ligat clericos et est etiam in foro ecclesiastico observanda . . . fortius est lex scripta servanda in foro ecclesiastico et debet etiam clericos ecclesiasque ligare'.[5] He reminds his

[1] loc. cit., no. 7. The 'lex humana', for Lucas, is primarily the Roman law as it stood at his time.

[2] C. X, 39, 9, no. 41. Lucas refers to the *Decretum Gratiani*, *causa* xvi, *quaestio* 3, *canon* 17, which contains a letter of Pope John VIII (872–882) and wherein the words quoted by Lucas occur. The second reference concerns *causa* xxv, *quaestio* 1, *canon* 10, wherein Pope Pelagius (555–560) is reported to have said: '. . . legibus ministremus, quibus nos etiam subditos esse sacrae scripturae praecipiunt'.

[3] See *infra*, pp. 84–7.

[4] C. XI, 71, 1, no. 7.

[5] He continues: 'Cum longe majoris auctoritatis sit lex scripta, maxima Romana, quam consuetudo'. He notes duly that Bartolus is opposed to this view, in which he seemed to follow, as Lucas implies, the canonist Hostiensis.

readers that even St. Peter judges ecclesiastical matters according to secular law which was definitely created by non-Catholics. Lucas says: 'Nam et sic beatus Petrus, princeps Apostolorum, causas ecclesiarum secundum leges saeculi judicabat . . . quae tamen a non Catholicis latae erant'.[1] Finally, an unbiased study of the canon law books goes to prove that the highest Church authorities themselves fall back in their own affairs on Roman law: 'Si quis volumina canonici juris diligenter evolvat, inveniet causas ecclesiasticas per Romnos pontifices in defectu canonum Romanis legibus fore decisas'.[2] More than that: it is canon law itself which enjoins the Church to obey human law—that is, law issued by the secular authority.[3] Lucas states that this view is at variance with the opinions of Hostiensis and Bartolus. For these reasons he holds that civil (Roman) law extends also to clerical litigants appearing before the ecclesiastical judge. Its application is, however, conditioned. If the particular secular law is in open contradiction to canon law, the former can then not be applied: 'Ecclesia tenetur servare leges in negotiis clericorum cum canonibus contrariae directae non sunt'.[4]

(2) The secular status of the litigants entails absolute application of Roman law, notwithstanding the possibility that an appeal may have been made to the ecclesiastical judge to try the cause; the application of civil law to clerical litigants, on the other hand, is conditional. We may now turn to a discussion of the second criterion—namely, the character of the cause. That civil law has to be applied to temporal causes is a self-evident proposition. But Lucas insists also on the application of civil law to those spiritual causes which affect the social and public interest. He gives matrimony as a typical example of a spiritual cause affecting public interest. The application of secular law to causes like those is demonstrated by him by references to matrimonial causes which evoked many disputes and conflicts between ecclesiastical authority and law on the one hand, and civil authority and law on the other. They were, therefore, of especial interest to the practical lawyer. Lucas holds that, although, owing to their spiritual character, the ecclesiastical judge has to decide matrimonial causes, he has to apply civil law unless it is openly inimical to canon law. His theory is at variance with the generally accepted view, particularly in Sicily. Lucas refers to Andreas de Isernia, who taught that matrimonial causes have to be judged according to canon law and that they are of no concern to the secular authority, whether in the field of jurisdiction or in the domain of legislation. He reports Andreas de Isernia as

[1] C. X, 28, 2, no. 5.

[2] C. XI, 71, 1, no. 7.

[3] 'Unde secundum praecepta canonum tenetur ecclesia exequi, quod in humana lege continetur, 25. q. ideo', loc. cit., no. 7. The passage of canon law referred to is *causa* xxv, *quaestio* 1, *canon* 16, which reads: 'Ideo permittente Domino pastores hominum sumus effecti, ut quod patres nostri sive in sanctis canonibus sive in mundanis affixere legibus excedere minime debeamus'.

[4] loc. cit., no. 11.

having said that 'princeps saecularis nec principaliter nec incidenter aliquid constituere potest in matrimonio'.[1]

This opinion is not shared by Lucas. The problem as he sees it is this: the general application of civil law is the logical sequel of the universality of Roman law, which, by its very nature, covers all causes. But how can the application of civil law to matrimonial cases be justified when, on the other hand, the essentially spiritual character of matrimony is an established axiom? The detailed discussion of this problem necessarily leads us to his views on the respective spheres of secular and ecclesiastical powers and their limitations. He is wont to stress the strict separation of their respective spheres of power: neither may infringe upon the province of the other. The secular Ruler must not lay hands on ecclesiastical affairs, nor may the Church encroach upon temporal matters. The passage in which Lucas propounds this view runs as follows:

> Sicut Imperatori mensura statuitur, quod sua jurisdictione debeat esse contentus, nec ad ecclesiastica extendere manus suas . . . sic et ecclesiae esse debeat ordinata mensura, nec ad temporalia extendere manus suas. Ipsorum quippe officia sunt distincta . . . quare si ecclesia usurpat, quod suum non est, juste perdit etiam, quod suum est.[2]

Clerics should not interfere in worldly affairs: 'Clerici et monachi Deo militantes non debent se negotiis saecularibus immiscere'.[3]

That is the fundamental position of the two powers. But Lucas argues that there are spiritual causes—namely, causes which are essentially of a religious and divine nature—that are nevertheless of eminent interest to the secular authority. More than that: the secular authority is bound to take the greatest interest in those spiritual affairs which affect social life and eventually the existence and peaceful development of mankind. As indicated before, matrimony is of this character: 'Magnum debet legislatori studium esse de nuptiis'.[4] For the nucleus of human society is the human family, and Lucas is therefore impelled to declare: 'Studium vero nuptiarum totius est humanae sobolis'. The immortality of the human race is guaranteed only by matrimony which enjoys respect and is honoured precisely by virtue of its procreative function. It is the 'publica utilitas' of matrimony which necessarily warrants legislation, because 'ex filiorum procreatione renovata genera manent'.[5] In his truly idealistic manner he exclaims: 'Et plus debet lex civilis curare, ut adjectione hominum potius quam pecunia imperium augeatur'. Guided by ethical considerations, he advances the argument that the growth of human society should proceed only in the way which is legitimately provided by marriage.

[1] C. X, 39, 9, no. 18. Andreas de Isernia propounded this view in his commentaries on the Sicilian laws, lib. III, tit. 22, p. 230, col. 2 of the *Constitutiones*. [2] loc. cit., no. 26.
[3] C. XI, 71, 1, no. 16. [4] C. X, 39, 9, no. 16. [5] loc. cit., no. 15.

He says that 'augendam esse rem publicam, et multis legitimis hominibus frequentandam, quod non nisi matrimonio fieri potest'.[1] He alludes to the great social value, which the old Romans attached to matrimony.[2] Regarded as a social institution, matrimony requires legislative treatment by the secular authority. Consequently, secular law must be applied to matrimonial causes.

On the other hand, matrimony is a divine institution. It is the oldest sacrament, since it was instituted by God in paradise: 'Est sacramentum antiquissimum a Deo constitutum in paradiso'.[3] Matrimony constitutes the bonds of a 'natural friendship' between husband and wife, which friendship includes the 'honestum et utile et delectabile'.[4] Consequently, secular law which impinges upon this natural state or which contradicts the divine essence of matrimony must be considered 'periniqua et impotens'.[5] If the secular law-giver validly created law in contradiction to the divine nature of matrimony, the following question and answer would be justified: 'Quid est aliud quam reprobare opera Dei? Nefas est enim per nos, quod Deus instituit, impugnari.'[6] Nevertheless, the authority entrusted with the care of religious issues and of the divine law may validate opposing secular law either by consenting to it or by failing to protest against it: 'Sine consensu vel taciturnitate illius, qui jus poli habet in potestate, lex contraria non est valida'.[7] Unless,

[1] loc. cit.

[2] 'Unde apud Romanos mulctati sunt, qui ad senectutem coelibes venerunt, ut refert Valerius, lib. II, cap. 4', loc. cit., no. 17.

[3] Yet, according to Lucas, the origin of the priestly benediction at the wedding ceremony is to be found in pagan customs. He says that in former days the brides used to receive 'water and fire' at the ceremony: 'Ipsa festivitate nuptiarum accipiebant (scil. nubentes puellae) aquam et ignem' (C. X, 3, 3, no. 1). Amongst the faithful this custom is still preserved, though in a somewhat modified form. The blessing of the priest is done with holy water and incense, which supersede the former ordinary water and fire. He continues by saying: 'in cuius locum hodie apud fideles est sacerdotalis benedictio, quae fit etiam cum aqua benedicta et igne thuris incensi'.

[4] 'Sed inter virum et uxorem contrahitur naturalis amicitia, quae claudit in se honestum et utile et delectabile, ut dicit Philosophus 8vo Ethicorum', loc. cit., no. 17.

[5] loc. cit., no. 17.

[6] loc. cit., no. 17.

[7] loc. cit. We may safely assume that Lucas, on account of his conception of matrimony, came to touch upon problems which, as far as I was able to ascertain in the writings of fourteenth-century jurists, were not faced by his contemporaries, who still adhered to Ulpian's conception. See the paper 'Baldus's Conception of Law', in *L.Q.R.*, 1942, p. 394. It is interesting to note that Cynus, who in many respects was quite unorthodox, still persuaded himself into accepting Ulpian's view, in spite of the doubts which he himself had about the truth of Ulpian's conception: 'Matrimonium contrahitur per consensum, verbis expressum . . . vel literis inter absentes vel per nuntium et haec omnia sunt facta, vel si sunt jus, potius juris civilis'. But Cynus forces himself to justify Ulpian on three grounds: 'Primo modo, ut accipiatur natura, i.e., Deus. Et tunc bene verum est, quod de jure naturali . . . secundo modo, ut accipiatur natura, i.e., instinctus naturae, et dicendum est, quod matrimonium est de jure naturali occa-

in consequence of her vocation to create binding rules in the domain of spiritual matters, the Church has sanctioned the initially defective law of the secular legislator, it has no validity. Accordingly, it is not only an inapplicable, but also an invalid, law. Only that civil law which openly contradicts canon law is inapplicable to spiritual causes tried before the ecclesiastical judge. Provided that secular law is not openly inimical to canon law, the ecclesiastical judge is bound to adhere to it, whatever its contents may be and to whatever consequences its application may lead: 'In spiritualibus, puta in matrimonio, ubi lex non invenitur directo canonibus obviare, in foro etiam ecclesiastico est servanda . . . quod mundanis affixum est legibus, ecclesia minime debet excedere'.[1] As regards the application of civil law to matrimonial causes in particular, Lucas states the same thesis in almost identical terms: 'Lex etiam in matrimonio, ubi canon certum quid in contrarium non diffinit, in foro ecclesiastico est servanda'.[2] He declares that it is this inference which one has to draw from the purely legal point of view 'non obstantibus doctorum canonistarum opinionibus'. He continues by saying that civil law has to be applied even when the case concerns the substance and essence of matrimony: 'Etiam in causa', he asserts, 'quae tangit ipsam substantiam matrimonii, servanda est lex, quae non est directo contraria canoni.' In conclusion, his theory of the application of civil law to the outstanding spiritual cause, matrimony, is based on his conception of matrimony as an eminent social issue, which demands secular legislation and the application of secular law. The spiritual character of the cause, on the other hand, accounts both for the attachment of the condition—namely, that civil law is not in open contradiction to canon law—and for the exclusive competency of the ecclesiastical judge, because the secular authority has no power of jurisdiction in spiritual causes.[3]

Temporal causes, on the other hand, involve the unconditional application of Roman civil law, even when they are tried by the ecclesiastical judge. It has not infrequently occurred that purely temporal causes of secular litigants were brought before the ecclesiastical judge. It is justifiable for Lucas to ask which law should be applied in such a case: 'Quid, si coram ecclesiasticco judice inter

sionaliter, quia unusquisque habet suam mulierem propter fornicationem et sic ratione primi motus venit ad secundum, i.e., consensum. Tertio modo respondetur, quod etiam in consensu expresso . . . est affectio, quae est juris naturalis,' D. I, I, I, no. 18.

[1] C. XI, 71, I, no. II. Lucas obviously alludes to canon law, *causa* xxv, *quaestio* I, *canon* 16, see *supra* p. 79, n. 3, where the passage is transcribed.

[2] C. X, 39, 9, no. 24.

[3] 'Reges non habent potestatem in spiritualibus et ideo clavem regni coelestis non accipiunt, sed solum in temporalibus . . .', C. XI, 9, 3, no. 3. See also C. X, 16, II, no. 7. In England the ecclesiastical courts had undisputed jurisdiction in matrimonial causes, and canon law was administered, see Pollock and Maitland, vol. ii, p. 365. The temporal courts had no doctrine of marriage, 'although questions as to the validity of marriage might come incidentally before them', Holdsworth, vol. i, p. 622.

duos laicos litigatur de causa mera civili et temporali, an servabitur lex, quae directe contraria canoni ? '[1] His answer is emphatically in the affirmative: when even clerical litigants are to be subjected to Roman civil law, when appearing before their judge, Roman law is then all the more applicable to secular litigants: 'Fortius eas (scil. leges) observare tenetur (scil. ecclesia) in civilibus causis et negotiis laicorum . . . quamvis canonibus contradicant'.[2] Apart from these considerations, he continues, the formal criterion of the deciding judge cannot alter the material universality of Roman law. For, if the litigants had taken their cause before the ordinary secular judge, the application of civil law, however inimical to canon law, would have been beyond question.[3] This application of civil law by the ecclesiastical judge has, of course, practical consequences; he mentions, as an example, the prescription of the cause within three years instead of the canonical thirty years.[4]

In connexion with the foregoing problem Lucas treats of another problem, which is also intimately connected with the scope of civil law. His views on the alienation of devotional and sacred objects, which belong to the Church, represent an application of his principle that spiritual affairs should be left to the Church authorities. He asks whether the manifold regulations and restrictions of Roman law as to the 'res ecclesiasticae' are still applicable to the Church.[5] Although at first it would seem that secular law has to be applied—'videtur, quod sic'—he says that the application of civil law (which in many respects was considered as wholly the creation of pagan legislators)[6] must be made dependent on the approval of the Church.[7] For according to Lucas, it is God's will that the Church alone should be in a position to dispose freely of those ecclesiastical goods which are sacred objects and serve devotional purposes, without interference and usurpation by the secular authority: 'Nam ad sacerdotes voluit Deus, quae ecclesiae disponenda sunt, pertinere, non Imperatorem ingratum beneficiorum Dei contra dispositionem coelestis ordinis aliquid usurpare'.[8] The spiritual character and purpose of those

[1] C. XI, 71, 1, no. 11.

[2] loc. cit., no. 11.

[3] loc. cit., no. 11, and C. X, 39, 9, no. 29: 'Leges, etiam si directe contrariae canonibus, tamen servandae sunt in foro civili, ubi possunt sine periculo animae observari'. On the opposite view of Bartolus see *infra*, p. 90.

[4] loc. cit., no. 11: 'Ex his concluditur manifeste, quod . . . peribit instantia causae per lapsum triennii'. As regards matrimonial causes, the regulations of civil law, such as expression of the will, impediments, error, and the like, will have to be applied.

[5] 'Quaeritur, quid in alienationibus rerum ecclesiasticarum, in quibus cum multa solertia et religione Romani principes leges plurimas statuerint, an hodie sint servandae ?', loc. cit., no. 8.

[6] See for a typical remark Bartolus, D. 30, 58, no. 6: 'Nam jurisconsulti erant pagani et de praemio vitae aeternae non cogitabant'.

[7] 'In his alienationibus statuta Imperatorum non servantur, nisi sint specialiter per ecclesiam approbata', loc. cit., no. 8.

[8] loc. cit. Lucas accepts, therefore, the argument contained in *Decretum Gratiani*, *distinctio* xcvi, *canon* 11, whose author is unknown.

goods exempt them from a subjection to secular law, unless the Church authorities have approved of it.

The very antithesis of the above-mentioned case is that of the subjection to secular civil law of the Church's temporal goods, as for instance ecclesiastical estates: 'Bona clericorum et ecclesiae quoad imperium et jurisdictionem subjecta sunt principi saeculari'.[1] Consequently, legislation concerning the temporal possessions of the Church and clerics belongs to the secular legislator, because law-making is an effluence of his 'imperium',[2] and litigations about them, furthermore, have to be decided according to civil law. Legislative encroachments of the secular Ruler on the (temporal) property rights of the Church are, therefore, valid.[3] Legislation of this kind does not constitute law against the liberty of the Church.[4]

But this subjection of Church property to civil law has very important personal consequences, which should be presented here, even at the risk of a digression. Lucas maintains that it is justifiable for the civil law to establish the liability of the Church and of the clerics to carry out civic duties and public services. He advances the argument that it is not some subordinate official, but the highest legislative authority, the Emperor, who, through his civil law, orders the clerics and the Church to render public services. Since the law emanates from the very authority that is entrusted with its promulgation by divine mandate, the Church, being herself of God, is bound to obey the secular legal enactments: 'Neque enim rectores, consules aut communitates haec munera imponunt ecclesiis et earum rebus, sed scriptae leges per Romanos principes divinitus promulgatae, patet apertius, quod ecclesia, quae Dei est, eas implere teneretur'.[5] Apart from this consideration, the public interest calls for the Church and the clerics to make their contributions to the maintenance of the public and common good. The idea of the 'publica utilitas' once again furnishes our jurist with the material justification for his theory. Although not directly bearing upon our present topic, the elaboration of some details will illustrate his thesis and throw light upon its practical implications and his sociological conceptions.

He avails himself at the outset of his fundamental argument that at all events, theoretically, law implies equality of the citizens whose social life it regulates.[6] A practical consequence of his argument is the equality of the services which have to be performed for the sake of public safety and the maintenance of the State. Those services concern, above all, the payment of taxes: 'In solutione tributorum servari debet aequalitas. Tributa praestantur ob publi-

[1] C. XI, 3, 2, no. 2.
[2] 'Statuere est imperii . . .', loc. cit., no. 2.
[3] See *infra*, sect. IV.
[4] C. XI, 3, 2, no. 4: 'Laici, licet contra libertatem ecclesiae statuere nequeant, contra tamen ipsam ecclesiam seu eius bona statuere possunt', loc. cit., no. 4.
[5] C. X, 48, 2, no. 5.
[6] See *supra*, ch. III, sect. III.

cam utilitatem et publicae utilitatis gratia indicuntur et pro communi salute '.[1] Lucas borrows St. Augustine's argument that the rendering of public services and the fulfilment of civic duties have been ordered by Christ; civic duties are necessary for the maintenance of the State in times of emergency, particularly in time of war.[2] Lucas, therefore, thinks fit to allude to the words of the Gospel and says: ' Reddant igitur, quae sunt Caesaris, Caesari, et quae sunt Dei, Deo: cui tributum, tributum, et cui vectigal, vectigal '.[3] The Ruler fights for the common good, including the Church, and it is only just that the community as a whole makes its contributions: ' Unde princeps, qui militat pro utilitate communi, debet etiam de communibus vivere '.[4] Lucas bluntly asks this question: ' Et si conditio Caesaris, non civitatis, est censum reddere Caesari, quis talis est non subjectus sublimioribus, ut jura terreni regis putet esse solvenda et tributa huiusmodi non praestanda? '[5] Neither the Church nor the clerics should be exempted from paying taxes: ' Horum (scil. tributorum) quidem exactiones etiam ab ecclesiis decenter faciendae sunt '.[6] For payment of taxes and other public duties is beneficial to, and necessary for, the commonwealth and, consequently ' ipsisque ecclesiis '.[7] He reminds his readers of the axiom which appears to him a basic principle in public affairs—namely, that ' omnium in publicis functionibus aequalis debet esse inspectio '. This principle of equity opposes any agreement between the body politic and a citizen or a group of citizens whereby immunity from taxes is permanently granted: ' Non valent pacta, quae faciunt civitates concedentes immunitatem alicui '. The reason for the invalidity of such agreements is that ' reliqui ex hac immunitate gravantur, quod lex abhorret '.[8] In other words, immunity would impair the interests of other citizens[9]: ' Onerantur autem alii propter immunitatem unius '.[10] Thus immunity from those

[1] With particular emphasis on the *Policraticus*, lib. IV, cap. 1, C. X, 19, 8, no. 31.

[2] ' Et ideo Christus necessario jussit tributa reddi Caesari, quia propter bella necessario praebentur stipendia, dicit Augustinus, 23, q. 1, " quid culpatur " '—that is, *causa* xxiii, *quaestio* 1, *canon* 4. It should be noted, however, that this canon says ' monet reddi ', but Lucas writes ' jussit reddi '.

[3] C. X, 48, 2, no. 6.

[4] C. X, 18, 1, no. 10. See also C. XI, 46, 1, no. 15: ' Possessiones ecclesiarum materiali gladio de mandato ecclesiae defendendae sunt . . . bella quoque pro ecclesia sunt sumenda '.

[5] C. X, 19, 8, no. 31. He refers to St. Ambrose's dictum as reported in *causa* xi, *quaestio* 1, *canon* 27: ' Si tributum petit Imperator, non negamus '. It should be borne in mind that Innocent III had forbidden the lay powers to tax the clerics, see Dr. Previté Orton, *History of Europe*, pp. 51, 56.

[6] loc. cit., no. 31.

[7] ' Nam exactio ipsorum et militibus et privatis ipsisque ecclesiis et cunctae rei publicae utilis est et necessaria ', loc. cit., no. 31.

[8] C. X, 16, 6, no. 2.

[9] ' Immunitas concessa non debet esse cum alterius injuria sive damno ', no. 30.

[10] loc. cit., no. 30.

taxes and public duties which concern the 'publica utilitas' cannot be granted to the Church or the clerics.[1] Lucas is well aware of the divergence of his theory from the commonly accepted view which is held by 'doctores clarae dignitatis et auctoritatis',[2] but he rejects their opinion—'puto verius'—on the consideration that it would obviously be iniquitous if immunity were to be granted to the Church: 'Patet apertius, quod clerici et ecclesiae sunt ad subeunda onera huiusmodi rationabiliter debitores ex talium immunitate consurgens evidenter iniquitas'. He ends this passage with these words: 'Et hoc est de jure naturae'. Finally he argues, canon law itself lays down that the clerics should undertake those duties, 'quae bonum commune respiciunt'.[3] Treating of the legal basis of those civic duties of Church and clerics he says: 'Probo per jura inducta superius'. Now, it is interesting that he refers exclusively to passages of the *Decretum Gratiani*—namely, *causa* xi, *quaestio* 1, *canon* 26—in which Pope Innocent I expressed a similar thought to that of St. Ambrose in *canon* 27 and 28, viz., that the Church cannot refuse to pay taxes and to render civic duties; furthermore, Lucas refers to *distinctio* viii, *canon* 1, where St. Augustine is reported to have said: 'Humana jura Imperatorum sunt. Quare? Quia ipsa jura humana per Imperatores et reges saeculi Deus distribuit generi humano,' and lastly our jurist refers to *causa* xxiii, *quaestio* 8, *canon* 20—from which Gratian deduced the view that the Church should not claim any immunity from taxes and civic duties.[4] The contributions of the Church and the clerics should be relative—that is to say, 'pro mensura onerum et modo facultatum clerici et ecclesiae'.[5] Any other view appears to Lucas 'contra aequitatem, honestatem et justitiam'.[6] It would be iniquitous if the Church were allowed to derive benefit and emoluments from her estates, but were under no obligation to discharge civic duties which are connected with the

[1] 'Non est ergo immunis ecclesia ab his muneribus, in quibus publica versatur utilitas', C. X, 48, 2, no. 1.

[2] loc. cit., no. 2.

[3] The whole passage runs as follows: 'Item quia ipso jure canonico statuitur clericos in iis, quae respiciunt bonum commune, onera debere subire, ut patet in custodia civitatis, quod est munus personale', loc. cit., no. 2. Against the gloss he maintains that 'omnes generaliter compelluntur, quatenus cunctis vigilantibus melius valeat civitas custodiri, quae verba etiam clericos aperte includunt'. Once again, for confirmation he refers to canon law itself, *causa* xi, *quaestio* 1, *canon* 28. See also *infra*, p. 193.

[4] C. X, 19, 8, no. 2. It is worth while quoting Gratian's commentary: 'Porro alii sunt, qui . . . praedia, villas et castella et civitates possident, ex quibus Caesari debent tributa, nisi Imperiali benignitate immunitatem ab huiusmodi promeruerunt. Quibus a Domino dicitur: "Reddite, quae sunt Caesaris, Caesari, et quae sunt Dei, Deo". Quibus idem Apostolus: "Reddite omnibus debita, cui tributum, tributum, cui vectigal, vectigal".'

[5] loc. cit., no. 3: 'Auctoritate scriptae legis conveniuntur, ut pro mensura onerum et modo facultatum clerici et ecclesiae cum aliis contribuant in iis, quae bonum rei publicae sapiunt'. He says in no. 13 of the same passage that due regard should be paid to the divine office of the clerics which has to be said at certain times of the day.

[6] loc. cit., no. 5.

source of her emoluments; incidentally, the whole burden of those services might then fall upon the shoulders of a small number of the lay population which derives no benefit from that Church property.[1] Wherever the 'publica utilitas' is concerned, such as in the construction of public ways, buildings and bridges, aqueducts, or in the erection of city walls, and the like, the Church is bound to contribute her share.[2] Moreover, to stress the Church's duty he states in another passage in which he deals with war: 'Nec est omittendum, quod praelati, qui propter possessiones ecclesiae principibus obnoxii sunt, tributa bellorum sive aliarum rerum debent exsolvere'.[3] But he holds that immunity is to be granted from those services which are not exclusively undertaken in the public interest, and furthermore, from 'sordida munera'[4] as well as from extraordinary duties, ordinary duties being those which occur at regular intervals.[5] Lucas admits, however, that the secular judge has no power to compel the Church or the clerics to carry out civic duties, but, on the ground that they evade their duties as citizens, he stigmatizes their refusal to do so as sinful.[6] Lastly, common sense dictates that those who refuse to pay taxes may properly be styled of an alien temper.[7] The content of C. X, 15, 1, tempts our jurist to state: 'Immunitas concessa non valet, et notarius inde privilegium scribens, ignis crematione damnatur'.[8]

After this digression we may now envisage some of the practical implications which emerge from his distinction between temporal and spiritual causes. He points out that all causes concerning

[1] 'Esset autem contra aequitatem, honestatem et justitiam, si ecclesiae consequerentur emolumenta bonorum suorum, et onera, quae ipsa contingebant prius quam ad ecclesiam devenirent, reliqui laici forte pauci sustinere cogantur', loc. cit., no. 5.

[2] C. X, 19, 8, no. 8: 'Ecclesiae regulariter non sunt immunes ab his oneribus, in quibus est pietas vel publica versatur utilitas, puta in viis et itineribus extruendis ac de novo faciendis pontibus, fontibus et similibus . . . in portibus aquaeductibus et muris civitatum instaurandis . . . in his publica versatur utilitas'.

[3] C. XI, 46, 1, no. 17. See also C. XI, 59, 3, no. 9, where he emphatically states that no exemptions whatsoever may take place in time of war: 'Sed in bello gerendo nedum bona quorumcumque nobilium, sed ipsa bona, quae sunt de patrimonio principis, imo et ecclesiarum, a nullo onere, quinetiam nec ab angariis publici cursus expeditionis tempore excusantur'.

[4] C. X, 19, 8, no. 11. He describes them as follows: 'Sunt autem munera sordida, ut calcis coquendae, arenae fodiendae, custodia . . . calefactio balnei et similia'.

[5] 'Ordinaria, quae singulis annis nulla varietate negotiorum imminente praestantur, sicut econtrario illa sunt extraordinaria, quae casualiter veniunt, puta quia filius nascitur regi aut filia nubit vel maritat filius aut ab inimicis forsitan captivatur', loc. cit., no. 15.

[6] 'Igitur ex hoc manifesta ratione concluditur, quod clerici et ecclesiae, licet per saeculares judices nequeant ad haec onera subeunda compelli, peccant tamen, si illa subire detractant, nam sic peccant, qui censum regi sovere negant', C. X, 48, 2, no. 6.

[7] 'Alienus enim censetur ab humano sensu, qui solvere tributa recusat', C. X, 16, 4, no. 4.

[8] C. X, 19, 8, no. 31.

feudal property are temporal matters, belong to secular jurisdiction, and should therefore be decided by the secular judge, notwithstanding the fact that ecclesiastical litigants may be involved: 'Bona feudalia, de quibus etiam si ecclesia vel ecclesiastica persona convenienda sit, non coram ecclesiastico judice, sed coram temporali et saeculari trahentur. Nemo enim potest ultra formam suae jurisdictionis.'[1] The same holds good with regard to litigations about inheritance and testaments.[2] The limited effect of legitimation is a logical consequence of the strict separation of powers: individuals who are made legitimate by secular decree acquire no rights in the ecclesiastical sphere, and vice versa: 'Legitimatio facta per Papam ad bona temporalia non extenditur'.[3] Those legitimated by papal decree are entitled only to ecclesiastical rights: 'Papa legitimat quantum ad ecclesiasticas dignitates et res, princeps quoad saecularia, ad ecclesiastica non'.[4] The presupposition of valid legitimation is that he who grants it has jurisdiction in the secular or ecclesiastical field.[5] Furthermore, Lucas points out that the clerical authority has no power to invalidate the effects of infamy incurred by a civil condemnation—'infamiam irrogatam ex sententia judicis saecularis Papa abolere non potest'—because the Pope has no jurisdiction in these temporal matters: 'Eorum quidem ad Papam pertinet restitutio, quorum ad eum pertinet castigatio'.[6] By confining secular and ecclesiastical authorities to their proper spheres, Lucas tries to eliminate points of frequent conflicts and ruptures between the authorities.

An interesting sequel to Lucas's view of matrimony is his thesis that actions for a declaration of the paternity of a child have to be tried by the ecclesiastical judge. In cases in which the child has been begotten in adultery committed by the wife, or in which certain circumstances throw doubt on the validity of the marriage, the ecclesiastical alone is competent to decide. In short, if the point of dispute arises out of the state of matrimony itself—'pendet', as Lucas expresses it, 'ex matrimonio, quod dicatur matrimonium fuisse minus legitime contractum'—it is the ecclesiastical judge who has to deal with actions of this kind: 'erit cognitio judicis ecclesiastici'.[7] If, however, the child is born outside wedlock, so that the question of matrimony does not arise at all, it is the secular judge who is called upon to decide the question of the child's paternity: 'Aut

[1] C. X, 43, 4, no. 40. The principle that feudal litigation involving the Church should be dealt with by the secular judge was laid down in a Sicilian constitution by Charles II, see C. X, 58, 1, no. 13, and *Constitutiones*, p. 313.

[2] C. XI, 71, 1, no. 11, and C. X, 43, 4, no. 41.

[3] C. X, 43, 4, no. 40.

[4] loc. cit., no. 40.

[5] Cf. also no. 39: 'Ut manifestius loquar, quamvis Papa seu princeps possit naturalem vel alium illegitimum facere legitimum, non tamen habebit locum haec legitimatio in his, quae de alterius sunt jurisdictione'. The conclusion is inevitable: 'unde legitimatus a principe saeculari non intelligitur quoad ordines legitimatus'.

[6] loc. cit., no. 40.

[7] C. XII, 1, 1, no. 7.

non pendet ex matrimonio, ut quia dicitur partus suppositus vel ex certa concubina susceptus vel alia, *quae non fuit uxor* ', the decision is in the hands of the secular judge: 'tunc erit cognitio judicis saecularis et coram ipso tractabitur '.[1] The reason for this distinction is, Lucas points out, that in the one case the action concerns matrimony, whilst in the other the point does not arise. 'Et ratio diversitatis ', Lucas declares, 'quia ubi pendet ex matrimonio, est annexa spirituali causae.' It need hardly be said that here, too, Lucas demands the application of Roman law by the ecclesiastical judge, with the provisions set out above.

In this connexion it may be worth while to refer to a problem that was not touched by Lucas, but which Bartolus tried to solve. The latter, having obviously the practical needs of the application of law before his eyes, put the question to his hearers as to whether the secular or the ecclesiastical judge had to decide a preliminary question concerning matrimony. The example chosen by Bartolus was one of an action of inheritance; the presupposition for the plaintiff's success was that he was a legitimate child. Now, Bartolus declared, the legitimacy may be contested on the grounds of some defect of the marriage of his parents. Bartolus proposed a distinction for the purpose of determining who should decide this preliminary question. If the fact of marriage alone were disputed he held that the decision should be in the hands of the secular judge; matrimony then would not constitute a spiritual cause, but solely one of fact: 'Dico, quod illa questio, an fuerit matrimonium inter patrem et matrem alicuius, est super facto nec est causa spiritualis, et etiam potest tunc judex saecularis expedire '.[2] But if the point at issue concerned the validity of the marriage, the ecclesiastical judge then would have to be called upon to decide: 'Potest esse etiam questio super jure . . . an inter eos poterat esse matrimonium, tunc est quaestio spiritualis et judex saecularis non potest se intromittere '.

To conclude: Roman civil law extends to all temporal affairs whether of secular or of ecclesiastical persons. Its application is either absolute or conditional. It is absolute before all kinds of Courts which try temporal causes of secular litigants, and before the secular Court when it tries temporal causes of the Church and the clerics; it is subject to a condition—namely, that civil law is not openly inimical to canon law, before the ecclesiastical judge who tries spiritual causes of secular litigants or temporal causes of ecclesiastical litigants. We cannot do better than to quote Lucas's own concluding words: 'Tene ergo pro constanti, quod ubicumque lex non est directe contraria canoni aut contra libertatem ecclesiae, etiam in foro ecclesiastico est servanda et clericos et ecclesias ligat '.[3]

It may now be of interest to view briefly the difference between the theory of our jurist and that of his contemporaries.[4] The difference

[1] loc. cit., no. 7.

[2] Lecture on D. 2, 1, 2, no. 4.

[3] C. XI, 71, 1, no. 11.

[4] On the views of some of the earlier jurists see Dr. Carlyle, loc. cit., vol.

will now emerge in its proper perspective. He himself draws our attention to the generally accepted doctrine—which originated with the French jurist, Jacobus de Ravanis—that civil and canon law have to be applied before the corresponding Court: the Doctors maintain, Lucas says, 'ut leges serventur in foro civili, canones in foro ecclesiastico'.[1] He returns to the same subject in another passage in which he alludes to the superficiality of the common doctrine: 'Legistae super hoc dicunt brevius'. Here he says that the jurists usually distinguish between a 'ratio civilis' and a 'ratio canonica'. The application of civil law depends on the greater weight to be attached to the 'ratio civilis', and the application of canon law is to be judged by the same criterion; but when both 'rationes' have equal weight the nature of the Court determines which law has to be applied.[2] The difference between Lucas's theory and the common theory is obvious: the former sets out from the material universality of Roman law and carries this idea to its logical conclusion, whereas the latter makes the application of Roman law dependent on the formal and incidental criterion of the deciding judge.

This common view was not, however, shared by Lucas's great contemporary, Bartolus. The eminent reputation which this jurist enjoyed in the later Middle Ages, particularly on account of his opinions on the present topic, warrants a brief reference to him. The key-note of Bartolus's thesis is a territorial conception of Empire and Papacy with a territorially limited validity of civil law and a territorially unlimited validity of canon law. This thesis of Bartolus is based on a universal spiritual overlordship of the ecclesiastical authority, the Pope, whilst a corresponding universal temporal overlordship is denied to the secular authority, the Emperor. Consequently, according to Bartolus, canon law is applicable to all temporal matters 'in terris subjectis ecclesiae' and to spiritual matters without any territorial limitations, whereas civil law is applicable to temporal matters 'in terris subjectis Imperio' only[3]; even this applicability of civil law is restricted to those cases in which

ii, pp. 79 seq. The submissive attitude of the Glossators is noteworthy. Petrus in his *Exceptiones Legum Romanarum*, for instance, said, without drawing a distinction between secular and ecclesiastical judge, that 'in hoc capitulo notare potes, quod si canones sunt contrarii legibus canones tenendi sunt, non leges', quoted after Carlyle, loc. cit., p. 80, note 1. Azo held the same view, and simply stated: 'Cum et Imperator dicat sacros canones pro legibus observandos', *Summa Codicis*, IV, 33, 18.

[1] C. X, 43, 4, no. 41.

[2] C. X, 52, 6, no. 9: 'Si canon rationem sufficientem pro se habet et lex similiter sufficientem, quaelibet ipsarum legum in foris suis obtineat effectum; inducunt (scil. doctores) exemplum in numero testium in testamentis, in quibus per leges requiruntur septem, per canones vero tres'.

[3] Compare with this view Lucas's conception: 'Solus Imperator universis et clericis et laicis in temporalibus praeesse debet', C. X, 39, 9, no. 26.

its application would not lead to sin.[1] We cannot do better than to quote the main parts of Bartolus's lecture:

> Quaero [he says] quando lex contradicit canoni vel econtra, cui sit standum? . . . Tu dic, aut loquimur in spiritualibus et pertinentibus ad fidem, et stamus canoni . . . aut loquimur in temporalibus et tunc aut in terris subjectis ecclesiae et sine dubio stamus decretalibus, aut in terris subjectis Imperio et tunc aut servare legem est inducere peccatum, . . . et tunc stamus canonibus . . . aut non inducit peccatum et tunc stamus legibus.[2]

Lucas is consistent. Let us contrast this view of Bartolus with the axiomatic statement of our jurist: 'In his, quae bona temporalia tangunt, in quibus nulla jurisdictio est ecclesiae, decretales non vendicant sibi locum'.[3] For Lucas there exist no territorial limitations of either civil or canon law in their respective spheres. This is best illustrated, perhaps, by his thesis that, even in the Kingdom of Sicily, temporal matters must be dealt with according to civil law, the reason being that 'in causis enim saeculi rex major est sacerdote, sed econtra in causis Dei sacerdos major est rege'.[4] Bartolus, on the other hand, pleads for the application of canon law in temporal matters, because the Kingdom is papal territory: 'Nam ecclesia Romana exercet in illas terras jurisdictionem, quae erat Imperii Romani . . . administratio istarum provinciarum est alteri concessa'.[5] A further illustration of Bartolus's view is his treatment of legitimation. He, too, distinguishes between temporal and spiritual matters, and holds that the secular authority can legitimate only as regards 'temporalia', which right, however, cannot be exercised in Church territory; here the secular legitimation has no effects in temporal matters, whilst, on the other hand, the ecclesiastical authority is entitled to legitimate—with full effects—in spiritual matters regardless of territorial boundaries. 'The Pope also legitimates as regards "temporalia" in his distinct territory, but here the correspondence breaks down.'[6] Although Jacobus Butrigarius was one of

[1] Lucas, on the other hand, cuts short all arguments on the possibility of committing sin by obeying civil law. See the passage transcribed *supra*, p. 83.

[2] C. I, 2, 12, no. 2. The whole question is exhaustively and admirably treated by Woolf, loc. cit., pp. 72 seq., 99 seq. This author gives many more references from Bartolus's writings, including his *Consilia*. Woolf remarks that the inconsistency of Bartolus's doctrine is due to his 'extreme tenderness of giving offence to the Church and its laws', p. 86. See also *infra*, p. 172.

[3] C. X, 39, 9, no. 26.

[4] The term 'rex' is here the Sicilian King.

[5] Quoted after Figgis, 'Bartolus and the Development of European Political Ideas' in *Divine Right of Kings*, p. 357. Figgis refers to the sixteenth-century writer, Francois Hotman, as saying that Bartolus had no real belief in papal rights, but he was too near Rome to deny it, loc. cit., note 1.

[6] Woolf, loc. cit., p. 79, see also the passage quoted by him note 1.
It would be misleading to assume that Bartolus was the first to expound the theory of the territorially limited scope of civil law, or that he arrived at his thesis out of tenderness for the Church, as Woolf seems to suggest.

Bartolus's teachers, he propounded a view which was diametrically opposed to that of his pupil. Jacobus taught that the Ruler was not only entitled to grant legitimation outside the territory of the Church, but he could also, with full effects, 'in terris ecclesiae juridice hoc facere'.[1]

In England, the possibility of a conflict between civil and canon law, particularly on the subject of legitimation, was avoided by the 'national conservatism' of the barons sitting in the Parliament of Merton (1235-6). The English law as to legitimation was not 'secundum canones legesque Romanas'.[2] The uncompromising attitude of the barons at Merton is worth recalling, on account of their firm rejection, in their famous 'nolumus leges Angliae mutare', of any romanistic or canonistic principles. The ninth chapter of the Statute of Merton says, *inter alia*:

> Rogaverunt omnes episcopi magnates, ut consentirent, quod nati ante matrimonium essent legitimi sicut illi, qui nati sunt post matrimonium, quantum ad haereditatem, quia ecclesia tales habet pro legitimis, et omnes comites et barones una voce responderunt, quod nolunt leges Angliae mutare, quae usitatae sunt et approbatae.[3]

III

It is on the basis of the universality of Roman law that Lucas investigates a problem which was very topical in the later Middle Ages, but which was considered, as a rule, as a purely political problem.[4] Lucas's first approach to the problem is from the legal point of view, combining with this, however, the treatment of a political aspect. The problem arose as a result of the Crusades and related to the question of whether foreign peoples, such as the Turks, Saracens, and other alien nationalities, were to be subjected to Roman law: 'Quaeritur, an Saraceni et gentiles ligentur jure Romano', he asks.[5] For Lucas, to whom the universality of Roman

---

Cynus held the same view as did Bartolus later. Cynus dealt with legitimation in C. V. 5, commenting on the Authentica *Ex complexu nefario*, no. 4, where he said substantially the same as Bartolus: 'Quaeritur, numquid Imperator possit legitimare spurium? Glossa dicit, quod sic, quod intelligunt quidam quantum ad temporalia, non quantum ad spiritualia. Sed *in Papa econtra est*, ut in quantum ad spiritualia possit, non temporalia, nisi in terris temporaliter sibi subjectis.'

[1] See the report of Bartholomaeus Salicetus in his lecture on C. I, *Rubrica* no. 8.

[2] Holdsworth, vol. ii, p. 204. See also the literature referring to this point, quoted by Holdsworth, vol. i, p. 622, note 1.

[3] Quoted by Holdsworth, vol. ii, p. 218, note 1, see also Pollock and Maitland, vol. i, p. 168. On Bracton's romanesque views concerning legitimation see H. G. Richardson, 'Tancred, Raymond, and Bracton' in *English Historical Review*, vol. lix (1944), pp. 376–84. Bracton, writing his *De Legibus* after the Parliament of Merton, greatly depended on the canonist Raymundus de Pennaforte.

[4] See Woolf, loc. cit., pp. 28, 106.

[5] C. XI, 71, 1, no. 10.

law is an axiomatic truth, there can be no doubt that those 'foreign' peoples are bound by Roman law as the civil law *par excellence*. His argument is that the Saracens and similar nationalities should be subjected to Roman law in the same way as the Jews. His emphatic answer to the above question is noteworthy: 'Videtur aperte, quod sicut Judaei hoc jure ligantur, non minus Saraceni et gentiles'. But we may assume that it is his practical mind, his sense of reality, and the actual political conditions within the Empire which prevent him from propounding a dogmatic view which finds no justification in reality. Thus he arrives at a distinction into a 'de jure' and a 'de facto' reign of Roman law: 'Dicas, quod licet de jure ligentur, non de facto'. For when even the French King, who theoretically belongs to the Empire, refuses to acknowledge a superior legislator in temporal affairs, it is not surprising to find that those other nationalities which are outside the Empire, decline to recognize the Emperor and hence his law. Theoretically, since the Emperor is 'dominus mundi', both his reign and his law extend to these foreign nations; theoretically, the Empire should embrace all nations: 'Huic autem Imperio, scilicet Romano, omnes gentes subesse deberent'.[1] Lucas says that their exemption in practice from the observance of the Roman civil law is due not to their racial or national differences—'secta vero ipsorum non facit eos exemptos'—but to the weakness and lack of power on the part of the Empire, which is unable to enforce its law even within its own boundaries: 'Sed factio et potentia Imperiique Romani debilitas, ignavia et socordia, et hoc verum in regnis et locis eorum.'[2]

The conception of the universality of Roman law meant that, upon theoretical grounds, neither individuals nor corporate bodies such as the Church, nor states and nations, even if outside the Empire, could be exempted from it. But this very universality brought up the further problem of whether the Ruler himself is subjected to positive law and to his own enactments? There is no doubt for Lucas that the Ruler is subjected to natural and divine law. As to positive law itself, the Roman texts contained the famous dictum 'princeps legibus solutus est', but can this exemp-

[1] C. XI, 71, 1, no. 10.

[2] loc. cit., no. 10. In his commentaries on C. XI, 50, 1, no. 2, Lucas justifies this exemption on other grounds: 'Sunt aliqui reges liberi ab Imperio exempti, qui vel jugum numquam susceperunt vel susceptum rejecerunt . . . eos enim vocat Imperator socios et amicos . . . potissime liber et exemptus rex Francorum, qui superiorem in temporalibus non recognoscit . . . item rex Siciliae'. This opinion of Lucas is more in the line of the generally entertained view, see the passage of Andreas de Isernia, quoted by Dr. Carlyle, loc. cit., vol. v, p. 145. See also Bartholomaeus de Capua, who commented on the Sicilian laws, lib. I, tit. 1, pp. 4 seq.: 'Multi sunt reges exempti a Romano Imperio, qui vel ex praescriptione vel ex alia antiqua consuetudine vel de facto non recognoscunt Imperatorem, ut rex Franciae et Ultramontani'. But he holds that they are subjects of the Empire, not, however, 'sacramento fidelitatis' but 'ratione Imperii Romani, sub quo esse debent, cum et ipsi fuerint de imperio Justiniani'.

tion be justified in view of what Lucas conceives to be the universal character of civil law? He repudiates the idea that any person whatsoever can be exempted from legal obligation, and consequently the Ruler himself is not theoretically excluded from law. Lucas maintains that by scrupulously strict adherence to the laws which are to be a guide no less to himself than to his subjects he above all must set an example to his people. The conduct of the head of the State should be in harmony with the spirit and content of law, the creation of which is his vocational office. The sole meaning of the Roman dictum, Lucas argues, closely following John of Salisbury, is that the Ruler should be motivated to observe the law and to fulfil the duties incumbent upon him, not by fear of punishment threatened for non-compliance, but by his (innate) sense of justice.[1] Lucas holds that the Ruler's acceptance of the divine mandate to preserve ('custodire') the Empire implies along with it the duty to observe the law: 'Debeat (scil. princeps) . . . leges rei publicae custodire, secundum quas Imperium a Deo custodiendum accepit'.[2] His command carries its fullest weight, and finds all the readier acceptance and greater response if he himself faces its obligations: 'Justa est enim vocis auctoritas, si quod populis prohibetur, sibi licere non patiatur . . . curare debet, ut operum suorum sit conservator et regni et defensor justitiae, non eversor'.[3] It may be appropriate to quote just one more passage in which Lucas comes to speak of this particular problem:

> Officium enim cuiusque regentis non solum in danda, sed etiam in observanda disciplina consistit . . . omnes enim decet obedire legibus et secundum eas vivere, et omnes obediant legi et succumbant justitiae sanctioni. Imperator quippe recte et competenter exornare debet traditam sibi rem publicam.[4]

Practically speaking, Lucas says, the dictum of the Roman law means that the Ruler can never be forced to obey the law. But this privilege is granted theoretically to the Emperor alone, not to others: 'Nam is solus solutus est legibus . . . et ipse solus dicitur mundi dominus'.[5] Nevertheless, the Emperor is morally respon-

[1] Referring to the *Policraticus*, lib. IV, cap. 2, Lucas says: 'Princeps legis nexibus dicitur absolutus, non quia ei iniqua liceant, sed quia is debet esse, qui non timore poenae, sed amore justitiae aequitatem colat, rei publicae procuret utilitatem et in omnibus aliorum commoda privatae praederat utilitati', C. X, 26, 4, no. 3. On John of Salisbury's views see Dr. Carlyle, loc. cit., vol. iii, p. 113, and, in particular, R. L. Poole, *Illustrations of Medieval Thought and Learning*, p. 205.

[2] loc. cit., no. 2.

[3] loc. cit., no. 35.

[4] C. X, 7, 3, no. 3. In another passage he says: 'Rex debet in se legem pati, quam tulit in subditos et eo jure uti, quod in alios statuit . . . idem in se observare tenetur. Justum est principem legibus obtemperare suis, tunc enim jura sua ab omnibus custodienda existimantur (existimet?), quando ipse illis reverentiam praebet . . . alias potestas regia juste corrumpitur et ad terram trahitur, nisi legibus conservetur,' C. XI, 70, 5, no. 35.

[5] C. XII, 35, 14, no. 6. Thomas's opinion was not unlike that of Lucas,

sible to God, from whom he has received the mandate: 'Tenetur quippe Imperator Deo de Imperio reddere rationem'.[1]

On the other hand, in cases in which he acts under necessity, every individual is exempted from the observance of law. Necessity deprives an act of its unlawful character and justifies an otherwise illegal act. The idea upon which this justification rests is, once again, that of justice: it would be contrary to the idea of justice and equity if law insisted upon absoluteness of obedience, for necessity knows no law. Lucas expresses this conception in the following words: 'Necessitas, quae legem non habet . . . i.e., cessat lex, ubi necessitas venit et facit licitum, quod alias non esset licitum. Nam iniquum est, quod non dolo, sed necessitate contingit, non excusare'.[2] He adds that the concept of necessity comprises any just cause which presents itself as an obstacle to the legal mode of conduct.[3]

IV

The present chapter cannot be concluded without a brief review of Lucas's ideas on the abrogation of laws. Law which has been rescinded is inapplicable because invalid. Rescission of preceding law is valid, Lucas holds, when two conditions are fulfilled: firstly, that the preceding law has been expressly cancelled by its successor, or at least that annulment follows conclusively and necessarily from the text and content of the posterior law; secondly, that the legislative authority creating the new law is not hierarchically subordinated to that which has created the old law.[4]

---

but he does not refer to Thomas; see Prof. d'Entréves, loc. cit., p. 40. Thoughts very similar to those of Lucas are expressed by Salicetus, in his lecture on C. I, 14, 4, no. 1: 'Exemplis et operationibus virtuosis aliis indicatur et quanto quis est nobilior et potentior, tanto moralius et virtuosius debet se habere et speculum caeteris esse'.

[1] C. X, 26, 4, no. 5. Contemporary jurists did not deal with this particular problem at such great length as Lucas does. They all are agreed that the Ruler is free from any obligation to obey the law. See, e.g., Bartolus, C. I, 14, 4, no. 2: the Ruler submits himself to the law 'de voluntate, non de necessitate'. Baldus considers that it is a 'debitum honestatis' on the part of the Ruler to observe the law, although he makes use of a phrase which foreshadows the later development of the concept of sovereignty. He says that the *suprema et absoluta potestas principis* is irreconcilable with the idea of his being subjected to positive law, see Baldus on C. I, 14, 4, no. 1. This is perhaps still more clearly expressed in his lecture on C. III, 34, 2, no. 45, where he states the omnipotence of the Ruler in terms which are hardly distinguishable from those of Bodin: 'Est autem plenitudo potestatis arbitrii plenitudo *nulli necessitati subjecta nullisque juris publici regulis limitata*'.

[2] C. X, 31, 25, no. 2.

[3] loc. cit., no. 4: 'Nota, quod nomine necessitatis omne justum impedimentum continetur'.

[4] C. X, 39, 9, no. 26: 'Ad hoc, ut lex dicatur justa ratione correcta, duo necessaria sunt. Primum, quod corrigatur expresse. . . vel saltem, quod secunda corrigens totaliter, integraliter et directe sit contraria primae. Secundum est, ut is, qui vult legem praecedentem abrogare, habeat unde legitimam potestatem.'

The authority that abrogates (or amends) law must not be inferior to the authority that has issued the law. This thesis causes Lucas to investigate a problem which was, at his time, of particular importance and practical interest, and through which he practically and theoretically demonstrates the superiority in temporal matters of the secular authority over its ecclesiastical counterpart. He devotes no less that fourteen folio columns to the treatment of the problem of whether the ecclesiastical authority is competent to 'correct' civil law. The question related to the problem of whether the civil law which imposes infamy on the woman who marries within a year of her husband's death (*infra tempus luctus*) has been abrogated by canon law which expressly states that 'mulier nubens infra annum lugubrum, infamiam non incurrit'.[1] A similar problem arose in connexion with the regulation of canon law that matrimony is permissible between the ravisher and his victim,[2] whilst civil law, on the other hand, prohibits marriages of this kind.[3]

Lucas uses the former case to exemplify his doctrine of the superiority of the secular authority, even in matrimonial matters. He declares that the argument put forward by the canonists, namely, that the widow has no obligation towards her dead husband, because the marriage is dissolved—'mulier soluta est a lege viri'[4]—is not decisive. The canonists refer, he says, to some utterances in the *Romans* and in the *Corinthians* upon which they base their theory, and from which they conclude that 'per licentiam et auctoritatem Apostoli eius (scil. viduae) infamia aboletur'.[5] Lucas contests the

[1] See *Decretales*, lib. IV, tit. 21, cap. 4. The infamy was imposed by C. V, 9, 1. On the regulation of Roman law concerning the year of mourning see Greenidge, *Infamia*, pp. 176, 203, Professor Buckland, *Textbook of Roman Law*, p. 118, note 3, and Sohm–Mitteis–Wenger, *Institutionen des roemischen Rechts*, 17th ed., p. 526. The view of Sohm is not correct that the infamy had been abolished in the Middle Ages 'owing to the influence of the canonists', loc. cit., p. 526. In fact, the 'year of mourning' is still in many Continental legal systems an impediment to marriage.

[2] See *Decretales*, lib. V, tit. 17, cap. 7.

[3] Lucas says in his commentary on C. X, 39, 9, no. 18: '(Lex) etiam prohibet inter raptorem et raptam matrimonium contrahi, secus de jure canonico, quo permittitur, extra de rap. "accedens"'; this reference denotes the passage mentioned in note 2.

[4] loc. cit., no. 15.

[5] *Decretales*, lib. IV, tit. 21, cap. 4 *in fine*.

The gloss, too, adhered to the opinion of the canonists, see *glossa ordinaria*, C. V, 9, 1, s.v. *honorarias*, where the gloss says: 'Poena, quae imponitur mulieri eo, quod nimis festinanter nubit . . . hodie est sublata per dictum Apostoli'. But the jurists of the fourteenth century, as far as I could ascertain, almost unanimously rejected this opinion. See Cynus, ibid., who deals at great length with the views of Hostiensis, but puts forward as his answer to Hostiensis the argument that if Hostiensis were right, the woman would be punished on account of matrimony, a holy affair, 'sed certe non punitur propter matrimonium, sed propter nimiam festinantiam. Unde licet matrimonium sit licitum, festinantia tamen illicita est et contra bonos mores.' Bartolus was vague, and seemed to have inclined to the canonistic view. Baldus, on the other hand, held that canon law did not truth of this conclusion and asserts that St. Paul did not give any specific permission to the widow to marry within one year nor did he speak of abolishing infamy. It is only the canonists themselves, he says, who read this incorrect view into the apostle's words.[1]

Having refuted the basic canonistic argument, Lucas proceeds to solve this problem, dealing with it under three aspects. Firstly, he states, the reasons which have led the secular law-giver to impose the penalty of infamy upon the widow are still valid. Insecurity as to the paternity of a possible child would be the inevitable consequence of a legal situation which permits her to marry immediately after her husband's death. Lucas recalls a hypothetical case which caused a great stir amongst jurists and was forwarded to the Roman Curia. It is supposed that the following case had occurred : Within a fortnight of her husband's death a woman married two men consecutively. She bore a son some nine months after the death of her first husband. Lucas declares that the question 'talis partus, cuius judicabitur esse filius ? ' is well justified.[2] The wisdom of civil law cannot be disputed, he holds, and affirms : 'Tanta perlexitas et absurditas, nisi per observationem juris civilis, videlicet, quod mulier non nubat intra annum, vitari non potest '. Concluding this passage he again quotes the opposing views of the canonist Hostiensis with the apparent motive of demonstrating the inadequacy of canon law and doctrine.

Lucas's second argument is based on the idea of honourable conduct, which should be made material by the means of the law. He invokes Ulpian's precept of 'honeste vivere' and desires this postulate to be applied to the widow. It can hardly be said, he avows, that the widow who is in so great a haste to marry conducts

---

abrogate civil law. He reports that he himself was consulted in the affairs of 'dominus Pandulphus de Malatestis' (probably of Bologna) and had given this as his opinion, to which the Bolognese law faculty also adhered, namely, that marriage would be 'contra bonos mores', would make paternity doubtful, and would justify the suspicion that the widow 'in vita primi viri verbo vel facto aliquid inhonestum cum secundo viro commiserit et cum ipso secundo viro possit oriri materia perfidiae et discordiae', Baldus in his lecture on C. V, 9, 1, no. 21. In the same dramatic and spectacular way as that in which he delivered his lectures, Odofredus exclaimed rejecting the canonistic doctrine : 'O signori, nos dicimus . . . si mulier statim posset nubere, quando provocaretur vir ad iram, diceret " tace meretrix, quia statim nupsisti post mortem primi mariti, et ita faceres de me cras, si decederem ", quod lex non vult', Odofredus on C. V, 9, 1, no. 7. We may point out that none of the jurists treated this point as systematically as Lucas.

[1] 'Nec Apostolus expresse permittit mulierem infra tempus luctus ad secundas nuptias convolare, sed doctores canonistae ad hoc trahunt dictum eius', loc. cit., no. 29.

[2] 'Decidant (scil. canonistae) etiam quaestionem nostris temporibus ortam perlatamque ad sedem apostolicam de muliere, quae mortuo viro inter dies 15 alios duos viros superduxit (sic !), peperit deinde filium intra novem vel undecim menses ab obitu primi viri, talis partus, cui judicabitur esse filius ? Certe, si verum dicere volumus, tanta perplexitas et absurditas . . . .', loc. cit., no. 41.

herself in an honourable fashion.[1] Not only is it justifiable to assume her infidelity to her first husband,[2] but marriage so shortly after her husband's death is in any case bound to reflect on her moral character. She must appear as a lascivious woman, incapable of taming her sexual desires. Lucas says: 'Mulierem transire ad secundas nuptias infra tempus luctus satis est inhonestum, diciturque tunc mulier effusa concupiscentiis'. Relatives, grown-up sons of the widow, and the world at large would certainly have every reason to suspect adultery between her and her second husband during her first husband's life-time. Rightly, therefore, do the civil laws forbid marriage of this scandalous nature, because the widow must necessarily be regarded as unchaste, and must bring the whole family into disrepute. The honour of the deceased bids her, in Lucas's opinion, to wait the allotted year. He asks whether it were not proper and fitting for the Pope to prohibit marriages which lead to public scandal.[3] Our jurist points out that in items, which have so great a bearing on social and ethical aspects the principle of honourable conduct must not be disregarded by the law. The law would certainly endorse dishonourable conduct, if the canonistic views were accurate. He submits that the Church herself should be the guardian of honourable conduct and should take proper heed of these socially and morally important issues. Lucas holds that, on account of her continency, all praise is due to the widow who abstains from marriage: 'Cum ergo mulierem non transire ad secundas

[1] Lucas, in his gloss on King Robert's constitutions, p. 360 of the *Constitutiones*, draws our attention to the neglect of the principle by individuals who are in love, and he exclaims: 'Quid deceat, non videt ullus amans'. In the same gloss on p. 361 he gives the following description of a loving person: 'Tali amore ligatus parum dormit, minus edit et omnis eius actus in amantis cogitatione finitur; nihil beatum credit, quod illi sit odiosum'.

[2] 'Mulier secundo nubens dicitur fidem frangere priori marito.' This, according to Lucas, is also acknowledged by canon law: *causa* xxvii, *quaestio* 1, *canon* 1. The reference to this passage to prove his assertion testifies to the argumentative acumen of Lucas. The passage says that only a subjective element—i.e., the will—constitutes marriage, not the coitus. Consequently, this element has to be presumed even when one party abandons conjugal life, provided that he has still the will to matrimony. Adultery alone would not be sufficient to presume the abandonment of the will: 'Nam etsi jam corpore separatus est, tamen adhuc voluntate conjunctus est . . . non ergo, qui dimittit moechatur, sed qui alteram ducit'. Lucas applies this subjective element to the case in question. Gratian asked whether a woman who is betrothed to a man can 'renunciare priori conditioni et transferre sua vota ad alium?', *Rubrica*. It is, we may assume, this question of Gratian which led Lucas to see a parallel between the widow and the betrothed girl.

[3] 'Consanguinei vero aut filii, qui ex priore supersunt viri potentes, et celerati graviter inde turbati suspicantes de adulterio praecedente, vel non . . . hoc interdicunt (scil. leges) expresse dicentes eam taliter meretricari et tam ipsis filiis quam viro priori contumeliam irrogare; petunt, ut contineat saltem per annum, suo viro servans honorem, est enim honor defuncti mulierem ad secundas nuptias non transire . . . dicamusne Papam tunc prohibere non posse tale matrimonium, ut grave scandalum, quod videt inde parari, tollatur?', loc. cit., no. 31.

nuptias infra tempus luctus sit irreprehensible, imo laudabile, illud non impugnare, sed tueri catholica debet ecclesia '.[1]

The third argument is based upon the separation of powers. Lucas maintains that the Pope is the highest instance in all spiritual matters. Within the orbit of spiritual affairs he acts not ' ut homo, sed vice Dei '.[2] The same omnipotence must be conceded to the secular Ruler in temporal matters in which it is his turn to act ' vice Dei '.[3] The imposition of infamy in the case under discussion belongs to temporal jurisdiction, because temporal effects alone are involved. When the Pope is omnipotent in spiritual matters, ' quare ', asks Lucas, ' impedietur princeps saecularis, arcere viduam a secundis nuptiis, privans eam his, quae saecularia sunt, et ecclesiae non subjecta ? '—and he answers : ' certe ratio diversitatis reddi non potest, ergo idem jus '.[4] Moreover, the Pope can make new law in the spiritual sphere and can dispense even ' contra jus ', provided that his enactments are not disruptive to the structure of the Church organism or inimical to divine law or Holy Writ : why, then, should not the secular Ruler have the right to legislate in matrimonial matters, merely in order to ensure that the principle of honourable conduct be enforced and that public scandal be avoided ? ' Certe ratio diversitatis reddi non potest, ergo idem jus ', is again Lucas's laconic answer.[5] The sanction which civil law imposes is, according to our author, perfectly justified. It carries the first precept of the law, viz., ' honeste vivere ', into practical effect.[6] He believes that the sanction of infamy will be an effective means to lead the widow, perhaps against her will, ' ad honestatis rectitudinem '.[7]

With the following modest statement Lucas closes this long discussion, of which we have given only a very short summary : ' Auctor enim non ad doctrinam alterius, sed propriam, haec notavit '.

To conclude : the matrimonial laws are neither abrogated nor amended by the ecclesiastical authority. Those laws are intrinsically correct, and the Church has no competency to change secular law, for ' summus pontifex, quamquam in spiritualibus sit major principe saeculari, in temporalibus princeps saecularis major est eo '.[8]

[1] loc. cit., no. 30. He supports this argument again by referring to canon law itself : *causa* xxv, *quaestio* 1, *canon* 8, which starts off : ' Omne, quod irreprehensibile est, catholica defendit ecclesia '.

[2] loc. cit., no. 31. [3] loc. cit., no. 31. [4] loc. cit., no. 31.

[5] loc. cit. The whole passage runs as follows : ' Quare non et in matrimonio, non quod ipsum matrimonium annulletur, sed quod contrahatur honestius et sine scandalo poterit aliquid statuere, quo non observato et sic honestate violata in tam execrabilis festinantiae poenam privato bonorum, quae mere temporalia sunt, et in nullo subjecta ecclesiae, ut praemissum est, juste succedat ? ', no. 33.

[6] ' Potest jus civile incontinentiam secundarum nuptiarum punire bonis temporalibus, quae principi sunt subjecta, eo quod sunt contra primum praeceptum juris civilis, scil. honeste vivere ', loc. cit., no. 33.

[7] ' Justae ergo servandae sunt leges principum saecularium . . . ut metu ammissionis bonorum ipsorum cogantur ad honestatis rectitudinem festinares, loc. cit., no. 33. [8] loc. cit., no. 26.

A conflict between two legal enactments should usually be solved by the application of the maxim which Lucas offers, namely, that that law has to be given preference 'quae juri naturali aut praeceptis seu consiliis Evangelii vel Apostoli plus adhaeret'.[1] A case which was commonly understood as constituting a conflict between civil and natural law provokes the special interest on the part of our jurist, and leads him to an examination of the problem of whether an enactment that is not based on a just cause, and is understood to be inimical to natural law, has to be applied by the judiciary. The point in question concerns a law of the Ruler by which ownership of a thing is transferred from one person to another person, without just cause: 'Pone, princeps sine justa causa statuit aliquid contra jus naturae, puta, quod dominia de uno in alium transferantur, numquid talis constitutio est servanda?'[2] According to Lucas, the opinion of the jurists was not unanimous. The Archdeacon holds that this law is valid and therefore applicable, because it emanates from the proper authority[3]; the judiciary have simply to apply the law, not to pass judgement on the law, but to judge according to the law: 'Nec enim de ipsa lege principis, sed secundum ipsam, postquam facta est, judicandum est'.[4] Innocent IV and Hostiensis, on the other hand, maintain that law of this kind is inapplicable before either Court.[5] Lucas refers us to his solution, which he gives in his commentary on C. XI, 70, 5, no. 4. Once again he follows his own line of thought. The omnipotence of the Ruler as regards life and liberty of his subjects is a principle that cannot be questioned by anyone. When, by virtue of his functions, the Ruler has the power of life and death, no reasonable ground can be adduced, Lucas says, for denying him the actual power to dispose of things and to transfer property from one man to another. 'Et multo fortius', Lucas concludes, 'bona hominum tollere potest quam personas.'[6] Moreover, independent states ('civitates') have always exercised the right to take property away and to issue laws to this effect; and since the Ruler's power is greater than that of any 'civitas', the same right must be conceded to him.[7]

[1] C. X, 39, 9, no. 24. [2] C. X, 26, 4, no. 5.

[3] 'Vero determinat Archidiaconus . . . sunt enim leges divinitus per ora principum promulgatae . . . nec enim de ipsa lege principis, sed secundum ipsam, postquam . . .', loc. cit., no. 5.

[4] loc. cit., no. 5.

[5] 'Innocentius et Hostiensis scripserunt . . . quod talis constitutio nec in foro animae nec in foro judiciali est servanda', loc. cit., no. 5.

[6] The main parts of this passage are: 'Princeps est dominus personarum . . . et sicut Imperator est dominus mundi . . . ita et rex dominus regni. Sed si est dominus personarum, ergo et rerum . . . quemadmodum potest justificare et damnare personas, ut eis poenas leviet vel augmentet . . . sola voluntas eius justa causa est . . . et multo fortius bona hominum tollere potest quam personas,' C. XI, 70, 5, no. 4.

[7] 'Major est potestas principis quam populi, sed populus civitatis potest facere statutum et per suum statutum tollere dominium alicuius rei . . . ergo fortius poterit princeps donando rem alienam privare dominium', C. XI, 70, 5, no. 19.

In its result, this opinion of Lucas does not considerably deviate from contemporary views on this topic, but differs widely from them in the arguments which he adduces to prove the Ruler's power to transfer property.[1] His theory can be explained by his idea of the Ruler's overlordship. Lucas conceives the Ruler overlord, not, however, in the sense that he is owner of his subjects' goods,[2] but in the sense that the State (' civitas ') is in his absolute power: he has ' plenitudo potestatis '.[3] Lucas declares that a thing is spoken of as belonging to a person even if he has the mere protection of it: ' Interdum res dicitur alicuius quoad protectionem solam et servitium '.[4] In this sense, and in this sense alone, the State ' belongs ' to the Ruler: ' Et hoc modo ', Lucas continues, ' res publica dicitur esse principis '. Now it is in performance of his protectoral function that he can validly transfer property, even without an apparent just cause. For, however little the just cause may outwardly appear—and the Ruler is not bound to state publicly the reason for his enactment [5]—the presumption is that it does proceed from a just cause. To his subjects the legislative will is a sufficiently just cause, that is to say, obedience to the law does not entail sin, as long as the legislative will is carried out. In other words, the individual is covered by observing the law.[6] Lucas draws the attention of his readers to the activity of the Pope in his capacity as the highest ecclesiastical authority. Similarly, the Pope, Lucas says, is not bound to state publicly the ' cause ' of a specific action which may appear as unjust: ' Si Papa facit aliquid, quod videtur injustum, ubi nos rationem non possumus assignare, nihilominus illud justum sit '.[7] Thus the law which transfers property from one man to another is valid and enforceable. But the Ruler himself who takes away property without good cause and without being able to justify his action is morally responsible to God—' peccat gravius et mortalius '—because of the misuse of the powers entrusted to him. It is with this argument, namely, that ' sola voluntas eius (scil. principis) justa causa est ',[8] that Lucas meets the case of a property transfer ' sine justa causa '. In this way Lucas manages to uphold the absolute legislative authority of the Ruler. Lucas's argumentation is strangely reminiscent of Albericus Gentilis's ideas on the same topic.[9]

[1] For some outstanding opinions of contemporary writers, see *infra*, pp. 102–3.

[2] See also the passages quoted *infra*, ch. VIII, p. 187.

[3] For further details see *infra*, ch. VIII, section I.

[4] C. X, 31, 33, no. 19.

[5] See *supra*, ch. III, p. 54.

[6] To make himself perfectly clear, he refers to the duty of the wife to obey her husband. Whatever the husband bids her to do she is bound to do, and would otherwise commit a grave sin, because the husband's authority proceeds from God: ' Et sicut uxor parere tenetur viro aliquid in fractionem voti contra Deum praecipienti, alias mortaliter ipsa peccaret, cum tamen parendo nec etiam venialiter peccet, licet maritus jubendo mortaliter peccat . . . quod ex Dei auctoritate procedit ', loc. cit., no. 43.

[7] loc. cit., no. 42.

[8] See the passage *supra* in note 6, p. 100.

[9] See Dr. Carlyle, loc. cit., vol. vi, p. 453, note 1.

Moreover, Lucas's thesis approaches the concept of a 'full legislative sovereignty',[1] systematically elaborated by Bodin two centuries later. The idea so characteristic of medieval thought that legislation is concerned with the 'finding' of a precept, whose binding force comes 'from its supposed conformity to universal reason or to immemorial custom',[2] experiences a considerable modification and reformation in Lucas's system. Though still bowing before the weight of commonly accepted axioms, he envisages a concept of an absolute legislative power which can issue enactments in disregard of the limitations set by 'higher laws'. Such enactments are valid and enforceable as regards the citizens, but if issued without good cause the Ruler makes himself responsible before God.

We have said that, in its arguments, Lucas's theory differs widely from contemporary views on this topic, though in its result it is in line with most of fourteenth-century doctrines. Let us briefly scrutinize these opinions. The gloss [3] entertained a view that was, on the whole, rejected by the Post-Glossators. It said that the Ruler was not allowed to change the existing distribution of property by transferring the 'dominium' from one to another, because property was based upon the immutable *jus gentium*. The gloss was sharply criticized by Cynus for its rigid—and we may well add unrealistic—attitude. Cynus attacked the gloss on two points. Property, he said, was not only a matter of the *jus gentium*, but also of the *jus civile*, especially in its protection; and no one could maintain that the Ruler was not entitled to change the existing civil law. This was also conceded by the gloss, Cynus continued, and surely here the gloss contradicted itself, for, if the Ruler had the right to deny an *actio* in certain cases, he could therefore deprive property of its protection, and unprotected property was of no avail to its owner.[4] Cynus admitted, however, that the Ruler would not be entitled to a wholesale and universal transfer of property, but he could easily transfer property in individual cases.[5] But he counselled the Ruler not to take away property without good cause, a requirement upon which the *doctores ultramontani* had insisted; though he was realistic enough to recognize that the Ruler could, without good cause, validly transfer property *de facto*. 'Quando vult mihi tollere dominium rei meae sine aliqua causa de mundo, si quaeratur, utrum possit de facto?' Cynus asked and gave the laconic answer: 'Non est dubium'. *De jure*, however, the Ruler was not entitled to a property transfer without good cause: 'Sed utrum possit de jure

[1] McIlwain, loc. cit., p. 390.
[2] McIlwain, loc. cit., p. 390. See also the pungent remarks by Mr. E. Lewis, 'Organic Tendencies in Medieval Political Thought', in *American Political Science Review*, vol. xxxii (1938), p. 867.
[3] C. I, 19, 7.
[4] Cynus in his lecture on C. I, 19, 7, no. 12.
[5] 'Dici potest, quod licet imperator non possit totaliter facere, ut omnes amittant dominium, potest saltem particulariter facere, ut unus amittat et sic potest rescribere, quod res tua sit mea.'

et de potestate sibi per jura concessa, in veritate non potest'. As regards the administrators of the law, they had to observe such a decree of the Ruler.

An extreme point of view was adopted by Jacobus Butrigarius. He maintained that the Ruler could transfer property with or without good cause. His chief consideration was that the laws which protected property emanated from the same source which decreed the transfer—i.e., the Ruler, or as Jacobus put it, ' procedunt a pari potentia, ergo sicut potest istas leges tollere, ergo eodem modo possit dare alteri dominium rei meae sine causa '.[1] As usual, Bartolus himself was more cautious. He held that the Ruler, whose powers were entrusted to him by God, would not live up to the standard required of him if he took property away without good cause: ' Deus non dedit ei jurisdictionem peccandi, nec auferrendi alienum indebite '.[2] Baldus, writing towards the end of the century, pointed as clearly as Lucas to the future development of the idea of the *plenitudo potestatis*. We have already noticed how near Baldus came to the sixteenth-century conception of sovereignty [3] when he declared that the Ruler's *plenitudo potestatis* is ' nulli necessitati subjecta nullisque juris publici regulis limitata '. And the full implications of this view can be gauged from his attitude towards our present topic. He stated succinctly that the Ruler was entitled, with or without cause, to transfer property, precisely because he had the *plenitudo potestatis*.[4]

An obvious conflict between human law and its divine counterpart entails the invalidity of the former. Lucas illustrates this thesis by taking the issue of the duel as an example. He says that duelling is permitted by Lombard law (with which he has no patience),[5] but also (which is a far more serious matter) in certain cases by Sicilian laws. He denies them legal validity, since they are in direct opposition to the law of God: ' Constitutio ipsa est directe contra praeceptum Dei, id est, " non occidas " '. Moreover, duelling means tempting God.[6] It is true that those Sicilian constitutions were posterior to divine law, but no law-giver is entitled to abrogate divine law. The rules concerning the idea of the duel are not those of God, but of the devil. Those desirous of wielding arms are advised by Lucas to show their strength, valour,

[1] See the report of Bartolus in his lecture on C. I, 22, 6, no. 1.

[2] loc. cit., see also *Prima Constitutio*, no. 5, and the passages transcribed by Woolf, loc. cit., p. 46, note 2 and p. 47, note 1.

[3] See *supra*, p. 95, n. 1.

[4] C. III, 34, 2, no. 45; see also D. 1, 9, 12, no. 1, where he pointed out that the decree which transfers property is legally valid ' ex vi legis, quia omnis legum potestas est in pectore suo '. For earlier opinions see also McIlwain, loc. cit., p. 190, note 1, Carlyle, loc. cit., vol. vi, pp. 16, 84 seq., Gierke-Maitland, loc. cit., p. 79, and G. Meyer, *Das Recht der Expropriation*, pp. 97 seq.

[5] C. XI, 43, 1, no. 1.

[6] ' Item contra praeceptum aliud, ut Deus noster et dominus non temptatur, quid fit per pugnam ', loc. cit., no. 1.

and courage in the battle-field, and not against their neighbour. Hence killing in duel is murder. Those constitutions which permit duelling are neither reasonable nor just and are consequently not law: 'Praemissa etiam constitutio, licet posterior, est tamquam irrationabilis et injusta et contra paecepta Dei'.[1]

At this point one important observation must be made. It is true that human law cannot abrogate—that is, validly repeal—divine and natural law, because they are superior to human legislation. But human law can effectively derogate—that is, restrict—divine and natural law, provided that the legislator inserts a 'non obstante' clause. If he fails to do this, his enactment is not valid.[2] In consistence with his view, Lucas declares that the invalidity of this specific law is not caused by the lack of power on the part of the Ruler, but rather by the lack of will: 'Magis ex defectu voluntatis principis quam potentiae'.[3] In this point, too, the tendency of Lucas towards a 'full legislative sovereignty' becomes apparent. Enactments against preceding human legislation have full abrogating effect.[4]

[1] 'Non est lex, quae non justa . . .', loc. cit., no. 4. On the prevalent habit of duelling in England, even down to the seventeenth century, see Holdsworth, vol. i, p. 579. The ease with which men made use of their arms prompted the legislators in Tudor England to issue laws which prohibited the carrying of certain kinds of arms, see Holdsworth. vol. v, p. 304; vol. viii, p. 353.

[2] C. XI, 15, 1, no. 2: 'Imperator aliquando condit legem et tunc valet contra jus divinum et humanum, naturale et gentium, non ut abroget, sed ut deroget . . . aut contra divinum, naturale aut gentium, et non valet, nisi dicat "non obstante, &c." . . . si autem dixerit "non obstante, &c." et tunc valet, ut deroget, non ut abroget'.

[3] loc. cit., no. 2. The opinion of Jason de Mayno and Alciatus—see Dr. Carlyle, loc. cit., vol. vi. pp. 149, 301—that it was Baldus and Paulus Castrensis who first held this view, is therefore quite wrong. As far as the report of Jason goes, Baldus and Paulus Castrensis seem to have had in mind human legislation only, but not divine and natural law, cf. the passage quoted by Carlyle, p. 149, note 3. As regards the Pope, see *supra*, p. 99.

[4] loc. cit., no. 2.

CHAPTER VI

THE ADMINISTRATION OF LAW

I

THE central theme of Lucas's doctrine of legal administration is the conception that it is through coercive means that the idea of justice finds its practical realization and adequate expression. Judgement properly so called is solely that judicial decision which embodies and incarnates the idea of justice. The abstract idea of justice manifests itself in the judgement which, in its turn, commands authority precisely because the idea of justice is embodied in it. Judgements divorced from the idea of justice or in obvious disagreement with the notion of justice are devoid of any validity or authority. Lucas expresses this leading thought in these words: 'Judicium secundum propriam significationem nominis dicit denuntiationem juris sive justitiae'.[1] Through their concrete pronouncement backed by the coercive power of the body politic, the judiciary realize the idea and aim of law. They hypostatize, in their judgements, the idea of justice, upon which the concept of law rests. The judge is, so to speak, the mouthpiece of the law. It is he who transmutes the abstract legal term into a living reality, thereby making concrete what before was abstract.

Through the authoritative statement of the 'jus' in the concrete case, the judge's decision is declaratory in its character, Lucas holds; that is to say, he lays down what is right and just for the case in question, a conclusion which he draws from the application of the abstract legal rule to the concrete set of circumstances. Lucas conceives the judge primarily as an agency 'quasi jus dicens', because his interpretation and application, by opening up new vistas of legal thinking, give new shades of meaning to the law. It is in recognition of this half-creative activity on the part of the judge that Lucas is prompted to compare him with the legislator. He says that, superficially at least, there is some resemblance between the judge and the legislator, for both are engaged in the service of justice, although their common feature is at the same time their distinguishing criterion. Legislation is concerned, Lucas says, with the formulation of the abstract legal rule, judgement with the application of this rule to the concrete case; the character of the former is constitutive, of the latter declarative; the former establishes a universal, abstract regulation directed towards the future,[2] the latter contains its realization through application to the con-

[1] C. X, 70, 4, no. 6.
[2] C. XI, 26, 1, no. 8: 'Legislationes sunt de futuris et in universali'.

crete case.[1] The legislator creates the jural precept formulated on the basis of, and permeated with, the spirit of justice; the judge administers the same precept, and herewith gives real and coercive effect to the idea of justice.

In the eyes of Lucas, strict adherence to the law by the judge is the indispensable requirement for the realization of justice, because law is the only social force and institution in which the idea of justice finds articulate expression. That is the reason why our author insists that it is the duty of the judge to base his decision purely and solely on the law, and that is why he strongly deprecates any arbitrary decisions: 'Hoc autem signanter attendas, quod judex non debet judicare arbitrio suo, id est, prout sibi videtur . . . sed juxta leges et jura pronuntiare debet'.[2] The realization of the idea of justice is the paramount duty of the judge; he cannot realize this idea unless he strictly adheres to the manifestation of justice—that is to say, the law. Furthermore, this duty of strict adherence to the law is stressed by our jurist, in that he invites the judge to bear in mind that his individual opinion of the law should not bear upon its realization; his duty consists of delivering judgement on the basis of the law. The judge may not blend his judgement with his own private opinion or personal views on social issues. His office requires him to be simply the vehicle through which the idea of justice realizes itself, and law, because backed by the coercive power of the body politic, becomes an effective means for ordering social life. The idea of the reign of law, we may safely assume, furnishes the material basis of Lucas's thought. Not without reason, he adds, does he expound this thesis, since the law is the gift of God, and its disregard appears to him as a perversion of the divine order of things brought about by this divine gift and invention:

> Bonus judex nihil ex arbitrio suo facit . . . qui judicat, non suae voluntati obtemperare debet, sed tenere quod legum est. Nec immerito: quoniam per Imperatores leges humano generi Deum distribuisse manifestum est . . . nihil debent contrarium ex arbitrio suo dicere . . . postquam enim factae sunt leges, non de eis, sed secundum eas judicandum est.[3]

Since the judge speaks on behalf of the law in his decision, he is conceived by Lucas as delving into the very roots of human affairs and social interests. The inference he draws from this important function of the judge as administrator of justice leads him to postulate the requirement—not always adhered to at his time outside the Kingdom of Sicily—of the scientific training of the judge and of his complete familiarity with positive law. Not only the judge's

[1] Judges decide, Lucas says, 'de praesentibus et determinatis ad quod est amare vel odiri et quibus proprium commodum annexum est saepe', loc. cit. He notes, furthermore, that 'legislationes fiunt ex consideratis ex multo tempore, judicia autem ex subito et suborto'.

[2] C. XII, 49, 2, no. 11. This theme is repeated in many places.

[3] C. X, 52, 6. no. 7.

function as the practical executor of justice, but also his immense social responsibility and the danger that accrues to society from a misapplication, or lack of knowledge, of the law prompts Lucas to stipulate this requirement. In the metaphor of Justinian, he states that requirement in these words : ' Jura omnia in scriniis sui pectoris esse censentur '.[1] The judge, moreover, should be fully versed in contemporary doctrine and should penetrate into the texture of the law and the inner structure of legal thought ; his analyses should integrate the theory of law.[2] There is nothing more abhorrent to Lucas than a presumptuous and self-righteous attitude on the part of the judges: ' Nihil iniquius est quam impia sapere et sapientioribus quidem doctoribus non credere '.[3] If they were not scientifically trained, judges would be incapable of coping with their task of interpreting the law—and interpretation necessitates going behind the letter of the law and proceeding to its fundamental purpose and its principles. For there is no law, Lucas points out, which would meet all situations—' nulla lex ', he says, realizing the inadequacy of statutory enactments, ' videtur ad omnia sufficienter promulgari '[4]—and thus every law stands in need of its interpretation ' ut ad naturae varietatem et eius machinationes sufficiat '.[5] It is admittedly difficult, Lucas holds, to proceed safely through the labyrinth of the law and to discern clearly and to separate its intricate materials. Therefore, the interpreter has to go right down to the fundamental premisses : ' Difficile est silvam legis ingresso singularum quaestionum materias segregare, cum altera sic alteram ramulis quibusdam attingat, ut sine alterius inchoatione coepta nequeat explicari '.[6] The untrained judge, then, could never perform this task of interpretation by which he must discover the idea and meaning of the law : ' Hanc (scil. interpretationem) non facit nisi is, qui summe peritus '.[7] Lucas compares the untrained judge with a captain of a ship who ' remum tenere non novit ', and adds one of his typical remarks : ' Ergo quasi sal infatuatum a porcis conculcandum est '.[8] Accordingly, judges who prove themselves incapable of carrying out their duties should be mercilessly removed.[9] The untold harm

[1] C. X, 31, 33, no. 42.

[2] ' Item non debent indigere doctrina, sed aliorum esse doctores ', loc. cit., no. 38.

[3] loc. cit., no. 38.

[4] C. XII, 15, 1, no. 8.

[5] loc. cit., no. 8.

[6] loc. cit., no. 8.

[7] loc. cit., no. 8.

[8] C. X, 31, 33, no. 38.

[9] ' Nullus enim constituendus est judex, nisi sit peritus in jure. Etiam promotus ob defectum scientiae removendus est . . . nam populus, qui non habuit scientiam, ductus est in captivitatem . . . nihil autem tam indignum et impiissimum est quam ignorari jura et leges a magistratibus, qui in re publica praesunt . . . scientia est donum Dei,' loc. cit., no. 37.

The fact must be borne in mind that judges were appointed only for a certain period, usually one year. In order to secure independence and impartiality of the judge, who was, as a rule, a ' foreigner '—that is, no native of the province within which he had jurisdictional powers—judgeships were not permanent appointments. On the whole question see the exhaustive treatment by W. Engelmann, *Die Wiedergeburt der Rechtskultur in Italien*, pp. 53–72.

that untrained judges may do to society is made clear to Lucas's readers: 'Nemo amplius nocet quam qui perverse agens nomen et administrationem justitiae ac judicantis habet. Quis autem hoc poterit nisi peritus in jure.' [1] Following Lucas's train of thought, we may refer to his conception of the social purpose of law which bestows equality on the citizens; we have further noted that he considers law as the mightiest protection of the socially weak and inferior. The same train of thought is revealed in his conception of the judge as the true and efficient protector of citizens who would otherwise be left at the mercy of those members of society who wield great power and strong influence: 'Leges et earum ministri utiliores sunt pauperi et impotenti quam diviti et potenti'.[2] On the other hand, the office of the judge demands an inflexible attitude towards the supplications of the litigants and an impartial view of the implications of the concrete case. This function of the judge is again only the counterpart of the unbiased nature of law itself; just as the laws are 'inexorabiles', in the same way the judges 'nec moventur precibus, quin reddant unicuique juxta merita et demerita sua'; [3] or, as he says in another passage: the judge should be, as it were, immovable.[4] With particular reference to criminal jurisdiction our author observes a certain tendency on the part of the judges to diminish the penalty which the law contains as a sanction for its violation. He emphatically opposes this (unlawful) expansion of the discretionary powers of the judge. The judge, having sworn to preserve the law, would not be faithful to his oath if he diminished the legally fixed penalty. Proceeding on those lines would lead eventually to arbitrary decisions.[5] Since it alters the contents of the law, the diminution of the penalty is solely the prerogative of the legislative authority. It is quite different, Lucas says, in those cases in which the exercise of discretionary powers is based on the concession given to the judge by the law itself. He quotes as an example the power of the judge to remit the punishment by virtue of the specific legal enactment.[6] If, however, the law itself fixes a certain time limit, as for instance the period of ten days for lodging appeals against the judgement, the judge is not entitled to grant an extension of this period.[7] He would then transgress his powers,

[1] loc. cit., no. 38. With a reference to the *Civitas Dei*, 19, c. 6, Lucas says: 'Ignorantia quoque judicis plerumque est calamitas innocentis'.

[2] C. X, 70, 4, no. 6.

[3] loc. cit., no. 6. [4] C. XII, 1, 12, no. 13.

[5] 'Credo, quod judex nullo alio casu possit tempus a lege statutum minuere quam in his casibus, in quibus hoc sibi expresse ab ipsa lege permittitur, neque enim judex lege clementior esse debet . . . et cum sit minister legis et juret omnia secundum legem agere . . . non debet legem, a qua jus et imperium habet, in aliquo violare', C. XII, 57, 6, no. 18.

[6] 'Et hoc in dilationibus, quae licet certo modo ab ipsa lege praefinitae et constitutae sint, vertitur tamen in eis concedendis aliquod ministerium judicantis', loc. cit., no. 18.

[7] 'In aliis autem datis a lege, in quibus nihil agit ministerium judicantis, ut est dilatio decem dierum, quae datur ad appellandum, et similes, secus

and would have to account for this transgression. For Lucas, the test is whether the decision of the particular issue is within the ambit of a judicial decision proper (' ministerium judicantis ') or has been anticipated by the law itself. Lucas, however, gives the judge the right to commute the penalty, if he can adduce sufficient reasons.[1] In general, the legislator is advised to issue as many binding rules as possible, so as to restrict the discretionary powers of the judge: ' Quantum possibile est, omnia legibus determinanda sunt et quanto pauciora fieri potest, sunt committenda judicum arbitrio '.[2]

The sole duty, then, of the judge is the application of law pure and simple. He is called upon to preserve the integrity of the law, not to turn against it by evasive and carefully chosen arguments, however much he may think that these make for a better realization of justice than does the law. Obedience to the law is the judge's primary duty. Our jurist cries out, addressing the judges: ' Obtemperare autem non potestis, nisi id, quod in lege scriptum est, sequamini '.[3] Lucas compares the judge with a ' nervus, qui non frangitur, sed plicatur, non extenditur, nec lentescit . . . alias non est judex '.[4] The reasons and arguments upon which the judge bases his (just) decision are those of the law itself: he who correctly applies the law cannot fail in his duty: [5] ' Judex dicitur quasi jus dicens populo sive quod jure disceptat. Jure autem disceptare est juste judicare.' [6] Again addressing the judges themselves, Lucas reminds them that their decisons are to be taken, not so much as judgements of men, but rather of God; obviously having in mind the words of the Gospel, he exclaims: ' Videte, quid facitis non enim homimum exercetis judicium, sed Dei, et quodcumque judicaveritis, in vos redundabit '.[7] Thus Lucas concludes that the judge who proves to be a failure in his office should justly forfeit name, dignity, and any privileges granted to him on account of his office.[8]

In pursuance of his thesis that judgements properly so called manifest concretely the idea of justice, he states that judicial decisions which obviously violate the law, and are thereby at variance with

---

puto . . . in his enim quantumque subesset causa, non potest judex mutare legem, quam servare et custodire juravit ', loc. cit., no. 18.

[1] ' Potest judex cum causa commutare certam poenam a lege statutam ', loc. cit.

[2] C. XI, 25, Rubrica no. 8.

[3] C. XII, 45, 1, no. 53.

[4] C. XII, 1, 12, no. 13. Cf. also C. XII, 57, 6, no. 12: ' Judex debet esse justus et quasi immobilis . . . et non se flectet contra legem, sed eius integritatem custodiat '. Referring to Hieronymus's letter *Ad Rusticum Narbonensem*, our jurist says: ' Disciplina justitiae comparatur nervo, qui flectitur, sed non frangitur nec abbreviatur nec elongatur ', C. XII, 59, 7, no. 4.

[5] This point was of very great importance as regards the judge's liability for any miscarriage of justice, see *infra*, pp. 134–6.

[6] C. X, 31, 33, no. 2.

[7] loc. cit., no. 3.

[8] ' Si ergo non dicit jus vel justitiam non reddit, sed injuriam et injustitiam agit, furtis etiam se ac sceleribus maculando, nomen optimae dignitatis et privilegium perdit ', C. XII, 1, 12, no. 13.

justice, should be deprived of any legal effect: a palpable violation of the law—that is to say, judgements which flatly disregard law and justice—should be rendered incapable of practical execution. Moreover, no duty should be incumbent on anyone to carry out the judicial command contained in the decision, once the certainty is established that it plainly opposes the law: 'Ubi certum est, vel esse potest, quod judicis praeceptum justitiam non contineat, licitum est, non sibi obedire'.[1] In doubtful cases, however, the command of the judge has to be obeyed. But Lucas goes a step farther. He asserts that every private citizen has the right to resist any official, and consequently also the judge, when his decision or official enactment definitely opposes the law: 'Privatus potest impune resistere officiali, cum aliquid facit contra jura . . . et hoc quando certum est ipsum inique agere et manifeste contra leges. In dubio autem obediendum est judici.'[2] He adds that resistance includes the use of force: 'Dic, quod resistere comprehendit etiam actum manualem'. The theoretical justification for his view he finds in the fundamental juristic identity of the unlawful official action and the violation of the law by the robber: 'Tale judicium simile est violentiae latronum'.[3] Since self-defence and resistance against the robber are conceded to everyone, no reason can be adduced, Lucas declares, for denying the same right against the official or judge 'in tali casu'. On the other hand, the unjust treatment of a private individual by any official entails the automatic and authoritative intervention of the judge, who then appears in the rôle of a guardian of public order. Even without a special request from the party concerned, he must act by virtue of his official function, provided that the public interest is affected by the wrong the official has inflicted on the citizen. In cases which concern the private interest only, the individual should report his grievance to the judge, who will remedy the wrong: 'Si quis opprimatur ab aliquo officiali, potest recursum habere ad quemcumque judicem, ut mala acta faciat emendari'.[4] His official and automatic intervention in cases of public interest is based on his function as the guardian of law and public order.[5] The condition, however, is that the judge appealed to or the officially intervening judge is not subordinated to the

[1] C. X, 15, no. 19.
[2] loc. cit., no. 9.
[3] loc. cit., no. 13.
[4] He continues: 'Nam regulariter spectat ad judices liberare subjectos de vastantium manibus', C. XII, 61, 2, no. 2.

The function of every official is that he is useful to the whole community, see C. X, 1, 5, no. 15: 'Officiales dicti sunt ab officio, qui nulli officiunt, omnibus vero prosunt'.

[5] He asks if the judge can intervene 'absque petitione illorum, qui patiuntur injurias?' Although it might seem that they had no right of intervention, the question must be answered in the affirmative, 'ex eo, quod hoc respicit publicam utilitatem, quae attendenda et praeferenda est. Interdum officium judicis concernit publicam utilitatem et tunc debet ipsam judex sine postulatione partium expedire,' C. XII, 61, 2, no. 3.

official, who may also be a judge; the preservation of hierarchical authority may clearly be discerned as the reason for this condition.[1]

A further consequence of the unlawful judicial decision is the judge's liability for the miscarriage of justice: 'Judex, qui aut justitiam facere negligit aut jus scriptum ignorat et sic litigantes offendit, dicitur facere litem suam et punitur'.[2] The details will be discussed later.

The immense responsibility of the judge and the sublime nature of his office as the instrument which puts into effect the highest moral virtue, justice, necessitates his endowment with qualities of character which, as Lucas reminds his readers, only a 'nobilis vir' possesses. Nobility of mind and character rather than nobility of birth is the human prerequisite for any judge who deserves the epithet 'laudabilis judex'.[3] Lucas enumerates some of the qualities which, in his opinion, make up a 'nobilis vir' and which those to whom the administration of justice is entrusted are expected to have: impartiality, firmness of character, humanity, benevolence, caution, prevision, objectivity, liberal-mindedness, a genuine desire to render justice, an innate hatred of injustice, freedom from prejudice, absence of a presumptuous mind, an urge to aid those in distress—these are some of the general human qualities which should form the make-up of a 'laudabilis judex'.[4] Furthermore, the judge is expected to have certain technical qualifications, such as a critical attitude in evaluating the material of evidence, strongly developed powers of analysis and inference, maturity of judgement and skill in the investigation of facts—in short, 'memoria, intelligentia et providentia'.[5]

Before we proceed to an analysis of the judicial functions, we may briefly consider the current contemporary views on permissible resistance to the judge. In the beginning, two main lines of thought can be discerned. One school of thought, originating with Petrus de Bellapertica, maintained that a distinction has to be drawn between wrongful acts of the judge 'praeter officium suum': in this case the individual was conceded the right to resist;[6] and wrongful acts of the judge 'intra officium suum', in which case resistance was held permissible when the wrong was of an irremediable nature ('tale factum, quod reparari non potest'), otherwise no resistance was permitted. The other school of thought, led by Dynus, held that palpable violations of the law by the judge must be distinguished

[1] 'Nisi judex, ad quem recursus habetur, esset inferior. Nam consuetudine induci non potest, quod minor in majorem jurisdictionem habeat,' loc. cit., no. 2.

[2] C. XI, 57, 6, no. 4.

[3] That this is the meaning of a 'nobilis vir' follows clearly from the preceding passage, no. 12, C. XII, 1, 12.

[4] C. XII, 59, 7, no. 16.

[5] 'Ut faciliter non credant . . . et exquisite discutiant . . . ut proposita diligenter examinent . . . ut cum deliberatione pronuntiant . . . memoria, intelligentia et providentia', C. XII, 50, 3, no. 4. See also C. X, 31, 33, no. 38: 'Judiciaria potestas hoc postulat, ut quod debet judicare discernat'.

[6] See the report of Cynus in his lecture on C. VIII, 4, 1, no. 10.

from doubtful cases. Only in the former case resistance was allowed. Cynus combined the views of his French and Italian masters. He conceded the right to resist even in doubtful cases when the wrong inflicted was irremediable—that is, in Cynus's opinion, when no other lawful measures were left open to remedy the wrong: 'In dubio dicit (scil. Dynus) parendum, quod intelligo, ubi per aliud remedium juris potest reparari, quod judex facit'.[1] This doctrine of Cynus became generally accepted, as Baldus testifies.[2]

II

The performance of judicial functions presupposes the employment of certain norms of judicial reasoning. Those norms concern both kinds of judicial thought: the mental process which deals with the interpretation of the law (*quaestiones juris*), and secondly that sort of reasoning which evaluates the evidence (*quaestiones facti*). Both kinds have now to be discussed in greater detail.

(1) All interpretation, Lucas states, whether by the judge, the legislator himself, or by scholarship, should be guided by the following maxim: furtherance of the cause of truth by applying to the concrete case the idea inherent in the law, and thus rendering justice according to the law. The finding of the idea inherent in the individual law is the business of interpretation. The judge can fulfil his function as administrator of the law only when he bases his decision on the idea which pervades the individual law. This idea is to be discovered by legal interpretation which follows certain recognized principles. Lucas elaborates these in great detail.

The office of the interpreter consists, above all, in discovering the will of the legislator, the will that is inspired by the 'coeleste arbitrium'. The interpreter should discard his own views and opinions when engaged in the truthful exposition and explanation of the law. He should concentrate on the intention which the legislator had when framing the law: 'Commentatoris officium est non, quod ipse velit, sed quod sentiat ille, quem interpretatur, exponere, alias non interpres, sed adversarius illius, quem nititur explanare'.[3] The prime task of the interpreter is to reveal the intrinsic sense and inherent meaning of the law; he should keep permanently in mind the old Roman principle that the sense ('mens') and the legal bearing ('potestas') of the legal enactment determine its 'ratio'. All interpretation should furnish a working basis for the concrete judicial decision through which justice should be secured.

Here again the idea of a parallel between legislator and interpreter

[1] Cynus, loc. cit., no. 10 *in fine*.

[2] Baldus, *Repetitio* ad C. VIII, 4, 1, no. 34: No resistance is permissible 'si potest (i.e., the wrong) civili modo sine armis reparari secundum Cynum, Dynum et alios doctores'.

[3] C. XII, 15, 1, no. 10.

emerges. Simplicity of conception and naturalness of expression are a distinguishing mark of the interpreter, just as of the legislator. Nothing seems more repugnant to Lucas than the artificial, unnatural, rhetorical explanation of the law, which inevitably leads to a distortion of the sense and purpose of the law, and consequently to ideas more or less remote from the conception of true and natural justice. Moreover, naturalness means to Lucas reasonableness. Therefore, an artificial interpretation composed of juristic subtleties and sophistic niceties can never, in his opinion, satisfy the demands of reasonableness. The search for truth—that is, in the field of law and its administration, the search for, and the pursuit of, justice—can only be successful when the interpreter proceeds on the lines of simplicity, reasonableness, and naturalness, for they alone are the criteria which guarantee the attainment of the goal—justice. Those are the leading thoughts of Lucas concerning the interpretation of law: 'Veritas rerum,' he says with great emphasis, 'vocabulis et juris apicibus praeferatur'.[1]

Lucas, conceiving words as symbols of thoughts, exhorts the interpreter to draw out the idea and meaning epitomized by the word. Interpretation is concerned with the clarification and elucidation of the idea behind the word: 'Est autem interpretatio proprie aperta verbi aut intellectus significatio'.[2] The will of the Ruler as the legislator is expressed in words which are, however, only vehicles of expression: the means of conveying thoughts and the appropriate method of making public the Ruler's will. It is precisely for this reason that the interpreter has to take the words of the law as his starting-point and to use them as his working basis. For they constitute the medium through which the legislative will can be recognized. But Lucas is at great pains to emphasize that this postulate by no means implies that the interpreter is narrowly confined to a literal explanation: on the contrary, Lucas is anxious to impress upon the minds of interpreters that they should take words for what they are—that is, simply as a means of expressing ideas and concepts. And since without them nothing can be made known, they are as important for the formulating as for the discovering of the legislator's ideas and concepts expressed in the words of the law: 'Verba legis attentanda sunt', Lucas maintains, 'quibus deficientibus nec mens nec aequitas servanda est'.[3] The motto for the interpreter should be that 'non intentio verbis, sed verba intentioni servire debeant'.[4] Not inappropriately, Lucas compares the meaning of the word with the soul: 'Et sicut anima praefertur corpori, ita sensus verbis'.[5] Consequently, Lucas counsels the interpreter not to cling tenaciously to the literal expressions used by the legislator. He corroborates this view by pointing out the disadvantages and ill-effects of literal explanations which, once pure verbalism becomes a guiding principle, all too often entail the loss

[1] C. X, 47, 14, no. 4. [2] C. XII, 15, 1, no. 7. [3] loc. cit., no. 13.
[4] C. X, 3, no. 4, 10. [5] C. XII, 15, 1, no. 9.

of 'sensus veritatis' and inevitably lead to the paradox *Summum jus, summa injuria*. Not only may the legislator have used inaccurate expressions which, on closer inspection, convey a meaning that is at variance with his otherwise clearly recognizable intention, but the words may also have changed their meanings. Accordingly, Lucas advises the acceptance of that sense which the legislator clearly meant to give his law, in spite of any divergent meaning which literal interpretation might yield: 'Mens namque potentior est quam vox', Lucas rightly points out, 'plerumque etiam ipsa verbi propria significatio immutatur'.[1] The interpreter should take into account the consideration that differences in time and place call for differences in interpretation.[2] These differences may require such an interpretation, 'ut (lex) ad naturae varietatem et eius machinationes sufficiat'.[3] The general rule should be that words should be interpreted in the sense in which they are intelligently used. He draws attention to the danger of the uncritical acceptance of the not infrequent, but inappropriate use of words in daily speech: loose thinking and inaccurate modes of expression, rejected by intelligent use, may account for the change of meaning of words.[4] The isolation of words from their context is another danger which frequently besets the inexperienced interpreter.[5] Recklessness on the part of the interpreter, Lucas remarks, is a no less dangerous disposition, because it tends to lead to precipitate inferences not borne out by the actual text of the law. For the reckless interpreter is inclined to give a word an extrinsic and unessential meaning and to overlook the intrinsic idea.[6]

Any legal interpretation which approaches the explanation of law with preconceived ideas, or which boldly departs from the legal text, may aptly be styled 'prava'.[7] Since law is a delicately woven fabric, even a slight alteration or an otherwise negligible addition of words may entirely change its meaning.[8] Furthermore, the inter-

[1] loc. cit., no. 9.

[2] See C. XI, 18, 1, no. 16: 'Procedendum est secundum varietatem rationis; quod enim uno tempore fuit rationabile, variata causa posset esse irrationabile'.

[3] C. XII, 15, 1, no. 8.

[4] 'Cogimur enim verba in eo sensu retinere, quem solent recte intelligentibus generare . . . sensus autem verborum quandoque expresse colligitur, quandoque per sequentia, quandoque per praecedentia . . . non decet verborum definitionem procedere, cum plerumque abusive loquamur, nec propriis nominibus atque vocabulis semper utamur', C. X, 47, 14, no. 6.

[5] See the preceding note and C. XII, 29, 1, no. 13: 'Nedum significatio et rectus sensus verborum, sed etiam ordo, qui in ipsorum praelatione servatur, attendendus est'.

[6] 'Audaci mente constitutiones principum male interpretantur . . . non enim sensum extrinsecum alienum et extraneum debemus exquirere, ut quomodo ipsum ex auctoritate scripturarum confirmamus, sed ex ipsis scriptis sensum capere veritatis', C. XII, 15, 1, no. 12.

[7] 'Prava namque interpretatio dicitur, qua receditur a verbis legis', loc. cit., no. 13.

[8] 'Modica etiam verborum adjectio magnam juris diversitatem inducit', loc. cit.

preter himself should strive after a lucid and concise exposition which, as Lucas sarcastically remarks, would eliminate the need for an interpretation of the interpretation: a necessity too often arising out of the fondness of certain scholars for cloudy and hazy language, for involutions and for their own obscure word coinages.[1]

Those considerations lead our author to the postulate that the interpreter should endeavour to establish a 'shining' harmony ('consonantia luculenta') within the system of law—in spite of the entanglements and perplexities which the texture of the law admittedly offers to him. It is the obscurities arising from these that it is the aim of the interpreter to eradicate. Legal enactments issued at different times and by different legislators not infrequently account for such entanglements. The idea of a uniform and single purpose of law, unfolding itself in the whole legal order no less than in the individual law, of the eternal, unchangeable idea of right and justice, becomes once again the pivotal thought of Lucas.[2] The aim of all interpretation is the discovery of the principles and premisses upon which the individual law is erected. In their endeavour to bring harmony into the system of law by trying to disentangle it from its perplexities, some lawyers are prone to resort to subtle arguments. Those arguments are not, however, without danger, since subtle reasoning tends to produce a distorted, artificial, sophisticated, and unnatural interpretation containing the germs of unjust and inequitable decisions.[3] Though Lucas admits that not all subtlety in reasoning is to be condemned: that which can claim the support of reasonable arguments, thus conforming to the dictates of natural reason and fair-mindedness, may rightly be accepted and called 'laudabilis subtilitas'.[4] It behoves the scholar and the judge alike to employ that sort of reasoning, for both are engaged in the search for truth, which not infrequently necessitates piercing the texture of the law by sharp distinctions and subtle classifica-

[1] 'Clare autem, non involute aut per incognita verba debet loqui interpres, sed ita, quod intelligatur, ut ait Hieronymus Ad Damasum. Interpres videat, ne interpretatio sua indigeat interpretatione . . .', loc. cit., no. 12. Cf. also no. 17: 'Bonus doctor vulgi more loquatur, ut ambiguitates obscuritatesque vitet, non sic dicat ut a doctis, sed ut ab indoctis dici solet'.

[2] 'Imo debet lex confusa in consonantiam erigi luculentam . . . et earum caligo rectis judicum definitionibus insidians exstirpari. Et cum verbum dubium interpretamur, debemus illud accipere in potiori suo significato', C. X, 47, 14, no. 6.

[3] 'In ipsarum constitutione seu interpretatione sic procedendum est, quod a natura non devient', loc. cit., no. 4. See also no. 6: 'Etenim magis placet in legibus simplicitas quam difficultas' (with a reference to the *Policraticus*, lib. VII, cap. 12) 'non debet subtilis ratio, quae ad absurditatem induceret, aequiorem sententiam impugnare'.

[4] 'Subtilitas est duplex, una bona et laudabilis, quae scilicet ex ingenii virtute procedit, a ratione paritur et aequitate non devians. Hanc debet habere doctor in interpretando . . . sic etiam laudanda est subtilitas, quam judex ad veritatis indaginem tenetur impendere . . . judices enim laudabiles et electi, cum ex justitiae examine ad judicium prorumpunt, intus subtile judicium respiciunt,' C. XII, 15, 1, no. 16.

tions. Once again Lucas sees a parallel between the legislator and the interpreter: reasonable subtleties—those based on natural reason, which is the safest guarantee for equity—are the criterion both of a far-sighted legislator and of an experienced interpreter.[1] In the sphere of legislation, reasonable subtleties will diminish at once the danger of loopholes in the law and the possibility of escaping its obligations through fraudulent means: whilst in the province of the administration of the law, the judge will preserve the unity of the body of law by finding out the reasons for divergent legal enactments; provided he approaches the problem 'subtili animo', Lucas says, he will be able 'diversitatis legum rationes excutere'. Lucas draws our attention to the necessity which may sometimes exist for the legislator to speak in subtle language, in order to cover a wide range of conditions.[2] Subtlety in reasoning, then, is all the more imperative, in order to enable the interpreter to discover the true intentions of the legislator.

Contrasted with the 'laudabilis subtilitas' is that interpretation which we may call hair-splitting. The 'illaudabilis et mala subtilitas', as Lucas styles it, is characterized by the artificiality of the arguments and by the desire to make unsubstantial distinctions and classifications, of no essential bearing upon the subject-matter itself. That hair-splitting interpretation is born of excessive, not to say morbid, zeal for arguing for the sake of arguing, and is stigmatized by Lucas as pernicious and destructive to the idea of law; to it he attributes not only the continued existence of the trite proverb 'summum jus, summa injuria', but also a restriction of the free display of the intentions and the initiative of parties in concluding contracts. Owing to the harmful effects of arguments based upon sophistry, the deciding judge should not admit them as defences ('exceptiones').[3] In strong words Lucas denounces that interpretation which is undertaken solely for the sake of subtle reasoning with no further aim in mind, which is devoid of the urge to penetrate constructively into the texture of the law, and which is distinguished by the desire to parade shrewdness and stratagems rather than by the intention to explain and understand the law and its nature.[4] He condemns fiercely those scholars who try, at least in

[1] 'Ordinata et rationalis subtilitas est habenda in conditione legum et causarum decisione . . . fraudulentibus actibus proprium est legis resistere subtilis . . . decet enim ad decisionem quaestionum perspicuo jure procedere . . . et diligenter indagare . . . subtilique animo diversitatis legum rationes excutere . . .', loc. cit., no. 16.

[2] 'Et ideo decuit leges obscura eloquentia interdum scribi, ut in eis proficere noster intellectus, non solum inventione, sed etiam exercitatione deberet, prout etiam de divina scriptura dicit Augustinus, quarto de doctrina Christiana', loc. cit., no. 16.

[3] 'Et ideo tales subtilitates a judicibus non admittuntur', loc. cit., no. 17.

[4] He adopts the words of St. Peter Damian and exclaims: 'Illud, quod scribit Petrus Ravennas in quodam sermone: "Odibilius nihil est subtilitate, ubi est sola subtilitas, quid enim prodest in illis expendere dies suos, quae nec domi, nec militiae nec in foro nec in claustro nec in curia nec in ecclesia nec alicubi prosunt"', loc. cit., no. 17.

the lecture-hall, to impress the minds of the students of law with their own hair-splitting arguments, unintelligible to their hearers, and entirely useless from the point of view of creative legal science.[1]

Lucas regards analogical interpretation as an instance of the extension of the specific idea (*ratio*) underlying a particular law to cases which are not directly covered by the explicit declaration of the legislator. The judge is entitled to resort to this method of interpretation when the legal text and the purview of the enactment admit of the conclusion that the specific idea and purpose of the law apply to the case under consideration, although it is not covered by the explicit wording of the enactment. Similitude justifies this procedure: 'Ubi enim eadem vel major est ratio, trahitur lex ad casum similem etiam non expressum'.[2] This extension is permissible on the ground that the legislator, had he known of the concrete set of circumstances, would have proceeded likewise.[3] It is the idea behind the law which warrants its extension to cases not explicitly embraced by the legal text, but whose application is justified from the wider viewpoint of the whole legal order.[4] The employment of the logical figure 'a majori ad minus' and its counterpart is only a further step in this method of reasoning. Lucas treats these figures on the pattern of a *multo minus* and *multo magis* relationship.[5] A logical conclusion of this kind may be based either

[1] 'Sunt nonulli, qui in legibus nihil abscuritatis habentibus ingerunt quaestionem ex studio et ad suam intentionem obscuritatem introducunt . . . et hi vocantur callidi et fatui . . . hi sunt, qui grandi aut torto naso, &c. . . .', loc. cit., no. 17, see *supra*, ch. II, p. 20.

The same objections hold good with regard to the mechanical interpretation of law which often leads to the paradox *summum jus, summa injuria*, cf. no. 2 of this passage and C. X, 76 Rubrica no. 11: 'Decidere quippe quaestiones non per casum legis expressum, sed per argumenta legalia et exquisitas rationes contra manifestam aequitatem, vel quia ex personarum et rerum qualitatibus ratio contrarium suaderet, non multum reputo sapientis'.

[2] C. XII, 15, 1, no. 15. See also no. 14: 'Extendere potest etiam doctor, ubi eadem est ratio et omnimoda similitudo, si tamen coaptatur id verbis et menti'.

[3] 'Idem jus servandum est, licet statutum non sit, quia verisimile est statutum fuisse, si hoc quaesitum fuisset', C. X, 5, 2, no. 9.

[4] This conception was already expressed by Dynus de Mugellano, *De regulis juris*, reg. 88, no. 22: 'Mihi autem videtur'—he disagrees with the gloss on this point—'quod cum mens nihil aliud sit quam ratio, quae legislatorem movit, tunc verba legis non extendantur nisi ad eum casum, ad quem extendatur ratio'. The gloss laid down that only a 'ratio scripta' may justify an extension of a law to other cases, and hence a deviation from the actual wording of the legal text, see gloss on C. I, 14, 5; but, as far as I could see, the gloss was rejected.

[5] Contemporary scholarship spoke usually of an extensive and a declarative (restrictive) interpretation. See, e.g., Jacobus Butrigarius: 'Si mens se habet in plus quam verba et tunc: aut verba possunt extendi ad id, quod mens licet improprie extenditur, et talis interpretatio dicitur extensiva . . . si autem mens se habet in minus quam verba, restringuntur verba ad mentem, et hoc appellatur interpretatio declarativa', D. 1, 1, 29, no. 4. See also my remarks in *Revue d'Histoire du Droit*, vol. xvii, pp. 65–9.

on the subject-matter itself, or on the legal argument, or on the text of the law.[1] According to Lucas, the legislator is at full liberty to lay down legal rules by way of examples. It is then the business of the interpreter to detect whether the actual case, though not covered by any of the exemplifications of the law, is still governed by the 'ratio' underlying the law: 'Sufficit enim legislatori aliqua enumerare gratia exempli, et constitutio legis tunc ad etiam non expressa trahenda est, si tamen eadem ratio est'.[2] But Lucas utters a warning against an interpretation which in fact amounts to a correction or amendment of the law—a danger against which the interpreter using the analogical method must guard himself. Correction or amendment of the law, since it constitutes new law, is the office of the legislator, never of the interpreter.[3] Similarly, creation of legal fictions is the sole prerogative of the legislator. The judge has to apply fictions, but cannot validly create them, because they change truth into falsehood. Only the Ruler, by virtue of his legislative omnipotence, can lay down fictions: 'Solus princeps fingit, quod in rei veritate non est'. These considerations apply, however, only to genuine legal fictions—that is, to *praesumptiones juris ac de jure* which do not admit of any proof to the contrary.[4] The analogical interpretation comprises also the figure of the 'argumentum a contrario'. Lucas does not raise any objections against the employment of this kind of interpretation, and says that argumentation 'a contrario sensu' is valid.[5] But can the reverse be inferred only from the wording of the legal text or from its underlying sense also? 'An autem argumentum a contrario sensu procedat ex significatu verborum vel ex subaudito intellectu?'[6] He refers us to Jacobus Butrigarius, whose theory our jurist adopts. The legal text itself may provide the basis for an argumentation 'ex contrario sensu', when a conditional clause is employed in the legal text, because the lapse of the conditional disposition brings about the opposite proposition. But if there is no such conditional clause—'dictio "si"'—the interpreter is permitted to assume the reverse 'ex subaudito intellectu', as long as the 'ratio' is still preserved.

Lucas realizes that cases frequently occur which cannot be decided on the strength of positive law or dealt with by any legal rule and in which no admissible method of interpretation is helpful. New situations arise which the legislator cannot possibly have foreseen, and which cannot be classified under any positive legal enact-

[1] 'Quod tribus praecipue modis vel causis attendi potest, puta ex majori propositione et conclusione, et ex forma vel qualitate verborum, ex majori, quia argumentum a majori incipit . . .', C. XII, 19, 15, no. 3.

[2] C. XI, 54, 1, no. 13.

[3] 'Correctionem non facere potest, nisi legislator', C. XII, 15, 1, no. 14.

[4] See C. XI, 70, 5, no. 42: 'Ubicumque lex aliquid praesumit et probationem contrariam non admittit, quinimo ex vigore huiusmodi potestatis cedit naturae veritas potentiae fictionis'.

[5] C. X, 31, 45, no. 5.

[6] loc. cit., no. 5.

ment without distorting or correcting the law. On the other hand, the judge has no power to refuse judgement by reason of the silence of the law. In deciding cases of this kind the judge assumes the rôle of the legislator himself: his criterion is the 'arbitrium boni viri' and the basis of his decision is equity. The interpreter should bear in mind the consequences and effects of his decision, the exigencies of time and place, the character of cause and person involved: 'In casibus quidem, in quibus jus non invenitur expressum, procedendum est aequitate servata, ut semper in humaniorem partem judex inclinet, prout postulant loca et tempora et personae'.[1] Here again Lucas is anxious to stress the need for natural conceptions and simple reasoning—the safest guides for attaining the aim of all administration of the law.[2]

Viewed against the background of contemporary scholarship, Lucas's doctrine of interpretation appears at once more elaborate and more cautious than that of other jurists. Although there is no fundamental discrepancy between him and his contemporaries, the latter were inclined to neglect the significance of words. They were, above all, concerned to refute the narrow views of the gloss, and in their endeavour they tended to go to the other extreme by over-emphasizing the importance of the 'mens legis' and underrating the significance of the 'verba legis'. Lucas's chief postulate is the harmony of the whole legal order; this harmony should be obtained by discovering, through the medium of words, the intentions of the legislator and the specific purpose of the individual law. The other jurists stressed the significance of the 'ratio legis' so much that the importance of wording and text came to be pushed into the background. Whilst Lucas urges a consonance of legal text and meaning, his contemporaries do not appear to be greatly interested in this harmony. Lucas tries to steer a middle course and to establish a balance between text and meaning. We may profitably refer to some statements of eminent jurists. Cynus laid down the rule that a disregard of the words is permissible as long as the meaning of the law is preserved.[3] Still more outspoken are Raphael Fulgosius—'vis et potestas legis in sola mente et legis sententia consistit, non in mente et verbis, sed in mente tantum et non in verbis'[4]—and later Ludovicus Romanus: 'Sufficit enim

[1] Cf. also C. X, 75, Rubrica no. 11: 'In multisque non potest absolute responderi, quia plura possunt oriri, quae pro bono sunt aestimanda, ideoque huiusmodi varietates viri boni arbitrio dirimendae sunt . . . quare talia discutienda sunt consideratis causis, locis et temporibus et personis'.

[2] We find the same idea expressed by Angelus de Ubaldis in a *Consilium* which is also signed by his brother, Baldus de Ubaldis: 'Adducamus ipsam rerum naturam, id est, discretam et naturalem rationem, ad quam argumentis deficientibus recurrendum est, quoniam per hanc homo est homo', *Consilium*, no. 110, no. 5. Similar thoughts are expressed by Baldus himself in C. VI, 50, 1, no. 1: 'Et ideo ad naturalem rationem est recurrendum, quia optimus legis clipens est ratio naturalis'.

[3] 'Licet offendere verba legis', Cynus, C. I. 1, 5, no. 4.

[4] C. I, 1, 5, no. 1.

menti disponentis satisfactum esse, quamvis non verbis '.[1] It is probably owing to the tendency of contemporary scholarship to over-emphasize the importance of the 'ratio legis' at the expense of the significance of legal text that Lucas warns the interpreter against bold and rash interpretations which frivolously neglect the text of the law and render an explanation of the law that is faithful neither in letter nor in spirit to the intention of the legislator. He reminds his readers that 'verba legis non proferuntur frustra, sed ut aliquid operentur', and consequently 'a verbis non recedendum est'.[2]

The main types of interpretation are, Lucas considers, authentic, judicial, customary, and scientific interpretation. The law is authentically interpreted by the legislator himself.[3] The judiciary are bound to apply this interpretation. Lucas recommends an appeal to the legislator by the judge whenever the words of the legal enactment or its meaning are obscure: 'Si omnino obscura et incerta sunt, recurritur ad eius latorem'.[4] The second type refers to the interpretation which the law has received by the Courts, in particular by the Supreme Court of Justice in the Kingdom. But Lucas emphasizes that judicial interpretation does not, as a rule, limit the freedom of the judge to interpret the law for himself, nor does it exempt him from his duty to interpret the law. On the contrary, no judicial interpretation, even the interpretation by the Supreme Court, has binding effect on any other Court. For the judge is strictly forbidden to adhere simply to the decisions of other Courts. Lucas, like all other Post-Glossators, bases this prohibition on the principle that precedents constitute no justifiable basis for judicial decisions: 'Judiciaria seu judicialis interpretatio', says Lucas, 'non tamen extenditur ad causas alias, quia res inter alios acta non praejudicat aliis'.[5] The judge, as the administrator

[1] *Consilium*, no. 433, no. 2: 'Mentem enim legislatoris verborum cortici praeferre debemus'.

[2] C. X, 3, 4, no. 10. He admits, however, that the interpreter is allowed to depart from the text '*si certum est* de contraria intentione seu voluntate'.

[3] C. XII, 15, 1, no. 5.

[4] loc. cit., no. 15.

[5] That was common theory based on Justinian's dictum that 'non exemplis, sed legibus judicandum est' (C. VII, 45, 13). See also Baldus in his lecture on C. VII, 45, 13, proemium: 'Nota, quod judex non debet sequi sententias, nisi in se habent rationem, et tunc non sequitur eas, quia sit hoc vel illo modo judicatum, sed quia jus ita vult'.

The jurists distinguished between an interpretation which had become customary through judicial practice and through precedents; the former is binding, the latter are not. One statement may suffice. Cynus, C. VIII, 53, 2, no. 13: 'Verum est, quod res inter alios acta non nocet aliis virtute rei judicatae, sed quia consensus majoris partis populi consecutus est, et ex hoc consuetudo resultat, quae pro lege habetur, unde virtute illius aliis praejudicare potest'. Even invalid judgements, therefore, introduce the custom: 'Sententiae nullae in quantum nullae sunt, non sunt aliquid et nullum effectum habent virtute sententiae, sed consensus totius vel majoris partis populi, qui ex his colligitur, cum diuturnitate temporis bene habet of the law, must be conceded full liberty in its explanation and interpretation. In cases in which positive law contains divergent regulations on the same topic, Lucas counsels the acceptance by other judges of that interpretation which the law has previously received. This view is probably due to his desire to have some degree of uniformity of judicial decisions preserved within one and the same territory: 'Si jus scriptum diversimode aliquem casum disponeret et esset interpretatum in uno loco, etiam ad vicinos extenditur'.[1]

The third type of interpretation—that is, the customary interpretation—is binding upon the judge. Lucas argues that, once the binding force of customary law has been recognized, no reason can be adduced which could deny the same effect to customary interpretation.[2] Again, probably for the sake of uniformity of judicial decisions, Lucas advises the acceptance in one province of an interpretation which has become customary in a neighbouring province: 'Talis (scil. consuetudinaria) interpretatio procedens in uno loco extenditur ad loca vicina'.[3] The fourth type is called by Lucas the 'professoria interpretatio'. His sceptical mind warns the administrator of the law against the blind acceptance of the academic interpretation, although in many cases it will come nearer to the truth than any other interpretation, and must therefore be classed as 'probabilis'. Nevertheless, whenever the judge is in a position to support his decision with better and profounder arguments, he is at full liberty to deviate from the doctrinal interpretation, for nobody is compelled to 'stare verbis magistri'.[4] But, if in doubt, he is well advised to adhere to the academic interpretation.[5]

Lucas's principles of interpretation, which we have summarized, should not only govern the interpretation of law in the strict meaning of the term, but also the interpretation of contracts, wills, and all other declarations of individuals which produce effects in the legal sphere. Here, too, the interpreters should avoid tenaciously clinging to the words, but should interpret them in a liberal and generous sense which will ensure equitable decisions.[6] Generally

---

effectum, ut consuetudinem inducat', see also no. 9 of the same lecture. See also my remarks in 'Bartolus on Customary Law', in *Juridical Review*, 1940, pp. 276–9.

[1] C. X, 28, 1, no. 3.

[2] The duty to adhere to an interpretation which had become customary was generally accepted in medieval jurisprudence. See *supra*, p. 120, n. 5, and Baldus, D. 1, 1, 37, no. 2, and C. IX, 1, 4, no. 4: 'Nec minus potest consuetudo quam ars interpretatione sermonis'. The gloss expressed a similar view: 'Si quidem certo modo per consuetudinem intellecta, eius intellectui stabitur', gloss on C. I, 10, 14.

[3] C. XII, 15, 1, no. 6.

[4] loc. cit., no. 6.

[5] 'Professoria seu magistralis professorum seu doctorum', Lucas says, 'non est necessaria, sed probabilis, quia nemo cogitur stare verbis magistri', loc. cit.

[6] 'Verba non tenaciter et stricte, sed amplius et benigne sunt interpretanda', loc. cit., no. 7. He refers to 'verba testatoris, stipulatio, pactum et contractus, sententia,' &c.

speaking, Lucas maintains, wherever doubt arises as to which of several possible interpretations should be accepted, the judge is advised to resort to that interpretation which proves itself more liberal-minded and serves the interests of equity rather than succumbing to an unyielding 'rigor juris'.[1] He is anxious to stress that the 'ratio aequitatis' should always be preferred to the inflexible 'ratio stricti juris'.[2] Interpretation is, therefore, conceived by Lucas merely as a means by which the judge can effectively transplant the idea of equity into the reality of social life.

(2) The other kind of judicial thought consists in adequately evaluating the evidence presented to the judge in the course of the judicial proceedings. Searching for truth and furthering the cause of truth again constitute the supreme task of the judge.[3] All evidence serves as a means for establishing the truth.[4] It is the office of the judge to discover the truth relating to acts and circumstances by appropriately sifting the evidence and assessing its real worth, for the 'officium judicis', as Lucas says, 'est, quod veritas non lateat'.[5] Evidence, he declares, always refers to external matters. His definition of testimony runs as follows: 'Testimonium est omne id, quod ex re externa sumitur ad faciendam fidem'.[6] The subject of all testimony is the factual knowledge of the witness. Consequently, the witness should not be asked whether Peter is the owner of a certain thing, or whether he is a drunkard, or an irascible person. For the answers to these questions constitute a conclusion from certain facts, a conclusion which it is the office of the judge to draw.[7] But, if the witness should state that Peter is the owner of the contested thing, or is a drunkard, or should make some similar statement, the judge has then to inquire

[1] loc. cit., no. 12. See also C. X, 5, 2, no. 6: 'Ineptum est regulam non fallere, si aequitas videatur'.

[2] This somewhat liberal idea appears already in the writings of the early jurists, such as Hugolinus, though they dealt with justice, not with equity, see the passage transcribed by Dr. Carlyle, loc. cit., vol. ii, p. 17, note 2. Azo treats this particular question from the point of view of equity. *Brocardica*, Rubrica 76: 'Certum est aequitatem stricto juri esse praeferrendam . . . aequitatem dico, lege, non cuiusquam ingenio excogitatam'. The reference to an equity derived from the law clearly shows Azo's endeavour to limit the implications arising out of the idea. Lucas, probably for the same reason, insists on the '*ratio* aequitatis' which alone is to be preferred to the '*ratio* stricti juris', not *any* equity.

[3] Andreas de Isernia makes an interesting remark on this point: 'Judex sagaciter debet de cunctis circumstantiis perquirere et diligenter, quia ad eum spectat veritatem perquirere . . . et *ex officio* repetet testes, non ad petitionem partis', commentaries on Frederick II's *Constitutiones*, lib. I, tit. 14, p. 23.

[4] That was, of course, a generally recognized principle, but it is nevertheless interesting to see how some of the jurists reasoned. See Andreas de Isernia, loc. cit., lib. I, tit. 28, p. 49; he speaks of the judge as a seeker for truth and says: 'Ad veritatem semper oculum debet habere judex, quia verum amamus . . . et Christus, dominus noster, dixit, "ego sum veritas", non dixit "ego sum sententia".'

[5] C. XI, 5, 3, no. 12.

[6] C. XII, 29, 7, no. 3.

[7] C. XII, 35, 13, no. 15.

further into the source of his knowledge, or, as Lucas expresses it, into the 'causa scientiae'. It is sufficient, Lucas says, when the witness states that he saw Peter buying wool out of which he himself made the garment whose ownership is contested.[1] That is the very reason, he declares, why persons under fourteen years of age cannot be witnesses, because they are presumed to be incapable of giving testimony about the source of their knowledge. This presupposes reasoning powers involving conclusions and other logical operations that cannot be expected from a child under fourteen years.[2] The whole weight of the testimony lies in the source of the witness' knowledge, Lucas holds with Innocent, Hostiensis, and Guillelmus de Cuneo. 'Tota vis esse videtur in causa scientiae, quam testis in suo testimonio reddit, an sit sufficiens, secundum Innocentem, Hostiensem et Guillelmum de Cuneo.'[3]

The cause of truth cannot, however, be furthered, if the judge is tied by presumptions and other rules restraining his freedom in assessing the worth of the various proofs. He must be unfettered and truly free when weighing up the value of evidence, particularly that of contradictory statements. Only in the most difficult cases should the judge resort to presumptions, by which Lucas means inferences and conclusions to be drawn from certain statements or from documentary evidence.[4] Presumptions in the proper meaning of the term can never be the basis of judgements.[5] Only where direct evidence is notoriously difficult to obtain, such as in adultery, the judge may admit evidence based on hearsay[6] and other

[1] loc. cit., no. 17: '. . . videlicet sufficientem causam sui testimonii reddat sic dicendo "scio, quod Petrus est dominus talis rei, quia vidi et praesens fui, quando emit lanam, de qua fecit sibi vestimentum, de quo agitur". Hoc enim probat casu dominum non ratione primae partis, sed ratione secundae, id est, causae scientiae, quam deponit.'

[2] loc. cit., no. 18: 'Per hoc impubes non potest esse testis, quia non habet huiusmodi judicium, nec est rationis capax'. Lucas refers us for some more explanations to his commentaries on C. XII, 55, 1, no. 15, where he says: 'Et haec ratio, quare non potest impubes testimonium ferre, quia non potest reddere causam scientiae, quam oportet reddere testem, scil. quia non est capax rationis. Item, quia nondum potest uti libero arbitrio . . . nec est consilii capax.' Although this is the general rule, Lucas declares that in criminal proceedings, which involve far greater issues than their civil counterparts, the witnesses must be over twenty years of age, so as to ensure correct statements: 'Non potest minor 20 annis in criminibus testis esse, at in civili sufficit aetas 14 annorum', C. XI, 65, 4, no. 6.

[3] C. XII, 35, 13, no. 17. He could also have referred to Cynus, C. IV, 20, 4, who said: 'Si non reddit causam sui dicti rationabiliter, non valet (scil. testimonium)'.

[4] 'Ubi difficiles et quasi impossibiles sunt probationes testium vel instrumentorum', shall the judge resort to presumptions, C. X, 26, 1, no. 16. See also C. XII, 29, 7, nos. 4–16, where he has a long discussion on the scope of the testimony of testamentary witnesses.

[5] 'Ex praesumptionibus nemo damnatur', C. XII, 50, 3, no. 13.

[6] It should be pointed out that, in medieval England, hearsay evidence was never admissible, see Holdsworth, vol. ix, p. 215; see also Pollock and Maitland, vol. ii, p. 622.

'probabiles praesumptiones', but there is no obligation on the judge to adhere to that kind of evidence, which has only corroborating value in the eyes of Lucas.[1] Another difficult case concerns the proof of internal elements, such as criminal intent. External evidence may permit of the conclusion that the accused had criminal intent, but direct evidence is rarely available.[2] Since in these and similar cases no definite, directly applicable rules can be laid down, Lucas declares, the decision of whether certain internal factors are to be taken as proved must be left to the discretion of the judge.[3] For intentions, aims, and the like cannot be 'seen'—'neque propositum neque mentem alterius quis videre possit'[4]—and cannot therefore be made the object of direct observation; these factors have to be inferred from external criteria. Lucas advises the judge to take into account not only the juridically relevant actions, but also time, place, the personal status of the individuals involved, and all other accompanying circumstances which may be of value for diagnosing the existence of those internal factors.[5]

First-hand experience has taught him that witnesses make, albeit not always intentionally, wholly false statements; sometimes they mix truth with falsehood in their statements. This observation also applies to documentary evidence which may be wholly or partly false.[6] It would be highly dangerous for the correct administration of the law, and for the cause of truth and law altogether, if the judge were allowed to fall back on legal presumptions or on rules which indicate under what conditions a statement may be taken as true. 'Et ideo', he concludes, 'non sine ratione committitur arbitrio judicis, quanta sit fides testibus adhibenda.'[7] Consequently, quantity of evidence is not decisive in itself. The sole criterion is the trustworthiness of statements. In case of contradictory statements, therefore, the judge is not bound to follow the statements of the majority of witnesses, provided that he is not convinced their statements contain the truth.[8] Lucas notes that the judge should

[1] 'Difficilis est probatio per aliquem sensum corporis, ut in adulterio, quod non nisi cum magna difficultate videtur. Tunc etiam admittitur probatio per famam et alias probabiles praesumptiones,' C. XII, 35, 13, no. 14.

[2] 'Sic etiam probatur dolus ex perspicuis indiciis', loc. cit., no. 16.

[3] 'Nam perspicuis indiciis probandum est, quae facti qualitatem indicant, ex quibus vir bonus aestimabit, intelliget, arguet, cognoscet et conjecturabitur . . . unde cum super his certa regula dari non possit, necessario fuit relinquendum judicis arbitrio', C. XI, 47, 7, no. 23.

[4] C. X, 33, 3, no. 26.

[5] 'Valde difficilis est probatio . . . ad perfectam autem huiusmodi commissorum notitiam solum ad opera respicere non debemus, sed et ad tempus, causam, voluntatem personarumque differentiam et quantacumque alia ipsis operibus acciderunt, perfectissime requiramus; non enim ad veritatem possumus aliter pervenire', loc. cit., no. 26.

[6] C. X, 69, 2, no. 13.

[7] 'Judex non sequitur plures testes, imo interdum numero pauciores, si eorum testimoniis lucem veritatis adesse conspiciat', C. X, 31, 33, no. 52.

[8] loc. cit., no. 13.

personally interrogate the witnesses, because, in this way, he can obtain direct impressions: a principle, he declares, which is not always adhered to, because it has been observed that the judge leaves the interrogation to the scribe, whose duty is the recording of statements, not the interrogation of the witnesses.[1] Direct interrogation by the deciding judge is highly advisable, he emphasizes, in civil causes, but is to be insisted upon in criminal proceedings. No delegation should take place whereby some other judge is entrusted with the interrogation: 'Nec potest ipsorum (scil. testium) audientia delegari'.[2] The reason is that in criminal matters greater issues are at stake than in civil proceedings. Therefore, all care should be taken to ensure that the judge who is to pass judgement eventually, investigates and closely scrutinizes the details by means of his direct interrogation.[3] The direct impression which witnesses make upon the judge—through the kind of response they give to questions, through their behaviour before the Court, through the firmness of their statements and the like—best enables him to appraise the trustworthiness of their statements:

> Ipse namque judex debet testes examinationi subjicere, ut magis scire valeat, quanta sit fides eis adhibenda . . . plurimum quidem in excutienda veritate etiam vox ipsa et cognitoris subtilis diligentia affert.[4]

Within the ambit of procedure, too, he thinks that way is the safest which involves the least possibility of causing harm to the parties concerned.[5] In criminal procedure it is therefore wiser to acquit the guilty than to condemn the innocent, once the judge has doubts as to the veracity of the evidence adduced to prove the accused's guilt.[6] Lucas advises the criminal judge to investigate most carefully the cause and motive of the crime as well as the personal circumstances of the criminal: 'Sapienter et quasi astute interroget peccata et circumstantias peccatorum'.[7] Direct evidence should be preferred and taken wherever possible: 'Ergo est primo exquirenda veritas et perfectius ex ore illorum, qui rei notitiam habent'.[8] Documentary and indirect evidence should be taken only

[1] 'Quamvis enim judex possit committere tabellioni receptionem testium quantum ad scribendum, non tamen quantum ad examinandum', C. X, 1, 2, no. 7.

[2] C. XI, 65, 4, no. 6: 'Testes in criminali sunt coram judice inducendi'.

[3] loc. cit., no. 6: 'Ratio est, quia in criminalibus gravius est periculum, et ideo subtilius est consulendum'.

[4] loc. cit., no. 7.

[5] 'Igitur, quia in dubiis et perplexis via tutior est eligenda . . . et quotiens nihil sine captione accipi potest, eligendum est, quod minimum habet iniquitatis', C. X, 69, 2, no. 13.

[6] 'Cum sanctius sit impunitum relinqui facinus nocentis quam innocentem condemnare', loc. cit., no. 13.

[7] C. XI, 5, 3, no. 5: He continues: 'Ut capiat vulpeculas, id est, delinquentes occulte et fraudulenter'.

[8] He says here also that monks cannot be exempted from their duty to appear as witnesses, loc. cit., no. 8.

in an auxiliary capacity; 'causa criminis subtiliter est investiganda', Lucas exclaims, because only in this way will it be possible to establish the truth.[1] His complaint that 'hodie veritas quasi est in luto necata' vividly illustrates his dissatisfaction with contemporary conditions prevailing among the judiciary.[2]

The cause of truth is certainly not assisted, Lucas further complains, when the judge resorts to torture in cases in which its use is illegal. Lucas's humanitarian sentiments are too much outraged by that institution for him to acquiesce in it without protest. But contemporary opinion tolerated it, and Lucas is well aware that opposition to it would be of no avail. He therefore tries to restrict its use to a tolerable minimum—that is, to cases in which the law itself admits it. Over-eagerness on the part of a certain type of judge,[3] Lucas holds, is the main cause of the illicit use of torture in criminal proceedings. He reminds them of the Imperial statute by which the judge illegally resorting to torture is to be sentenced to a fine of £20 and to be declared perpetually infamous.[4]

Lucas is at great pains to emphasize the rôle which the conscience of the judge plays in judicial decisions. The supreme principle should be that his judgement must be in accord with his own conscience. Lucas bases this postulate on the dogma—to which, as he points out, the Church also adheres—that the decision of the doubtful case must be left to the dictates of the individual conscience. The Christian Faith would not admit of any discrepancy between judgement and conscience. Any other view appears to Lucas un-Christian. Therefore, Lucas asserts, all legal enactments lay down that the judge should deliver judgements in accordance with his own conscience: 'Nam et qui contemnit conscientiam, non est plene Christianus'.[5]

However simple and clear-cut this thesis may appear in theory, its practical application not infrequently presents a far-reaching

[1] Direct evidence was also preferred by Cynus in his lecture on C. IV, 20, *Rubrica*: 'Probatio vivae vocis magis est dignior quam vocis mortuae'. If there is a choice between statements to be rendered by a witness and those contained in a document, the judge should always hear the witness.

[2] loc. cit., no. 12.

[3] He characterizes this type of judge in the following way: 'Nimis periculosum est judicibus, potissime juvenibus aut inanis gloriae cupidis aut crudelitatem eorum praetio distrahentibus potestatis arbitrariae frena laxare', C. XII, 49, 1, no. 6.

[4] 'Statuit Imperator, quod omnes judices . . . abstineant a tortura illicita . . . judex autem, qui contra hoc fecerit, punitur 20 lib. auri et perpetua infamia', C. X, 69, 2 proemium. We may recall here that Bartolus, according to rumours, had to give up his assessorship owing to over-severity in torture, see Woolf, loc. cit., p. 396.

[5] The whole passage runs thus: 'In dubiis ecclesia potius relinquit aliquem suae conscientiae, quam in eis aliquid contra conscientiam suam statuere velit . . . certi sumus, quod fides Christi vera est, sine qua nulla potest esse alicui salus. Faciunt omnia jura dicentia judicem debere secundum conscientiam suam judicare. Nam et qui contemnit conscientiam, non est plene Christianus,' loc. cit., no. 5.

problem. Not in his official capacity, but as a private citizen, the judge may have acquired some substantial and real knowledge relating to the very case tried before him. And yet, the facts as they appear on the basis of Court evidence may be at variance with his own truthful knowledge of the facts; indeed, the official trial seems to establish facts which are a complete perversion of the truth known to the judge by virtue of his privately acquired knowledge. How is the judge to proceed in a case of this kind? Lucas asks, 'an judex in judicando teneatur conscientiam sequi, an allegata et probata, ubi haec invicem se collidunt'?[1] In accordance with his thesis he maintains that, if he wants to be a Christian and to fulfil the obligations imposed upon him as a Christian, the judge has to set aside the results of the official trial and the facts established by the official evidence, and to base his decision on his private knowledge, which conforms to the truth. Before we proceed to discuss Lucas's theory in detail, we may profitably refer to the generally entertained views on this topic.

Lucas himself draws our attention to the common view, with which he entirely disagrees: 'In contrarium est communis positio theologorum, canonistarum et legistarum, scilicet quod secundum allegata et probata, et non secundum conscientiam'.[2] He mentions St. Thomas Aquinas and Cynus as the outstanding representatives of this school of thought. They try to solve this problem, Lucas says, by introducing a criterion which enables them to distinguish between the public character of the judge's function and his position as a private citizen. The laws governing either side of his personality are different: in his official capacity he is a 'persona publica' and has to take cognizance only of those facts which, during the course of the proceedings, have been publicly proved and established, whilst his privately acquired knowledge is of no concern to his judicial activity: he has to base his decision on Court evidence through which alone facts appear sufficiently proved. It will be well to quote the relevant passage of Lucas:

> Cum enim judex sit persona publica, tenetur conscientiam sequi publicam fundatam super eo, quod sibi constat ut judici, scilicet juxta merita probatorum, non privatam, quae fundata est, quod sibi constat, ut privatae personae, ut dicunt omnes, et maxime idem sanctus doctor.[3]

[1] loc. cit., no. 5.

[2] loc. cit., no. 5.

[3] loc. cit., no. 5. Lucas quotes St. Thomas's *Summa Theologica*, 2, 2, q. 67, art. 2. Here St. Thomas says in his 'conclusio': 'Cum judicium ad judices spectet, non secundum privatam, sed publicam potestatem, oportet eos judicare, *non secundum veritatem*, quam ipsi, ut personae privatae noverunt; sed secundum quod ipsis, ut personis publicis, per leges, per testes, per instrumenta et per allegata et probatas res innotuit'. Thomas refers to St. Ambrose as having had the same idea. Cynus, in his lecture on C. II, 11, no. 3, says that already Placentinus and Jacobus de Ravanis distinguished between the private and public character of the judge. Cynus himself holds that the judge should pass sentence against his own conscience: 'Judex innocentem secundum probata condemnare debet, licet in veritate suam

Lucas strongly repudiates this common view: 'Puto posse melius non sine ratione distingui'. Above all, on account of the artificiality of the argument, the distinction between a public and a private character of the judge must be rejected, Lucas asserts with great vigour and conviction. Deeply imbued with the Christian Faith, he considers the position of the judge before God as the Supreme Judge on the day of the last judgement. There, he says, the judge cannot plead that, contrary to his better knowledge, and therefore against his own conscience, he acted not as a private citizen, but as a public servant ('tamquam alius'). It is he himself who is responsible for all his actions, whether they are commanded by a 'publica' or by a 'privata conscientia'. 'Damnabitur ipse ut ipse', Lucas reminds his readers and academic opponents, 'non tamquam alius et ipse poenas debitas sustinebit nec eas poterit alteri delegare.' [1] There are no two kinds of conscience, and the conscience which the judge has will be his only witness before God: 'Nam quando Deus erit judex, alius testis a conscientia nostra non erit'.[2] He concludes by saying that the commonly accepted view is hypocritical: their arguments, he asserts with great indignation, resemble fig-leaves which are used to hide a diseased conscience; instead of curing the wound, contemporary science covers it with a veil.[3]

It is certainly true, Lucas continues, that the judge cannot decide on the sole basis of his own knowledge. 'An judex possit secundum solam conscientiam judicare', he asks, and answers the question in the negative. Without any further evidence or testimony, the judge could not, Lucas argues, condemn Titius even when he himself observed Titius committing a crime. Therefore, there must be no judgement '*secundum* solam conscientiam'.[4]

---

innocentiam noverit ut privatus, quia non apparet innocens eo modo, quo debet, scilicet per acta, imo contrarium apparet per acta, scilicet nocens, ergo ut nocens puniendus est'. He adds that this is also the right decision according to divine law, as he heard Aegidius saying in a public disputation: 'Dicunt theologi, quod non peccat judex. Et hoc audivi in disputationibus publicis definire per fratrem Aegidium, magistrum theologiae ordinis Eremitarum'.

Bartolus in his commentary on C. II, 11, no. 4, *in fine* simply adopts the arguments of the theologians: 'Et ita dicunt theologi'.

Before the time of Placentinus the distinction between the private and public character was known to the Glossators Martinus and Joannes Bassianus, see the gloss *Authentica* 'De mandatis principum', Collatio i, tit. 4, cap. 3.

[1] loc. cit., no. 10. Here he says also: 'Non debet aliquid contra conscientiam agere, ut aedificet ad gehennam . . . judicium tamen conscientiae suae effugere non potest'.

[2] He continues, loc. cit.: 'Deus tunc judex et testis est'.

[3] He exclaims: 'Parcant mihi tales allegationes inducere, quod quis facit ut alius, non ut ipse, nihil aliud est quam cauteriatis conscientiis ex herbarum foliis texere perizomata et non adhibere medicamen vulneri, sed velamen', loc. cit.

[4] 'Puta judex asserit, et verum est, quod vidit Titium occidere Gaium vel furtum facere, vult eum ex solo ipsius visu absque aliis probationibus judicare, certe non poterit', loc. cit.

The very antithesis of this case is judgement ' contra conscientiam '. Lucas is in the position to refer to his own experience when he was a judge in Ruvo, a small place near Bari. The judge, Lucas reports, witnessed the murder of Gaius by Titius; Sempronius, who was in the company of the judge, was charged with the murder. The witnesses unanimously stated in Court that Sempronius committed the crime: accordingly, Sempronius was proved to be the murderer. But, Lucas holds, the judge should override the evidence and should abstain from passing sentence on Sempronius—' dico indubitanter, quod judex non tenetur eo casu Sempronium innocentem contra suam conscientiam judicare '—because, whatever official evidence may prove, he knows perfectly well that Sempronius is innocent.[1]

In support of his theory, Lucas refers to the arguments regulating the execution of judicial decisions. He says that if the judge who is entrusted with the execution of the judgement has certain knowledge about the nullity of the decision to be carried into effect—e.g., that it is based on false testimonies or documents or that the case was tried before a judge who had no jurisdiction—he is bound to stop the execution. It is precisely his knowledge of the nullity of the decision which forbids him to carry out the execution: ' Ergo majori vel aequa ratione ', Lucas concludes, ' judex non cogetur contra suam conscientiam judicare '.[2] He forestalls a possible objection to his thesis—namely, that the judge who has to carry the decision into effect is inferior to the deciding judge, and could in this way undermine the authority of his superior, with the result that ' regendi frangatur auctoritas '—by pointing out that the inferior judge does not defy the authority, but the judgement, of his superior, which is based on false testimony of private individuals, and the like. To maintain that, in spite of his certain knowledge about the truth, the inferior judge has to carry out the execution, would be, in Lucas's opinion, ' vere justitia nimia, quae improbatur a Deo '.[3]

[1] ' Aut quaeritur, an judex possit et debeat contra conscientiam judicare, cum vera sua conscientia probationibus factis coram eo resistit, puta vidit judex Titium percutere Gaium et occidere, de quo Sempronius accusatur, qui tempore ipsius patrati homicidii erat cum judice in loco remoto ab ipso loco maleficii et verissime hoc constat judici, ut mihi de facto quadam vice accidit Rubi; constat autem per testium depositiones, quod Sempronius, quem judex scit esse omnimode innocentem, illum occidit et tunc dico indubitanter, quod judex non tenetur eo casu Sempronium innocentem contra suam conscientiam judicare ', loc. cit.

[2] The whole passage runs like this: ' Executor, si scit sententiam nullam, ut si lata est auctoritate falsarum literarum, propter quod judex, qui tulit, non habuit jurisdictionem . . . vel per falsa instrumenta vel per dolum adversarii . . . has exceptiones tenetur admittere et supersedere in executione . . . ergo majori, &c. . . .', loc. cit., no. 7.

[3] His argument is this: ' Neque enim decet eum, quem oportet esse subjectum sui examinare processum, ne, dum nimium in hoc servaretur humilitas, regendi frangatur auctoritas . . . secus autem est in judice, qui in non judicando contra conscientiam aut recusans contra conscientiam

Lucas sees a confirmation of the rightness of his view in the condemnation of Christ. The guilt of Pilate appears to our jurist to lie in his failure to follow his conscience and in his succumbing to the clamours of the Jews; he passed sentence on Christ knowing perfectly well that he condemned one who was innocent. He followed the evidence officially and publicly given, instead of delivering judgement in conformity with his knowledge, and therefore with his own conscience.[1]

To sum up: the judge's own privately acquired knowledge cannot furnish the sole basis of his decision. If his own better knowledge of the truth proves the evidence given in Court to be wrong, he must on no account base his decision on the Court evidence. This thesis of Lucas permits us to conclude that he accepts the conception of the judge as a seeker for truth in all its implications. The common doctrine appears to him to thwart the aim of all judicial activity—namely, the pursuit of justice.

In this context it is interesting to refer to a problem which at the time was hotly disputed amongst the scholars of the Bolognese law faculty. Paulus Castrensis reports that they considered an aspect of the question which was different from that of Lucas. They were called upon to decide the problem as to what the judge should do if he saw from his window how Titius killed Seius, and if the official evidence taken in Court did not prove Titius' crime. The Bolognese doctors decided that the knowledge of the judge is of no concern and that he must 'judicare secundum acta et probata, non secundum conscientiam'.[2]

There is one more point of interest. Of what value were the records relating to the proceedings in Court? Could they be considered as a sufficient basis of evidence in proceedings which occurred at a later date? Lucas investigates this problem, which was important from a practical point of view. He distinguishes between criminal and civil causes. If the first proceedings concerned a criminal charge, the records then furnish full proof, whereas in the

---

condemnare hominem innocentem, superiorem aliquem non contemnit, sed privatos homines contra veram sui conscientiam deponentes non sequitur . . . hoc esset vere . . .', loc. cit., no. 7.

[1] 'Huiusmodi etiam conclusionem perfecte colligimus in damnatione Jesu Christi. Scimus enim, quod Pilatus cum reputans innocentem, nimium conatus fuit eum eripere de manibus Judaeorum, de quo Augustinus super illud Matth. 27. Videns autem Pilatus, quod nihil proficeret, sed magis tumultus fieret, &c., dicit saepius autem Pilatus, cum Judaeis egit volens, ut dimitteretur Jesus, quod paucissimis verbis testatur Mattheus . . . de quo Papa Leo in sermone de passione. Excessit ergo Pilati culpam facinus Judaeorum, sed nec ipse evasit reatum, qui reliquit proprium judicium et in crimen transivit alienum. Et Ambrosius super illud Luc. 23.'

We may safely assume that this particular problem later led to the introduction of the legal institution by which the judge is automatically excluded from partaking in the trial of a case about which he has acquired substantial knowledge in his capacity as a private citizen.

[2] See Paulus Castrensis, *Consilia*, IIa pars, cons. 299, no. 4.

latter case they have value only as presumptions: 'Tunc faciunt (scil. acta) praesumptionem, non autem plenam probationem'.[1] The reason for this distinction is that Lucas attributes to criminal proceedings, owing to their thoroughness, accuracy, and wider range of evidence, far greater weight than to civil proceedings.[2]

III

It may be of interest to show briefly some of the fundamental principles governing the proceedings.

Litigations, Lucas declares, greatly resemble war and can properly be termed 'cognitionalia certamina'.[3] They are settled by authoritative decisions based upon the power of reason and justice, whilst wars are characterized by the use of naked force, or, as he expresses it, 'per vim beluarum'. Consequently, Lucas thinks, litigations are more appropriate to the nature of man than wars ('proprius hominum'). This is the reason, he states, why many a regulation concerning litigation is derived from natural law, particularly 'defensiones judiciales dicuntur competere jure naturae'. The general idea justifying litigations is that 'vim et injuriam propulsare juris est naturalis'.

(1) The machinery of the legal administration is set in motion by an act of the judge—that is, by the issue of the summons or citation. It is the first official act of the judge and the foundation of all further proceedings. Any act which the judge performs before citation has no official character: 'Antequam nihil agitur, quod veram speciem et figuram habeat judicii vel instar . . . est (scil. citatio) fundamentum omnis judiciarii'.[4] In civil proceedings the first step has to be taken by the plaintiff who submits his claims—'oblatio libelli'—upon whose examination the judge issues the summons. Lucas says that once the plaintiff has submitted his claim, all further action has to be determined by the only competent authority, the judge. With the submission of the claim the case ceases to be a private affair of individuals and henceforth rests with the proper authority. Lucas firmly insists on this principle: nobody is compelled to appear before the judge unless the latter has issued his judicial command, which need not, as a rule, be written. If, however, the law prescribes a written citation in specified cases, the oral delivery of the summons carries no effect.[5] The issue of

[1] C. XII, 50, 20, no. 14.

[2] See *supra*, p. 125.

[3] C. XII, 1, 17, no. 31.

[4] C. XII, 19, 14, no. 5. In no. 12 of the same passage he says: 'Citatio itaque est fundamentum et initium judicii, ut praedictum est, sine quo superaedificari non potest'.

[5] 'Dic, quod est jus commune, ut quilibet citetur cum praecepto judicis habito sine scriptura . . . est speciale ut sententia, id est, epistola citatoria detur in scriptis, alias non valent isti citari', C. XII, 1, 17, no. 35.

the judicial summons is the first official and judicial action, and is called the 'interlocutoria sententia'.[1] The judge has to refuse a summons when the plaintiff has not stated his claim in definite and fixed terms.[2] The citation must be served to the defendant in person, otherwise it is not valid.[3] It cannot be served when the defendant is outside the province, because the judge has no jurisdictional authority outside his territory with which to enforce the command contained in the citation.[4] Proceedings can be continued only in respect of those claims for which a citation has been issued. If new claims are submitted, a new citation has to be delivered.[5]

(2) Lucas finds a guarantee for the impartiality of the judge in the right of either party to object to the judge on legitimate grounds. The judge who appears to be interested in the cause to be tried by him can be objected to by the litigants. That was a generally acknowledged principle based upon Roman law. Lucas adopts it, but goes one step farther. The common doctrine maintained that, once a judge has been appointed by the supreme authority (Ruler, &c.) 'ex certa scientia', any right to object to this judge must be denied to the parties. This principle was later extended even to the ordinary judge.[6] Lucas disapproves of this restriction imposed upon the parties, and holds that, even in the case of a specially appointed judge, he may be objected to 'ex justa causa'. For this is a natural right, the exercise of which cannot be denied, even by the highest authority: it is a special form of defence of which nobody can rightly be deprived. Consequently, even in spite of the explicit declaration of the supreme authority, such a judge may be successfully objected to by the litigants.[7]

[1] 'Praeceptum enim quo quis citari jubetur, interlocutoria sententia dicitur', loc. cit., no. 35.

[2] 'Nisi autem certe sit petitio, judex reum citare non debet', loc. cit. He adds that this matter is better known to the canonists than to the legists.

[3] 'Hoc etiam sciendum est, quod citatio facienda est personaliter.'

[4] 'Extra provinciam non est facienda citatio, quamvis sciatur, ubi sit is, qui citandus est'; he implicitly adopts the decretal 'Pastoralis cura', *Clem.* ii, xi, 2: Cynus rejected it as yet another error of the canonists, Bartolus half-heartedly accepted it (C. I, 3, 31 and D. 48, 17, 1).

[5] 'Haec autem nota, quod si aliquis citetur in causa super uno articulo, interim ad alios actus contra eum procedi non potest, nisi iterum citetur.'

[6] The elder doctrine adhered to the view that the ordinary judge can also be objected to by the parties. This view was held in particular by Jacobus de Arena and Martinus. See Cynus, in his lecture on C. III, 1, 16, no. 3: 'Alii, ut Jacobus de Arena videntur sentire, quod ordinarius possit recusari cum causa. Et sic procedit opinio Martini.' Later it was held that the parties can insist that the ordinary judge consults another judge, see, e.g., Bartolus, ibid., no. 2: 'Veritas est, quod non potest (scil. ordinarius) recusari, ut removetur, sed ut sibi aliquis adjungatur'. The same thought was expressed by Baldus and Angelus.

[7] 'Nam licet in rescripto principis exprimatur, ut judex recusari non possit, nihilominus ex justa causa poterit recusari. Recusatio enim species est defensionis, quam, cum sit de jure naturae, princeps in suo rescripto etiam expresse tollere nequit,' C. X, 31, 66, no. 1. The right of defence was usually held to be a natural right, see Bartolus himself, D. 24, 3, 49, no. 4:

(3) The principle of equality, Lucas holds, should be preserved in judicial proceedings through the equal treatment of the parties—no favouritism and no special privileges: 'Quod non licet uni, non licet alteri'.[1] The uniformity of treatment demands that the evidence should be given in the presence of the other party: 'Aequalitas est in judiciis observanda, unde debent ambae partes in eodem loco subire probationis onus'.[2] The examination of the cause submitted to the judge should be carried out when both parties are present.[3] The 'aequalitas naturalis' accounts also, in Lucas's opinion, for the principle in all proceedings—viz., that the scope of evidence should be as wide as possible: the public interest no less than the cause of truth demand the greatest possible maximum of proof. 'Facultas enim probationum non est angustanda', Lucas declares, 'imo pinguius amplianda . . . nam in hoc publica versatur utilitas: et haec est aequitas naturalis.'[4] It is precisely for this reason that, in criminal proceedings, the accused who is incapable of being witness in his own case can give testimony about the other defendants involved in the same case.[5]

(4) Judgement should be delivered after all the available evidence has been exhausted and the proceedings have gone to the very root of the matter.[6] The judge should be 'in mentis tranquillitate', and should guard himself against the influencing of his judgement by sudden emotional outbursts or fits.[7] Probably speaking out of experience, Lucas wisely suggests that the judge should always endeavour to persuade the parties to finish the litigation by a compromise rather than to let the judge pass sentence.[8] Lucas's aversion to presumptions makes him declare that the absence of the defendant, although a valid citation had been issued against him, is not a sufficient reason to presume an admission of guilt.[9] Furthermore, Lucas states, conclusive proof is required to sentence a defendant, be it in civil or criminal causes: in doubt the judge should not pronounce judgement against the defendant, for 'non dicitur quis convictus in dubio, nisi contra quem clare et manifeste constat'.[10] Conclusive proof can be obtained by the unimpeachable testimony of witnesses, by true documents or by a genuine confession of guilt.[11]

'Defensio est juris naturalis, quod non potest tolli'. But he did not consider this item to be an item of defence.

[1] C. XII, 19, 12, no. 30.
[2] loc. cit., no. 30.
[3] 'Causae enim cognitio fit utraque parte praesente', C. XI, 47, 23, no. 3.
[4] C. XI, 61, 7, no. 3.
[5] loc. cit., no. 3. He continues and says: 'Unde et hac ratione latrones de aliis interrogantur, qui alias testes esse non possent'.
[6] 'Ante plenam negotii discussionem sententia non est ferenda . . . sed post plenam veritatis investigationem ferenda est', C. X, 41, 4, no. 1.
[7] loc. cit., continuing: 'non ex furore proferre debet'.
[8] 'Judex, inquantum potest, debet attendere, ut causam prius concordia quam judicio terminet', C. X, 75, 1, no. 4.
[9] C. XI, 58, 9, nos. 1 and 2.
[10] C. X, 31, 62, no. 4.
[11] loc. cit., no. 5.

(5) The execution of judicial decisions, Lucas says, is in the hands of a judge. He is bound to carry them out even when the decision appears to him unjust or inequitable. The judge entrusted with the execution has no right of reviewing the proceedings of the deciding judge. The admissibility of a defence alleging an injustice of the decision would only lead, Lucas rightly remarks, to a multiplication of suits, and eventually to a loss of prestige on the part of the law.[1] But, if objections are made on the ground that the judgement is null and void, and if the nullity of the decision can be proved, the judge is bound to abstain from any further action.[2] If the ecclesiastical judge—who was not allowed to use force in order to carry out the decision of an ecclesiastical authority—requests the secular judge to execute the judgement, Lucas concedes the latter no right to review the proceedings of the former.[3] Nevertheless, although the secular judge in such cases is ' merus executor et subditus ecclesiastico judici ', he is advised by Lucas to abstain from the execution of the canonical judgement, if he knows that it is palpably unjust.[4] It is clear that Lucas wants to have preserved the independence of the secular judge, even when he is a mere executor. We will return to the point of independence of the secular judge shortly. The judge dealing with the execution is entitled to ask for military assistance, if the need arises.[5]

(6) If the trial has begun before several judges, Lucas holds that it has to be brought to an end by the same tribunal. A majority of votes suffices for passing sentence: ' Si dissentirent, plurium sententia obtineret '.[6]

We may now briefly consider the liability of the judge in respect of a faulty judicial decision. Lucas, following D.5.1.15, elaborates and develops Ulpian's thesis of the judge ' qui litem suam facit '. The office of the judge consists in rendering justice through the application of the law: miscarriage of justice exposes him to a prosecution for injury which he has inflicted in his official capacity as the administrator of law. The right to prosecute the judge at the end of his tenure must be conceded to everyone, Lucas asserts, not only to the party which has suffered damage: ' Licentia datur

[1] It is true, our author says, that ' tenetur inferior exequi sententiam latam a judice, licet sciat eam injustam. Nam illud verum in executore, ne lites consurgent ex litibus,' C. X, 35, 1, no. 7.

[2] See *supra*, sect. II, p. 129.

[3] ' Quaeritur, an judex saecularis eo casu, quo invocatur eius bracchium per ecclesiasticum judicem, possit ipsius examinare processum . . . arguo, quod non, et hoc tenet Innocentius et Archidiaconus . . . et idem tenet in simili Cynus secundum Jacobum et Petrum . . .', C. XII, 1, 5, no. 2.

[4] C. XII, 29, 1, no. 11: ' Si sciret injuste sententiam latam, debet ab ipsa executione potius abstinere, juxta consilium Innocentii '.

[5] C. XI, 46, 1, no. 3.

[6] Lucas gives here a very detailed account of the proceedings before a collegiate tribunal; but since he deals mainly with questions of adjective law, the presentation of his views on this topic is beyond the scope of this essay.

unicuique judicem post finitum officium accusare '.[1] Lucas stresses the detriment to the public interest caused by a miscarriage of justice and states that it is the duty of everyone (' omnes tenentur ') to report the judge to higher authority and, if need be, to the Ruler himself.[2] The judge who, after his tenure has come to an end, attempts to escape from the province within which he has had jurisdictional powers, can rightfully and legally be apprehended and taken into custody by the competent provincial authority.[3]

Lucas comprises both wilful and negligent miscarriage under the general concept of a disregard of the law. According to Lucas, the judge is guilty of a wilful miscarriage of justice when he violates the law by not applying the appropriate legal rule, hence warping justice, when he refuses to admit evidence that ought to be admitted, when he examines witnesses in a biased manner, when he passes different sentences in spite of a legal identity of the causes, when he protracts the proceedings without due cause, when he resorts to the illicit use of torture, and the like—in short, every wilful disregard of the law and wilful non-compliance with the duties which he has sworn to fulfil renders him both liable to punishment and responsible for the damage inflicted by him.[4] Acceptance of bribes is considered by our jurist as one of the most abominable crimes the judge can commit. Immediate dismissal appears to Lucas the only adequate measure, but he counsels that the judge, who automatically loses his reputation as the guardian of law and justice, should give satisfaction to those who have suffered through his corrupt judicial activity, before undergoing punishment himself.[5]

Ignorance and lack of legal knowledge expose the judge to charges based on negligent disregard of the law. The miscarriage of justice results, Lucas thinks, from the judge's neglect, after accepting his office, of his duty to become fully acquainted with the obligations which his position imposes upon him,[6] above all with the law he is called upon to administer. For the administration of law does not simply consist of mathematical calculations: the professional knowledge of the judge should be on a higher plane than the corresponding knowledge of the land-surveyor who simply allots land by measurement: ' Magis quoque tenetur judex ', Lucas says in the same passage, ' scire leges quam mensor scientiam metiendi '.[7]

[1] C. XII, 57, 7, no. 2.

[2] ' Imo tenentur etiam ad hoc omnes, ut principi referatur et cognoscat, quod auro justitiam vendidit ', loc. cit., no. 2.

[3] ' Si post depositum officium de provincia fugerit, ante redditam rationem et obtentam licentiam discedendi, potest per provinciales auctoritate propria capi ', loc. cit., no. 2.

[4] C. XII, 49, 2, no. 3.

[5] C. XII, 1, 12, no. 10. The temptation to bribe judges and the actual acceptance of briberies by judges seem also to have occurred outside Italy. For similar contemporary English conditions see Holdsworth, vol. ii, pp. 564–5.

[6] C. XII, 49, 2, no. 8.

[7] loc. cit., no. 8.

Consequently, the satisfactory discharge of his duties presupposes his complete familiarity with contemporary doctrine. But since, owing to divergent interpretations, a great number of legal issues are controversial, the problem arises whether the judge may be found guilty of a miscarriage of justice if he follows a doctrine he ought to have recognized as erroneous ? [1] Lucas thinks that a distinction should be drawn : provided he follows a doctrine which appears to him humane and charitable, the judge should not be held liable for any damage inflicted through erroneous application of the law in those issues which do not concern divine justice and good faith. Even if this doctrine were proved to be wrong, Lucas says, no blame can be attached to the judge who errs in matters not directly bearing upon divine justice and good faith : 'Non est peccatum errare, i.e. aliud pro alio putare'.[2] But in issues which are within the ambit of divine justice and good faith, the judge must adhere to that theory which can claim to be scientifically conclusive, sound, well-founded, and aims at a clear and truthful exposition of the 'ratio legis'; of two theories that one must be preferred, Lucas suggests, 'quae meliori ratione nititur'. Lucas would not even penalize that judge who follows a doctrine which at first sight seems to meet all the requirements of a sound doctrine, but which proves, on closer inspection, to lead to inequitable judgements.[3] The presupposition for recognizing which of two theories is sounder and more reasonable is the judge's training in legal science and legal thought. Consequently, inability of the judge to appraise theories according to their juristic and scientific merits exposes him to prosecution and makes him liable for all damage inflicted.[4]

There is one more point of interest—namely, the relationship of secular and ecclesiastical judges. We have already noted (and we will return to the point later) that Lucas considers the strict separation of ecclesiastical and secular powers as an essential principle and a basic presupposition of a smooth working of the social and political organism. The practical consequence is that secular and clerical judges are entirely independent of each other. Lucas takes upon himself the task of testing the correctness of his views by a practical example. He is interested in the question as to what effects a

[1] 'Quaeritur, quid si super aliqua juris quaestione diversa sit inter doctores opinio : an excusetur judex, si erroneam in pronunciando sequatur', loc. cit., no. 9.

[2] 'Responsio : in his, quae non sunt contra Deum et bonos mores humanior opinio, etiam si sit erronea, si judex eam sequitur, est excusandus . . . nam sic et in his rebus, in quibus nihil interest ad capessendum regnum Dei, non est peccatum errare, i.e., aliud pro alio putare', loc. cit., no. 9.

[3] 'Sequenda videtur doctoris opinio, quae prima facie justa videtur, licet postea ex subtilitate rationis inveniatur iniqua', loc. cit., no. 9.

[4] 'Non ergo videtur judex excusandus, qui ex defectu proprio intellectus et imperitiae nescit inter opiniones doctorum discernere, quae meliori nititur ratione, cum non debuerit assumere officium judicandi, si non viderit in hoc se opportuna definitione peritum', loc. cit.

merely ecclesiastical condemnation of a *cleric* has upon the secular judge. For instance, as a consequence of the perpetration of some crimes, a bishop condemned a cleric to degradation—that is, loss of his ecclesiastical position—and handed the cleric over to the secular judge to be dealt with and punished. Lucas asks, ' an saecularis judex debeat eum et causam eius et crimina iterum examinare ? ' Most emphatically Lucas answers in the affirmative : ' Responsio, de jure civili nulla est quaestio '.[1] The legal basis of his view Lucas finds in an enactment of the *Authenticum*, which provides for such a case and lays down that the secular judge has to bring the matter to an end after his own examination.[2]

This opinion, though strictly derived from positive law, is opposed by the canonists, ' qui dominare et revereri cupiunt ',[3] in particular by the Archdeacon. They maintain that the proceedings before the ecclesiastical judge furnish a sufficient basis for a condemnation, without any further examination, by the secular judge.[4] Nevertheless, Lucas holds, the canonistic view is palpably wrong from the pure legal point of view. The canonists are not in a position to quote one single legal authority, whereby the secular judge is prohibited from examining the case *ab initio*. Instead, they consider the enactment of the *Authenticum* to be abrogated or corrected by posterior legislation, but omit to quote the posterior law. Lucas concludes : ' Quicquid domini canonistae dicant, puto, quod judex saecularis eum debeat iterum examinare '. He admits that the canonists are ' auctoritates insignes ', yet ' non tamen propter eas a textu legum recedendum est '.[5] He holds that a jurist should have every reason to blush with shame when he maintains a law to be corrected, but fails to quote the legal basis for this correction : ' Erubescendumque est legem correctam dicere et corrigentem non allegare '.[6] In fact, the law of the *Authenticum* had never been repealed, and is therefore still valid. The canonists are to be censured for their disregard of civil law, which, as Pope John VIII himself declared, is venerable.[7]

But there are still other considerations. The purely canonical

[1] C. XII, 29, 1, no. 5. Andreas de Isernia was far less outspoken on this point. He wrote in his commentaries on Frederick II's *Constitutiones*, lib. I, tit. 1, p. 4 : ' Attende tamen, quod non omni requisitioni debet parere. Hodie tamen peccatis exigentibus plures sunt praelati mali quam boni '.

[2] *Authenticum*, collatio IX, tit. 6, cap. 21 : ' Competens judex comprehendat et secundum leges litem examinans causae finem imponat '.

[3] C. XII, 29, 1, no. 5.

[4] They assert, Lucas says, that ' acta habita coram episcopo fidem faciant coram judice saeculari ', and that ' consequenter absque ulteriori examinatione sit ad poenam legitimam condemnandus, tamquam de notorio, cuius crimen factum est notorium seu manifestum per probationes legitimas coram suo judice factas ', loc. cit., no. 5.

[5] loc. cit., no. 6.

[6] loc. cit., no. 6.

[7] ' Arguendi sunt doctores huiusmodi volentes contra expressam legem, quam canones venerandam dicunt ' ; he refers us to *causa* xvi, *quaestio* 3, *canon* 17, which contains the letter of Pope John VIII.

condemnation—i.e., the degradation of the cleric by the ecclesiastical authority—may result from some error or false application of the law or some other factors which entail its invalidity. Can the secular judge reasonably be expected simply to adopt the decision of bishops, particularly at a time when most bishops are venal and readily sacrifice their obedience to God for money—' tempore, quo praelati plurimi, licet ex Dei judicio constituti, plus tamen pecuniae obediunt saepe quam Deo '?[1] Furthermore, Lucas draws his reader's attention to canonical degradations which cannot claim the support of the law, because the bishops degraded the cleric ' extra casus in canonibus expressos '.[2] Finally, great issues are at stake in criminal proceedings which make careful investigations all the more imperative. ' Puto verius ', says Lucas, ' cum de periculo hominis et salute conscientiae hic agatur, est in hoc cautius procedendum.'[3] Moreover, the jurisdictional power and authority of the secular judge are not dependent on the ecclesiastical authority, but directly derived from God.[4] For all power in the strict meaning of the term is derived from God, and this idea, Lucas points out, is laid down in canon law itself.[5] Now, if the secular judge merely accepted the evidence taken by the ecclesiastical judge, without any further examination, he would implicitly admit that he is inferior to, and dependent on, his clerical counterpart; he would, moreover, neglect his duty to seek the truth.

Another fundamental condition for the smooth and frictionless working of the judicial organism, according to Lucas, is that judges should keep within the bounds of the jurisdictional powers allotted to them. Interference on the part of judges with matters appertaining to the jurisdiction of other judges and still under judicial consideration inevitably leads to a confusion and disturbance: ' Conturbat enim corporis ordinem totum, qui non suo officio contentus subripit alienum '.[6] A practical application of this principle of non-interference is that judges who deal with criminal matters should keep aloof from deciding civil matters, because they do not belong to their jurisdiction—unless the decision of the civil cause by the criminal judge is warranted by the law: ' Sic enim non debet criminalis judex civilibus causis intervenire ', Lucas says, ' nisi lex hoc mandat '.

[1] loc. cit., no. 11. Cynus's verdict was similar, see C. IX, 26, 1, n. 4: ' Male servat curia Romana, quae vendit praesidatus suos, in quibus propterea justitia est venalis, sed si dici licet, curia Romana habet pecuniam bono et aequo cariorem '.

[2] loc. cit., no. 11.

[3] loc. cit., no. 11.

[4] ' Quinimo nedum saecularis judex, qui habet potestatem suam a Deo sicut et judex ecclesiasticus '. Lucas refers us to canon law, *distinctio* xcvi, *canon* 6, in which passage Pope Nicholas said: ' Cum ad verum ventum est, ultra sibi nec Imperator jura pontificatus arripuit, nec Pontifex nomen imperatorium usurpavit '. About this letter see also *infra*, ch. VIII, sect. I, p. 171.

[5] Lucas quotes canon law, *causa* xxiii, *quaestio* 1, *canon* 4: ' Non enim est potestas nisi a Deo, sive jubente, sive sinente '.

[6] C. XII, 60, 2, no. 2.

IV

As we may well expect, Lucas treats of the judicial organization in the Kingdom of Sicily at very great length. A short sketch summarizing his views on the actual conditions may fittingly conclude the present chapter. As a consequence of Frederick II's reforms the judicial organization in the Kingdom was fundamentally different from that in Northern and Central Italy. The administration of justice in the Kingdom did not lie in the hands of one official, such as the podestà in the other parts of the peninsula, but was entrusted to a diumvirate composed of the 'praeses' and the 'judex', also called 'assessor' or 'consiliarius'. Both officials constituted what we may call a judicial board, and both of them took part in the proceedings. The valid judgement was constructed by the joint efforts of 'praeses' and 'judex'. Their respective spheres of power and function were, however, distinct.

According to the writings of our jurist, the 'praeses' functions as the official invested with the proper coercive authority to conduct the trial. He is appointed by the Chief Justice of the Kingdom ('praefectus praetorio') [1] and exercises jurisdiction on behalf of the King. Lucas postulates 'religiosa constantia' as a personal qualification of the 'praeses'.[2] He need not be legally trained or versed in legal doctrine, but should have high personal qualifications, such as are expected of every official to whom great responsibilities are committed. It is he who conducts the trial, determines what evidence should be taken, and who delivers judgement, for which he alone is responsible. Not inappropriately, Lucas says of him that he has two keys: 'Duas claves habere videtur, per unam quarum intelligitur scientia discernendi, per alteram auctoritas judicandi'.[3] Trial, proceedings, and all necessary examinations pertaining to the cause have to be carried out jointly by both officials simultaneously: 'Audit enim praeses et una cum consiliario causam examinat'.[4] Judgement has to be pronounced publicly, otherwise it is not valid.[5]

The function of the judge is consultative. The 'praeses' is bound by law to take into account the professional advice of the judge. Disregard of this legal duty entails not only invalidity of the judgement, but also the punishment of the 'praeses ex arbitrio regis'.[6] There seems to have been, however, a certain tendency on the part of the 'praesides' to circumvent this duty, and hence to neglect the legal advice of the judge; in fact, Lucas reports, one has

[1] 'Praefectus praetorio', says Lucas, 'repraesentat reverantiam principis . . . creat praesides et alios magistratus vice Imperatoris . . . unde Imperator sibi loquitur in plurali', C. XII, 4 Rubrica no. 1.

[2] 'Sciendum est, quod praesides religiosam constantiam debent habere, C. XI, 36, 2, no. 1.

[3] C. X, 31, 33, no. 64.

[4] loc. cit.

[5] 'Sententia praesidis lata non publice . . . non valet nec sententia dici potest', C. X, 1, 2, no. 12.

[6] C. X, 31, 33, no. 64.

sometimes the impression that the office of the judge is merely nominal.[1] Probably caused and furthered by personal motives and ambitions,[2] this kind of administration on the part of those very officials who are called upon to preserve the integrity of the law makes law a mockery.[3] Moreover, since the judges are paid out of public funds, their employment would mean sheer waste of public money.[4] Nor would that 'praeses' act in the spirit of the law, let alone comply with its letter, who should seek the advice of some jurists who hold no official or public appointment.[5] Apart from these considerations, the unification of two distinct offices in one hand—for that is what this practice amounts to—is illegal and punishable.[6] The presence of the judge is necessary throughout the proceedings, so as to enable him to give his legal advice relating to all the facts and circumstances of the cause.[7] For, whilst the 'praeses' wields all authority and actually conducts the trial, the judge's function consists in the examination of the claims and proofs submitted, in drafting the orders of the Court, and the like—in short, it is he who performs the legal and juristic part of the proceedings.[8] Lucas concludes that the 'praeses' has to take into account the legal advice of the judge in all causes, whether civil or criminal—'in cognitionibus causarum omnium tam criminalium quam civilium'.[9] The 'praeses' would not be entitled to proceed alone without the assistance of the judge, even with the latter's explicit assent;[10] it is true, says Lucas, that in the absence of the

[1] 'Figuratum', loc. cit., no. 64.

[2] The 'praeses', we may safely assume, not infrequently misused his powers for political purposes. It was, we may further assume, for political reasons that he was inclined to neglect the professional, legal advice of his judge, who was not concerned with the political aspect of the case being tried before them.

[3] 'Si praeses non teneretur assessoris consilium sequi, jam tale officium frustra foret inventum, et leges, quae ipsum statuerint, vivae aut mortuae, ludibrio forent', loc. cit., no. 39.

[4] '. . . item assessores salarium habent de publico . . . inutiliter autem talia salaria praestarentur eo casu, quod lex abhorret', loc. cit., no. 40.

[5] 'Non debet praeses omisso consilio assessoris sui vel per curiam sibi dati . . . uti consilio aliorum, cum id sit rationi et honestati contrarium et quod absque tali consilio ageretur, irritum esse debet', loc. cit., no. 40.

[6] 'Improbum et difficile est, ut unus homo duorum gerat officium . . . imo punitur, qui de alterius officio quid usurpat', loc. cit., no. 43.

[7] 'Non ergo sola praesentia assessoris videtur sufficere, imo praesentia eius exigitur, ut eius consilium consequator . . . quod ergo sine consilio fit, irritum est', loc. cit., no. 45, with a reference to the *Policraticus* about the necessity of hearing the counsel of someone with professional knowledge.

[8] 'Officium assessoris consistit enim in examinatione causae, id est, in cognitionibus, postulationibus, examinationibus, libellis, edictis proponendis, &c. . . . cum ipse habeat causam examinare, et de ipsa cognoscere, ergo rationabilius est eius consilio decidenda', loc. cit., no. 43.

[9] loc. cit., no. 63.

[10] 'Nulla autem lege vel constitutione cavetur, quod justitiarius possit audire solus etiam ex commissione judicis et causam examinare', loc. cit., no. 64.

judge the 'praeses' is the office-bearer in name, but cannot actually dispose of his authoritative powers, which receive, so to speak, their juristic and legal integration from the judge: 'Nam praeses absque assessore nomen habet officii, non officium vel eius executionem'.[1] Nor is the judge authorized to perform any judicial acts in the absence of the 'praeses'.[2] In short, the validity of trial and judgement presuppose the joint and simultaneous activity of both officials. Lucas records that this principle is also applied in the Supreme Court of Justice, and remarks that the stereotyped formula of judgements contains the names of the 'Magister Justitiarius' and of the judges partaking in the creation of the judgement: 'Unde in magna curia pronunciatur sic: "Nos talis magister justitiarius et talis et talis ipsius magnae curiae judices condemnamus vel absolvimus. . . ."'[3] Furthermore, the Court of Appeal is composed on the same principle: the place of the 'praeses' is taken by the 'praefectus praetorio', that of the judge by the 'quaestor'.[4]

It is easily perceptible that the peculiar structure of the judicial board created its peculiar problems, particularly the problems arising out of a disagreement between 'praeses' and judge. Lucas devotes much space to a solution of this problem, but a detailed discussion would be beyond the scope of this essay.

[1] loc. cit.

[2] 'Judex etiam per se solus nequeat suum judicatus officium ministrare', loc. cit.

[3] loc. cit., no. 64. [4] loc. cit., no. 64.

CHAPTER VII

THE IDEA OF CRIME

I

PENOLOGICAL investigations have proved that medieval jurists developed the sparse and shadowy Roman ideas on the subject of crime and punishment into fully-fledged theories.[1] The Roman texts merely provided some undefined and ambiguously expressed penological ideas, these, moreover, being dispersed throughout the whole length of Justinian's codification. It was through the efforts of the Post-Glossators that the elements constituting the concept of crime and the reasons justifying punishment of the criminal were systematically and scientifically investigated, the means of research at these jurists' disposal, however, limiting and sometimes narrowing the field of their researches. Nevertheless, their investigations could have greatly profited by concurrent and preceding canonistic scholarship, particularly as regards the idea of 'peccatum', if the legists had, to any appreciable extent, availed themselves of the results achieved by their canonistic colleagues.

Without disparaging the achievements of his contemporaries, we may say that it is largely due to Lucas's thorough-going study and perusal of the canonistic researches [2] that his theory of crime and punishment is far in advance of his time and his theory shows more than one fundamental resemblance to twentieth-century penological thought. Lucas's main thesis—a striking illustration of the progressive nature of his penological ideas—postulates a close interrelationship between criminal, crime, and punishment. In his opinion, it is not the wrongful act itself that justifies punishment of the perpetrator; on the contrary, the external wrongful act is viewed by our jurist solely as a symptom of the internal factors which give birth to the crime: 'Nec factum, sed causa facti attenditur', remarks Lucas.[3] Starting out from this conception of crime, he is necessarily driven to refute all retributive, retaliatory, or vindictive

[1] See, in particular, the works by Professor W. Engelmann, *Der geistige Urheber des Verbrechens* (1911), *Irrtum and Schuld nach der italienischen Lehre und Praxis des Mittelalters* (1922), Dahm, *Das Strafrecht Italiens im ausgehenden Mittelalter* (1931) and H. Kantorowicz, *Albertus Gandinus und das Strafrecht der Scholastik* (1907).

[2] See the remark of Lucas in his commentary on C. XI, 52, 1, no. 14: 'Verum, quia jure canonico multa praemissis rationabilia et decora satis accedunt, ex quo plurima in hoc scripto inserta sunt, materiam ipsam eo jure mixtis etiam aliis melius prosequamur'. On the neglect of the canonistic literature see also my remarks in *Revue d'Histoire*, vol. xvii, p. 31.

[3] loc. cit., no. 5. We may be tempted to perceive in such and similar utterances—which abound in Lucas's commentaries—ideas not unlike those which prompted Liszt to his famous war cry: 'Nicht die Tat, sondern den Täter bestrafen wir'.

conceptions of punishment, and to lay down as his thesis that punishment should fulfil a useful purpose. This purpose can be no other but the prevention of future crimes—' cohibere a peccato ', as Lucas expresses it.[1] This aim can be achieved, he thinks, by the moral improvement of the offender—' ut ipse, qui prius odio habebatur, corrigatur exemplo '—and by inculcating a fear of punishment in potential criminals : ' (ut) alii terreantur exemplo '.[2]

The preventive idea inherent in punishment is expressed in the following words : ' Nemo enim prudens ideo punit, quia peccatum est, sed ne peccetur ; revocari enim praeterita non possunt, futura prohibentur '.[3] This statement, which is reiterated in many places and expressed in Lucas's typically unassuming style, anticipates, by four centuries, the postulates of Beccaria, who was to submit his stirring ideas to a more responsive public. With Lucas the preventive idea of punishment is the corner-stone of his penological thought. If we interpret Lucas's thoughts correctly, punishment should be, as it were, prospective. Here again he sees a parallel between the judge and the legislator, because both are concerned with the well-being of society. Their duty consists in taking measures which should effectively prevent future crimes. The former fulfils this duty by taking into account all the individual factors which ' caused ' the crime, whilst the latter will take such legislative measures as promise, in general, the fulfilment of the goal of all penal policy—namely, the prevention of crime. By attaching strong sanctions to the law, the Ruler ' timorem justum transgressoribus infert '. Besides a prudent penal legislation, Lucas considers a strong and well-organized public administration essential for the suppression of crime. In particular, subordinate officials, who have themselves no jurisdictional powers, are called upon to report all unlawful conduct to their superior ; this duty applies, above all, to the bailiffs, magistrates, soldiers, and policemen. After the above-quoted passage, in which he announces his preventive ideas, he continues :

> Ad hanc ergo justitiam plenius exequendam constituti sunt reges et principes ac magistratus inferiores et sub eis inferiores alii, qui punire nequeunt crimina, sed superioribus ea nuntiare tenentur, ut sunt curiosi et stationarii, ergo in regno baiuli et magistri jurati ac similes.

Lucas lays down the principle that the officials who neglect their duty should be held responsible in the same way as the criminals themselves : an application of his basic idea that there is no fundamental difference between the criminal and the officials who—from whatever motive—neglect their duty to prosecute criminals : ' Paria enim sunt aliquid malum facere et per alios id factum, cum ad hoc teneretur ex officio, non publicare '.[4]

[1] C. X, 16, 3, no. 3. [2] loc. cit., no. 3. [3] C. X, 75, 1, no. 7.

[4] loc. cit., no. 7. He continues : ' Si huiusmodi officiales corrupti precibus, pretio, amore vel timore delinquentium crimina commissa neglexerint nuntiare, eadem poena qua et ipsi delinquentes sunt puniendi '.

According to Lucas, the element which is constitutive of crime is of a solely subjective nature, viz., the evil intention of the wrongdoer. In his opinion, that intention must be considered as evil which is detrimental and destructive both from the moral and religious and from the social point of view. Criminals, he says, ' in Dei et aliorum perniciem debacchantur '.[1] It is not, therefore, to be wondered at that Lucas advances the idea that every crime is an offence committed against society in general and thus constitutes a public wrong. The idea of crime as a private offence is herewith implicitly rejected: ' Ipso jure etiam omne crimen est publicum '.[2] The prosecution of criminals is the concern, not of private citizens, but of society, he asserts. Accordingly, fines imposed upon criminals flow into the coffers of the State, and are not to be considered as a means whereby the wronged party obtains satisfaction: ' Poena, quamvis pecuniaria venit ab aliquo exigenda, est fisco applicanda '.[3] It is true, Lucas says, that the internal attitude of the criminal is sufficient reason to punish him *in foro conscientiae*, because ' Deus enim non ex operibus judicat, sed ex cogitationibus et ex corde '.[4] But human society needs an external manifestation of the criminal's evil intention, and that is the only reason why an external act is required. Thus the external wrongful act is considered by Lucas merely as a symptom of the criminal's state of mind: ' Lex enim opus requirit, sed gratia voluntatis '.[5] The best illustration of his view that it is the internal attitude of the offender, not his external act, which constitutes crime, is furnished by his conception of criminal attempt. In the passage in which he makes the statement just quoted he continues by saying: ' In maleficiis quippe spectatur voluntas, non exitus. Regula illa punitur affectus, etsi non sequatur effectus.' In other words, the offender's action presents itself as criminal precisely because it springs from an unlawful intention, not because it is harmful and unlawful in itself: ' Verum causa, non materia vel exitus actuum, sed intentionis propositum culpas discernit et merita '.[6] For the essential criterion is the intention of the offender: ' Ex voluntate et proposito maleficia distinguuntur ', Lucas says, and refers to Hadrian's famous rescript,[7] stating that ' in eis non exitus, sed voluntas attenditur '.[8] In another passage he reiterates his principle in these words: ' Nec tantum attendenda sunt, quae fiunt, quantum quo animo fiunt '.[9] He declares that however praiseworthy and good an external act may be, it cannot have full moral value unless it springs from a good intention: ' In bonis factis voluntas attenditur, nec enim sufficit benefacere, nisi ex bono

[1] C. X, 16, 3, no. 3. [2] C. X, 10, 5, no. 13. [3] C. X, 6, 2, no. 11.
[4] C. XII, 50, 3, no. 2: Lucas obviously refers to *Matt.* v, 28, when he says: ' secundum illud " qui viderit mulierem ad concupiscendam . . ." '. A similar thought was expressed by Albertus Gandinus, see p. 211 of the edition by H. Kantorowicz.
[5] C. XI, 53, 1, no. 12. [6] C. XI, 52, 1, no. 3.
[7] D. 48, 8, 14. [8] C. XI, 61, 2, no. 8.
[9] C. XI, 52, 1, no. 3, with a reference to canon law, *causa* xv, *quaestio* 6, *canon* 1, para. 6, which contains a similar statement.

fonte procedat, id est, bona voluntate '.[1] The same principle necessarily applies to evil actions, such as crimes: 'Nec potest dici caro corrupta, nisi etiam animus sit corruptus '.[2]

Lucas's thesis that the internal attitude is the sole constituent of crime is best illustrated by his treatment of actions against the 'bannitus'—that is, a person who is outlawed as a consequence of some crime.[3] The common view was that the killing the 'bannitus' was legally permissible.[4] The jurists found the juristic justification in the dictum of Roman law that 'juris executio non habet injuriam '.[5] They argued consequently that, since the law itself permitted the killing of a 'bannitus', the perpetrator could not be punished for his action, which in itself is within the province of lawful acts. Lucas is not satisfied with this objective orientation.

It is quite true, he affirms, that from the objective point of view the action of the killer was not forbidden. But it is not the wrongful act which constitutes crime, nor can, on the other hand, the performance of a legally permissible act be the sole reason for impunity, unless the agent acted 'ex zelo justitiae'. If his action had sprung 'ex odio et fonte nequitiae', he is liable to be punished, even though he committed an act which, at first sight, seems legally permissible. In other words, only those individuals are entitled to kill the 'bannitus' who are impelled by the same motive as that which underlies the law wherefrom the right (to kill the 'bannitus') is derived. Those individuals act, so to speak, on behalf of the law; and this function makes it imperative that they pursue the right with an intention corresponding to that of the law—that is a 'zelus justitiae'. In default of this motive, killing a 'bannitus' is simply murder. The generally entertained view declared, however, that the intention of the killer is of no concern to the judge: killing a 'bannitus' was considered lawful without taking into consideration the motive which impelled the killer. Albericus de Rosciate refers to the common doctrine and practice, and writes that the killing of a 'bannitus' is not punishable, no matter what reasons motivated the perpetrator: 'Vidi servari et statutum (scil. statutum municipale) interpretari, et qualitercumque et quomodocumque sit interfectus bannitus, impunitum sit'.[6]

[1] loc. cit., no. 3. He refers again to canon law, *distinctio* lxxxvi, *canon* 14, which says: 'Nec satis est iterum bene facere, nisi id ex bono fonte, hoc est, ex bona voluntate, profiscatur'.

[2] loc. cit., no. 3.

[3] Albericus de Rosciate in his *Dictionarium* said that just as excommunication excludes the member from the Church, in the same way the ban excludes man from civil society: 'Bannitus suam civitatem amittit . . . sicut excommunicatio dejicit a communione ecclesiae . . . sic et bannum dejicit a communione publica'.

[4] Many municipal statutes expressly declared killing a 'bannitus' lawful, see the statutes referred to by Dahm, *Strafrecht Italiens*, p. 99.

[5] See the detailed report of Lucas in his commentary on C. XII, 53, 1, no. 62; cf. also my references in *Revue d'Histoire du Droit*, loc. cit., pp. 52–3.

[6] Albericus de Rosciate, *De statutis*, lib. IV, 20, no. 4; see also Bartolus in his lecture on D. 48, 5, 22, no. 2, and Baldus, *Consilia*, III, 9, no. 3.

Thus Lucas's view of crime is subjectively orientated. The lawful or unlawful character of the external act is not a sufficient basis upon which to estimate its criminal character. The decisive element is the individual's intention. This is certainly a very advanced view of the *Schuldprinzip*.[1]

Punishment, we noted before, aims at the moral improvement of the offender. No vindictive and retaliatory aims should influence the judge when he tries a criminal case. For he is bound to follow God, Lucas argues, and the ' natura divinitatis ' is utterly opposed to any retributive measures. God, Lucas says, ' non vult mortem peccatoris, sed ut convertatur et vivat '.[2] Lucas is anxious to stress the purposive nature of punishment. There is a parallel, he asserts, between the punishment inflicted by society and that imposed by parents upon their children: both punishments are meted out in order to ensure that the wrongdoer ' ne peccet ulterius '.[3] But the judge dealing with criminals should always keep in mind the public interest, since every crime is a public wrong : ' Hoc solum attendatur, quod vita hominum corrigatur . . . quicquid etiam in his (scil. criminibus) agitur, ad rei publicae utilitatem referendum est '.[4] For from the purely secular point of view crimes are punished in order to protect the interests of society (' ad bonorum custodiam ').[5] Lucas regards an efficient criminal justice as one of the most effective guardians of public order. Delinquency spreads easily, he observes, and, unless perpetrators of crimes are effectively brought to book, society will eventually decay : ' Quare si (quod absit !) publicam solicitudinem vigoremque negligimus, perdit desidia disciplinam . . . etenim vitium propagatur, nisi per correptionem disciplinae correptio subsequatur '.[6] Nevertheless, judges should not punish in the spirit of vindictiveness, ' sed pro commodo rei publicae ac zelo justitiae '.[7] They should mete out punishments according to the exigencies of society and according to the interest of the public. Now, these very interests demand the conversion of the criminal himself into a useful member of society. Consequently, punishments are ' medicinae '[8]—that is to say, corrective measures—and the function of the judge is to attend to the ' wounds ', in order to

[1] It is interesting to note that modern German penal science, before it became the instrument of politics, arrived at very similar conceptions through the theory of the *subjektiven Unrechtselemente*. See Mezger, *Strafrecht*, 2nd ed., p. 170 : ' Aeusserlich gleiches Tun kann das eine Mal Recht, das andere Mal Unrecht sein, je nach dem Sinn, den der Täter mit seinem Tun verknüpft, je nach der seelischen Lage oder Einstellung, in der er die Handlung vollzieht '. The Germans, however, thought that this recognition is a very modern acquisition, see Mezger, loc. cit., p. 168 : this theory ' gehört erst der neuesten Zeit an. Die ersten Anregungen hat H. A. Fischer (1911) gegeben.' See also *infra*, p. 155.

[2] C. XII, 45, 1, no. 44.

[3] loc. cit., no. 47.

[4] loc. cit., no. 47.

[5] C. X, 16, 3, no. 4.

[6] loc. cit., no. 4. Lucas refers to, and borrows, the argument of *causa* xxi, *quaestio* 2, *canon* 2.

[7] C. XII, 53, 1, no. 60.

[8] C. X, 16, 3, no. 4.

cure them, however much against the 'patient's' will: 'Judex quippe debet crimina delinquentium tamquam vulnera, licet invitus, attingere. Nam ea, nisi tacta et tractata, sanari non possunt.' [1] The judge's foremost concern is the prevention of crimes.[2] The elimination of the cause of crimes—not infrequently of an economic nature, Lucas observes—will bring the realization of this aim nearer: 'Cum ad officium pertineat judicantis nedum commissa delicta punire, quinetiam opportunitas adimenda est'.[3] The 'punitive' treatment, which seems to dawn on Lucas's mind, pursues the moral improvement of the delinquent by directing him to ethically good actions. For 'corrigere', our jurist maintains, aims at 'ad bonum dirigere'.[4] But, apart from the alleged corrective influence of punishment on the criminal himself, its aim should also be deterrence—that is, inculcation of the fear of punishment into potential criminals.[5] Lucas does not omit to point to the educative influence of punishment. For the punishment of the criminal gives an unmistakable warning to those who have approved of the crime, although without participating in it and without being caught by the machinery of justice; at the same time, punishment vividly demonstrates the wrongful nature of certain actions to those citizens who are not acquainted with the law. 'Punitionis exemplum', Lucas declares, 'et ad recordationem admonet conscios et ad considerationem cogit ignaros.' [6]

Yet the chief concern of punishment is the criminal himself: it is he who has to undergo 'punitive treatment'. Punishment, thus conceived, presupposes the judge's exact knowledge of the circumstances which caused the crime. It is only, therefore, an application of Lucas's fundamental principle that he lays down the following postulate: 'Causa enim, quae instigat delinquentem, est semper in puniendis criminibus attendenda. Magis etiam causa facti quam ipsum factum inspicienda est.' [7] The motive of the perpetrator is the sole element which designates his act as wrongful. Furthermore, Lucas's view of a corrective treatment makes him stipulate that the punishment should be commensurate to the criminal's motive, or, as he expresses it, should not be 'durius quam causa deposcit . . . imo correctio debet esse moderata'.[8] Wherever the motive of the delinquent expresses no evil intention, no reason can be adduced, says Lucas, to inflict punishment on him. Consequently, the judge is bound to investigate 'qua cogitatione et spe animus ad maleficium profectus sit, quo animo quisque faciat'.[9]

[1] loc. cit., no. 3.

[2] 'Potestas judicialis in hoc statuta est, ut non solum puniat delicta commissa, verum ut prohibeat, ne de caetero committantur', C. X, 75, 1, no. 7.

[3] C. XII, 40, 2, no. 5. [4] C. XII, 35, 13, no. 1. [5] See *supra*, p. 143.

[6] C. X, 16, 3, no. 3, referring to one of Orosius's letters to St. Augustine.

[7] C. XII, 45, 1, no. 8. Repeated in many places, see, e.g., C. XI, 52, 1, no. 5.

[8] loc. cit., no. 3. He continues: 'Cavendum est, ne major sit poena quam culpa'.

[9] C. X, 19, 3, no. 6.

Before we proceed farther, we may profitably cast a glance at contemporary thoughts on the main ideas discussed in the preceding pages. Concurrent penological thought was still under the decisive influence of the retaliatory or retributive conception of punishment, unmistakably expressed in Roman law, which laid down that punishment is 'noxae vindicta'. Following this idea, the writings of the jurists abound in expressions—never used by Lucas—manifesting the retaliatory idea of punishment, such as 'ultio', 'satisfactio', 'vindicta', and similar terms.[1] Theological and canonistic research were also permeated with the retaliatory conception of punishment.[2] In other words, the motto 'punitur, quia peccatum est', so sharply repudiated by Lucas, was an axiom to his contemporaries, whilst its antipode, 'punitur, ne peccetur', was neither expressed nor even hinted at in contemporary commentaries, with the notable exception of Jacobus de Belvisio, who seemed to have vaguely conceived of a corrective (preventive) idea inherent in punishment; but Jacobus did not elaborate the concept or recognize it as a keynote of penological thought. Jacobus said: 'Poena criminalis fuit inventa principaliter propter malos mores hominum corrigendos'.[3] In accordance with the retaliatory principle, the jurists laid stress on the postulate that punishment should be meted out according to the external wrong caused by the criminal. The preventive idea was practically absent in the fourteenth-century penological thought, although the idea of deterrence seemed to have had some adherents. Bartolus, for instance, did not appear to be satisfied with the purely retaliatory conception when he stated: 'Poenas inferre bonum est propter exemplum, ut unius poena sit exemplum seu metus multorum'.[4] But, apart from these sporadic utterances, contemporary scholarship did not go beyond the idea of mere retaliation. None of the penological discussions reveals the comprehensiveness, clear conception, and logical consistency, which are characteristic of Lucas. Furthermore, the lectures and commentaries of the jurists do not show that they had clearly conceived crime as a public wrong. In fact, they had not yet quite clearly grasped the essential difference between crime and sin.[5] Accordingly, we shall search in vain for the conception that the public interest warrants the punishment of the criminal, a conception of so great importance to Lucas. There is nowhere a resemblance to Lucas's idea that the criminal must be punished 'pro commodo rei publicae'. Comparisons of his theory

[1] See Cynus in his lecture on C. IX, 27, 1; Bartolus, Baldus, and Albericus, ibid.

[2] Boniface VIII: 'Judex . . . poenam metiatur ex culpa, ut secundum quod excessus exegerit, vindicta procedat', quoted after Dahm, loc. cit., p. 287, note 12. See also Hinschius, *Kirchenrecht*, vol. v, pp. 643 seq.

[3] Jacobus de Belvisio, *Aurea practica criminalis*, lib. III, 26, no. 5.

[4] Bartolus, *Tractatus super Constitutionibus*, Rubrica 'Qui sint rebelles', no. 1. See also the passages of Odofredus and Angelus de Ubaldis transscribed in *Revue d'Histoire du Droit*, loc. cit., pp. 34 seq.

[5] See Dahm, loc. cit., pp. 84 seq.

with those of his contemporaries are, therefore, of little avail, because he sets out from premisses fundamentally different from those of his contemporaries. We may state in anticipation that none of his contemporaries conceived the true significance of those circumstances, which entail varying degrees of responsibility. This recognition, as we shall presently see, was possible for Lucas, because he holds that the element constitutive of crime is the evil intention of the criminal, and this recognition was impossible for the other jurists, because they conceived the wrongful act as the constitutive element.

The primary condition for any imputable unlawful act is that it is performed by a human agent: the punishment of animals is beyond the sphere of criminal jurisdiction: 'Quis sani capitis diceret animalia bruta proinde detineri?' [1] Animals are not held accountable for their actions: 'De suis factis nullam rationem redditura sunt, quia rationabilia non sunt'.[2] Only man, who is endowed with reason and the faculty of discerning right from wrong, can be made responsible, and has to accept reward or punishment, for his actions: 'Homines vero, quia rationabiles sunt facti et de se et de omnibus rebus, quas in usum praesentis vitae acceperunt, rationem reddituri sunt Deo et pro suorum actuum qualitate recipient aut poenam aut gloriam, et hoc puto verius'.[3] How far Lucas's views are in advance of those of his contemporaries may be gauged from the fact that the 'punishment' of animals was by no means unknown at his time, and that such cases occurred in certain European countries as late as the nineteenth century.[4]

The second condition for any imputable unlawful act is that it must be performed under circumstances in which the agent is free from psychical or physical compulsion: 'Peccatum non est, nisi voluntarium'.[5] In fact, to actions to which the individual is compelled, Lucas wholly denies the character of action; the criminal's motivation is not free. He must be in the full possession of those powers which enable him to exercise his will freely: 'Nec dicitur quis facere, quod facit invitus'.[6]

The constitutive element of crime—the evil intention of the perpetrator—warrants the infliction of varying degrees of punishment upon criminals who have committed superficially identical crimes: 'Unus quidem excessus gravius est in uno quam in alio puniendus'.[7] Responsibility, according to Lucas, varies according to certain circumstances, which influence the formation of the evil intention. He recognizes that, wherever the internal freedom of motivation is decisively influenced and restricted by circumstances, which lie

[1] C. XI, 61, 2, no. 8. [2] loc. cit., no. 8. [3] loc. cit., no. 8.

[4] See Liszt-Schmidt, *Lehrbuch des deutschen Strafrechts*, 26th ed., 1932, p. 155.

[5] C. X, 69, 3, no. 9. He refers to canon law, *causa* xxii, *quaestio* 5, *canon* 14, which says only: 'Omne peccatum ex voluntate nascatur'. Lucas generalizes this specific statement and says that no human action at all exists when the will is not free. See the text.

[6] C. XI, 9, 2, Rubrica. [7] C. XI, 52, 1, no. 8.

outside the individual's personality, his responsibility is diminished in proportion to the influence of those circumstances. Moreover, external circumstances may exercise such a decisive influence on the formation of the intention that the motivation is no longer free, and hence the individual cannot be held in any degree responsible for his action. Thus, in the opinion of Lucas, the notion of responsibility is flexible and elastic: the perpetrator's responsibility may be diminished by certain accompanying circumstances, which, when they exist in sufficient strength, may completely neutralize the freedom of motivation, and consequently lead to exculpation.

The following are examples of such extenuating circumstances:

(1) Provocation: 'Non enim quis debet esse proclivus ad homicidium committendum'.[1] Lucas envisages the case in which the husband kills his wife, whom he catches in the act of committing adultery.[2] It must be conceded, Lucas remarks, that the husband acted 'justo dolore concussus', and everyone knows, he says, that it is very difficult to be master of oneself in such situations.[3] Since, in a situation like this, the will of the murderer was not free, his responsibility is diminished: 'Non tamen excusatur a toto, sed a tanto', is Lucas's verdict.

(2) Anger is another factor which diminishes the responsibility of the offender, because actions performed in this state of mind do not fully reveal the offender's personality. He is, as it were, beside himself: 'Ira etiam saepe innocentes deducit ad peccatum . . . ex ira quippe fit homo extra corpus suum'.[4]

(3) Wrongs committed by order of a superior diminish the responsibility of the criminal. The son who commits some crime because his father has ordered him to do so cannot be fully exculpated. There is no legal enactment, Lucas argues, compelling the son to obey his father, but, on the other hand, the son is expected to obey his parents. Consequently, the conflict which arises in the son is taken into account, with the result that the punishment is diminished, because one can hardly say that the son wholly willed his deed: 'Quinetiam licet praecise filius cogi non possit, tamen obedire tenetur, et ideo qualisper excusatur; talia enim non libera voluntate exequuntur, quae mandantur'.[5]

Totally different aspects are opened up, Lucas continues, when the order of the superior is accompanied by the threat of death in the case of its non-fulfilment. Lucas wholly accepts the arguments put forward by Cynus, to whose commentaries he refers his readers. Cynus envisages the case in which a master, who suspects his wife of adultery, orders his servant to murder her; in case of non-compliance

[1] C. XII, 53, 1, no. 62.
[2] loc. cit., no. 62. He continues: 'Ut patet in marito, qui uxorem in adulterio deprehensam occidit'.
[3] 'Quem (scil. dolorem) est difficile temperare.'
[4] C. X, 19, 2, no. 4. According to contemporary English doctrine, murder committed 'in sudden heat' was considered manslaughter, see Holdsworth, vol. iv, p. 303.
[5] C. XI, 52, 1, no. 9.

with his order the servant himself is threatened with death. Cynus asks whether the murder of the wife is imputable to the servant: 'Pone, quod Titius habebat uxorem odio, propter suspicionem violati thori, unde dixit servienti suo, quod illam interficeret, alias ipse occiderit eum. Serviens interfecit, numquid impune?'[1] There are strong reasons, Cynus says, for making the servant responsible, because it is better to suffer evil than to consent to it: 'Melius est omnia mala pati quam malo consentire'.[2] Nevertheless, he declares, this purely ethical—and theoretical—consideration is not the only one which should decide a grave matter like this. As usual, Cynus follows his teacher, Petrus de Bellapertica, for whom he always shows the greatest reverence. Petrus de Bellapertica, as Cynus reports, propounded a view which shows less an idealistic than a practical mind. Purely theoretical considerations cannot decide such a grave issue: insight into human nature, as it is, not as it should be, and a realistic appraisal of the unique situation in which the servant finds himself, seem to have guided Petrus, who pleads for total exculpation of the offender. This view is accepted by Cynus. The servant cannot be expected to sacrifice his life; whatever he does for the protection of his life must be within the ambit of permissible actions: 'Breviter indistincte dixit Petrus, quod serviens excusatur, quia facit ob tutelam sui corporis'. Cynus himself adds: 'Item, quia licet proprium sanguinem redimere'.

(4) Drunkenness. A distinction should be drawn, Lucas points out, between habitual and occasional drunkenness. In the former case the 'culpa' of the offender consists in his unwillingness to break himself of his habit.[3] His responsibility remains therefore unaltered: he is as responsible for actions performed in a state of drunkenness as for those performed in a state of sobriety. The latter case, however, involves a lessening of the criminal's responsibility, and, in so far as drunkenness is causative of the crime, he is exculpated: 'Nam ebrietas non assueta, licet excusat a tanto, non tamen a toto'.[4]

(5) Youth is another circumstance which has extenuating, because partly exculpating, effect. The child and the lunatic cannot be expected to act on the basis of a 'free will', nor have they the necessary faculty to distinguish right from wrong. They are not therefore liable to any punishment: 'Non exitus, sed voluntas attenditur . . . unde infans et furiosus occidentes hominem non tenentur'.[5] But the youth who is above the age of fourteen years is responsible for his actions, though, owing to his lack of comprehension and his immature intellect, he may not have grasped the full

[1] Cynus, in his lecture on C. VIII, 4, 1, no. 9, *quaestio decima*.

[2] Alluding to D. 4, 2, 8.

[3] 'Delinquens assuetus erat inebriari nec exinde corrigi volebat', C. XII, 37, 1, no. 6. There follows a long discussion as to how the judge can recognize habitual drunkenness, no. 7.

[4] loc. cit., no. 6.

[5] C. XI, 61, 2, no. 8.

import and weight of the wrong he has committed. Since entailing a lower degree of responsibility, this circumstance is taken into account by a proportionately lower punishment. On the other hand, high official position, age, and experience increase the responsibility of an offender and, therefore, the punishment: 'Aetas enim ad eruditionem multum habere facit differentiam . . . unde et qui perfectioris aetatis est et majoris sapientiae consiliique existit, honores consecutus est, et cognoscit criminum qualitates, majori poena dignus est'.[1] Here again, Lucas's pivotal thought comes to the fore—namely, his idea that punishments are 'medicinae' which must be adapted to the personality: 'Diversitas personarum diversam accipit medicinam . . . poenae, quae imponuntur, sunt ipsorum peccantium medicinae'.[2]

On the other hand, there are circumstances—'aliae circumstantiae', as Lucas says—which produce aggravating effects. They, too, are outside the personality of the offender. Their very existence throws light upon the offender, whose personality appears far more reprehensible than it would appear if these circumstances had not been existent at the time of committing the crime. Such aggravating circumstances may be connected with the time at which a crime is committed, with the way in which the criminal proceeds in order to carry out his intention, and with the quantity of the wrongs inflicted.

The commission of a crime at night-time is an aggravating circumstance, because it reveals a greater moral corruptness than the commission of the same crime in bright daylight: 'Nam qui male agit, odit lucem'.[3] It is to be presumed, Lucas says, that the criminal himself has chosen night-time, and, therefore, the choice of this time is a symptom of his depravity: 'Praesumitur autem ipse delinquens tale tempus pro idoneo ad committendum maleficium elegisse'.[4] Crimes committed in war-time are to be punished with more severity than if they had been perpetrated in time of peace: 'Attenditur temporis qualitas, ut pacis ac belli'.[5] Lucas demonstrates this principle by referring to desertion. A soldier who commits this crime in war-time deserves severer punishment, because his action reveals a more reprehensible attitude than it would have done had he committed it in time of peace.[6]

Particular attention, Lucas continues, should be paid by the judge to the 'qualitas criminis'—that is to say, the judge should carefully inquire into the way in which the crime was actually

[1] C. XII, 45, 1, no. 42.

[2] C. XI, 52, 1, no. 8. Cf. with this highly advanced theory of Lucas the superficial reasoning by which Bracton exculpates the infant and the imbecile: 'Cum alterum innocentia consilii tueatur, et alterum facti imbecillitas excusat', quoted by Holdsworth, vol. ii, p. 259.

[3] C. XI, 58, 8, no. 2.

[4] loc. cit., no. 2.

[5] C. XI, 52, 1, no. 12.

[6] loc. cit., no. 12: 'Attenditur temporis qualitas, ut pacis ac belli. Nam aliter punitur, qui in pace deseruit, quia militiam perdidit, aliter, qui in bello, nam capite punitur'.

perpetrated: the kind of weapons used by the offender, the kind of wounds inflicted; furthermore, he should investigate which part of the body was injured, whether the victim was permanently mutilated, whether much loss of blood was caused, and the like.[1]

Persistence in criminal behaviour, as, for instance, adultery committed over a considerable period of time, is a circumstance which has aggravating effect: 'Commisit aliquis adulterium, in quo longo tempore perseveravit'.[2] This is only an application of his general principle that 'temporis quantitas' is a highly important factor for assessing the criminal's guilt: 'Nam aliter punitur, qui diu manserit in peccato, aliter, qui modico'.[3] But punishment should be cumulative. The criminal should be charged with one crime only, but punishment should take the persistence into account: 'Hoc casu accusatio una et poena una locum habebit, sed augebitur'.[4]

The personality of the persistent offender resembles that of the habitual offender. Habitual delinquency exhibits the same features as any other habit—viz., that it is the individual's second nature.[5] In habitual offenders Lucas recognizes a particularly dangerous class of criminals: for the most part incorrigible they easily infect others with their habit—'inficiunt alios'.[6] The repeated perpetration of a crime reveals a very strongly developed criminal personality and shows that the measures previously taken against the criminal have been of no avail. He therefore deserves a more severe punishment than the first offender: 'Gravius punitur delictum iteratum'.[7] The sooner the criminal habit is recognized, Lucas declares, the better prospects are offered for a rehabilitation of the offender, for, unless a bad habit is checked in time, it becomes ingrained, and its elimination is accordingly all the more difficult.[8]

At the other end of the scale are circumstances which completely neutralize the freedom of motivation. Unfree motivation cannot furnish a basis of responsibility. Necessity is an example which, Lucas observes, occurs very frequently. It exculpates the offender from all criminal responsibility: 'Nec debet trahi ad opprobrium malae voluntatis, quod conditio necessitatis extorsit', says Lucas, summarizing the whole problem of necessity in a nutshell.[9] When they are committed under duress, even perjury and breach of oath

[1] 'Item attenditur qualitas criminis, puta in armis et vulneribus illatis, et cum quo instrumento . . . item in qua parte corporis quis percusserit . . . an ex percussione sit, membrum mutilatum vel debilitatum vel sanguis multus effusus', loc. cit.

[2] C. XII, 52, 2, no. 2.

[3] C. XI, 52, 1, no. 12.

[4] C. XII, 52, 2, no. 2. See also C. X, 31, 18, no. 7: 'Ex perseverantia quidem, quae committitur in delictis, modica poena pecuniaria in capitalem augetur'.

[5] See the passage quoted *supra*, ch. IV, p. 62.

[6] C. XII, 45, 1, no. 57.

[7] C. XII, 52, 2, no. 1.

[8] C. X, 16, 3, no. 3: 'Si pravae rei habitus, antequam diu patescat, non clauditur, usu fit latior . . .'

[9] C. XI, 52, 1, no. 6.

are not considered punishable offences.[1] Furthermore, he propounds the view that necessity knows no law: 'Necessitas moderamen non diligit'.[2] Consequently, the thief who steals because the force of necessity drives him to commit theft, cannot be held responsible for his action: 'Unde propter necessitatem famis quis excusatur a furto'.[3] Economic necessity, Lucas remarks, is a frequent cause of crimes. But he draws attention to a general desire to acquire money by illegal means. This desire, he observes, is the most frequent cause of crimes. This case, of course, should be kept apart from the case of necessity, since it is a common experience, he states, that 'pecunia (est) cunctorum criminum mater et incentiva litis'.[4] But if economic duress is genuine, Lucas expects the judge to see to the removal of this cause, so as to prevent future crimes: 'Dum mater criminum, necessitas, tollitur, peccandi ambitus relinquetur'.[5]

Actions undertaken in self-defence do not spring from an evil intention. The individual is not to be held responsible for actions of this kind, because he is pursuing his right of private defence against unlawful attack: 'Licitum est, repellere seu propulsare injuriam'. The guiding principle should be this: the defender should not use more force than is necessary to repel the attack: 'Moderamen (inculpatae) tutelae est illud, quo omisso violentia repelli non posset'.[6] But the right of self-defence ceases to exist as soon as the attack itself has ceased—e.g., through the attacker's flight. If, in such a case, the defender inflicted injury, his action would then not spring from the desire to ward off an attack, but from that of taking vengeance on his adversary: 'Quid, si me percutias, poterone te fugientem in continenti repercutere?' Lucas answers that the defender's action 'non ad defensionem, sed ad ultionem fieret, quod juris regulis prohibetur'. In other words, the right exists only against an actual and immediate attack. Lucas does not mention any other attacks but those upon life which make self-defence permissible.[7]

Lucas also postulates a duty of defence in those cases in which the attack is not directed against one's own life, but against that of another individual. If the third person does not take defensive measures against the wrongdoer, he himself becomes liable to punishment. In Lucas's opinion, he who is able to repel unlawful attacks and does not do so, is no better than the criminal himself, and should

[1] C. XII, 42, 1, no. 4.

[2] C. XI, 61, 2, no. 8. See also the passage quoted *supra*, p. 95.

[3] loc. cit., no. 8.

[4] C. XI, 47, 5, no. 3.

[5] C. XI, 61, 2, no. 8. According to contemporary English law under Edward III, crimes committed under compulsion were not punishable when perpetrated in time of war or rebellion, Holdsworth, vol. iii, p. 372.

[6] C. XII, 40, 5, no. 8.

[7] Generally speaking, the plea of self-defence in contemporary English law led only to a mitigation of punishment, not to total exculpation; see Holdsworth, vol. iii, p. 372. It was only by a statute of Henry VIII that killing the aggressor in certain specified cases became justifiable, Holdsworth, ibid., p. 314.

be treated accordingly: 'Alium defendendo non solum possumus, sed etiam debemus committere homicidium; qui enim perituro succurrere potest et non succurrit, occidit'.[1] We may point out that this view of Lucas is in flat contradiction to contemporary theories, which held that no duty is incumbent upon anyone to render assistance to an individual who is attacked. We may quote Bartolus as a typical representative of the common view. He says: 'Si aliquis occidat aliquem me praesente et eum non adjuvarem, cum possem, non teneor, nisi alias essem conscius vel particeps sceleris'.[2]

This brings us to another category of actions, which may be performed in pursuance of some right. Lucas holds that, although from a mere objective point of view certain actions have the semblance of wrongful conduct, they do not involve liability to punishment if they are undertaken with a good intention. Certain persons, such as teachers, parents, husbands, have the right to punish; when they pursue their right 'causa correctionis et disciplinae', and for no other reason, they are not criminally responsible for those acts:

> Causa enim in puniendis criminibus est nimium attendenda, quae videlicet instigavit hominem ad peccandum . . . si causa correctionis et disciplinae, ut si magister verberet discipulum suum, quod potest; et sic est in parente et marito,[3] qui causa correctionis possunt inferre verbera, includere et flagellare.[4]

The right to punish is based on the intention, which is pursued with the punishment of the child, &c. If a motive other than that of education has prompted punitive measures, they are outside the realm of permissible actions. No one is entitled to any action—however much he may plead that, objectively speaking, it is based on

[1] C. XII, 42, 1, no. 8.

[2] Bartolus, D. 29, 5, 1, no. 2. The same idea is expressed by Baldus, D. 1. 1, 3, no. 21, Albericus de Rosciate, ibid., no. 7, and Gandinus (ed. H. Kantorowicz), pp. 182, 230.

[3] The right to punish wives—provided that the husband has a praiseworthy intention—is based by Lucas on the superior quality of the man and the inferior quality of the woman, inferior because she is not made in the image of God: 'Unde potest vir uxorem tenere vinculis et castigare . . . non est enim mulier ad imaginem Dei facta, sed vir'. Here, too, Lucas follows canon law, to which he refers his readers for confirmation: *causa* xxxiii, *quaestio* 5, *canon* 13, which says: 'Mulier non est facta ad imaginem Dei. Sic enim dicit (scil. scriptura): "Et fecit Deus hominem, ad imaginem Dei fecit illum". Hinc est inde Apostolus: "Vir quidem", ait, "non debet velare caput suum, quia imago et gloria Dei est; mulier autem ideo velet, quia non est gloria aut imago Dei".'

[4] It is interesting to compare a statement by a modern penologist on the same subject. M. E. Mayer, *Der allgemeine Teil des Stafrechts*, 2nd ed., p. 186, also held that the punishment of a pupil by a teacher may be unlawful if the motive was vengeance: 'Die Rechtswidrigkeit einer Züchtigung kann zum Beispiel darauf beruhen, dass der Lehrer sich am Vater des Schülers rächen will, während sie rechtmässig wäre, wenn sie Züchtigungszwecken diente'. This view became later generally accepted, see Mezger, loc. cit., p. 228, Liszt-Schmidt, loc. cit., p. 212.

positive law—unless his action springs from a motive substantially agreeing with that of the law, which concedes the right. As we may well expect, this thesis of Lucas is fundamentally opposed to the theory of his contemporaries on this point. They are unanimous that, as long as the parents &c. keep within the bounds of the right which is conceded to them, they act lawfully. Their intention is of no concern. Not even the transgression of the right is accepted by Baldus as an indication of an evil intention: 'Si autem excedit modum, tenetur non tamquam dolosus, quia non praesumitur in eo dolus, sed tamquam culpabilis'.[1] Lucas concludes the discussion on the present topic by advising the judge who deals with criminal affairs to investigate most carefully as to whether or no some worthy motive prompted the individual to act in a seemingly wrongful way: 'Et breviter', he sums up, 'ubicumque honesta causa potest impellere aliquem ad crimen committendum, hoc attente pensandum est'. Thus, throughout his system of penal thought, Lucas applies his basic principle uncompromisingly, the principle, namely, that it is the 'why', the motive, which impresses upon actions the mark of criminal character.

Nevertheless, no worthy motive on the part of the individual can be discerned, Lucas asserts, in the case of euthanasia. Even if the moribund gives his assent, the criminal character of the action is beyond dispute: 'Quinimo moribundum, licet volentem, non licet occidere'.[2]

Ignorance about the wrongful character of the action performed does not render the agent liable to punishment, because actions of this kind have not sprung from an evil intention. Lucas is wont to stress that all punishment presupposes the exercise of free will and the full knowledge of, and insight into, the legal consequences of the act performed: 'Illa quidem peccata veniunt punienda, quae libero mentis arbitrio et delinquentis proposito committuntur'. The inevitable conclusion is, he says, that 'ignorans non offendit. Et hoc est regulare, ubicumque agitur de dolo in crimine puniendo.'[3] Consequently, ignorance (mistake) of law reveals no evil intention and necessarily leads to the offender's exculpation. 'Nam tunc', he argues, 'quaelibet ignorantia, etiam juris, excusat.' Ignorance must be conceded, when the agent is not cognizant with the criminal character of his act: 'Dicitur autem quis ignorare, quando non cognoscit illud esse peccatum, quod facit'.[4] In order to make his position perfectly clear, he reiterates the statement that nobody can be made responsible for his otherwise criminal conduct 'nisi scit se injuriam facere'.[5] In other words, he demands the full knowledge

[1] Baldus in his lecture on D. 9, 2, 5, no. 3. The same idea was expressed by his brother, Angelus de Ubaldis, in his commentary on D. 21, 1, 16, no. 3.

[2] C. XII, 53, 1, no. 61.

[3] C. XII, 45, 1, no. 60.

[4] C. X, 69, 3, no. 8.

[5] The basis for this general remark is contained in canon law, *causa* xxxiv, *quaestio* 1, *canon* 5: 'Si virgo nesciens viro nupserit alieno, hoc si semper nesciat, numquam ex hoc erit adulteria'. See Lucas on C. XII, 45, 1, no. 18.

of the perpetrator as to the unlawful character of his action: 'Nemo enim sine scientia peccat'. It is a sign of inhumanity to punish an individual who is ignorant of the true character of his conduct: 'Insciumve teneri satis incivile est'.[1] Here again Lucas carries his basic principle to its logical conclusion. His way of reasoning once more reveals the utter sincerity of his mind and a courage of conviction so alien to modern penologists.

Akin to this problem is another question—namely, error as to the ownership of stolen objects. An individual removes objects, which he believes to be his: 'Quaeritur, quid etiam, si aliquis furto subtraxit rem alienam, quam esse suam putabat, an possit accusari de furto?'[2] The individual had no evil intention—'quia dolo caret, qui in his principaliter exigitur'—and he is therefore not responsible: 'Quod enim animo malo non fit, poenam non meretur'. The presupposition is, Lucas emphasizes, that the agent can adduce good reasons for his mistake: 'Haec vera sunt, si non quaesito colore ignorantiae hoc fecit, sed justis rationibus ductus'.[3] The solution of the antithetic problem is not quite clear. Lucas asks, 'Quid econtra, subtraxit suam rem, quam putavit alienam, an excusabitur de furto?' Although the 'prava voluntas' would call for the punishment of the offender, Lucas cannot bring himself to the point of laying this down as his conclusion. Instead he reverts to the common view, which is 'verius'—viz., 'quod probato ipsum rem suam subtraxisse, non teneatur'.

In accordance with his basic view of crime, Lucas recognizes that there is no fundamental difference between the actual perpetrator of the crime and those other individuals who have taken part in it in some other capacity: 'Facientes et consentientes par poena constringit'.[4] Accessories before or after the fact are liable to the same punishment, provided that their activity was causal and sprang from an evil intention. Thus not only the instigators to the crime —'qui facientes suis suggestionibus provocant ad delictum'—and those who give effective aid to its perpetration—'consocii et ministri'—but also any person who has contributed in any way whatsoever to the criminal event: 'qui causam malorum praebet'. Even those individuals are liable to the same punishment as the actual perpetrator, who, without displaying any effective activity, are merely present at the perpetration of the crime and are a contributory cause, precisely by virtue of their presence: 'Qui enim facientibus sunt tempore delicti et animo delinquendi, licet nihil egerint'. In this context, two of Lucas's principles assume the greatest importance. In the first place, he rightly realizes that no intrinsic reason can be adduced for drawing a distinction between those who employ agents for the commission of a crime and those who perpetrate a crime with their own hands: 'Qui per alium faciunt, per seipsos

[1] C. XII, 45, 1, no. 7.
[2] C. XII, 45, 3, no. 4.
[3] A few lines later he says: 'Debet enim, qui excusandus est, justis rationibus ductus hoc putare'.
[4] C. XI, 7, 10 Rubrica.

facere videntur et dicuntur '.[1] Secondly, criminal responsibility is incurred by those individuals who, although in a position to prevent the perpetration of a crime, failed to do so ; according to Lucas the omission of effective prevention of crime puts the individual concerned on a footing with the criminal himself: 'Qui enim patitur, quod prohibere potest, ipse facere videtur '.[2] A practical application of this principle is the liability of public officials who neglect their duty.[3]

The treatment of a plurality of individuals implicated in a crime leads our jurist to a statement on the delictal responsibility of a corporation, such as a township. Wrongs committed by a corporation makes those in a responsible position liable to punishment, the reason being that they were able to prevent the crime : ' Delinquente universitate puniuntur majores eo, quod prohibere possunt '.[4] The whole corporation cannot be said to have acted with an evil intention —' non potest dici universitatem dolo peccare '—and therefore only the officials and counsellors—e.g., of a town—should be punished : ' Sic etiam puniuntur consiliarii et officiales civitatis '. Admittedly, Lucas's doctrine is as little clear and convincing as that of his contemporaries, who followed, as a rule, the ' fiction theory '. Oldradus de Ponte, another Bolognese jurist, asserted the capability of a corporation to commit a crime, because it is a fictive person. He declared that, although corporations ' non habeant veram personam, tamen habent fictam fictione juris . . . et sic eadem fictione animam habent et delinquere possunt et puniri '.[5] Bartolus, on the basis of the fiction theory, was less bold and declared somewhat reluctantly that the whole corporation was responsible : ' Si quaeris, an universitas possit delinquere, respondeo : proprie non potest delinquere, quia proprie non est persona . . . tamen hoc est fictum positum pro vero, sicut ponimus nos juristae '.[6]

II

Although not directly bearing on the conception of crime, the exposition of some principles governing the proceedings in criminal matters should not be omitted.[7] Here, too, Lucas shows his detached mind and complete independence of thought. The opposition to some well-established institutions places him on an

[1] C. XII, 40, 5, no. 8.
[2] C. X, 75, 1, no. 7.
[3] See *supra*, p. 143.
[4] C. XII, 60, 3, no. 4.
[5] Oldradus de Ponte, *Consilium* 65, no. 7.
[6] Bartolus in his lecture on D. 4, 2, 9, no. 4. His opinion was generally accepted in the sixteenth century, see Clarus, *Opera Omnia*, lib. v, quaestio xvi, no. 7. On the English view of punishing corporations, see Holdsworth, vol. iii, pp. 488 seq., and, on the whole question, Gierke, *Das Deutsche Genossenschaftsrecht*, vol. iii, pp. 342 seq.
[7] There is a very short review of the general development of criminal procedure in the Sicilian kingdom in A. Esmein, *History of Continental Criminal Procedure*, p. 291.

equal footing with the great reformers of four centuries later. Above all, Lucas transfers his basic ideas of crime and of the criminal to the sphere of criminal procedure.

We have already had opportunity of pointing out that, because they impede the search for truth, Lucas is utterly opposed to (legal) presumptions.[1] In the province of criminal proceedings, it is not therefore surprising to find him reiterate and re-emphasize that the judge must on no account rely on presumptions. The fact alone, he declares, that an individual has once acted in a criminal manner, is by no means sufficient reason to presume further delictal conduct. The judge must not base an important decision, such as the condemnation of an accused criminal, upon mere presumptions, but solely on evidence: 'Semel malus in uno actu, gradu et genere malitiae, non debeat praesumi malus in aliis generibus malitiae'.[2] More than that: Lucas holds that, even if an individual has shown an evil personality in one type or category of crime, the commission of other crimes must not be inferred from this fact alone: 'Non videtur possibile, quod homo, qui est malus in uno, quod peccet in omnibus'.[3] The basis for Lucas's view is the following consideration. He recognizes that every human creature is endowed with certain innate dispositions, propensities, or character traits: 'In corpore humano sunt quatuor humores, ex quibus corpora conficiuntur humana'.[4] The disposition to do evil may find an outlet in one direction only and may be recognized in one situation only, whilst in others the same individual with the same propensities may act in a most virtuous manner: 'Humores non aequaliter se habent in homine, sed superabundant in uno et in alio deficiunt'. Consequently, he says, 'multi peccant in luxuria, in aliis autem virtuose agunt, sic et multi peccant in avaritia, qui non peccant in luxuria'. Although not quite clearly stated, Lucas's idea seems to be that recidivist offenders commit, as a rule, one type or one category of crime only, whilst the commission of other types of crime appears quite alien to their psychic make-up.[5] The practical lesson, which, in his opinion, should be drawn from this common experience, is that the motto 'once a criminal, always a criminal' can find no place in criminal proceedings. The mere fact of a previous conviction is no basis for presuming that the individual is guilty of some other crime alleged to be perpetrated by him. His guilt must be proved by the evidence available.

This brings us to Lucas's views on torture—a topic which, he says, is truly a delicate matter ('res fragilis').[6] We have already pointed out Lucas's innermost aversion to that institution so freely

[1] See *supra*, p. 123.
[2] C. XI, 47, 7, no. 29.
[3] loc. cit., no. 29.
[4] loc. cit., no. 29.
[5] Modern penological research, especially that carried out by Liszt and his followers, which is based on statistical material, arrives at the same recognition. Habitual criminals, as a rule, commit crimes either against life or against property, but very rarely against both.
[6] C. XII, 49, 1, no. 3.

made use of in his day. Within the ambit of criminal proceedings, Lucas declares, torture is used to an extent that is not warranted by law. The cause of truth can never benefit from the use of torture, he is anxious to stress. Torture, in his opinion, is only admissible as an accompaniment of punishment—viz., after his final condemnation to induce the criminal to make good the damage he inflicted, if restitution is feasible. Lucas says: 'Nota hoc tormenta inferri non ad inquisitionem veritatis, sed ad poenam. Sic et pro vilibus furtis fur torquendus est, donec illa restituat'.[1]

He is well aware, however, that his advocacy of the restricted use of torture does not meet with general approval: 'Regulariter autem', he continues, 'quaestio potius infertur ad veritatis investigationem, quam ad criminis punitionem'. In fact, the jurists seemed little perturbed by this inhuman institution. Lucas, however, avows that confessions of guilt, extorted through the subjection of the criminal to the torture, can have no value as evidence. For confessions should be given without external compulsion and, therefore, of the criminal's own accord: 'Confessio enim non compulsa, sed spontanea fieri debet. Omnis etiam confessio, quae fit ex necessitate, fides non est.' Lucas expresses his abhorrence for those judges who base their decisions on mere suspicions or confessions obtained by the employment of torture: 'Pessimum enim est de suspicione aut extorta confessione quemquam judicare'. He puts confessions which were obtained by threats or by resort to fraudulent means on an equal footing with those obtained by the use of torture: 'Nota, quod paria sunt confessionem extorqueri per vim aut per metum et per fraudem'.[2] In short, confessions before a judge should be voluntary. In the opinion of Lucas, confessions otherwise obtained should not suffice as evidence against the criminal. Lucas's fearless stand against an institution so strongly entrenched in the minds of the fourteenth century reveals once more the utter sincerity of his thinking and the depth of his humanity. Moreover, in his firm rejection of this inhuman institution, he once again anticipates, by four centuries, his fellow-countryman, Beccaria.[3]

Accusations against criminals, Lucas says, should be preferred, not in a spirit of vengeance or of hatred, but in one of justice. For accusations, which set in motion the judicial machinery against the criminal, serve the public interest, and thus promote the well-being of society: 'Accusator, qui ad accusationem non invidiae livore, sed

[1] loc. cit., no. 3. The general doctrine relating to torture is contained in 'Reflections on Medieval Torture' in *Jur. Review*, 1944, pp. 123–38.

[2] loc. cit., no. 6.

[3] If any proof were needed of the high standard of Sicilian legislation, it would be furnished by the rules concerning the use of torture. Lucas mentions a Sicilian statute which permits torture only in case of the gravest crimes—that is, for those crimes for which relegation of the criminal is the legally provided sanction, loc. cit., no. 9. But even then torture may be used only as an accompaniment of punishment itself with the aim to compel the delinquent to make good the wrong.

justitiae zelo procedit, salutis publicae custodiam gerit '.[1] It is the objective interest in the maintenance of public order and peace within society—' pro pace servanda '—not the subjective interest of the accuser, which should prompt an accusation against a criminal. Accusations from personal motives are styled as ' damnabiles ' by our jurist: ' (Accusatio) quae autem procedit a carne, id est carnali intentione, puta odio vel nequitia, damnabilis est '.[2] The sole object of accusations is ' ut mali puniuntur et boni quiete vivant '.[3]

Lucas goes one step farther. He holds—and his view is merely a corollary of his conception of crime as a public wrong—that it is the public interest that calls for official accusations—that is to say, for accusations which are preferred against criminals by the public authority itself, and not by the wronged party. But this official accusation is still in the hands of the judiciary: ' Eadem ratione ', Lucas continues, ' cogitur quis alium accusare de crimine officio judicis, licet non jure actionis.' Nevertheless, we are bound to observe the progressive nature of Lucas's thought, which leaves behind the typical Roman and medieval notions of crime and advances the conception of crime as a public wrong, once again anticipating, by centuries, the development in legal thought. His view of the public character of crime makes him declare that compositions between the criminal and his victim do not affect the public nature of his wrong, and cannot, therefore, lead to his acquittal: ' Offensus enim pacem aut remissionem faciendo non potest injuriam publicam remittere, sed suam tantum '.[4]

In general, the judge who deals with criminal matters is primarily concerned with the public interest, whilst the motive behind all his official activity should be the ' zelus justitiae '.[5] He will act in the spirit of justice when he pursues a middle course, thereby prudently and cautiously avoiding the pitfalls of extremes: ' Sit igitur judex in his (scil. criminibus) cautus et prudens, ut sequatur medium, in quo est virtus. Nam medietas in omnibus est laudanda, extrema autem neque recta neque laudabilia sunt.' [6] The judge should show human understanding for human weaknesses, and his judicial actions should be born out of a ' spiritus lenitatis '—provided that he is convinced that the case deserves leniency and clemency. This would not be advisable, Lucas maintains, probably remembering his own experience as a judge, in the cases of hardened criminals upon whom leniency had previously made no impression.[7] The

[1] C. XII, 45, 1, no. 35. [2] loc. cit., no. 36. [3] loc. cit., no. 12.

[4] C. XII, 53, 1, no. 41. On the ' striking contrast ' between the English system and the so-called continental system, see Holdsworth, vol. v, p. 177. It should be pointed out, however, that even in modern times one can hardly speak of ' a continental system ', unless the distinction between the accusatorial and inquisitorial principle denotes the difference. Many modern continental systems exhibit both features, and thus the contrast becomes meaningless. [5] C. XII, 45, 1, no. 49. [6] loc. cit., no. 49.

[7] ' Misericordiam impendere prohibemur impoenitentibus et obstinatis in malo ', loc. cit., no. 57.

judge should not be moved by the supplications of accused criminals who, without genuine repentance, are only desirous to obtain the least severe treatment.[1] But the judge endowed with the faculty of good observation can discern whether the accused is genuinely repentant or only simulating repentance. The defendant's reactions during the proceedings, Lucas holds, will give a sufficient opportunity for gauging the genuineness of his repentance: the defendant's physiognomy, the tone of his voice, the way in which he confesses his guilt, and the tears he sheds as an external sign of his sorrow over the wrong he committed—all these symptoms, Lucas thinks, may indicate the genuineness of repentance. In such cases the judge may reasonably be justified in taking the course of leniency. Lucas says: 'Neque enim ad misericordiam judex adducatur, nisi ei signa doloris seu verbis, sententiis, voce, vultu cum lachrymatione denique supplex . . . tunc enim cessare poterit virga rigoris et succedat spiritus lenitatis'.[2]

[1] loc. cit., no. 50.

[2] loc. cit., no. 50.

CHAPTER VIII

SOCIAL AND POLITICAL CONCEPTIONS

I

POLITICS and Law were not distinct branches of learning in the Middle Ages. It would be highly misleading to style any one of the Post-Glossators as a political thinker, although they all touched upon issues which, according to modern modes of thinking, lie in the province of political science. In the first place, the treatment of political questions by the medieval jurists is due to the fact that Justinian's law books contain topics which would be held nowadays as purely political, such as the enactment in C.I, 1, 1, where the universal lordship of the Emperor is laid down as an axiomatic principle. Secondly, the actual conditions in the medieval Empire provoked thinking in political terms : the political conditions of the Empire were bound to have repercussions on legal science, for the divergence of legal systems in many parts of the Empire, the ensuing conflict of laws, and the question of the application of law, raised problems which were intimately bound up with the relations of the Empire to the Papacy, Kingdoms, and *Civitates*.[1] Finally, by viewing law as a social phenomenon, medieval jurisprudence was forced to elucidate some basic principles relating to human society, and thus was led to consider topics which, under modern conditions, would be dealt with, not by the lawyer, but by the sociologist.[2] Nevertheless, when they ceased to affect the juristic import of his investigations, all political and social problems ceased to arouse the interest of the lawyer. The medieval notion of law itself was far wider

[1] Bartolus furnishes a good example of the attitude of the pure lawyer towards political questions. Treating of the forms of government in his tract *De regimine civitatis*, he says in no. 6 : ' Haec investigato necessaria est juristis ; quoniam domini universales, dum de reformatione civitatis tractant vel juristas consulunt vel eis committunt, vel cum ipsi assident apud eos, de regimine civitatis quaerela proponitur '. See also his speech *In Doctoratu Joannis de Saxoferrato* (his brother), partly transcribed by Figgis, ' Bartolus and the Development of European Political Ideas ' in *Divine Right of Kings*, p. 349, note 1, and Woolf, loc. cit., pp. 14, 19. See also the remarks of Prof. Barker, ' Medieval Political Thought ' in *The Social and Political Ideas of some Great Medieval Thinkers*, ed. by Prof. Hearnshaw, p. 16.

[2] Professor d'Entrèves, loc. cit., p. 13, points out that it would be a great mistake to suppose that the basis of medieval political science was purely religious. This basis would have proved insufficient for rational inquiries, abundant as they were. ' The problem of politics would have been entirely shifted on to the plane of religious duty, which obviously allows of little discussion.' It seems that, as far as the Post-Glossators are concerned, their basis was far more philosophical and legal than purely religious.

than the modern one, and comprised provinces which nowadays would come under the heading of politics and morals.[1]

Without disparagement to medieval legal scholarship, it may be justifiable to assert that Lucas's political, and particularly his social disquisitions are superior to those of his contemporaries. His investigations in this field are not only distinguished by originality of approach and his characteristically profound and penetrating analyses of intricate problems, but above all by his endeavour to elucidate the fundamental, abstract, and general principles underlying the concept of the body politic as an organized entity. Unlike his contemporaries, he looks beyond the topical and actual, and tries to go down to the premises of human society, which—to his mind—is marked by the reign of law and justice. The entire reconstruction of his social thoughts would require a study of its own, but we may attempt to reconstruct some of his more fundamental views.

Our jurist, somewhat apologetically, submits that the scientific treatment of political problems is not, strictly speaking, the office of the lawyer; this matter is 'moralior seu magis politica', he writes, than 'legalis'.[2] The origin of the human race is traced to the primary, creative act of God. The first human social relation, he asserts, was that of man and wife, though it must not be assumed that this society was created simultaneously. God did not create each independently of the other, but created the one out of the other. On this first natural society Lucas writes: 'Primaque naturalis humanae societatis copula, vir et uxor, quos nec ipsos singulos Deus condidit et tamquam alienos junxit, sed alterum creavit ex altero'.[3] In this original creation God pursued definite, preconceived, aims applicable to all human society. He created His human society ('sua societas') with the aim and object of binding its members together by the ties of kinship and likeness.[4] Lucas envisages the whole of mankind as one large family. In his further investigations he arrives at the conclusion that, apart from these biological features, reason and speech constitute the true bond of all mankind, because these two endowments enable man to have social intercourse: 'Breviter', he says in the same passage, 'summum humanae societatis vinculum est ratio et oratio, quae docendo, dicendo, communicando, disceptando, judicando, conciliat inter se homines'. Although so strongly influenced by St. Augustine and the Stoic theses, our jurist does not seem to adhere to the theory of the sinful origin of the earthly State.[5]

[1] See also Holdsworth, vol. iv, p. 223.

[2] C. XII, 55, 2, no. 1.

[3] C. XII, 19, 2, no. 6.

[4] 'Deus ex uno voluit omnes homines condere, ut in sua societate non solum similitudine generis, sed etiam cognationis vinculo tenerentur', loc. cit., no. 6.

[5] This theory of the sinful origin of the State did not greatly appeal to the scholars of the fourteenth century. Baldus, for instance, when treating of the origin of the Empire, says in his lecture on C. VII, 37, 3, no. 8, that

Lucas's central theme in his conception of human society is its organic structure. Society and individual are one and the same phenomenon, only perceived under different aspects, for, in his opinion, the former cannot exist without the latter, and the latter is dependent on the former. If we may employ modern terminology, both constitute the social organism. Lucas compares the structure of human society with the constitution of the human body. Just as the one human body is composed of its various constitutive organs, in the same way human society—the social organism, the 'res publica'—is composed of its various constitutive parts.[1] He illustrates this thesis[2] at some length. The function of the Ruler, he says, resembles that of the head of the human body, whilst governmental institutions, such as the senate, are not unlike the human heart; the executive and administrative officials are the eyes, ears, and tongues of the body politic,[3] since they are auxiliary, yet constituent, parts of the human body. The peasants are likened to the feet of the human body: 'Pedibus vero solo jugiter inhaerentibus agricolae coaptantur', with more references and quotations from the *Policraticus*. The function of the stomach of the body politic is fulfilled by the fisc, which 'nourishes' the various organs of the body politic by furnishing them with salary.[4] Hence all the different departments, officials, institutions, and the like, which he sees in the administration of the body politic, are not only likened to, but also partly identified with, the organs of a living structure.

This organic idea of the body politic is of the greatest importance. Firstly, since every citizen constitutes a vital link in the machinery

---

although Innocent IV did not know where the Empire had its origin—'Innocentius dicit, quod nescit unde imperium habuit originem'—one can safely assume that it originates in the divine Being: 'Potes dicere quod habuit initium ab ense permissu divinu'. I could not find any jurist who alluded to St. Augustine's famous dictum. Not even the jurists who were papal extremists referred to this idea; on their views see *infra*, p. 173.

[1] 'Sicut enim corpus unum est et membra habet multa, omnia autem corporis membra, cum sint multa, unum corpus sunt . . . et eodem typo multa rei publicae membra unum corpus sunt, i.e., res publica', C. XII, 55, 2, no. 1.

[2] In which he follows the *Institutio Trajani* of pseudo-Plutarch.

[3] 'Princeps obtinet instar capitis, cordis locum senatus habet, a quo bonorum et malorum procedunt initia. Oculorum, aurium et linguae officia sibi vendicant judices provinciarum et praesides. Officiales et milites, qui semper assistunt principis lateribus, bracchiis assimilantur,' loc. cit., no. 1. Referring to the *Policraticus*, lib. V, cap. 2, he says in his commentary on C. XII, 3, 3, no. 3: 'Princeps in re publica, quae pro quoddam corpore ponitur, obtinet vicem et officium capitis'. On John of Salisbury's organic theory see Prof. McIlwain, loc. cit., p. 321, and E. F. Jacob, 'John of Salisbury and the Polycraticus', in *The Social and Political Ideas of some Great Medieval Thinkers*, pp. 65 seq. The clergy has no organic function in Lucas's doctrine, see *infra*, p. 186, n. 3. The organic theory was also adopted by St. Thomas, see De Wulf, *History of Medieval Philosophy*, vol. ii, p. 28.

[4] 'Fiscus est pars rei publicae . . . et obtinet in corpore rei publicae instar stomachi, a quo membra singula recipiunt nutrimentum, et in quem omnia congeruntur', C. XI, 58, 7, no. 9.

and working of the social organism, any wrong or offence committed against one citizen suffices to disturb the organism, and, furthermore, even entitles society to take appropriate action against the wrongdoer, whether an individual or a corporate body, such as a 'foreign' State. Lucas puts the following question to his readers: 'Illata est injuria in civem ex aliqua civitate, an possit ipsa civitas indicere bellum injurianti?' He gives an affirmative answer to the question for the following reasons: 'Nam sicut, qui aurem tetigit, totum tetigisse videtur . . . ita et qui civem offendit, qui est pars corporis civitatis, totum ipsum corpus offendisse videtur'.[1] Secondly, the structure of the social organism entails the close interdependence of all its members. Availing himself of the Aristotelian and Stoic thesis that 'homo sociale animal communi bono genius est',[2] he says that everything created and produced 'in terris' is for the common good and the good of man. Furthermore, the social function of man consists in his rendering services to his fellow man, for man does not exist for his own sake, Lucas says in the following passage in which utilitarian and communistic ideas may clearly be discerned: 'Dicimus, quae in terris gignuntur, ad usus hominum creata omnia, homines autem hominis causa fuisse generatos, ut ipsi inter se alii aliis prodesse possint. In hoc ergo debemus naturam sequi et communes utilitates afferre in medium.'[3] The idea of co-operation between the members of society appears, as we shall presently see, axiomatic to Lucas. It is precisely this recognition on the part of Lucas which makes him assert the need for the subordination of the individual to the demands of society and of the common good: the condition for the smooth working of the social organism is the common and identical aim of all citizens. Thirdly, his emphasis on the social necessity of civic duties is another aspect of his organic conception. Everyone is obliged to contribute to the promotion of the common good: neither must he shirk work destined to further the common good nor must he selfishly try to evade perils when the common good demands that he confront them.[4] The practical application of this view is

[1] C. XII, 55, 2, no. 1.

[2] C. X, 37, 1, no. 6, referring to Seneca's *Liber de Clementia*.

[3] C. XII, 8, 2, no. 1. This idea that everything created on earth is created for the sake of man is also a fundamental tenet of the *Rex Pacificus*, the document ascribed to the Masters of the university of Paris (1302), see *infra*, p. 175. But I could not find this idea employed by any other authority of the fourteenth century, nor can it be presumed that Lucas knew of the *Rex Pacificus*. On the interpretation of Wyclif's communistic ideas, conceived from an entirely different angle, see now Dr. Coulton, *Studies in Medieval Thought*, pp. 195 seq., and Workman, loc. cit., vol. i, p. 261.

[4] 'Nota, quod unusquisque tenetur suae patriae utilitatibus providere, quinetiam pro sua re publica nullos labores effugere et pericula non vitare . . . Arist. Octavo Ethic.', C. X, 43, 2, no. 2.

Lucas's idealistic mind causes him to complain of the inactivity, selfishness, and the disregard by some members of society for the requirements of the public interest. In a delightful note our jurist passes some scathing the obligation on the part of every citizen to military service and to all other public duties which the State orders.[1] Patriotism is conceived by Lucas as being derived from the love of the native soil, and, therefore, natural. Consequently, civic duties should not be felt as a burden on the citizen, but should be freely given in return for all the fatherland gives the citizen.[2] For it is precisely by the collective efforts of the whole society that the individual member can live. We shall soon have opportunity of discussing the purpose for which, in the eyes of Lucas, this body politic exists—the purpose, namely, of furthering the individual's happiness and of enriching the human creature. This close interrelationship, interdependence, and interplay of the individual and the whole is the key-note of Lucas's social and political ideas. The State, to employ modern terminology, is not an abstract idea, but a living reality. The ' res publica ', Lucas declares, is ' quoddam corpus universitatis '.[3]

For the presupposition for a peaceful and prosperous development of society, Lucas finds, is the belief in Christian ideas and ideals. ' Fides est fundamentum nostrae salutis.' [4] Faith, since it is the gift of God, not a matter of our own free choice, is the element that unites all men for a common purpose, makes them strive after an identical, recognized end and forms the strongest moral link in social relations. Moreover, Faith overcomes all stormy conflicts arising out of a militant Church, and makes us comprehend things which our limited intellectual capacities cannot grasp.[5] Wherever Faith is lacking, there can be no true justice,[6] and societies not inspired by it are bound eventually to disintegrate. Neither physical

---

comments on certain types of citizens both in the cloister and the world at large. In the monastery, he says, there is much abuse of sacerdotal power, and it is precisely through such abuses that the whole edifice of religion crumbles ; there is the indifferent bishop, the idling student, the obstinate old man, the eccentric monk, the inevitable rumour within the cloister, the exquisite food, the irreverence in front of the altar, and the like. In the world at large other types can be found : the wise man without good works, the rich man without charity, the woman without chastity, the baron without virtue, the pugnacious Christian, the unjust ruler, the undisciplined common folk, and above all, the people upon whom the law makes no impression. C. XI, 41, 4, no. 9. For conditions in the monasteries see also Previté-Orton, loc. cit., pp. 249 seq. and 435, and on contemporary English monasteries, see Trevelyan, loc. cit., pp. 47 seq.

[1] Mr. E. Lewis, ' Organic Tendencies in Medieval Political Thought ', in *American Political Science Review*, vol. xxxii (1938), p. 855, seems to think that this idea was not clearly conceived before Aeneas Sylvius (died 1464).

[2] ' Naturae quippe est, ut unusquisque natale diligat solum et nihil dulcius habet patria, ut dicit Hieronymus super Jeremiam ', C. X, 37, 1, no. 4.

[3] C. XII, 49, 4, no. 1.

[4] C. XII, 59, 9, no. 5.

[5] ' Fidei vero affectus multiplex est. Nam fides in unum fideles connectit, quos diversitas meritorum tenet . . . omnes procellas militantis ecclesiae superat . . . rem publicam magis quam sudores corporales gubernat . . . per ipsam res publica magis quam labore et sudore corporis conservatur ', loc. cit., no. 5.

[6] ' Ubi etiam sana fides non est, ibi justitia esse non potest. Nam et sine fide virtus falsa est, etiam in optimis moribus,' loc. cit., no. 5.

exertions nor material acquisitions on the part of the citizens nor territorial aggrandizements on the part of the Rulers can compensate, in Lucas's opinion, for a lack of Faith.[1] Because it alone guarantees the pursuit of justice and the attainment of peace, the true happiness of society rests on Faith. It effectively promotes understanding and friendship between the members of society, which latter element is a powerful barrier against political strife.[2] More than that: the idea of an organized society is substantially constituted by the internal peace, friendship, and the salutary mutual relations existing between its members [3]—in short, the test of the prosperity of a society is that of unity, not that of efficiency, which so easily leads to tyranny. Obedience to law is conceived by our jurist as merely an external symptom of these constitutive elements. It is the will—a will, which is the direct effluence of moral and religious affections—of society's members to obey the instituted authority and to preserve the law. This will makes them citizens in the proper meaning of the term.[4] For a *civitas* is a multitude of individuals united in their will to live according to the law.[5] The element constitutive of organized society is a co-operative will, an identical purpose and a common aim on the part of all its members. The idea of a freely concluded contract can consequently cause no surprise: 'Generale quoque pactum est societatis humanae regibus obtemperare'.[6] Here we are bound to observe that Lucas, although setting out from the organic conception of human society, does not stop at this point. He combines this conception with the other one—viz., the idea of a co-operative will, which, in his opinion, is the leaven of human society. It is precisely this co-operative will which animates, enlivens, interrelates, and knits together the various elements and organs of society. Thus, his point of view is an amalgamation of the theory of the organic structure of society with the idea of a social contract, which contract is concluded, not between people and Ruler, but between

[1] C. XII, 50, 23, no. 1.

[2] Cf. C. XI, 31, 1, no. 1.

[3] He explains the term 'societas' of C. X, 31, 19, and says: '"Societatem", id est amicitiam, pacem, foedus, quae omnia debent in civibus immaculate persistere. Amicitia namque videtur civitates continere.'

[4] loc. cit., no. 1.

[5] 'Civitas est hominum multitudo seu collectio ad jure vivendum . . . civitas nihil aliud est quam concors hominum multitudo', C. X, 10, 1, no. 4. Modified Ciceronian ways of thinking are expressed in this passage: 'Est autem populus humanae multitudinis coetus juris consensu et concordi communione sociatus. Unde populus est collectio tam nobilium quam ignobilium,' C. XI, 48, 1, no. 1. See also C. XII, 19, 2, no. 4: 'Societas requirit concordiam animorum'. Similar ideas occurred, however, as early as the twelfth century, see Dr. Carlyle, loc. cit., vol. ii, p. 77, note 2, where he transcribes the definition of human society given by Hugolinus.

[6] C. XI, 71, 1, no. 1. On this interesting point see also Gierke-Maitland, *Political Theories*, p. 89 and p. 187, note 306, and Dr. Carlyle, loc. cit., vol. v, pp. 442 seq., Figgis, *Divine Right of Kings*, pp. 1, 113 seq., 251 seq.; cf. also Prof. Barker, loc. cit., p. 21, on the pact between Ruler and people.

the members of society themselves. But in all his commentaries there is no trace of a 'status innocentiae' of human society—the basic Thomistic principle [1]—nor, as we mentioned before, any allusion to the sinful character of the earthly State. It would be inaccurate to say that Lucas belonged to the theorists of the social contract; nor can he be reckoned amongst the followers of the theory—in spite of his faithful adherence to John of Salisbury [2]—which proclaims the purely natural-organic structure of human society. But Lucas's theory is certainly organic in this sense, that it stresses the interdependence and harmony of individual and society, that it visualizes an organic growth and development of society, that it considers sociability of the members of society as fundamentally necessary for its existence and prosperous continuity, and, lastly, that his conception sets out from an intrinsic unity of the body politic, like the unity of the human body. His theory is not organic in the sense that it distinguishes between the purpose of the individuals and that of organized society, and envisages Ruler and public officials as organs who derive their authority from the community and are responsible to it.[3] This interpretation would have been entirely alien to Lucas.

For, he holds, it is precisely man's purposive life—the will to a common end—which makes authoritative guidance imperative. It is this consideration which necessitates the institution of governments. Governments guide citizens by issuing authoritative commands, which bring about order and security: without these twin premises there can be no society in the proper meaning of the term, Lucas affirms: 'Nihil est tam necessarium civitatibus quam principatus, sine quibus impossibile est esse civitatem. Et sine his (quae ad bonum ordinem et ornatum) impossibile est habitare.' [4] Moreover, diversity of needs and desires of the citizens calls for an authority that stands above the community and is vested with the power to issue authoritative commands which, based on the idea of justice and equity, harmonize the needs and desires of individuals. Therefore, 'Deus unicuique genti praeposuit rectorem'.[5] We have only to recall Lucas's views on the political capabilities of the people. It is in the same line of thought that he finds monarchy

[1] See the brilliant exposition of Thomistic principles by Prof. d'Entrèves, loc. cit., pp. 19 seq., particularly p. 29 and, contrasted with Marsiglio's thought, p. 52. See also De Wulf, loc. cit., vol. ii, p. 28.

[2] See, e.g., *Policraticus*, lib. VIII, cap. 17 and 18.

[3] On the antithesis of individualistic and organic theories in medieval lore see the penetrating analyses of Mr. E. Lewis, loc. cit., pp. 849–76. This author raises very grave objections to Gierke's 'organic' doctrine which is 'fundamentally inaccurate' (p. 849), 'erroneous' (p. 871), 'founded on very doubtful evidence' (p. 853), and 'obscures, if it does not misinterpret' (p. 858). It may be, as Mr. P. W. Duff remarks, that Gierke, 'a most persuasive writer', is a preacher and a historian who sometimes exaggerates, *Personality in Roman Private Law*, pp. 209, 222.

[4] C. XII, 59, 8, no. 3.

[5] C. X, 16, 3, no. 4, with a reference to *Ecclesiasticus*, xvii.

the best form of government. It is the monarch who is best suited to regulate social life, to co-ordinate the activities of all citizens, and to lead them, by wise and prudent legislation, to the path along which they can pursue their aim. 'Princeps solus', Lucas maintains, 'melius exercet imperium quam plures'.[1] It is the monarch alone who can adequately take charge of the public welfare, prosperity, and the common good: 'Subjectorumque salutem nullus alius quam princeps melius tueri potest'.[2] It is he alone, Lucas is firmly convinced, who is qualified to repress social perversity effectively. Lucas sees in the repression of this perversity the presupposition for the well-being of the body politic, because its constructive and creative forces can then come into full display. The idea behind the power of the Ruler is this: 'Potestas quippe regia constituta est, ut mali coerceantur a malo, et boni inter malos quiete vivant'.[3] The Ruler's function resembles that of the human soul: just as the soul guides man, in the same way the Ruler guides the destiny of the people entrusted to his care.[4] The Monarch's authoritative commands—that is to say, the law—put an effective check on egoistic desires perilous for the tranquil development of society. Laws are made by the Ruler, Lucas avows, 'ut appetitus noxius sub juris regulis limitetur'.[5] The idea of a true leadership by the Monarch is ever present in Lucas's mind. We will return to this point later.

The supreme Ruler, the Monarch, receives his authority from, is instituted directly by, God without any intermediary. His power is independent of the Pope: 'Sibi Deus res humanas regere deputavit'. This view admits of only one conclusion, he says: 'Nec eius potestas dependet a Papa'.[6] On the extremely controversial point of medieval political thought, the allegory of the two swords, Lucas once again follows his own convictions, in spite of the great sway which John of Salisbury [7] had over him. Lucas repudiates the idea that the Pope possesses both swords: 'Satis incongrue diceretur papam utrumque gladium et jurisdictionem

[1] C. XII, 59, 8, no. 3, and C. XII, 60, 2, no. 11: 'Dualitas ad rei destructionem parata . . . unitas vero ad conservationem'.

[2] loc. cit., no. 3.

[3] C. XI, 71, 1, no. 1.

[4] C. XI, 9, 1 Rubrica.

[5] 'Sicut anima regit corpus et conservat, ita rex statuitur ad regni gubernationem et regimen, et sicut anima est salus et vita corporis, sic et rex . . .', C. XII, 43, 3, no. 12.

[6] C. XI, 71, 1, no. 11, where he refers to the *Decretum Gratiani, distinctio* xcvii, *canon* 1, which contains a letter of Pope Boniface to the Emperor Honorius (420). The Pope said in this letter that 'Deus noster meum sacerdotium, vobis res humanas regentibus deputavit'. It is apparent that Lucas takes these words as his starting-point.

[7] John of Salisbury was a staunch adherent of the view that the Pope possesses both swords. John's prince is merely the agent of the 'sacerdotium', see *Policraticus*, lib. IV, cap. 3, Dr. Carlyle, loc. cit., vol. iv, p. 333, and R. L. Poole, loc. cit., p. 206.

habere '.[1] In another passage he returns to the same problem, and says that the Ruler is bearer of the plenitude of all temporal power, which is granted to him by God directly: 'Excellentia potestatis eorum (scil. principum) a Christo descendere significatur, et ut ipsi sub Christo regnent '.[2] For it was Christ Himself who 'actibus propriis et dignitatibus distinctis officia potestatis utriusque discrevit '. Lucas not inappropriately refers to Gratian's *Decretum*, which contains a letter of Pope Nicholas I to the Emperor Michael; [3] our jurist simply adopts the argument and the wording of this letter written by the highest ecclesiastical authority in, or about, the year 865. The statement that 'jus utriusque potestatis Christus actibus suis discrevit' occurs frequently in Lucas's investigations of this topic.[4] The nature of the government of the world is twofold—namely, 'pontificalis' and 'regalis'.[5] In another context he comes to speak of the same problem, and states that the secular authority and Imperium descend directly from God—'Imperium enim a Deo est'—and that all secular authority is distinctly separated from ecclesiastical authority: 'Et distincte est eius (scil. principis) potestas ab ecclesiae potestate'. [6] Rulership, therefore, has no sacramental character.[7] A practically important application of this strict separation of powers is the complete independence of secular and ecclesiastical judges, since both judges eventually receive their powers from God.[8] Closely allied with this view is his further thesis that the ecclesiastical authorities have no power to release anyone from the obligations imposed by the secular authority. This, Lucas points out, is particularly true in respect of the payment of taxes and the rendering of civic duties, since these obligations were especially mentioned and insisted upon by Christ. Once again, Lucas wishes to make it clear that this view, however much

[1] C. XI, 70, 5, no. 57, where he refers to the passage pointed out in note 3.

[2] C. XI, 9, 3, no. 3, referring to the *Romans*, xiii.

[3] C. XI, 71, 1, no. 11. The letter is included in Gratian's collection, *distinctio* xcvi, *canon* 6. It is interesting to note that this passage of the *Decretum* was hardly referred to by the partisans of papal claims. Ægidius Colonna's tract *De ecclesiastica potestate* did not refer to it. As far as could be ascertained, the extremist Henricus de Cremona dealt with the passage in his tract *De potestate Papae*, but did not attach any importance to it, because Nicolas I wrote out of humility of mind: 'causa humilitatis hoc dicit'; see also Carlyle's lengthy discussion of this tract, loc. cit., vol. v, pp. 398 seq., and the long passage quoted by him p. 401, note 1, see also McIlwain, loc. cit., pp. 247 seq.

[4] See, e.g., C. XII, 16, 2, no. 2.

[5] loc. cit., no. 2.

[6] C. XII, 29, 1, no. 11.

[7] C. XI, 9, 3, no. 3. It must be borne in mind that Cynus adhered to a similar conception: '. . . a Deo procedit Imperium et Sacerdotium . . . et Deus est dominus omnium, ergo temporaliter sub Imperio omnes populi omnesque reges sunt, sicut sub Papa sunt spiritualiter', Cynus in his lecture on C. I, 1, 1, no. 3. See also Baldus, ibid., nos. 1–12. But Lucas does not refer to other authorities.

[8] 'Saecularis judex, qui habet potestatem suam a Deo, sicut et judex ecclesiasticus', C. XII, 29, 1, no. 11. See also *supra*, pp. 136–8.

it may be in disagreement with current ideas, is simply derived from, and in complete agreement with, that of ecclesiastical authority —namely, St. Ambrose. Lucas says on this point: 'Et ideo sacerdotes putare non debent regis terreni leges solvendas, cum ipse Dei filius censum Caesari jusserit esse solvendum, 11 q. 1, magnum'.[1]

At this point we may profitably cast a glance at the views which Lucas's great contemporary, Bartolus, had on this important point.[2] The latter's view may be summed up in these words: 'In its result it endorses to the full the extremist view of Papalism;[3] complete inferiority of the Emperor, temporally and spiritually, to the Pope'.[4] Bartolus still adhered to the all-embracing position of the Pope because 'apud Christi vicarium est uterque gladius, scilicet spiritualis et temporalis'.[5] The temporal rulership had been handed over to the Emperor by the Pope: 'Transfertur per papam in principem saecularem'. In the lectures on the *Digestum novum*, he simply adopted the doctrine of the canonists and said: 'Nam ecclesia tenent, quod Imperium dependeat ab ecclesia pulcherrimis rationibus, quas omitto'.[6] Lucas, on the other hand, insists on the equal rank of either power in their respective spheres. That is best illustrated perhaps by the metaphor which our jurist constantly uses—namely, that the Ruler is the common father, whilst the Church is the common mother.[7] We may here recall that while Bartolus maintained a temporal overlordship of the Pope in all territories belonging to the Church,[8] Lucas, faithful to his principles, holds that the Church has no authority in temporal matters—'salvo judicio veritatis et reverentia clavium', he adds somewhat apologetically—because concession of such authority would be 'ultra mensuram aequitatis'.[9]

[1] C. XI, 71, 1, no. 11. He refers to the *Decretum Gratiani*, *causa* xi, *quaestio* 1, *canon* 28, with which his diction is in agreement; a similar idea is expressed in *canon* 27, but Lucas does not refer to it.

[2] On the theories of Andreas de Isernia—essentially agreeing with those of our author, but not so elaborately worked out—see Dr. Carlyle, loc. cit., vol. v, p. 359: 'In Imperio nihil temporale habet (Papa), nisi quantum Imperator sibi concedit'. On the other great Neapolitan jurist, Barth. de Capua, see text.

[3] Woolf, loc. cit., p. 100.

[4] Woolf, loc. cit., p. 94.

[5] Quoted after Woolf, p. 87.

[6] D. 48, 17, 1, no. 5. These reasons were obviously those set forth in *Unam Sanctam* to which he expressly referred in his lecture on *Authenticum*, coll. i, tit. 6, no. 2.

[7] C. X, 43, 3, no. 4.

[8] See *supra*, pp. 90–1.

[9] It is true that the Pope is 'proprietarius' (C. XI, 70, 5, no. 55) of the Sicilian kingdom, but Lucas does not concede to him authority in temporal matters. See also *supra*, ch. V, p. 91. Lucas concedes to the Church the administration of public affairs only in case of an actual or legal vacancy of the *Sicilian* throne: 'Vacante regno de jure vel de facto, ut quia est inutilis, haereticus vel excommunicatus . . . nam regno alias non vacante, si diceremus ecclesiam posse in eo (scil. regno) materialem gladium exercere (salvo judicio veritatis et reverentia clavium), esset ultra mensuram aequitatis; cum eadem ratione posset extendere potestatem suam ad alios regni fructus, quod in justitiam successionis beati Petri cadere non videtur', C. X, 39, 9, no. 27.

We may here note, however, that Lucas's viewpoint on this controversial issue was not unique amongst the jurists of the Southern seat of learning. The great Neapolitan jurist, Bartholomaeus de Capua, wrote that there are two authorities which preside over mankind.[1] The one is the spiritual power possessing the spiritual sword: 'Unus, videlicet qui spiritualibus praeest, utpote dominus Papa, cui attributus est gladius spiritualis'; whilst the other wields all temporal power by means of his temporal sword: 'Et alter, qui praeest temporalibus, utpote princeps, cui datus est gladius temporalis'. This view Bartholomaeus de Capua derived from the *Authenticum*, in which the two powers are designated as *sacerdotium* and *imperium*. Both powers proceed from one and the same ultimate cause: 'Ex uno eodemque principio utraque procedentia humanam exornant vitam', says the enactment in the *Authenticum*.[2] In order to make his position quite plain, he says a few lines later, after the above-quoted passage that the King is the supreme authority in all temporal matters, just as the Pope is the highest authority in spiritual affairs: 'Idem etiam intelligendum est de rege in regno suo, in quo in temporalibus non habet superiorem . . . et sicut papa in spiritualibus, ita princeps in temporalibus habet plenitudinem potestatis'.[3] About the relationship between King and Pope in the Kingdom of Sicily, Bartholomaeus declares that the King is a 'ligius Romanae ecclesiae', and that the Kingdom of Sicily *was* the patrimony of St. Peter and the Church: 'Regnum Siciliae fuit (!) patrimonium Petri et Romanae ecclesiae'.

With the views of Bartholomaeus de Capua and Lucas, both maintaining the independence of the Ruler from the Pope and their equal ranks in either sphere, let us briefly contrast the extreme views of some other contemporary scholars from the northern universities. Apart from Bartolus, the extreme section amongst the jurists is perhaps best represented by Joannes de Lignano, Richardus Malumbra, and Oldradus de Ponte. They all rejected the idea of equality of the Ruler and the Pope, and insisted on the superiority of the latter over the former. As Bartholomaeus Salicetus testifies—'audivi confirmari per Joannem de Lignano, dum in cathedra hanc quaestionem pertractaret'[4]—Joannes de Lignano reasons that since the celestial government, the 'machina coelestis', is characterized

[1] Bartholomaeus de Capua, *Commentaria in Constitutiones*, lib. I, tit. 1, p. 4: 'Sunt duo humano omni generi praesidentes'.

[2] *Authenticum*, *Collatio* I, tit. 6, *praefatio*: 'Maxima quidem in hominibus sunt dona Dei a suprema collata clementia: sacerdotium et imperium; et illud quidem divinis ministrans, hoc autem humanis praesidens ac diligentiam exhibens. Ex uno . . .'

[3] He continues and says that both powers are 'distinctae, quod nec spiritualium dominus se de temporalibus intromittat, nec temporalium dominus spiritualibus se immisceat'. He claims that 'rex Siciliae in regno suo est monarcha et habet omnia jura ad imperatorem spectantia'. It appears, therefore, inaccurate to attribute the idea of 'rex in suo regno imperator' to Oldradus, as both Albericus and Bodin did.

[4] Salicetus, C. I, *Rubrica* no. 7.

by monism, the terrestrial government, the 'machina terrestris'—must also be constituted on the monistic principle. But it would not be 'conveniens' if that one superior authority were the Emperor, because he could not direct spiritual matters. 'Non est conveniens, quod imperator sit ille, quia divinis praeesse non potest.' Consequently, it is of necessity that the Pope, holding the place of the divine Ruler, hands over the temporal government of the world to the secular Ruler.[1] Similar thoughts are expressed by Richardus Malumbra; the Pope is 'dignior' than the Emperor, and thus superior to him, because he alone commands authority in spiritual matters which are 'perfectissimae'. Accordingly, the Pope's authority concerns the soul, 'quae est immortalis', whilst the Ruler's authority governs merely the corporeal, 'quod est mortale et corruptibile'. And Oldradus de Ponte, perhaps the most extreme juristic writer of the period,[2] declares that all spiritual and temporal power is vested in the Pope: whoever assumes temporal authority without the consent of the Pope, 'praedo est',[3] and every action resulting from such usurpation must be called 'furtivus' and 'illicitus'.[4] For Christ had put into the hands of St. Peter and his successors the governance of both the celestial and terrestrial kingdom: 'Beato Petro et successoribus suis tradita sunt utriusque regni gubernacula coelestis scilicet et terreni'.[5] True to his fundamental thesis, Oldradus maintains, therefore, that temporal authority is not directly derived from God, but handed over through the medium of the Pope. 'Dico', Oldradus says, 'quod imperium est a Deo non immediate, sed per debitam et subalternam emanationem a vicario Jesu Christi.'[6] God is the 'causa prima' of all power and authority, but the 'vicarius' constitutes the 'causa secunda' and is 'quasi quoddam agens instrumentale'.[7]

A comparison between these staunch partisans of the papal cause and their contemporary colleague, Cynus, reveals a striking difference of opinion. Cynus, in his lectures on the *Digestum vetus*, entertains no doubt that, because the Empire was constituted by God as the 'agens universale', the Ruler, though coming from the people—'imperator a populo est'—is not only 'Deus' on earth and a 'divina persona', but also derives his powers from God

[1] 'Ergo summus pontifex necessario erit ille, et maxime, quia locum tenet ille coelestis principis, a quo cuncta reguntur.'

[2] He was consulted by Pope John XXII on the legal validity of the appointment of the anti-pope Nicholas V (1328), see Baluzius, *Vitae Paparum Avenionensium*, tom. i, col. 707, and Oldradus's consilium no. 65 and no. 85. Oldradus advised John XXII that Nicholas 'tamquam excommunicatus et praecisus est a communione ecclesiae repellendus'.

[3] *Consilia*, cons. 191, no. 1: 'Constat etiam jurisdictionem et administrationem imperii esse penes papam; quicumque eam sibi sine superioris authoritate usurpat, praedo est'.

[4] Cons. 180, no. 8.

[5] loc. cit. He continues: 'Quicumque ergo sine voluntate successoris beati Petri terreni regni gubernacula assumit, rem illicitam committit'.

[6] loc. cit., no. 15.

[7] loc. cit., no. 15.

directly, without any intermediary: 'Ab ipso Deo immediate processit, unde inter imperatorem et Deum non est ponere medium'. Nor is it absurd to uphold this idea: 'Nec absurdum est,' Cynus continues, 'quod sic a populo et a Deo, tamquam ab agenti universali, sicut aliter dicimus, homo hominem generat; vel melius dico, quod imperator a populo est, sed imperium, cuius praesidatu imperator dicitur divinus, a Deo'.[1] That is, incidentally, the reason why the Ruler's laws are 'divinae'.[2]

In this context, the question of the Ruler's coronation becomes specially interesting. Lucas declares that the King's coronation visibly establishes his spiritual bond with God, from whom he receives his commission. The coronation is a symbolic act. It ratifies the fact of succession—be it by election or by hereditary rights—so that the King is now virtually in possession—'realiter assecutus', as our jurist expresses it [3]—of those rights which emanate from his divine mandate: 'Ea, quae sunt praecipua regiae dignitatis', are Lucas's words. Coronation is an act of confirmation, ostensibly completes the Ruler's bond with God and makes it spiritually effective: 'Et ideo inungitur, ut potestas in eo plenior ex Dei benedictione descendat'.[4] Thus coronation is the external sign between Ruler and God. The declarative nature of coronation is also explained by Lucas in another passage, in which he deals with the purely significative character of the crown. He draws a parallel between the Ruler's crown and the ceremonial signs of other institutions. Just as matrimonial rings are simply the external sign, not the constituents, of marriage, just as the tonsure of the

[1] See Cynus, D. 1, 1, 14, no. 4.

[2] It is worth mentioning that the current political literature had very little influence upon the jurists. The document entitled *Rex Pacificus*, ascribed by Bulaeus, *Historia Universitatis Parisiensis*, tom. IV, p. 935, to the Masters of the university, is, as far as could be ascertained, never referred to; John of Paris's tract, Marsiglio's *Defensor Pacis*, and Dante's *De Monarchia* were referred to by Albericus de Rosciate, though he did not adopt their arguments, see his commentaries on C. VII, 37, 3, no. 19. It will be recalled that the *Rex Pacificus* and the other treatises dealt with all the arguments ingeniously put forward by canonists and theologians, and destroyed them one by one. The line of argument in the *Authenticum* (see *supra*, p. 173), of Bartholomaeus de Capua, Cynus, and Lucas himself, is very similar to that of the *Rex Pacificus*, the ideas in which tract are based upon a dualistic principle of government. A comparison between Lucas and Marsiglio would be of little avail, since both set out from different premisses and reach conclusions which have very little in common. On the other hand, there is a remarkable similarity between Lucas, Dante, and Bishop Lupold of Bebenburg, who all maintained the independence of the Empire, but whilst Dante, as an Italian patriot, found the Italian, and Lupold, as a German, the German, answer to 'the problem of the Empire', Lucas is concerned with the purely abstract political problem of rulership in its relation to the pope.

[3] C. X, 74, Rubrica no. 7.

[4] With a reference to *Isaias* ix, 6, he says also: 'Ex hoc confertur sibi gratia et virtutis augmentum . . . augetur in eo gratia fortitudinis contra hostes extrinsecos', loc. cit.

clerics is the external mark, not the constituent, of their clerical status, and just as the circumcision of the Jews differentiates them from non-Jews, but does not in itself make them Jews—in the same way the crown of the Ruler is merely the external and visible sign of his sovereign dignity, not its constituent element: 'Ita et corona signum est regis, non tamen constituit regem . . . corona regis designat plenitudinem imperii et est eius insigne, tamen non tribuit imperium'.[1]

Coronation expresses the recognition of the Church that the Ruler is a Christian Ruler qualified to rule over a Christian people.[2] For it is he alone who, in temporal matters, acts 'vice Dei' on earth. Yet it is precisely his function as God's representative on earth, as His vice-gerent, which has given rise to the doubt whether any approbation and coronation are necessary at all. Indeed, Lucas says, there are some who hold that the Ruler 'ex solo nomine a solo Deo et vice Dei in terris plenitudinem potestatis habere ac sine ulla examinatione, benedictione et coronatione omnia posse'.[3] But Lucas is dissatisfied with this purely mundane conception of the Ruler. He, too, sets out from the function 'vice Dei', and says that it is the actual character of his function which makes imperative his recognition and approbation by the Church of God. But approbation presupposes examination of the candidate's moral character. For how should an excommunicated, a heretic, or an apostate king be able to act 'vice Dei'? And how should the Church be expected to crown an excommunicated personality? Lucas thus fully adopts the arguments set forth by Innocent III.[4]

Consequently, through coronation, the Ruler attains the full possession of all those prerequisites by whose virtue he can rightly claim to be God's representative. There is one more point of interest. In what legal position is the Ruler before the confirmative and declarative act of coronation has taken place? Are his acts preceding his coronation invalid? Or have they the same validity as after coronation? In the latter case the necessity of a coronation might well be questioned. Bartolus, indeed, decidedly maintained that coronation does not affect the validity of any act performed before his coronation.[5] Before Bartolus the same view was held by

[1] C. X, 58, 1, no. 7: 'Et sicut annuli sunt signa matrimonii, non tamen faciunt matrimonium . . . et idem tonsura clericorum, quae est signum ordinis, et non ordo, circumcisio, quae est signum Judaeorum, non tamen facit Judaeum . . . habitus, qui non facit monachum, sed professio, licet signum est monachationis . . . ita et corona . . .'

[2] C. X, 74, Rubrica no. 8. [3] loc. cit., no. 12.

[4] *Decretales*, lib. I, tit. 6, cap. 34, which says, *inter alia*: 'Est enim regulariter et generaliter observatum, ut ad eum examinatio personae pertineat . . . numquid enim, si principes non solum in discordia, sed etiam in concordia sacrilegum quemcumque vel excommunicatum in regem, tyrannum vel fatuum, haereticum eligerent, aut paganum, nos inungere, conservare ac coronare hominem huiusmodi deberemus. Absit omnino . . .'

[5] See the long passage quoted by Woolf, loc. cit., p. 31, note 1.

Cynus, who closely followed Jacobus de Arena.[1] According to these jurists, then, coronation meant simply a change of title, if the spiritual side of the ceremony is left out of account.[2] And Louis of Bavaria, in his quarrel with John XXII and Benedict XII, was bold enough to declare that the papal coronation of the elected Ruler was quite superfluous. This is the standpoint expressed in his famous decree *Licet juris utriusque*. It caused a great stir (' magna concertatio ') in Avignon amongst the prelates and the ' laicos in utroque jure peritos ', according to the report of Albericus de Rosciate, who witnessed the disputes amongst them during his stay at the Roman curia, when the decree was promulgated (1338).[3] Louis, after declaring that the Ruler's power was directly derived from God, stated that if there was a unanimous election or a majority vote, the Ruler became Emperor automatically : ' Imperator ex sola electione eorum, ad quos pertinet, verus efficitur imperator nec alicuius alterius eget confirmatione seu approbatione, quoniam in temporalibus superiorem non habit in terris '.[4]

Lucas's thesis, on the other hand, is consistent. He draws a parallel between the Pope and the Ruler as regards the effect of coronation upon their sovereign status. The only difference between them, according to Lucas, is that the Ruler has to undergo an examination, whilst, for obvious reasons, a corresponding ex-

[1] Cynus in his lecture on C. VII, 37, 3, no. 5 *in fine* says : ' Ex electione rex est, licet propter consecrationem pontificalem et coronationem appellatur Imperator . . . consecratio Papae operatur, ut spiritualia bona sive dona et spiritus sancti gratiam consequitur . . . ante coronationem Papae rex facit legem . . . cum princeps vice populi eligatur ab his, ad quos spectat electio de jure . . . eiusdem est potestatis et vigoris electio ab eis facta de principe, cuius erat electio facta de populo '.

It should be noted that Dr. Carlyle does not adequately deal with the doctrines of Cynus ; nor have the French jurists, Jacobus de Ravanis and Petrus de Bellapertica, who exercised so great an influence on the Italian school through the medium of Cynus, been regarded in Carlyle's work.

[2] Cf. also Woolf, loc. cit., p. 33, and see Cynus's words. How far these thoughts expressed in the fourteenth century resemble those current in the sixteenth century, may be gauged from the opinion of a political writer, Servin (1596), according to whom ' coronation and unction are mere ceremonies and no essential part of the regality ', Figgis, *Divine Right of Kings*, p. 122.

[3] See Albericus' commentaries on C. VII, 37, 3, no. 16 : ' De hoc fuit magna concertatio tempore Joannis XXII et successoris sui Benedicti XII inter eos et dominum Ludovicum de Bavaria electum in imperatorem, et me existente tunc in Romana curia audivi magnos praelatos et etiam alios laicos in utroque jure peritos in hanc opinionem inclinare tamquam veriorem, et super hoc dominus Ludovicus fecit legem, quae sequitur.'

[4] Albericus, loc. cit. On the importance of this decree see McIlwain, loc. cit., p. 277. The silence of the *Golden Bull* (1356) on papal confirmation of the election is as significant as Louis's outbursts. It is not generally known that this decree is printed in Albericus's commentaries. The decree is noteworthy for its unrestrained language ; the Pope is called the ' antiquus hostis ', who by ' pravas assertiones ' as well as by ' pestifera dogmata ' does his best to make sure that peace will not return within the Empire.

amination of the Pope can be dispensed with. But, just as the latter does not receive the plenitude of spiritual powers before his coronation—'Papa ante coronationem spiritualia et praecipua non exercet'—in the same way the Ruler does not possess the plenitude of temporal powers before his coronation. Before his examination and the ceremony of coronation by the Church of God, the Ruler cannot claim to act as His representative, and consequently his acts do not possess divine sanction. For his specific sovereign rights are precisely the effluence of his divine commission. Yet it cannot be said that the Ruler has validly received the mandate—'realiter assecutus'—before the Church has approved of him. Therefore, the exercise of his specific sovereign rights depends on his approbation and coronation by the Church. Hence Lucas arrives at a distinction. Before coronation those acts of the Ruler are valid which are necessary for the maintenance of public order and discipline—acts, that is to say, within the ambit of administrative government. 'Credo autem', says Lucas, after expressing his dissatisfaction with the other views, 'quod ea, sine quibus regnum gubernari non potest, puta executio justitiae et huiusmodi, possit rex administrare, etiam ante benedictionem, consecrationem et coronationem.' [1] Specific sovereign rights, whose exercise is the effluence of his divine mandate, and which receive therefore divine sanction, are not within the scope of his powers before coronation. For instance, new legislation, abrogation of laws, new fiscal policy, conferment of privileges, and the like, cannot be validly exercised. [2]

[1] loc. cit., no. 9. The papal extremist, Oldradus de Ponte, denied the uncrowned Emperor even the exercise of acts falling within the ambit of administration. Cons. 180, no. 12: 'Praeceps est nimium et immatura ingestio eius, qui ante efficacem commissionem gladii utitur gladio . . . et ante administrationis decretum se administrationi impudenter (!) se immiscet'.

On the other hand, some canonists, such as Joannes Andreae, held a view which did not greatly deviate from that of the imperialists. Joannes Andreae taught, as Salicetus reports, 'quod principes Alemanniae judicaverunt, quod rex Romanorum post electionem concordem *omnem habet potestatem*, quam imperator, dicentes quod coronatio et unctio nihil addit', see Salicetus, on C. VII, 37, 3, no. 7. Joannes died 1348.

A century later the professor at the university of Perugia, Philippus Corneus, declared that it is ridiculous ('puto ridiculum esse') to say that the elected Ruler was limited in the exercise of his rights and powers before coronation. Corneus propounded the view that the Ruler, once legitimately elected, 'ante coronationem omnemodam jurisdictionem habeat prout postea'; he is, consequently, in no need of any coronation, since not only the old Roman Emperors were not crowned by a Pope, but also Justinian himself never came to Rome to receive the crown from the hands of a Pope. And no one could entertain any doubt that Justinian and all his successors in the East were rightful Emperors; Justinian's laws were observed throughout the world. See Philippus Corneus, *Consilia*, tom. iii, cons. 1, nos. 12–19.

[2] 'Leges autem novas condere, veteres abrogare, novam monetam cudere, privilegia concedere et alia insignia, in quorum executione consistit pondus et gravitas regiae dignitatis, exercere non possit.'

Of great practical importance was the grant of privileges and donations to princes and barons before coronation. Our jurist denies them legal validity and effect.

We may profitably sum up this topic by contrasting the views of Cynus, Bartolus, and our jurist. Though they are all typical representatives of fourteenth-century legal thought, their diverging views on the position and function of the Ruler throw interesting light on the lawyer's political thought. Cynus, we have seen, in close adherence to Jacobus de Arena, and having been probably influenced by the democratic attitude of the French school of thought, maintained that, by virtue of the still valid *Lex Regia*, the Ruler receives his powers from the people through election and acts 'vice populi', and hence is a representative of the people who have laid the government into his hands.[1] At the other end of the scale is Lucas. To his mind, the government of the people is entrusted to the Ruler by a direct grant of God; hence he acts 'vice Dei'. Bartolus takes up an intermediate, though not always an adequately clarified, position. In his opinion, neither God nor people have given a mandate to rule. This mandate has been given by the Pope, who, as Christ's vicar, possesses both swords and transfers the temporal government to the secular Ruler; but, as far as could be ascertained with reasonable certainty, Bartolus does not go so far as to say that the Ruler acts 'vice Papae'.

As regards the specific sovereign rights, we have already had opportunity to point out that Lucas considers the legislative powers of the Ruler as inalienable. But legislation is only one of his many prerogatives as a sovereign, none of which are transferable. Lucas devotes much space to an enumeration of those rights which are

---

It is noteworthy that Baldus, apparently through independent means, arrived at the same distinction. In his *additio* to his lecture on C. VII, 37, 3, he deals with our present problem, and argues against Jacobus de Arena by saying that a distinction has to be drawn between the Ruler's plenitude of power and his administrative faculties: 'Ante coronationem non habet plenitudinem potestatis, licet habeat generalem administrationem. Ista quaestio disputatur hic per Jacobum de Arena, sed ipse non distinguit inter plenitudinem et generalem administrationem, sicut ego (sic!) facio.'

In his commentary on the peace of Constance, Baldus maintained that in this treaty it was 'expressum, quod rex Romanorum etiam ante coronationem potest concedere privilegia: iste enim Henricus non erat coronatus imperator, quia pater vivebat', col. 166.

The thirteenth-century canonist Joannes Teutonicus propounded a view that was similar to that of Lucas. Joannes, according to the report of Salicetus, loc. cit., maintained that the elected became Emperor through election, but the exercise of his sovereign powers depended on papal confirmation: 'Nam electio facit imperatorem, sed non habet exercitium, nisi per confirmationem'. But a colleague of Joannes reproached him, and said that this was his theory, because he was a German: 'Joannes Faventinus dixit, quod iste sic dixerat, quia teutonicus erat', Salicetus, loc. cit.

[1] See the passage transcribed, *supra*, p. 177, and: 'Electo a populo per legem regiam omne jus utriusque potestas competit merito', loc. cit., no. 5.

preserved for the Ruler alone, theoretically speaking for the Emperor. Apart from legislation, such sovereign rights are declaration of war, command of the armed forces, the coining of money, imposition of taxes, grant of immunity from taxes (in special cases only), appointment of officials, introduction of new revenues and extraordinary taxes, remission of penalties,[1] release from ban, conferment of privileges and their withdrawal, jurisdiction on final appeal, revocation of special laws granted by predecessors, and the like.[2]

A special problem—particularly concerning the nature of sovereignty—arose in connexion with territorial donations by the Ruler to a private citizen. The problem concerned the question as to whether sovereign rights are simultaneously handed over by a transfer of territory, and hence by acquisition of dominion. Lucas asks which rights are understood to have been transferred by a donation: 'Pone, rex donat tibi castrum simpliciter dicens "dono tibi hoc castrum", utrum intelligatur omnia jura, quae habet in eo, in te transtulisse?'[3] In consistence with his views on the personal character of sovereignty, he distinguishes between rights which can be possessed by any private citizen and those which only the Ruler possesses by virtue of his function as a sovereign. The former are understood to have been implicitly and simultaneously transferred by the donation of the sovereign, the latter cannot be validly transferred, even if the Ruler wished to do so; they can only be delegated, so that they can be exercised 'auctoritate regis'. Lucas answers the above question in these terms: 'Dicas omnia jura, quae possunt cadere in privatum, in te transtulisse videntur, quae autem non cadunt in alium quam in regem, et quae ipse rex etiam si vellet expresse a se et majori dominio rei publicae, cuius gubernationem accepit, non posset eximere, ut est potestas condendae legis et alia similia, non intelligitur concedisse'. Sovereign rights, properly so called, are inseparable from royal power, because they are 'velut regis ossibus inhaerentibus'.[4] God has given the Ruler himself the mandate which creates a personal bond with God, establishes a trusteeship, and, in consequence, is inalienable: 'Quorum omnium (scil. sovereign prerogatives) auctoritas et potestas est solis regibus et principibus a Deo concessa'.[5] In his commentary on C. X, 35, 1, yet another argument appears: he says that if an ecclesiastical estate which had been incidentally granted

[1] Baldus declared that every judgement was understood to contain the clause 'salva suprema potestatis imperatoris', C. VII, 50, 3, no. 1.

[2] C. XII, 35, 14, nos. 1 seq.

[3] C. XII, 46, 1, no. 5.

[4] loc. cit., no. 5. He treats also of the same problem in his commentary on C. XII, 29, 1, no. 18, and says here: 'Dicas plenius, quod omnia, quae rex ibi habet, videatur donare, quae tamen possunt per privatum et subditum possideri; quae vero sunt regalia mere, ut potestas condendae legis, creare magistratus et tabelliones, monetam cudere et similia, quae quidem non possunt cadere in privatum, donasse nullatenus intelligitur, quia ista velut regis ossibus inhaerentia nequeunt a potestate regia separari'.

[5] C. XII, 35, 14, no. 9.

immunity from taxes or other civic duties were transferred to some other private individual, the immunity would instantly come to an end, because 'si vero mutatur personae conditio, mutatur conditio rei '.[1] The idea of the 'publica utilitas', once again, makes any other view, in Lucas's opinion, untenable: 'Quia in praestatione functionem publica versatur utilitas', he concludes this discussion. He avails himself of the very same argument to prove that sovereign rights are not understood to have been transferred by a donation of the kind envisaged by him. In another passage in which he treats of this problematic transfer of prerogatives he remarks that 'haec est specialis prerogativa principis (i.e., legislation), quae in singularem successorem non transfertur . . . quia mutatione personae mutatur conditio rei '.[2] Lucas clearly distinguishes between a transfer and a delegation of sovereign rights.[3] The theory that the exercise of sovereign rights, such as jurisdiction, follows from the actual possession of certain territories, is not unknown to Lucas, as is shown when he says that some believe 'quod jurisdictio adhaeret territorio'.[4] It was especially Bartolus who conceived of territorially limited sovereignty, particularly as regards jurisdictional powers. He, too, envisaged the problem of a donation by the Ruler in the form of a territorial transfer, but applied to this donation the rules governing donations between private individuals. Hence he was led to conclude that all rights flowing from the possession of that (formerly royal) territory had been transferred: in particular, he stated, the Ruler had thereby renounced his right of exclusive jurisdictional powers: 'Si princeps vel alius concederet tibi universaliter unum territorium, videtur tibi concedere universaliter jurisdictionem, quia sicut ille, qui concedit rem singularem, dicitur dominium rei singularis concedere'.[5] But Bartolus hastened to add that this envisaged universal transfer of territory does not convey universal jurisdictional powers—that is, over any territory—but only over the transferred territory: 'Ex hoc patet', Bartolus wrote a few lines later, 'quod jurisdictio non cohaeret proprie territorio; pro tanto dicitur, quod cohaeret territorio, quia terminatur territorio'. Lucas, on the other hand,

[1] He continues: 'Unde si res ecclesiastica, pro qua non subit onus collectarum ecclesia, perveniat ex locatione in censum vel emphyteusim ad laicum, non erit ipse laicus immunis ab onere collectarum pro ipsa, quia mutata est conditio possessoris, ergo et conditio rei'.

[2] C. XI, 29, 2, no. 3. Bartolus, on the other hand, held that a donation of this kind entailed a transfer of sovereign rights, see Figgis, loc. cit., p. 561, and also Woolf, loc. cit., pp. 134 seq.

[3] C. XII, 59, 8, no. 5. Here he speaks of a prescriptive acquisition of jurisdictional powers and says: 'Puto, si privatus exercet jurisdictionem aut merum imperium *auctoritate regis*, et alius privatus vellet contra eum illa praescribere, ac sibi jus proprium vendicare, ut ea *non auctoritate regia*, sed propria exerceret, praescriptio non procedat'.

[4] C. XII, 29, 2, no. 18.

[5] Strangely enough, neither Figgis nor Woolf refer to this passage of Bartolus, D. 2, 1, 1, no. 16.

anxious to preserve the unity of sovereign power, rejects this territorial conception of sovereignty, and declares that sovereign rights are inalienable and not transferable, even if the Ruler wished to transfer them. They can be exercised on his behalf only. This 'territorial conception' of Bartolus seems to have been, at least implicitly, rejected by Baldus, his pupil. Baldus, heavily leaning towards a strengthening of royal and imperial power, propounded the view that jurisdictional powers could be exercised on behalf of the Ruler only; they were inseparable from the supreme power. 'Nam in eis (scil. jurisdictionalibus),' said Baldus, 'semper auctoritas superioris reservatur, et nisi eius auctoritate non potest exerceri, cum in eo resideat suprema potestas inseparabilis.' [1]

The personal character of sovereign rights is, furthermore, a bar to their prescriptive acquisition. Lucas argues at great length on this point, and states that within the purview of 'regalia' there can be no prescription against the instituted authority. Not only would prescription of this kind disturb the social organism, he holds, but would also obviously be against the public interest and would be contrary to the idea of obedience.[2] Consequently, the prescriptive acquisition of sovereign rights, such as public ways, taxes, revenues, jurisdiction, and the like, is not possible according to Lucas. He reports, however, that other jurists held that these rights can be acquired 'longissimo tempore'. That was the view of Dynus and his pupil Cynus, who believed that 'per tanti temporis patientiam fingitur princeps permisisse'.[3] But apart from the reasons adduced above, Lucas holds that 'in his (scil. regalibus), quae debentur sibi (scil. principi) super aliis ratione praeexcellentiae principalis' no prescription can ever be allowed. Once again Lucas's predilection for, and insistence upon, instituted authority cause him to oppose current views which, to his mind, would upset the structure of the social organism as he conceived it. The following statement significantly epitomizes his reasons: 'Sic enim tota excellentia et praeeminentia potestatis imperialis et regiae deperirent, quod est omnino cavendum, cum sint a Deo'.[4] Whether clandestine or open, the usurpation of sovereign rights, particularly of the right of jurisdiction,[5] constitutes, according to Lucas, the *crimen laesae majestatis*: this crime is committed not only by a factual injury to the sovereign, but also by the exercising of authority that had not been granted—that is to say, 'si quis fecerit ut regi subjectus, quod in eius imperium potestatemve non veniat, sed rex sua jurisdictione privetur'.[6]

There is one aspect of fiscal policy that deserves mentioning—

[1] He continued: 'Unde potest jurisdictiones supprimere aliorum, non solum singularium personarum, sed etiam civitatum', Baldus in his lecture on C. VI, 14, 3, no. 34; see also his *Consilia*, tom. I, cons. 64.

[2] 'Contra principem in hoc non currit praescriptio. Item, quia talia usurpare est contra debitum obedientiae, quam omnis privatus et subditus regi tenetur impendere', C. XII, 59, 8, no. 4.

[3] loc. cit., no. 6.

[4] C. XII, 35, 14, no. 12.

[5] C. XI, 53, 1, no. 38.

[6] loc. cit., no. 38.

viz., the change of the value of money by the Ruler. It is true that he alone is entitled to a fiscal measure of this kind, but the exercise of his right depends on the consent of the people. It is very difficult to reconcile the following statement with Lucas's basic principles: 'Et nota', he states, 'quod monetam sine consensu populi rex mutare non potest'.[1]

Throughout our exposition we have employed the term sovereignty, although this notion belongs to the terminology of the sixteenth century rather than to that of the fourteenth century. But there can be little doubt that it is this very concept which our jurist struggles to work out, to clarify, and to express. His theory of the power and function of the Ruler is a recognition of the absolute sovereignty of the Monarch—a theory which became fashionable in in the later sixteenth century.[2] In many respects we may clearly discern a resemblance of Lucas's ideas to those of Jean Bodin two centuries later.[3] Lucas's doctrine—quite in the fashion of two centuries later—is conceived politically rather than legally, whilst his great contemporaries, such as Bartolus and Baldus, were still busying themselves finding the legal basis (and background) of the political realities of their day. Lucas approaches the political problem from political aspects, whilst they try to tackle it from the purely legal point of view. That is precisely the reason why his political theory, especially that of sovereignty, is in advance of his century.[4]

The idea of civil liberty and its preservation by the Ruler is a cardinal tenet of Lucas's conception of government. For liberty is, as he expresses it, 'lumen vitae nostrae', whilst servitude is 'mortis imago'.[5] The just Ruler will uphold and guarantee individual freedom, and will further the cause of freedom by interfering as little as possible. There is nothing on earth more precious than civil liberty, and there is nothing more detestable than slavery: Lucas, indeed, thinks that death should be preferred to servitude.[6]

[1] C. XI, 10 Rubrica, no. 4. In this context it is interesting to observe that Jean Bodin propounded an idea not unlike that of Lucas, but in respect of taxes. Bodin, in spite of his partisanship for the absolute monarchy, maintained that 'princes could only impose taxes with the consent of their subjects', Dr. Carlyle, loc. cit., vol. vi, p. 488.

[2] Aeneas Sylvius's theory of inalienable sovereignty prepared the ground ideologically, though there is no fundamental difference between his and Lucas's theory.

[3] See Dr. Carlyle, loc. cit., vol. vi, pp. 417–429. The close resemblance of Lucas and Bodin becomes still more apparent in the exposition of the latter's doctrine by A. W. Dunning, loc. cit., vol. ii, pp. 96 seq., especially pp. 101–103. See also Mr. J. W. Jones, loc. cit., pp. 81 seq. and Figgis, 'Political Thought in the Sixteenth Century' in *Cambridge Modern History*, vol. iii, p. 747.

[4] The idea of sovereignty does not necessarily require an articulated State in the modern twentieth-century sense, see Professor Powicke, 'Reflections on the Medieval State', in *Transactions of the Royal Historical Society*, 4th series, vol. xix, 1936, p. 12.

[5] C. XI, 48, 1, no. 10, referring to *Policraticus*, lib. VII, cap. 17.

[6] loc. cit., no. 10.

Earthly goods and material commodities exist for the sake of man, whose liberty, dignity, and personal value, being immaterial, are immeasurable in quantitative terms: 'Salus atque libertas aestimari non potest'.[1] Lucas believes that the liberty, happiness, and prosperity of the individuals depend, to a very marked degree, on the adequate payment of wages for the work performed by them. This right of adequate wage he finds expressed in *Leviticus* xix. 13, and is, therefore, an issue of the divine law itself: 'De jure divino debetur unicuique merces pro labore, juxta illud Levit. 19: "non morabitur apud te opus mercenarii tui usque mane"'.[2] The same holds true of civil law: 'Idem jure civili', Lucas declares.[3] Work should be rewarded according to the kind of services rendered ('juxta mensuram laboris'), and something more than a mere pittance ('mercedula') should be doled out.[4] Nevertheless, our jurist is fully aware that material values do not constitute in themselves happiness, but he conceives them to be a contributory cause to happiness. Nothing seems to him more incompatible with a true conception of life than the craving for money, in the possession of which the vulgar opinion sees the measurement of felicity. Money and temporal goods should be only means to the end, he holds, and not ends in themselves; they should not be striven after 'cum studio et affectu singulari'.[5] The value of the human creature is incomparable to that of any material creation: 'Personae quippe hominum sunt rebus caeteris digniores,' Lucas avows.[6] Since Christ, King of kings, voluntarily chose death for the liberation of man from the servitude of the devil, the good and just Ruler will

[1] 'Homines . . . quorum gratia bona omnia sunt inducta . . . et qui sunt bonis omnibus digniores . . . eorum salus et libertas aestimari non potest', loc. cit.

[2] C. XI, 70, 5, no. 21. On the philosophers' views see De Wulf, vol. i, pp. 305–6.

[3] loc. cit., no. 21. Lucas refers to C. IX, 41, 17, and to canon law, *causa* 1, *quaestio* 2, *canon* 10. This is a very interesting example of Lucas's way of reasoning. Both laws, the civil as well as the canon law, are concerned with special cases only. When he refers to the passage in the *Codex* which deals with criminal proceedings against persons of a certain status, he obviously has in mind the quite insignificant words, which are used in an entirely different context: 'habeat hanc mercedem laboris multorum munerum testimoniis commendata devotio'. The passage in canon law, too, deals only with a special case—namely, with the reward for work performed by clerics: 'Clerici omnes, cui ecclesiae fideliter vigilanterque deserviunt, stipendia sanctis laboribus debita secundum servitii sui meritum per ordinationem canonum a sacerdotibus consequantur'. This was a rule laid down by the council at Agde in France in the year 505. Both these examples show clearly how Lucas, in the true fashion of the Post-Glossators, generalizes special cases.

[4] He alludes to some obsolete law which appears to diminish this right: 'Tamen lex mortua his juribus detrahit, cum pro magnis laboribus statuat mercedulam dari'. But he does not say to which law he alludes.

[5] 'In pecunia juxta vulgi opinionem, qui putant omnia mensurari nummismate omnemque felicitatem exinde provenire, consistunt divitiae temporales, quae, si sunt cum studio at affectu singulari, ignominiosae sunt', C. XI, 47, 5, no. 3.

[6] C. XI, 70, 5, no. 21.

not shun any exertions to preserve and increase the liberty of his subjects.[1] In the development of his argument, Lucas says that the Ruler encroaches upon liberty by revoking causelessly any privilege—that is to say, right—granted to, and enjoyed by, a particular individual or a particular group of individuals. By virtue of his position, function, and mandate he is bound to follow God as his example: God would never revoke anything granted to man, and in the same way the Ruler should never, without a 'justa causa', revoke any privileges.[2] On the other hand, if the public policy or the common weal demands action of this kind, the Ruler is entitled to impinge upon the rights of individuals. Expropriation of private property [3] and the withdrawal of privileges in the public interest are quoted by Lucas as typical examples of justifiable encroachments on liberty.[4] But, because they infringe upon the rights of others, Lucas stresses the necessity of a 'justa causa'—which is pre-eminently the consideration of the public interest—in all expropriations. He draws a parallel between expropriations and remissions of penalties by the Ruler, who is left very much freer in his dealings with the latter: 'In remissione poenarum, quae debentur ex crimine, plus potest rex quam in donando rem alienam'.[5] The reason is that 'remissiones poenarum aut parum aut nihil laedunt alium'. But even here the Ruler has no full liberty of action: if by judicial decision the condemned is bound to give satisfaction to the injured party, the Ruler should then not remit the penalty, unless the judicial command concerning satisfaction has been carried out.[6]

The principle underlying the Ruler's mode of government should be that of equity.[7] His aim should be the welfare of his people and the promotion of the common good: 'Tutela et procuratio rei publicae', in these words Lucas epitomizes the primary task of the

[1] 'Ipse Christus, rex regum, ut hominum genus diabolo serviens erueret a servitute, voluntarie mori voluit et dignatus est', C. XI, 48, 1, no. 10.

[2] 'Princeps Deum imitari tenetur . . . sed Deus non revocat beneficia collata per eum . . . non est verisimile, quod revocare velit, sed magis liberalitatis accumulare fasciculum . . . ergo rex, si Deum imitari vult, donata revocare non debet, neque potest', C. XI, 70, 5, no. 34. That is particularly true with regard to privileges granted to the Church: 'Et ideo princeps privilegium, quod semel concedit ecclesiae, aufferre non potest'.

[3] It is important to observe that the Ruler is bound to pay compensation for expropriated goods. 'Pro utilitate publica potest rex capere bona cum pretii solutione', loc. cit., no. 19. See further in the text. Baldus, too, insisted on compensation, see C. VII, 13, 2, no. 3. This became then the general doctrine, see Paulus Castrensis, D. 39, 1, 5, no. 11, and Ludovicus Romanus, *Consilium*, 310, no. 4. Albericus de Rosciate, however, denied this right, D. 8, 6, 14, no. 1.

[4] loc. cit., nos. 44–57. Lucas devotes four columns to examples and illustrations of cases in which the Ruler is entitled to withdraw privileges and to confiscate property. The main criterion is: 'ex legitima vel honesta causa, puta ratione publicae utilitatis'.

[5] C. XI, 70, 5, no. 36.

[6] 'Sed rex non potest remittere poenam debitam delinquenti, nisi primo satisfaciat parti laesae', loc. cit., no. 36.

[7] 'Omnis actus regius debet super aequitate fundari', loc. cit., no. 34.

Ruler.[1] Lucas compares him with the soul of the human body, since his function is like that of the human heart. Government resembles pastoral care.[2] Wise government avoids harshness, which merely exasperates the people and incites them to rise against the instituted authority: 'Populus enim leniendus est verbis clementibus et sic servit. Duris autem exasperatur atque rebellat.'[3] The Ruler should strive to avoid being a taskmaster ('exactor'), and he should be desirous of proving himself a divine leader of his people by his superior understanding of their needs, instead of ruling by violent and harsh methods or by brutal suppression: 'Debent quippe reges', Lucas says, 'studere, ut non exactores, sed Dei rectores nominentur, non in subditos saevire crudeliter, sed illos amplecti regaliter'.[4] Lucas compares the Ruler with a father loving his children and a shepherd watching over his flock.[5] Taxation, in particular, should be reasonable, Lucas holds; the Ruler should abstain from imposing unreasonable, new, or crushing burdens on his subjects, hence exploiting them for his own personal benefit 'sub colore justitiae'.[6] The maintenance of public order and the promotion of the common good are once again the decisive criteria for the imposition of taxes. Nobody can rightfully claim to be exempted from them. As we pointed out before, the right of taxation is the effluence of the Ruler's sovereign power. The question as to whether, through imposing taxes, a 'natural obligation' is created between Ruler and his subject, does not evoke the interest of Lucas—though it was still very much disputed by his contemporaries.[7] But another question aroused the interest of Lucas—

[1] C. XII, 43, 3, no. 12. In other places he speaks of the Ruler as a protector.

[2] 'Sicut anima regit corpus et conservat, ita rex statuitur ad regni gubernationem et regimen, et sicut anima est salus et vita corporis, sic et rex et huiusmodi principes, si recte principantur, sunt salus et vita regnorum . . . et sicut se habent medici ad corpora, sic se habent reges et legumlatores ad animas subditorum, ut patet per Arist. 4 Polit', loc. cit., no. 12.

It is significant that, in spite of his predilection for John of Salisbury, Lucas does not follow him in this point. In his discussion on the organic structure of society, John said that the function of the heart is performed by the clergy. Lucas fails to give the clergy any 'organic' function within the body politic; see E. F. Jacob, loc. cit., p. 65, McIlwain, loc. cit., and Poole, loc. cit., pp. 207, 208.

[3] C. X, 19, 2, no. 16. He refers to a proverb of the inhabitants of Salerno: 'Juxta proverbium Salernitanorum "in manu passorum, mel in ore",' loc. cit., no. 17.

[4] C. X. 18, 1, no. 11.

[5] 'Similis est operatio regis ad subjectos patris ad filios, pastoris ad oves; paterno enim more pie debet regere populum et clementer', loc. cit., no. 11.

[6] loc. cit., no. 11. In no. 3 he says: 'Debeant (scil. principes) potius bonis parentum moribus eis (scil. subditis) veluti filiis thesauros praeparare . . . est enim princeps communis pater omnium'.

[7] See the passage of Baldus transcribed by Dr. Carlyle, loc. cit., vol. vi, p. 86, note 1. On the whole the jurists were not greatly interested in the problem of taxation. About the literature of the publicists see Gierke-Maitland, loc. cit., p. 190, note 323, and p. 191, note 325.

namely, that of whether the (Christian) Ruler is entitled to impose taxes on his Christian subjects. Indeed, Lucas says, canon law seems to lend support to the idea that the Ruler cannot, without sin, impose taxes on his Christian subjects: 'Videtur, quod . . . non possunt absque peccato facere exactiones sive pecuniam in suos subditos Christianos, ad id 16 q 1 praedicator'.[1] But Lucas finds sufficient establishment of this kingly right in the divine appointment and in the function of the Ruler. He answers: 'Sec circa hunc articulum considerari oportet, quod principes terrarum a Deo sunt instituti.'

It is true that the Ruler is 'dominus mundi'—that is to say, overlord over person and property. But, from the point of view of our jurist, it would be entirely misleading if this designation were taken as a literal expression signifying the Ruler's ownership. Overlordship means to Lucas trusteeship: it is as their guardian, their protector, their leader in all temporal questions concerning the community at large that God entrusts people and things to the Ruler. That is why Lucas says that the Ruler cannot lay any personal claim on the property of his subjects, but that he has the right and duty of protection: the Ruler, he declares, 'in bonis subjectorum nullum jus habet, sed protectionem solam, juxta veram opinionem'[2] (C. X, 47, 4, no. 34). Only in a very wide and vague sense can the Ruler be spoken of as the owner, not of the people's goods, but of the State itself. He argues, we may recall, that the term 'belong' can also be applied to persons who have the mere protection—and therefore no property in the juristic sense—of an object. In this very wide sense the Ruler can be envisaged as the owner of the State: 'Et hoc modo res publica dicitur esse principis'.[3] The people's goods, of which they are owners, are in his trust. This protectoral function of the Ruler may best be illustrated by the passage of Lucas in which he says that the Ruler wields all temporal power—'exercet imperialem potestatem'—for the sake of protection.[4] Through his temporal sword the peace-loving and law-abiding citizens enjoy security. The Ruler has the duty to protect the life and property of the citizens entrusted to him by God: 'Quemlibet in sua possessione tueri'.[5] Or as he expresses it in another passage: 'Gladii princeps potestatem accepit a Deo, non super bonos et malos indifferenter, sed in eos, qui gladio male utuntur'.[6] There is some resemblance between the function of the Ruler and that of a tutor, Lucas states.[7] This aspect of the Ruler's position as regards the property of his subjects explains why he is, by virtue of his trusteeship, permitted to expropriate possessions for the common good, but, on the other hand, obliged to

[1] C. XII, 29, 1, no. 8, canon law: *causa* xvi, *quaestio* 1, *canon* 64.
[2] He obviously means Bulgarus's famous reply to Frederick I.
[3] C. X. 31, 33, no. 19. See also *supra*, p. 101.
[4] C. X, 16, 3, no. 4.
[5] C. X, 75, 1, no. 8.
[6] C. XII, 45, 1, no. 33.
[7] C. XI, 28, 1, no. 1.

compensate the owner of them. His permission is derived from the consideration of the public interest—hence the requirement of a 'legitima causa'—on whose behalf he encroaches upon the rights of his subjects; his obligation follows from his not being owner of the expropriated goods. Moreover, the Ruler is not entitled to impose servitudes upon his subjects' possessions,[1] for such actions would not be within the province of protection, properly understood: 'Non enim hoc esset protegere, sed destruere'.

The Ruler who, without just cause, restricts the freedom of his citizens, is a tyrant. Tyranny, according to Lucas, consists essentially in the misuse of the mandate and of the powers entrusted to the Ruler by God. The Ruler's disrespect for the liberty of his subjects leads to an enslavement of his people. The tyrant governs, not by laws and decrees based on justice and equity, but by violence and oppression: the idea of law, the idea of justice and righteousness, are alien to him. 'Tyrannus', says Lucas, closely following John of Salisbury, 'est, qui violenta dominatione populum premit'.[2] Disregard of the law by the very authority who is called upon to govern on the basis of justice and equity entails deprivation of civil liberty, and hence insecurity on the part of the citizens. For, according to Lucas, only under the reign of law can true security and liberty flourish.[3] Selfishness is a characteristic feature of the tyrants, Lucas maintains. Again, taking the *Policraticus* as his trusted adviser, Lucas strongly affirms that tyrannicide is a justifiable, nay, a praiseworthy deed, not only according to human law, but according also to divine law.[4] He is well aware that this opinion is not one which may command general approval;[5] he remarks sarcastically: 'Juste itaque tyrannus occiditur, licet quidam vel timidi vel nimium justi contrarium dicant'. But he feels that 'pater coelestis terrenusque de ipsius (tyranni) interitu consolatur'.[6] It is not only his dependence on force which distinguishes the tyrant from the just Ruler, but also unnecessary confiscations which amount

[1] 'Cum princeps non sit dominus rerum singularum privatorum . . . non ergo princeps, qui solam protectionem habet, imponet rebus singularium servitutes', C. X, 39, 4, no. 3. Opposing the general opinion, Oldradus, cons. 87, demanded a just cause for the confiscation of Jewish property.

[2] C. X, 31, 42, no. 2. It is interesting to note that Lucas applies the term 'dominatio' to the government of a tyrant only, see, e.g., C. X, 70, 4, no. 13.

[3] See also *supra*, ch. III, p. 44.

[4] 'An sit licitum etiam divina lege tyrannum occidere . . . verum divina ultio non diu permittit has sui furoris et iracundiae virgas longius vivere . . .', loc. cit., no. 4. On John of Salisbury's views see A. W. Dunning, loc. cit., vol. i, pp. 187, 188, and R. L. Poole, loc. cit., pp. 205, 208, 209.

[5] This surmise was well justified. Paris de Puteo, professor of laws at the university of Naples, dutifully records Lucas's opinion, and adds that even St. Thomas is supposed to have said 'quod meritorium est, occidere tyrannum', but himself rejects these views on account of the decision of the Council of Constance (1415), Paris de Puteo in his tract 'De sindicatu' in *Tractatus*, tom. vii, fol. 217, no. 17. About St. Thomas's views see Carlyle, loc. cit., vol. v, p. 93, and d'Entrèves, loc. cit., pp. 35 and 38.

[6] On Bracton's theory of tyrannicide, see Schulz, loc. cit., p. 153.

to pillaging, the levying of heavy and unjustifiable taxes and similar destructive acts.[1] The removal of this 'publicus hostis' is only in the public interest, since tyrannical government leads to the eventual destruction of society as a whole.[2] It is probable that Lucas has in mind contemporary conditions in parts of the Empire when he cries out: 'O utinam, qui sunt reges, illud bene portarent et non intumescerent in offensam Dei et perniciem subjectorum'.[3]

But Lucas observes that it is not only the tyrant who encroaches upon the liberty of the subject, but also sometimes 'minor' rulers, such as barons and counts. Lucas puts on record that the citizen may lawfully be deprived of his liberty only by the proper authority—that is, by officials who have the power to imprison, such as bailiffs, magistrates, and governors of the provinces. No private citizen is authorized under any circumstances to take another private citizen into custody or otherwise to deprive him of his liberty. 'Privatus autem nullus', writes Lucas, 'potest aliquem pro maleficio capere'.[4] This principle suffers only one exception: the perpetration of a crime by a vassal whose master is allowed to imprison him; this privilege is granted to the master alone. But the master has the duty to commit the vassal to the proper authority within two days, unless security is given for him.[5] Officials, too, are only empowered to imprison criminals for crimes committed, but not yet punished. Lucas does not mention any other reason for imprisonment. In particular, the idea that a threat to public order constitutes an offence is a conception still alien to him, and the aim of promoting 'security' and the avowed purpose of 'protective custody' would not, in his opinion, have justified the deprivation of an individual's liberty.

Thus incarceration is permitted only by the competent authority and for a legally recognized reason—i.e., crime. The right to imprison rests only with the public authority to which this specific

[1] 'Omnis ergo princeps, licet sit legitime institutus, debet tamen vitare opera tyrannorum, quae sunt injustis legibus populum subjectum opprimere, collectis et tributis indebitis aggravare, rebus propriis spoliare, muneribus indebitis angariare', C. XII, 63, 1, no. 74.

[2] Because of the absence of law, Lucas goes even so far as to deny a State governed by a tyrant the character of an organized entity: 'Nulla est societas cum tyrannis et potius summa destructio est', loc. cit., no. 71. For an explanation of the medieval idea of tyrannicide, see McIlwain, pp. 285–6.

[3] C. XII, 35, 14, no. 6; he continues: 'Licet autem princeps habeat plenitudinem potestatis, melius tamen faciat circa regimen rei publicae, si eius onera cum aliis partiatur'. On the views of Bartolus see Figgis, 'Bartolus and the Development of European Political Ideas' in *Divine Right of Kings*, pp. 363–6.

[4] C. XII, 57, 1, no. 1. On the English practice see Holdsworth, vol. ii, pp. 101–2, and the measures taken against unlawful arrests, ibid., p. 448.

[5] loc. cit., no. 1. This was also laid down in a law of Charles II, see *Constitutiones*, p. 335, cap. 'amplius'. Lucas says: 'Nisi esset vasallus capientis. Nam tunc pro maleficio patrato poterit eum dominus capers, non tamen detinere ultra duos dies et illum in defectu fidejussoriae cautionis captivum transmittere ad praesidem provinciae debet'.

right has been conceded. Imprisonment follows from the rights of public authority. Thus imprisonment by unauthorized persons, such as private individuals or officials to whom this right has not been given, particularly imprisonment for debts, is prohibited.[1] Lucas observes a tendency to circumvent this prohibition by concluding a treaty between creditor and debtor to the effect that, if the debt is not paid by a certain date, the debtor may be imprisoned for his debt. Now, the problem was whether upon the application of the creditor such a treaty could be enforced by an authorized official, such as the judge.[2] Lucas's answer is emphatically in the negative: 'Videtur aperte, quod non; cum talis consuetudo censeatur iniqua, ut hic, ergo et pactum iniquum est et sic nullum'. The intrinsic reason is that privately disposing of one's own personal liberty is condemned by the law: 'Contractus super homine libero procedens improbatur a lege'. But apart from this material consideration, Lucas holds that there are legalistic reasons against the validity of imprisonment for debts. If it were true that the judge could order imprisonment solely on the basis of a private agreement, then imprisonment would be a matter of private arrangement and would be withdrawn from the jurisdiction of the proper public authority: 'Si ex auctoritate pacti, certum est, quod jus carcerandi et potestas non procedunt a jure publico'; the only juristically tenable idea is that imprisonment 'non competit nec procedit ex pactis privatorum'. But imprisonment is indeed the manifestation of a right possessed only by public authority. A treaty between creditor and debtor cannot be held to be within the purview of the rights of public authority, nor can it furnish the judge with a legally valid title to imprisonment. A private treaty cannot alter the rights of other individuals; nor can it encroach upon the rights which are conferred only upon the appropriate public authority: 'Nec pactum vel dispositio potest tollere jus alienum, id est, publicum, quae sunt jurisdictionis vel imperii'.[3] In conclusion, a private contract invoking the help of an authorized person cannot validate the otherwise invalid and prohibited incarceration by private individuals: 'Ex quibus manifeste concluditur', Lucas sums up, 'quod cum actus iste incarcerationis sit prohibitus in substantia et forma, quod pacto non potuit validari'.

Lucas complains that the previously mentioned 'minor' rulers

[1] Lucas deduces this also from C. XII, 22, 1 *in fine* and from C. X, 19, 2.

[2] C. XII, 22, 1, no. 5. 'An vigore huius pacti possit judex instante creditore in carcere ponere debitorem?'

The system prevailing in contemporary England resulted generally in the creditor's being able to take the debtor's body in execution, see Holdsworth, vol. viii, p. 231. Holdsworth also says that, in England, constraint of the debtor's person became a more general method of execution than in many other countries in Europe, ibid.

[3] loc. cit., no. 8. 'Cum ipse actus incarcerationis sit judicis, et eius potentia procedens sit ex jure publico, auctoritate publici juris nullam communinionem habens cum privatis et potentia privatorum, sicut jus tertii non tollit pactum alterius . . .'

usurp the authority which is granted to officials only, by depriving persons of their liberty and by keeping them detained.[1] Those rulers—if they can be so called—exercise no official rights and should be punished for the wrong they have inflicted on the citizen. That wrong, in Lucas's opinion, is no less than the *crimen laesae majestatis*. For imprisonment is the effluence of public authority,[2] and since this specific right has not been granted to the wrongdoer, his action must be considered an offence against the public authority embodied in the person of the supreme Ruler: 'In hoc enim offendit et minuit majestatem, et ideo acrius est plectendus, quia non sibi concessam a domino potestatem abutens usurpare non timuit'.[3] Legally authorized officials who use their powers to detain citizens for reasons other than those of crime, commit a no less heinous offence than the 'minor' rulers. Such an official transgresses the limits of his powers: 'Concessa sibi capiendi et includendi abutitur potestate . . . taliter delinquendo excedit terminos suos'.[4]

Imprisonment, however, does not mean that the individual is entirely unprotected, or that he has lost all rights, especially those which he has by virtue of his dignity as a human creature. It is precisely on humanitarian grounds that Lucas urges the individuals responsible for the prisoner to take proper care of him.[5] For there is a presumption, Lucas declares, that if death occurs in prison, the individuals in charge of the prisoner are to be censured: 'Mortuus in carcere praesumitur custodis culpa vel negligentia mortuus'.[6] Thus, in case a prisoner is moribund, the warder should convoke witnesses in front of whom he should declare that the present moribund prisoner has not met with any injuries at his (the warder's) hands.[7] The warders are in duty bound to take all possible precautions for the well-being of the prisoner entrusted to their care: 'Notandum est', Lucas writes, 'quod custos debet in captivorum custodia solertissime vigilare'. The warder would pay with his head if he neglected his duty: 'Custos enim sui capitis tenetur adhibere custodiam'. On the grounds of equity, Lucas states, following Bartolus, the prisoner must be allowed to appoint a lawyer who will take charge of all legal steps connected with his cause.[8] This is only a corollary of the general principle that the accused

[1] loc. cit., no. 3: 'Quis includit seu capit alium, quasi habens publicam potestatem vel ut ipsam usurpet, ut plurimi comites et barones fecerunt hactenus . . .'

[2] loc. cit. 'Custodia exercetur, cum quis ponit aliquos in carcere veluti personas accusatas . . . et sic agit hoc per modum imperium exercendi'.

[3] loc. cit., no. 4. He refers to *causa* xxiii, *quaestio* 8, *canon* 33, which deals with a similar topic.

[4] loc. cit., nos. 5 and 6.

[5] C. XII, 37, 17, no. 4: 'De humanitate congrua, quam custos in custodia captivorum debet habere'.

[6] loc. cit., no. 6.

[7] loc. cit., no. 7.

[8] loc. cit., no. 8. 'Et ideo dominus Bartolus notat . . . quod captivus positus in carcere pro crimine capitali potest in omnibus, quae ad prosecutionem causae pertinent, constituere procuratorem, praeterquam ad sententiam audiendam'.

cannot be deprived of his defence: 'Omnis omni tempore defensio reo danda est . . . defensionem quocumque tempore postulando reo negari non oportet'.[1]

We have somewhat digressed from our proper subject,[2] and may now consider the executive. The transaction of the public affairs is in the hands of officials who have received their mandate from the proper authority, that is, from the Ruler—'a solo principe tamquam a capite in omnia rei publicae membra honorum et potestatum munera diffunduntur'[3]—and hence indirectly from God, the source of all power. To use modern terminology, the organs of the executive represent the supreme Ruler, on whose behalf they act. The governor of the province, the 'praefectus praetorio', is appointed by the Ruler, and every subordinate official is created by him who, says Lucas, 'principis reverentiam repraesentat', and therefore any subordinate official 'sic per medium praefectum repraesentat reverentiam principis'.[4] The hierarchical order, and consequently subordination, of all offices is strongly insisted upon by Lucas.[5] A sequel of the idea of representation is his view that a wrong committed against any official constitutes a wrong against the supreme authority: 'Laeditur majestas, ubi aliquis collateralis Imperatoris offenditur'.[6] On the other hand, precisely because they represent the Ruler, the officials are charged with the duty to act impartially in the spirit of justice and equity.[7] The consideration of the common good should be the motive force of all their actions.

Our employment of the term 'organ' in this context and in the preceding pages must not lead to the assumption that the public officials are organs of the community in the sense in which the term is used in modern terminology or in that sponsored by Gierke. In our investigations the term 'organ' signifies an official appointed by superior authority. His function towards the people is the same as that of the Ruler himself—viz., protectoral. Lucas sees in the protection of the people by the officials merely the concrete realization of the protectoral idea inherent in true leadership. Just as tyrannicide is permitted, in the same way resistance to officials is lawful under the same conditions. The officials are created, not from below, but from above; they represent, not the people, but the Ruler; they are set over the people by the Ruler and are responsible to him alone. This conception of the function of the officials is merely a sequel of Lucas's ideas on rulership.[8]

[1] C. XI, 40, 5, no. 3.

[2] The reason for our digression is identical with that of Lucas: 'Haec omnia, licet extra materiam legis, nosse utile est', loc. cit., no. 7.

[3] C. XII, 35, 14, no. 1. See also C. XI, 70, 5, no. 35: the Ruler is 'fons et origo omnium temporalium potestatum'.

[4] C. X, 1, 9, no. 25, C. XII, 4, Rubrica no. 1, and C. XI, 46, 1, no. 22.

[5] See C. X, 31, 33, no. 43, C. XII, 60, 2, no. 2, and nos. 4, 11.

[6] C. XI, 71, 1, no. 1.

[7] C. X, 1, 5, no. 15.

[8] As far as Lucas is concerned, Gierke's assertion that the temporal magistrate is a representative of the people, loc. cit., pp. 58, 61, is not correct. This point of view of Gierke has been sharply criticized by E. Lewis, loc. cit., p. 858.

II

Lucas deals at very great length with the fundamental principles relating to war and peace. It may be of some interest to summarize briefly his views on this important and topical subject. It must be borne in mind, however, that the modern concept of war is closely linked up with international law, which presupposes the existence of sovereign, independent States. The notion of international law, in the modern sense, is of course unknown to Lucas. He is less interested in the vexed problem of whether the *civitas* is entitled to wage war against another *civitas* than in the fundamental principles which underlie the concept of war. Apart from considerations which ensue from the peculiar political structure of the Empire in the fourteenth century, Lucas lays down certain principles which, properly speaking, concern the notion and essence of war, regardless of time and place.

From the outset Lucas distinguishes between just and unjust wars.[1] But we should be ill-advised if we simply adopted his terminology of 'justum' and 'injustum bellum'. Closer examination of his thoughts reveals that his concept of a just war also comprises the notion of the legality of war. Moreover, in his opinion, a war may still be unjust in spite of its legality. The criteria which render a war unjust, in spite of the fulfilment of certain 'legal' premises by the belligerents, are of an objective and a subjective nature: these criteria concern the cause for which the war is waged and the intention corresponding to the cause. He quotes as examples of just wars the restitution of wrongs inflicted upon the body politic or upon only a single citizen, the repelling of invasions, the recovery of goods which have been illegally or unjustly seized by the enemy, and, above all, the securing of liberty which is the 'most just' cause: 'Est ergo justissima causa bellum gerendi pro propria libertate'.[2] The defence of the liberty both of individuals and of society as a whole, is the paramount duty of the Ruler. This duty also comprises, Lucas avows, the defence of the Faith and of the liberty of the Church herself; even the temporal possessions of the Church enjoy the armed protection of the body politic.[3] Even if their cause is just, an evil intention on the part of the belligerents deprives the war of its just character: 'Intentio quoque mala justum bellum facit injustum'.[4] In Lucas's eyes such evil intentions are

[1] Holdsworth, vol. v, p. 31, points out that in medieval days war was considered *prima facie* a moral wrong and that, if undertaken, it needed to be justified. Although it may seem that 'this truth had little effect upon the international practice of the Middle Ages', Holdsworth observes that the salutary practical effects of speculations about a just war cannot be overlooked, ibid., p. 32.

[2] C. XI, 46, 1, no. 14.

[3] loc. cit., no. 14: 'Imperator pro subjectorum libertate et pro recta ad Deum religione bella gerendi suscepit . . . sic et pro libertate ecclesiae. Possessiones ecclesiarum materiali gladio de mandato ecclesiae defendendae sunt'. This duty of the Ruler is counterbalanced by the obligation of the Church to contribute to the taxes and public services. See also C. XII, 63, 1. no. 73.

[4] C. XI, 46, 1, no. 11.

the lust for power or domination,[1] the desire to wage war for the sake of revenge, the aim to inflict unnecessary harm to the enemy [2]—in short, any intention that is incompatible with a properly conceived idea of justice and fair-mindedness. A 'bona intentio', in Lucas's opinion, is a necessary prerequisite for a war, which can claim to be just. The great importance which Lucas attaches to this subjective prerequisite outweighs the significance of its objective counterpart.

The legality of war requires the fulfilment of certain formal conditions. In the first place, the authority to declare war must be vested with the power to do so. According to Lucas, it is only the supreme Ruler, the Emperor, who has the lawful authority to call his citizens to the arms. Wars declared by lesser authorities are no wars in the strict meaning of the term. Secondly, the individuals who are called to the arms must be under a legal obligation to undertake combatant duties.[3] Lucas distinguishes accordingly between the 'persona indicentis' and the 'persona obedientis'.[4] Thirdly, the individuals, against whom war is waged, must have given reasonable cause; they must have, as Lucas expresses it, 'deserved war'.[5]

[1] Later scholars, such as Paulus Castrensis, held that war may justly be waged for the sake of domination, if it is intended to bring peace, tranquillity, and prosperity to foreign nations. Paulus argued that otherwise all wars by which the Roman Empire obtained its greatness and glory would have been illicit; moreover, Christ Himself approved of the Empire as it stood at His time. D. 1, 1, 5, no. 4: 'Puto etiam, quod licet de jure divino non liceat bellare pro subjugando bellantes . . . de jure tamen gentium unus populus liber non recognoscens superiorem posset contra alium liberum, si faciat ad bonum finem, ut illos bene regat et gubernet. Aliter bella, quae exercuit populus Romanus ad hunc solum finem pro gloria imperii, non fuissent licita, nec ipsorum principatus et monarchia, et tamen est verum, quia Christus approbavit, dum dixit "reddite, quae sunt Caesaris".' The Augustinian and Thomistic influence on Lucas is conspicuous.

[2] 'Quinque sunt, quae faciunt bellum injustum, scilicet nocendi cupiditas, ulciscendi crudelitas, impacatus atque impaccabilis animus, feritas rebellandi et libido dominandi', loc. cit., no. 11. Paulus Castrensis employed almost the same words as Lucas: 'Interficientes aliquem in bello licito non delinquunt nec tenentur in foro conscientiae . . . nisi occidentis esset prava furore vel iracundia, scil. nocendi cupiditas . . .' He ended: 'Haec enim sunt quae in bellis jure culpantur', loc. cit., no. 6.

It is most certainly an exaggeration to say with Nys, *Origines du Droit International*, p. 188, that medieval wars were characterized by unheard-of acts of barbarity, by the use of poisoned arms, mutilation of prisoners, destruction of towns, and recourse to treachery and deceit. These general indictments are a gross exaggeration, and the following is wrong: 'The unimpeachable evidence of moralists, poets, lawyers, statesmen, soldiers can be appealed to, and their evidence is the same', Nys, p. 190.

[3] The clerics, for instance, were mostly exempt from military service.

[4] loc. cit., no. 12.

[5] loc. cit., no. 12. The prerequisite of a reasonable cause was, of course, capable of many and diversified interpretations. All wars against the infidels could be justified on this ground, though it will be recalled that Innocent IV was not inclined to attribute justness of the cause to wars which were waged against the Saracens; if they did not harm Christians, Christians had no right to seize their lands and goods. See Nys, loc. cit., p. 144.

Warfare does not mean—Lucas is anxious to stress this point—that the belligerents are at full liberty to do what they think fit. Any wrong committed in the course of the war and not directly bearing upon its outcome should be mercilessly and adequately dealt with: murders, robberies, plunderings, use of force against civilians, rapes, and the like, are crimes which should be as severely punished as if committed in peace-time: war does not give any licence to the soldiers.[1] Once the enemy has been rendered harmless by his being taken prisoner, he should be treated in a humane way: 'Hosti in bello capto miserendum est, dummodo futurum periculum non timeatur'.[2]

The aim of war should be peace through the complete defeat of the enemy—that is, victory over him. Victory, in Lucas's opinion, is the 'subjectio repugnantium'.[3] No war can be just if its aim is not peace.[4] 'Bellum geritur, ut pax acquiratur.'[5] This aim of war, he points out, should never be lost sight of even during the war: 'Bella non crudelitate et cupiditate, sed pacis studio geruntur.'[6] For peace is far more difficult to achieve, he thinks, if war is waged in a cruel and lusty manner. The activity of those responsible for the outbreak of war should be curbed and the individuals themselves punished; whilst those members of society who were not responsible for war should be aided, so that a peaceful intercourse in society at large again becomes possible.[7]

The peace, which follows war, is to be concluded between the heads of the belligerent societies.[8] The reason why the Rulers themselves should conclude the peace treaty is that 'sine regali quidem providentia impossibile est civitatibus pacem dare'.[9] A necessary condition for the reasonableness and sobriety of the peace treaty is, Lucas wisely suggests, that tranquillity of mind which can best be found in a place remote from the agitation and turbulence necessarily created by the passion of war.[10] 'Veritatis examinatio' is a principle, our jurist affirms, which should constantly be kept

[1] loc. cit., no. 8. He says that the soldiers should be punished according to the kind of crimes they have committed, either the *lex Cornelia de sicariis*, or the *lex Julia de publica vi*, &c. He reports that murder in wartime is punished with death in the Kingdom of Sicily.

[2] loc. cit., no. 17.

[3] loc. cit., no. 17. Bartolus maintained that Christians under allegiance to Rome belonged, at least theoretically, to the *populus Romanus*, and could not therefore become slaves.

[4] C. XII, 63, 1, no. 2.

[5] C. XI, 46, 1, no. 17: 'Regulariter justa bella pro pacis studio quaeruntur (? geruntur), ut mali coerceantur et boni subleventur'.

[6] C. XII, 63, 1, no. 7.

[7] loc. cit., no. 7.

[8] loc. cit., no. 8. 'Reformatur et componitur inter plures principes invicem discordantes atque bellantes'.

[9] loc. cit., no. 22.

[10] 'Quaeritur, quae sunt in reformatione pacis attendenda? Responsio, tractatus componendae pacis in tranquillitate animi familiariter secrete habendus est . . . nam in bello contentus ferri, in pace veritatis examinatio . . .', loc. cit.

in mind by the contracting parties.[1] The validity of the peace treaty depends on the sincerity and the goodwill of the parties to keep their promises: 'Pax', Lucas reminds us, 'in charta conscripta non valet, nisi fuerit in corde radicata'.[2] Satisfaction should be given for wrongs inflicted—'juxta mensuram injuriae'[3]—in accordance with the principles of justice, reasonableness, fair-mindedness.[4] The effectiveness of peace treaties can be enhanced, Lucas believes, when they are solemnly sanctioned by oath which, as a sacramental act, binds the contracting parties closer to each other.[5]

Peace within society, Lucas is convinced, is an indispensable condition for the prosperity and the felicity of the citizenhood.[6] He deplores the restless and unstable political conditions in some parts of Italy. He observes that rebellions, tyrannies, and seditious movements are regrettably frequent.[7] God, Lucas says, punishes societies which lacerate themselves by internal turbulations—'scinduntur semetipsas'—by letting loose upon their citizens the 'furor teutonicus' or some other scourge—'furorem teutonicum aliudve flagellum inducit Dominus super eos'—and He will punish them until their citizens abstain from their frivolous and destructive

[1] loc. cit., no. 22. [2] loc. cit., no. 25. [3] loc. cit., no. 25.

[4] He says: 'Intellige, quod satisfactio fiat competenter juxta mensuram injuriae . . . et arbitrio boni viri . . . nihil in hoc statuens contra Deum aut bonos mores', loc. cit., no. 25.

[5] loc. cit., no. 30: 'Ut validior sit ipsa pax, est reformanda cum juramento. Nam omne, quod venit in pacis foedere, tunc subsistit solidius, cum id roborat interpositio juramenti et omne, quod amicorum animos reconciliat, tunc fidelius durat, cum eos sacramenti vincula ligant.'

[6] It would lead us too far away if we attempted to go into details. This idea of peace is very characteristic of fourteenth-century political thought. It is noteworthy, particularly with reference to modern pronouncements, that the Austrian publicist Engelbert, abbot of the Benedictine monastery at Admont, in his treatise *De ortu et fine Romani Imperii*, written early fourteenth-century, postulates three freedoms as conditions of peace: freedom from want, freedom from fear, freedom from trouble. See the passage transcribed by Woolf, loc. cit., p. 282, note 7.

[7] Lucas deplores the political conditions in Rome particularly, and he says: 'Haec civitas multa sortita est nomina . . . quorum pauca in effectu vera sunt hodie. Item dicitur gloriosissima . . . item augustissima . . . item caput civitatum . . . sed, ut praedixi, ex praedictis nominibus pauca vel nulla conveniunt; potius ei congruit illud Esaiae "quomodo facta est meretrix civitas fidelis, plena judicii",' C. XI, 12, 1, no. 5. Rome's government was 'a deluded parody of the classical past', Dr. Previté-Orton, loc. cit., p. 351.

Other jurists, in particular Bartolus, grieved at that state of affairs in Italy, though there is, in Lucas, a distinct note of satisfaction when he refers to the conditions in Sicily which, in his opinion, compare favourably with those prevailing in other parts of Italy. Bartolus called the Roman government a 'res monstrosa', and in his treatise *De regimine civitatis* he said: 'Hodie Italia est tota plena tyrannis'. On the whole question see Woolf, loc. cit., cap. II, sect. III *passim*. Woolf holds that it was 'this terrible problem'—the tyrannical governments—which caused Bartolus to compose his treatise on tyranny. It is interesting, however, that Bartolus is totally unaware of John of Salisbury's views on this topic, whilst Lucas draws on the *Policraticus* so extensively.

activities.[1] The effect of peace on earth is that through it 'ad aeternam (scil. pacem) pervenitur'.[2] A breach of peace does not justify retaliatory measures; the violation of the peace by one individual does not entitle the victimized party to retaliation. Lucas argues that if someone burnt down his neighbour's house, the latter would by no means be entitled to retaliate by burning his adversary's house. The only permissible reaction is defence within the limits of the law. Lucas thinks that all self-help would lead to lawlessness.[3]

In this context, Lucas's view of reprisals is worth mentioning. His fundamental axiom is that as long as the way prescribed by the law is still open, reprisals are not permissible either against communities or against individuals: 'Ubi pro justitia potest ad superiorem recursus haberi, non est locus repressaliis'.[4] The question as to whether the members of a corporation can be subjected to reprisals, if the corporation has committed some wrong, constituted a topical problem at Lucas's time. He lays down as a principle that reprisals can be taken against the guilty members of that corporation only. Since only a certain number of individuals are guilty of wrongs, it is against the principle of justice and equity to extend their liability to their innocent fellow members. He states that 'quod universitas alicuius municipii debet, singuli de ipsa universitate non debent'.[5] Lucas points out that this principle is at variance with the views presented by Bartolus 'in tractatu repressaliarum, quem noviter vidi'.[6] Bartolus wrote in this treatise that the citizens of a *civitas* can rightfully be captured, provided that a wrong has been inflicted by its Ruler. The *civitas* and its members were considered by Bartolus as co-responsible for the actions of its Rulers. Lucas refers us to Bartolus: 'An possit capi homines . . . scripsit dominus Bartolus . . . quod possunt'. Lucas thinks

[1] loc. cit., no. 20. In his commentary on C. XII, 45, 1, no. 59, Lucas says: 'Propter iniquitates nationes delentur a Deo'; he refers to *Deuteronomy* ix.

[2] loc. cit., no. 34.

[3] loc. cit., no. 69: 'Quaeritur, quid si alter paciscentium frangit pacem, an alter ipsam impune frangere possit? . . . Non tamen ego debeo ipsam violare . . . nam licet comburas domum meam, non tamen debeo comburere tuam. Et licet facias proditionem mihi, non tamen debeo illam committere contra te, qui tibi fidem promisi . . . sed possum me defendere, ut sic is, cui primo contra pacem fecit, ex eo damnari possit, non autem id, quod fecit alter in recompensationem mutui criminis in utroque communicare.'

[4] C. XI, 56, 1, no. 2. Lucas is silent on the question as to what action should be taken if there is no 'superior' who can be approached. The common opinion was that if a wrong had been committed and there was no superior authority, reprisals became lawful. See, e.g., Salicetus in his lecture on C. IV, 12 *Authentica* 'Sed Omnino': 'Pro solutione distinguunt communiter doctores, aut post neglectam justitiam per dominum . . . aut non potest haberi (scil. recursus ad superiorem), quia superiorem non recognoscunt de jure vel de facto, et tunc sunt permissae (scil. repressaliae).'

[5] loc. cit., no. 2.

[6] loc. cit., no. 3.

that the reason for Bartolus's opinion is that 'dominus et civitas justitiam facere negligens est debitor justitiam postulantis. Igitur vasalli et homines sui propter hoc delictum eius poterunt capi.' [1] Lucas disagrees with this view—'puto melius distingui'—and he applies his own principle. Reprisals can be rightfully taken only against those members of the *civitas* who have countenanced, or partaken in, the commission of the wrong by the Ruler. From the point of view of justice there is then no difference between them and the Ruler, who actually perpetrated the wrong. He writes: 'Aut tales homines favent domino suo circa injustitiam exercendam seu justitiam denegandam, et tunc possint capi et affligi, sicut et ipse dominus. Aut non favent . . .' For the general principle is that the individuals composing a corporate body are not responsible for the deeds of their rulers or other members: 'Contra personas singulares, quae non deliquerunt, nullo modo repressaliae concedi possunt'.[2]

[1] Lucas could have added Albericus de Rosciate's view. He too justified reprisals against whole communities, 'nam ex delicto domini punitur familia, et civitas, quae eius dominio subest', C. IV, 12, *Authentica* 'Sed Omnino'.

[2] loc. cit., no. 2.

CHAPTER IX

CONCLUSION

WE have attempted to represent, in a varying degree of detail, the leading thoughts of Lucas de Penna, the Neapolitan scholar without an academic chair and without an academic public. He was a lonely figure grappling with the intricacies of law, keeping himself aloof from the more turbulent and ostentatious life which the position of an academic teacher entails, who wrote solely for his own delight and, we may reasonably assume, out of an innate urge to find the truth underlying the idea of law. It is due precisely to his craving for knowledge and for a better understanding of the various and complicated forces by which social life is effectively regulated that his doctrines reveal everywhere a genuine spirit of profound scholarship, permeated by an unshakable and unerring sense of morality. His scholarly mind was repulsed by the superficiality and commonplaces which he condemned in contemporary scholarship. He knew that his doctrines and disquisitions could not appeal to the broad public. He undertook the laborious and unspectacular task of commenting upon the neglected *Tres Libri* merely to satisfy his own thirst for knowledge, as he so often points out in his commentaries. As a practical lawyer, he strongly felt the inadequacies of current legal thought. Out of an inexhaustible urge for creative and constructive work he wrote his prolific commentaries. The very fact that there was no necessity for him to undertake this difficult task, which he set himself, bears testimony to his scientific zeal. And this fact the more deserves our regard, because it is in this that the internal value of his work lies.

He was no innovator, no revolutionary thinker, and no zealot. But he was an independent thinker who applied his almost incredibly rich mental and spiritual equipment to the problems of his day. It is not, then, to be wondered at that his conclusions often anticipated the future development of legal and political thought, and that he brought forward the very same arguments which were so lavishly employed some two centuries later. Immersed as he was in the ideological structure of the fourteenth century, he himself was unable to evaluate fully the social and political implications of which his conclusions permit. And yet he saw legal, social, and political problems from a detached and higher standpoint. Though it is true of him, as of so many medieval personalities, that he was ' standing upon the ancient ways ', he nevertheless conceived of a social and political structure whose scientific elaboration was reserved for the thinkers of the sixteenth century. He laid down principles of law, which should be directive in any country, and yet should take full cognisance of national and racial differences. His theory of law and of politics revolves round the idea of justice. And this idea cannot be different wherever the Christian faith, as opposed to some ' dogmatic conviction ', holds sway over any community. The recognition of the force of ideas and the thorough-going application, which they experienced in his system of thought, reveal at once the mentality of fourteenth-century scholars and the spirit of their work. Though not consciously and clearly perceived by him, his system is rooted in the recognition of the power of ideas that—to use one of Lord Acton's happy phrases—' give life and motion, that take wing and traverse seas and frontiers '.

Imbued as he was with the spirit of Christianity, the fulfilment of the precepts of justice appeared to him the safest path to the final salvation of mankind. He conceived justice as a principle divinely infused into man enabling him to pursue a life in society worthy of a Christian whose end is preconceived. The instrument which transforms justice into a workable social reality is the law. And those who are chosen to administer it should be inspired by the ' zelus justitiae ' which is the token of the legislator, judges, professors of law, interpreters, public officials—in short, they all have to play a vital part in the practical realization of that idea of justice concretely manifested in law.

It is precisely his deeply religious mind, together with his desire to lay down principles for the political security and peaceful development of the restless and troubled Italian lands, which made him a determined supporter of the absolutist conception of government and the Ruler, and which made him impatient of the will of the people. It was inconceivable to him that an indefinite, amorphous, and chaotic mass of individuals should have the right, or the qualification, to issue binding rules, or the power to transfer any authority to the Ruler. For, in this latter case, the Ruler would still be responsible to the people, who have the power to revoke their mandate and to depose him. This idea was certainly the stumbling-block which prevented Lucas from conceiving that any authority could be derived from the consent of the people. Setting out from the *a priori* principle that, in the last resort, all rulership and authority are a divine mandate, he was necessarily driven to a theistic conception of government—that is, of a government set over the people by divine commission. His idea of the Ruler as a guardian and protector is merely another way of expressing the idea of the divine government of the world: God who rules over the Universe has chosen the Ruler as His vicegerent and His representative on earth for the administration of temporal affairs, amongst which legislation is the most vitally important. God creates His laws through the medium of the Ruler. The Ruler, standing as he does above the law, is responsible to God alone for any miscarriage of government. This theory of the Ruler's absolute power, in its articulate expression having no parallel amongst Lucas's contemporaries, shows a close resemblance to the theory, fashionable two centuries later, of the divine right of Kings. Sixteenth-century political thought tended ' to substitute for a theory of delegation a conception of the King as holding his authority directly from God. This conception is the very essence of what is called the divine right of Kings [1] . . . the Prince delegate was transformed into the Prince of divine appointment.' [2] It was precisely this conception which Lucas struggled to express in his commentaries and which caused the lengthy arguments with his academic opponents. Tyranny is nothing else but the intentional misuse of the powers entrusted to the Ruler by God. Tyranny is perverted rulership. The tyrant, therefore, can claim no divine sanction of his commands and is, furthermore, a menace to the people he is called upon to lead. Because in the interest and the preservation of society, his removal is consequently a dictate of justice.

At this point we feel bound to disagree with the gist of the statement made by the great authority on medieval political conceptions, Dr. A. J. Carlyle. He states that ' positive law was the expression of the will or the consent of the whole community, including the King '.[3] This statement certainly cannot be applied to Lucas (nor, we venture to add, to certain other civilians, such as Baldus). Dr. Carlyle's further remark that ' the conception of writers like Bodin and Barclay, that the King was the legislator, represented an alien and intrusive principle ' should not be allowed to pass without protest. If this were true, how much more true would it be of Lucas, who lived two centuries before Bodin and Barclay. Yet the medieval character of Lucas's mind and mode of reasoning can in no way be doubted.

That is also the reason why we have to express our disagreement with the gist of Gierke's statement—namely, that ' medieval doctrine gave to the Monarch a representative character ',[4] and that ' it is a distinctive trait of medieval doctrine that within every human group it decisively recognizes an aboriginal and active Right of the group taken as a Whole '.[5] From this dogma Gierke deduces the following statement : ' It was in the province of Temporal Power that the Right of the Community first assumed a doctrinal form. An ancient and generally entertained opinion regarded the Will of the People

[1] J. W. Allen, *History of Political Thought*, p. 367.

[2] J. W. Allen, loc. cit., p. 283. In this context the profound truth of the general remarks by Dr. Previté-Orton, loc. cit., p. 213, clearly emerges in its full weight. He says, surveying the ruling legal conceptions in the fourteenth century, that ' the right to rule came from God. . . . This religious view . . . gave an overwhelming sanction to kingship, and it is easy to see how it could produce later absolution and refute the rival theocracy of the Papacy.'

[3] loc. cit., vol. vi, p. 511, and in many other places.

[4] Gierke-Maitland, loc. cit., p. 61. ' It was admitted on all sides that . . . every power of a political kind appeared always more clearly to bear the character of a constitutional competence of some part of the body politic to " represent the Whole ",' loc. cit,

[5] loc. cit., p. 37.

as the source of Temporal Power.'[1] Precisely because Lucas was medieval through and through, we feel bound to disagree with Gierke, since those *general* statements can in no way be applied to Lucas. It was the latter's axiom that the Ruler was a representative, not of the people, but of God, who had set him over the people. There is no trace of the opinion in Lucas's commentaries that he would concede to the people any sovereignty or any communal or political rights which they had not as individuals. The statement of Lucas in which he denies the people all political rights lacks neither clarity nor precision. Lucas conceived of an individual responsibility only, and this conception precludes all further consideration of a collective responsibility of the people as a whole—even if the idea of a collective responsibility had been known to Lucas.

The question now arises as to what influence was exercised upon Lucas by the vast auxiliary material at his disposal. That exerted upon him by Aristotle and John of Salisbury is so conspicuous and palpable that no further explanation is necessary. If Lucas depended in any way on one particular philosophy, it was on the Aristotelian. In all fundamental questions he is as rigorously and faithfully Aristotelian as any other late medieval thinker. To Lucas, Aristotle was the fountain of all knowledge and wisdom. The *Policraticus*, 'probably the most perfect and the most complete summation of the political speculations of the past centuries',[2] was his guide to all social ethical problems. Yet Lucas preserved his independence of mind and refused to follow John blindly: his insistence upon the necessity of strict separation of secular and ecclesiastical powers, and upon their equality of rank, is one important point in which John was not followed by his Neapolitan admirer. In the case of the other extra-legal material it would be rash to pass judgement upon the extent of its influence on Lucas. We may venture to suggest, however, that, unlike the case of Aristotle and John of Salisbury, there was no direct and obvious influence of any one philosophy or philosopher. It is probably true that Lucas's mind was decisively shaped by the absorption of the whole vast literary apparatus, which he had digested the better to be able to tackle legal problems. In his mind Ciceronian, Augustinian, Gregorian, Thomistic, and other medieval ideas were fused into a rounded whole whose central theme and orientation were dictated by the idealistic aspects of Christian cosmology. The Christian idea was the underlying motive power of his researches and the basis upon which he built his system of thought. For him Christianity was perfect Truth.

It is precisely on account of this conviction that he was unsparing in his often sarcastic criticisms of existing conditions within the

[1] loc. cit., p. 38. Mr. E. Lewis, loc. cit., p. 867, remarks that Gierke's idea of popular sovereignty seems 'open to grave objections'. Certainly, Gierke's idea—stated in these general terms—must be challenged, at least as far as Lucas's theory is concerned.

[2] McIlwain, loc. cit., p. 324.

Church. On this point his independence of thought and his fearlessness on the one hand, and the transitional character of his period on the other hand, become increasingly apparent. It is true that he still conceived society as a *respublica christiana*. But within a few decades the ideological foundations of a Christian commonwealth, so vigorously and emphatically asserted at the very beginning of the century in which he was born, were to receive shattering blows. Is it, then, to be wondered at that the idea of a ' plenitudo potestatis ', comprising as it did both the temporal and spiritual government of the world, was flatly rejected by Lucas, and that he came to conceive of a strict separation of powers, whereby each power was to be kept strictly within the bounds allotted to it ? This interpretation of the Gelasian principle—hardly before so coherently and energetically insisted upon by jurists—is the first point of his political theory which we must underline. The Monarch's power is independent of the Pope, because both powers are of equal rank ; both are equipped with the ' plenitudo potestatis ', each in his own sphere. But new and very significant ideas were beginning to take shape. The frontiers between the temporal and the spiritual were fluid, and the harmony between the two omnipotent powers was disturbed precisely because of the fluidity of the frontiers. Lucas felt the weakness inherent in the distinction between the temporal and the spiritual, a weakness which he was convinced could be overcome by the introduction and application of a criterion that would, from the social and political point of view at least, lead to satisfactory results and, above all, would safeguard a frictionless and salutary co-existence of the two Powers. This criterion, which had lingered in the minds of jurists ever since the revival of legal studies, was that of public utility, a concept which, when applied to the highly controversial Gelasian principle, gives it entirely new meaning and plays havoc with traditional views. In Lucas's system of thought, it was the criterion of public utility which marked off the temporal from the spiritual proper. We have only to recall his views on matrimony, with their far-reaching legal and legislative consequences, his insistence on the civic duties of the Church and the clerics, his ideas concerning the abrogation of civil law by the ecclesiastical authority, his emphasis upon the independence of the secular judge, and many more items of Lucas's doctrines, in which the principle of public utility is actually the deciding element and the intrinsic reason for the strangeness and novelty of his views, for their deviation from contemporary doctrines, and for the lengthy treatment which they received in his system, often apparently out of proportion to the importance of the concrete issue involved. Small wonder, then, that, through the introduction and thorough-going application of this criterion, entirely new lines of thought were opened up. The ground of delimitation and apportionment came to be gradually, yet decisively, shifted in favour of the secular power. The pendulum was beginning to move in the direction from which it never swung back. In the background lurked the ascendancy and final superiority of the secular authority, which was to find it increasingly easy to justify an ever-growing expansion of its powers by the attractive appeal to public utility. In the criterion of public utility we may well detect one—if not the most important—germ from which the concept of the modern State arose.

It may be quite true that Lucas did not himself clearly perceive the disintegrating process, which was dramatically unfolding itself before his eyes, but it was the inner force of ideas, shaping mind and reality, which led him to propound theories and statements which two centuries later became the common property of all progressive political thinkers. Sixteenth-century political thought had undoubtedly cast its shadow as far back as the middle of the fourteenth century. Lucas's concern, however, lay primarily—if not exclusively—with the law, the gift and invention of God, pronounced through the mouth of an absolute and yet, theoretically, severely restricted Monarch. In this he saw the safest guide to the attainment of man's end. His concern with the human, positive law made him categorically refuse to the Church any authority in matters affecting society at large. His system is a solemn pronouncement of the purely spiritual character of the Church and of the purely temporal character of the secular governments, epitomized by the Ruler who acts 'vice Dei'. It is true that Lucas curtailed the Monarch's powers and submitted him to higher laws. But this curtailment was more a theoretical speculation than an actual restriction. For when it comes to the real test, Lucas unhesitatingly declared that the Ruler had the power, not only to derogate divine and natural law, but also to issue law which—it was alleged by concurrent doctrine—violated natural law. The concept of a full legislative authority emerges clearly.

The advance in thinking, which his system represents, is not only marked in the political field properly so called. Lucas would certainly have been most surprised to find his political outlook earmarked as being in advance of his time. But we are nevertheless justified in calling his political system advanced, firstly, as juxtaposed with that of his contemporaries, and, secondly, as compared with the political thought current in the sixteenth century. It is not so much the political conception as such—i.e., the absolutism of the Monarch—which marks an advance, because this conception was latent amongst his contemporaries, especially Baldus, as the argumentation and method through which he established the all-powerful position of the Ruler. The main feature of his argumentation is the employment of those arguments whose authenticity and reliability his opponents could hardly doubt. But, as we said before, it is not only in the political field that he stands above his contemporaries. In the sphere of law proper, in the theory of the nature of law, of its application and administration, of its practical execution—everywhere he carried the one fundamental idea—i.e., justice—to its strictly logical conclusion. Hence he presented a theory of law, unsurpassed either in its scope or in its comprehensiveness by his great contemporaries. A thorough knowledge and experience of the actual working of the law in the daily life of citizens, an experience gained by his practical activity, and a pronounced abhorrence to the disregard of the right and just, enabled him to see more problems than the others saw, and moved him to seek a remedy for the removal of deficiencies, glaring as they appeared to him as a practical lawyer, imbued with a deep moral sense. The remedy seemed to him to be the unconditional application of the idea of justice in its somewhat mitigated form of equity. It is precisely this idea which caused him to propose a theory of the exercise of rights which, if carried to its logical conclusion, would play havoc with our own traditional views on the 'objective' nature of law. Moreover, his conception of crime and punishment is a convincing test of the broad-mindedness and humanity with which its author was imbued: the idea that punishment should be commensurate to the guilt of the criminal, that its primary aim is to make him once more a useful member of society, and that responsibility for a crime varies according to certain accompanying circumstances—all these are ideas which were out of the range of his contemporaries' vision, and which mark an advance of penological thought still current in the nineteenth century. The use of torture was as repugnant to him as it should be to a man of the twentieth century.

Yet in spite of all these great achievements of this legal philosopher we are bound to admit shortcomings, logical and substantial inconsistencies, fallacies of arguments and other defects, particularly in some of his political axioms when the argument sometimes appears artificial and not wholly convincing. But we may assume that these defects were caused by the emergence of ideas which were superimposed upon firmly entrenched ideas and which made the latter appear in a fundamentally different light. The transformation, reformation, and modification of basic principles do not seem to have been adequately recognized by Lucas. Moreover, these superimposed ideas, which slowly forced their way into the scholar's mind, were not always apprehended in their contradicting and overlapping effects. This, we think, is the reason why Lucas's doctrine is not always free from inconsistencies, but, at the same time, a defect of this kind is pardonable in an age of transition when values and ideas are beginning to take new shape. The fourteenth century was indeed a period which exhibited the typical traits of a cultural crisis, enhanced, if not conditioned, by the repercussion of political events; it became increasingly difficult for man to perceive the inconsistencies of thought inherent in the peculiar mixture of old and new ideas. Unlike its predecessor, that century was not an age of unchallenged assumptions: very slowly and imperceptibly, reasoning *a priori* gave way to modes of thought more in harmony with the requirements of critical and objective scholarship. But ideas so firmly rooted in men's minds for many centuries recede but slowly, grudgingly, and resistingly into the background. In this contest between the ancient and the new thought, each striving for absolute recognition in men's minds, the former challenges and attempts to displace the latter from its permanent habitations and forms which have been crystallized and moulded during past centuries. We must not be surprised, then, that a crisis of such magnitude as we witness in the fourteenth century necessarily showed itself in individual thinkers and scholars—however much they might have attempted to adopt a detached point of view—and that this crisis produced a corresponding instability and disturbance in the balance of individual thought.

Nevertheless, the great value of this jurist's work lies less in the fundamental principles upon which he based his system of legal thought, than in the application of those principles, and less in novel thoughts than in the method by which he elaborated and clarified ancient—not to say outworn—traditional ideas. A distinguished though lonely scholar, an independent thinker, a fearless writer, a seeker after truth and justice, a true Christian—these epithets might well be applied to Lucas de Penna, an illustrious figure in the Pantheon of medieval Italian jurisprudence.

APPENDIX

EPITAPH [1]

D.O.M.P.

LUCAE DE PENNA SEPULCHRUM

I.C. EMINENTISSIMI

QUEM

PENNA IN SAMNIO GENUIT

PARTHENOPE EXCOLUIT

SIBI AEMULA ADSCRIPSIT GALLIA

UNIVERSA SUSPEXIT EUROPA

MUTIUS PANSA PHYLOSOPHUS ET MEDICUS

NE SUUS HONOS IN PATRIA MAGNO DEESSET CINERI

EX HUMILI LOCO IN HANC EXTULIT LUCEM

ELOGIUM POSUIT ET APOLOGIAM CIVIS PRO CIVE

CONSCRIPSIT

AMORIS ET GRATI ANIMI MONUMENTUM

ANNO JUBILEI MDCXXV.

[1] See *supra*, p. 8, note 5.

SOURCES AND AUTHORITIES

(a) *Original*

ALBERICUS DE ROSCIATE (*ob.* 1354), *Commentaria in Digestum vetus, Infortiatum, Digestum novum, Codicem*, Venetiis, 1585.
——, *Dictionarium*, Lugduni, 1548.
——, *Tractatus super Statutis*, Francofurti, 1606.
ALCIATUS, ANDREAS (*ob.* 1550), *Opera*, 4 tom., Basileae, 1582.
ANDREAE, JOANNES (*ob.* 1348), *Glossa ad Decretales*, Venetiis, 1581.
ANDREAS DE ISERNIA (*ob.* 1316), *Commentaria in Usus Feudorum*, Francofurti, 1598.
——, *Commentarium in Codicem et Authenticum*, August. Taurinorum, 1580.
——, *Consilia*, Francofurti, 1575.
AQUINAS, ST. THOMAS (*ob.* 1274), *Summa Theologica*, Parisiis, 1638.
ARCHIDIACONUS (Guido de Baysio, *ob.* 1313), *Lectura super Sexta Decretalium*, Venetiis, 1503.
AUTHENTICUM, see CORPUS JURIS CIVILIS.
AZO (*ob.* 1230), *Summa Institutionum et Codicis*, Basileae, 1563.
——, *Brocardica*, Basiliae, 1567.
BALDUS DE UBALDIS (*ob.* 1400), *Commentaria in Digestum vetus, Infortiatum, Digestum novum, Codicem*, Venetiis, 1616.
——, *Consilia*, Lugduni, 1548.
——, *Commentaria super Decretalibus*, Lugduni, 1547.
——, ' Commentaria ad Pacem Constantiae ' in *Volumen Legum Parvum*, Antverpiae, 1575.
BARTHOLOMAEUS DE CAPUA (*ob.* 1328), *Commentaria in Constitutiones Regni Utriusque Siciliae*, Lugduni, 1568.
BARTOLUS DE SAXOFERRATO (*ob.* 1357), *Commentaria in Digestum vetus, Infortiatum, Digestum novum, Codicem*, Lugduni, 1523.
——, *Consilia, Quaestiones et Tractatus*, Lugduni, 1552.
BODINUS, JOANNES (*ob.* 1596), *De Republica Libri Sex*, Francofurti, 1609.
BULAEUS, *Historia Universitatis Parisiensis*, tom. iv, Paris, 1668.
CACCIALUPUS, JOANNES BAPTISTA (*ob.* after 1472), *Succincta Historia Interpretum et Glossatorum Juris*, Lipsiae, 1721.
——, *De Modo studendi et vita Doctorum*, Basileae, 1500.
CASTRENSIS, PAULUS (*ob.* 1441), *Commentaria in Digestum vetus, Infortiatum, Digestum novum*, Lugduni, 1548.
——, *Commentaria in Codicem*, Venetiis, 1594.
——, *Consilia*, Francofurti, 1582.
CLARUS, JULIUS (*ob.* 1575), *Sententiarum Libri Quinque*, Francofurti, 1590.
CONSTITUTIONES ET ACTA PUBLICA IMPERATORUM ET REGUM, tom. ii, in *Monumenta Germaniae Historica*, Hannover, 1896.
CONSTITUTIONES REGNI UTRIUSQUE SICILIAE, Lugduni, 1568 (Quoted: *Constitutiones*).
CORNEUS, PHILIPPUS (*ob.* 1492), *Consilia*, 4 tom., Venetiis, 1572.
CORPUS JURIS CANONICI, 2 vols., Lipsiae, 1839.

CORPUS JURIS CIVILIS, ed. Gothofredus, Lugduni, 1683.
CYNUS DE PISTOJA (*ob.* 1336), *Commentarium in Codicem et Digestum vetus*, Francofurti, 1578.
DECIUS, PHILIPPUS (*ob.* 1536), *De Regulis Juris*, Lugduni, 1546.
DYNUS DE MUGELLANO (*ob.* 1299), *Commentaria in Regulas Juris Pontificii*, Lugduni, 1568.
FULGOSIUS, RAPHAEL (*ob.* 1427), *Commentaria in Digestum vetus*, Lugduni, 1554.
——, *Commentaria in Codicem*, Lugduni, 1547.
GLOSSA MAGNA, Venetiis, 1584.
GOMEZ, ANTONIO (*ob.* 1568), *Commentariorum Variarumque Resolutionum Juris Civilis, Communis et Regii Tomi Tres*, Francofurti, 1572.
HOSTIENSIS (Henricus de Segusia, *ob.* 1271), *Summa Decretalium*, Lugduni, 1548.
INNOCENTIUS IV (*ob.* 1254), *Commentaria in Quinque Libros Decretalium*, Venetiis, 1578.
JACOBUS DE BELVISIO (*ob.* 1335), *Aurea Practica Criminalis*, Coloniae, 1580.
LUCAS DE PENNA (*ob.* 1390), *Commentaria in Tres Libros Codicis*, Lugduni, 1597.
MENOCHIUS, JACOBUS (*ob.* sixteenth century), *De Recuperanda Possessione Commentaria*, Coloniae, 1614.
——, *De Praesumptionibus*, Coloniae, 1615.
ODOFREDUS (*ob.* 1265), *Commentaria in Codicem*, Lugduni, 1552.
OLDRADUS DE PONTE (*ob.* 1335), *Consilia*, Venetiis, 1515.
PETRARCA (*ob.* 1374), *Opera quae extant omnia*, Basileae, 1554.
PETRUS DE BELLAPERTICA (*ob.* 1308), *Lectura super Codice*, Parisiis, 1508.
PLACENTINUS (*ob.* 1192), *In Codicis Libros Novem*, Moguntiae, 1536.
RAYNERIUS DE FORLIVIO (*ob.* 1358), *Lectura super Digesto novo*, Lugduni, 1523.
REBUFFUS, PETRUS (*ob.* 1557), *Tractatus varii*, Lugduni, 1581.
ROMANUS, LUDOVICUS (*ob.* 1439), *Commentaria in Digestum vetus, novum, et Codicem*, Venetiis, 1580.
——, *Consilia*, Lugduni, 1565.
SALICETUS, BARTHOLOMAEUS (*ob.* 1412), *Commentaria in Digestum vetus et Codicem*, Venetiis, 1574.
SARISBERIENSIS, JOANNES (John of Salisbury, *ob.* 1180), *Policraticus*, ed. C. J. J. Webb, Oxford, 1909.
TIRAQUELLUS, ANDREAS (Tiraqueau, *ob.* 1585), *Opera Omnia*, Francofurti, 1574.
TRACTATUS ILLUSTRIUM JURISCONSULTORUM, 19 tom., Venetiis, 1584–86. (Quoted: *Tractatus*.)
VALLA, ROLANDUS A (late sixteenth century), *Consilia*, Francofurti, 1584.

(b) *Secondary*

ALLEN, J. W., 'Politics', in *Medieval Contributions to Modern Civilization*, ed. F. J. C. Hearnshaw, London, 1921.
——, *History of Political Thought in the Sixteenth Century*, 2nd ed., London, 1941.
D'ARCY, M. C., 'The Philosophy of St. Augustine', in *A Monument to St. Augustine*, London, 1930.

BALUZIUS, S., *Vitae Paparum Avenionensium*, 2 vols., Paris, 1693.
BARKER, E., 'Medieval Political Thought', in *The Social and Political Ideas of Some Great Medieval Thinkers*, ed. F. J. C. Hearnshaw, London, 1923.
——, Introduction to *The City of God*, ed. J. Healy, London, 1934.
——, 'The Conception of Empire', in *The Legacy of Rome*, Oxford, 1936.
BARRETT, H. M., *Boethius*, Cambridge, 1940.
BRIE, S., *Die Lehre vom Gewohnheitsrecht*, Breslau, 1899.
BRUNNER, H., *Deutsche Rechtsgeschichte*, 2nd ed., 2 vols., Leipzig, 1906–28.
BRYCE, J., *Studies in History and Jurisprudence*, 2 vols., Oxford, 1901.
——, *The Holy Roman Empire*, London, 1904.
BUCKLAND, W. W., *Textbook of Roman Law*, Cambridge, 2nd ed., 1932.
CALASSO, F., 'Studi sul commento ai Tres Libri di Luca da Penne', in *Rivista di Storia del Diritto Italiano*, vol. v, 1932.
CALISSE, C., *A History of Italian Law*, transl. by L. B. Register in *Continental Legal History Series*, vol. viii, London, 1928.
CANNAVALE, E., *Lo Studio di Napoli nel rinascimento*, Naples, 1895.
CAPASSO, B., *Sulla Storia esterna delle costituzione del Regno di Sicilia, promulgate da Frederico II*, Naples, 1869.
CARLYLE, A. J., *A History of the Medieval Political Theory in the West*, 6 vols., Edinburgh, 1902–36.
CHIAPELLI, L., *Vita e Opere giuridiche di Cino da Pistoja*, Pistoja, 1881.
——, *Nuovò Reserche su Cino da Pistoja*, Pistoja, 1911.
CHRIMES, S. B., *Sir John Fortescue*, Cambridge, 1942.
COULSON, JAMES E. E., *Bologna, its History, Antiquities, and Art*, London, 1909.
COULTON, G. G., *Medieval Panorama*, Cambridge, 1938.
——, *Five Centuries of Religion*, 3 vols., Cambridge, 1923–36.
——, *Studies in Medieval Thought*, London, 1942.
DAHM, F., *Das Strafrecht Italiens im ausgehenden Mittelalter*, Berlin, 1931.
DAWSON, C., *St. Augustine, Bishop of Hippo*, London, 1930.
——, *The Making of Europe*, London, 1932.
——, *Medieval Religion*, London, 1934.
DUFF, P. W., *Personality in Roman Private Law*, Cambridge, 1938.
DUNNING, W. A., *A History of Political Theories*, vol. I (Ancient and Medieval), London, 1919.
ENGELMANN, W., *Der geistige Urheber des Verbrechens*, Leipzig, 1911.
——, *Die Wiedergeburt der Rechtskultur durch die italienische Lehre des Mittelalters*, Leipzig, 1938.
D'ENTRÉVES, A. P., *The Medieval Contribution to Political Thought*, Oxford, 1939.
ESMEIN, A., *History of Continental Criminal Procedure*, London, 1914.
FIGGIS, J. N., *The Divine Right of Kings*, 2nd ed., Cambridge, 1934.
——, 'Bartolus and the Development of European Political Ideas', in *The Divine Right of Kings*.
——, 'Political Thought in the Sixteenth Century', in *Cambridge Modern History*, vol. iii.
GIANNONE, P., *Istoria civile del Regno di Napoli*, 4 vols., Naples, 1723.
GIERKE, O., *Das Deutsche Genossenschaftsrecht*, 3 vols., Berlin, 1868–81.
——, *Political Theories of the Middle Age*, ed. F. W. Maitland, Cambridge, ed. 1938.
——, *Natural Law and the Theory of Society*, ed., E. Barker, Cambridge, 1934.

GILMORE, M. P., *Argument from Roman Law in Political Thought from 1200–1600*, Cambridge (Mass.), 1941.
GILSON, E., *The Philosophy of St. Thomas Aquinas*, Cambridge, 1924.
——, *The Spirit of Medieval Philosophy*, London, 1936.
GIRARD, P. F., 'Les préliminairies de la renaissance du droit romain' in *Revue Historique du Droit Français et Etranger*, 4th series, vol. 1, 1922.
GIUSTINIANI, L., *Memorie storiche degli Scrittori Legali del Regno di Napoli*, Naples, 1787.
GOETZ, K., *Koenig Robert von Neapel*, Tübingen, 1910.
GREENIDGE, A. H. J., *Infamia*, Oxford, 1894.
HAMBURGER, M., *The Awakening of Western Legal Thought*, transl. by B. Miall, London, 1942.
HASKINS, C. H., *History of Medieval Science*, Cambridge (Mass.), 1927.
——, *Studies in Medieval Culture*, Oxford, 1929.
HAZELTINE, H. D., 'Roman and Canon Law in the Middle Ages', in *Cambridge Medieval History*, vol. v.
——, 'Commentators' in *Encyclopedia of the Social Sciences*, vol. iii, 1930.
——, 'Glossators', ibid., vol. vi, 1931.
HEFELE, K. J., *Conciliengeschichte*, vol. vi, Freiburg, 1890.
HINSCHIUS, P., *Das Kirchenrecht der Katholiken und Protestanten in Deutschland*, Berlin, vol. v, 1895.
HOLDSWORTH, W. S., *A History of English Law*, 12 vols., London, 1922–38.
HOLLAND, TH. E., *Jurisprudence*, 13th ed., Oxford, 1928.
HULL, R., *Medieval Theories of the Papacy*, London, 1934.
JACOB, E. F., 'Political Thought', in *The Legacy of the Middle Ages*, Oxford, 1927.
——, 'John of Salisbury and the Polycraticus', in *The Social and Political Ideas of Some Great Medieval Thinkers*, ed. F. J. C. Hearnshaw, London, 1923.
——, 'Sir John Fortescue and the Law of Nature', in *Bulletin of the John Rylands Library*, vol. xviii, 1934.
JOECHER, C. G., *Allgemeines Gelehrten Lexicon*, 6 vols., Leipzig, 1750.
JONES, J. W., *Historical Introduction to the Theory of Law*, Oxford, 1940.
KANTOROWICZ, H., *Albertus Gandinus und das Strafrecht der Scholastik*, 2 vols., Berlin, 1907–25.
——, 'The Quaestiones Disputatae of the Glossators', in *Revue d'Histoire du Droit*, vol. xvi, 1938.
——, 'The Political Sermon of a Medieval Jurist' in *Journal of the Warburg Institute*, vol. ii, 1938.
——, *Studies in the Glossators of the Roman Law* (in collaboration with W. W. Buckland), Cambridge, 1938.
KERN, F., *Kingship and Law in the Middle Ages*, transl. by S. B. Chrimes, Oxford, 1939.
DE LAGARDE, G., *Le naissance de l'esprit laique au declin de moyen âge*, vol. i, St. Paul-Trois-Chateaux, 1934.
LEWIS, E., 'Organic Tendencies in Medieval Political Thought', in *American Political Science Review*, vol. xxxii, 1938.
LEWIS, J. D., *The Genossenschaftstheorie of Otto von Gierke*, Wisconsin Studies, 1936.
LISZT, F., *Lehrbuch des deutschen Strafrechts*, 26th ed. by E. Schmidt, Berlin, 1932.

MCILWAIN, C. H., *The Growth of Political Thought in the West from the Greeks to the End of the Middle Ages*, London, 1932.
MAITLAND, F. W., *English Law and the Renaissance*, Cambridge, 1901.
——, *Collected Papers*, vol. iii, Cambridge, 1911.
——, *Selected Essays*, ed. by H. D. Hazeltine, G. Lapsley, P. Winfield, Cambridge, 1936.
See also Gierke.
MARITAIN, J., 'St. Augustine and St. Thomas Aquinas', in *A Monument to St. Augustine*, London, 1930.
MEYER, G., *Das Recht der Expropriation*, Leipzig, 1868.
MEYER, M. E., *Strafrecht*, 2nd ed., Heidelberg, 1923.
MEYNIAL, E., 'Roman Law', in *The Legacy of the Middle Ages*, Oxford, 1927.
MEZGER, E., *Strafrecht*, 2nd ed., Munich, 1932.
MOELLER, E., *Julius Clarus, der Kriminalist des 16. Jahrhunderts*, Breslau, 1911.
MONTFAUCON, B., *Diarium Italicum*, Paris, 1702.
MONTI, G., *Cino da Pistoja*, Pistoja, 1924.
MURATORI, L. A., *Annali d'Italia*, vol. viii, Milan, 1744.
NYS, E., *Origines du Droit International*, Brussels and Paris, 1894.
PANZIROLI, G., *De Claris Legum Interpretibus Libri Quatuor*, Leipzig, 1721.
POOLE, R. L., *Illustrations of the History of Medieval Thought and Learning*, London, 1932.
POUND, R., *Interpretations of Legal History*, Cambridge, 1923.
——, *Introduction to the Philosophy of Law*, Cambridge, 1937.
——, 'The Church in Legal History' in *Jubilee Lectures*, Law School, Catholic University of America, 1939.
——, 'The Revival of Natural Law', in *Notre Dame Lawyer*, 1942.
POWICKE, F. M., 'The Christian Life', in *The Legacy of the Middle Ages*, Oxford, 1927.
——, *Christian Life in the Middle Ages*, Oxford, 1935.
——, 'Reflections on the Medieval State', in *Transactions of the Royal Historical Society*, 4th series, vol. xix, 1936.
PREVITÉ-ORTON, C. W., *History of Europe 1198–1378*, London, 1937.
RADBRUCH, O., *Rechtsphilosophie*, 2nd ed., Leipzig, 1932.
RASHDALL, H., *The Universities of Europe in the Middle Ages*, ed. F. M. Powicke and A. B. Emden, 3 vols., Oxford, 1936.
READE, H. V., 'Philosophy in the Middle Ages', in *Cambridge Medieval History*, vol. v.
REEVES, J. B., 'St. Augustine and Humanism', in *A Monument to St. Augustine*, London, 1930.
RICHARDSON, H. G., 'Tancred, Raymond, and Bracton', *English Historical Review*, vol. lix, 1944.
RIVIÈRE, J., *Le problème de l'église et de l'état au temps de Philippe le Bel*, Louvain, 1926.
ROSS, W. D., *Aristotle*, 3rd ed., London, 1937.
SANDYS, J. E., *History of Classical Scholarship*, 3rd ed., Cambridge, 1927.
SAVIGNY, F., *Geschichte des roemischen Rechts im Mittelalter*, 7 vols., Heidelberg, 1850.
SCHIPPA, M., 'Italy and Sicily under Frederick II', in *Cambridge Medieval History*, vol. vi.

SCHOLZ, R., *Die Publizistik zur Zeit Philipps des Schoenen und Bonifaz' VIII*, Stuttgart, 1903.
SCHULZ, F., ' Bracton on Kingship ', in *E.H.R.*, vol. lx.
SCOTT, W., *Hermetica*, vol. i, Oxford, 1924.
SMALLEY, B., *The Study of the Bible in the Middle Ages*, Oxford, 1940.
SOHM, R., *Institutionen des roemischen Rechts*, 17th ed. by R. Mitteis and L. Wenger, Leipzig, 1930.
TOURTOULON, P., *Philosophy in the Development of Law*, New York, 1922.
TREVELYAN, G. M., *English Social History*, London, 1944.
ULLMANN, W., ' Der Versuch nach der italienischen Lehre des Mittelalters ' in *Revue d'Histoire du Droit*, vol. xvii, 1939.
——, ' Bartolus on Customary Law ', in *Juridical Review*, vol. lii, 1940.
——, ' Baldus's Conception of Law ', in *Law Quarterly Review*, vol. lviii, 1942.
——, ' The Influence of John of Salisbury on Medieval Italian Jurists ', in *English Historical Review*, vol. lix, 1944.
——, ' The Medieval Theory of Legal and Illegal Organizations ', in *Law Quarterly Review*, vol. lx, 1944.
——, ' Reflections on Medieval Torture ', in *Juridical Review*, vol. liv, 1944.
——, ' A Medieval Philosophy of Law ', in *Catholic Historical Review*, vol. xxxi, 1945.
——, ' A Medieval Document on Papal Theories of Government ', in *English Historical Review*, vol. lxi, 1945.
VINOGRADOFF, P., *Historical Jurisprudence*, Oxford, 1923.
——, ' Reason and Conscience in Sixteenth-Century Jurisprudence ', in *Collected Papers*, vol. ii, Oxford, 1923.
——, *Roman Law in Medieval Europe*, 2nd ed. by F. de Zulueta, Oxford, 1929.
WADDELL, H., ' John of Salisbury ', in *Essays and Studies of the English Association*, vol. xiii, Oxford, 1928.
WEBB, C. J. J., *John of Salisbury*, London, 1932.
WENLEY, R. M., *Stoicism*, London, 1922.
WHITTACKER, T., *Macrobius*, London, 1923.
WRONOWSKI, M. M., *Luca da Penne e sua opera*, Pisa, 1925.
WOOLF, C. N. S., *Bartolus of Sassoferrato*, Cambridge, 1913.
DE ZULUETA, F., *The Liber Pauperum of Vacarius*, London, 1927.
——, ' The Science of Law ', in *The Legacy of Rome*, Oxford, 1936.
——, ' Cino da Pistoja ', in *Encyclopedia of the Social Sciences*, vol. iii, 1930.
——, *Don Antonio Agustin*, David Murray Lecture, Glasgow, 1939.

INDEX

A

ABROGATION of law, see Law.
Absolutism, xxiv, xxxiv, 51 n. 1, 57, 64 n. 2, 95 n. 1
Accessories, 157–8
Accursiana, xv, xxxvii, see also *Glossa ordinaria*.
Accursius, xiv, xv, xxxvii, 34
Aegidius Romanus (Colonna), xxi, xxv, xxvi, xxvii, 32, 127 n. 3, 171 n. 3
Aeneas Sylvius (Pius II), 167 n. 1, 183 n. 2
Aggravating circumstances, 152–3
Alanus, 32
Albericus de Rosciate, xvi, xxiii, 53 n. 3, 63 n. 4, 68 n. 3, 145, 148 n. 1, 155 n. 2, 175 n. 2, 177, 185 n. 3, 198 n. 1
Alciatus, xxiii, xxxvi, 13 n. 7, 104 n. 3
Allen, J. W., 50 n. 4, 54 n. 2, 64 n. 2, 201 n. 1 and 2
Alvarus Pelagius, xxxiv
Ambrose, St., 30, 85 n. 5, 86, 127 n. 3, 130 n. 1, 172
Andreae, Joannes, 34, 68, 178 n. 1
Andreas de Barulo, 34
Andreas de Isernia, 10, 34, 73 n. 2, 79, 93 n. 2, 122 n. 3 and 4, 137 n. 1, 172 n. 2
Andronicus, 29, 38 n. 1
Angelus de Ubaldis, 39 n. 6, 42 n. 3, 63 n. 4, 119 n. 2, 148 n. 4, 156 n. 1
Animals, punishment, 149
Anselm, St., 32
Appeal, 108
'Archidiaconus', see Guido de Baysio.
Aristotle, xviii, xxi, xxv, xxvii, xxix, 2, 3, 4, 28, 29, 31, 36, 38 n. 1, 39, 41, 81 n. 4, 166, 186 n. 2
Attempt, criminal, 144.
Aufrerius, S., 13
Augustine, St., xviii, xxi, xxii, xxx, xxvii, xxix, 3, 16 n. 7, 28 n. 8, 30, 37, 46 n. 3, 51, 75 n. 6, 85, 86, 108 n. 1, 130 n. 1, 147 n. 6, 164, 194 n. 1
Azo, xv, xvi, xxix, 34, 37 n. 2, 38 n. 2, 40, 43 n. 3, 63 n. 2, 84 n. 4, 122 n. 2

B

Bailiffs, 143, 189
Baldus, xiii, xiv, xvi, xxii, xxiv, xxix, xxxvii, 12, 32 n. 7, 39 n. 6, 40, 42 n. 3, 43 n. 3, 73 n. 1, 104 n. 3, 145 n. 6, 148 n. 1, 155 n. 2, 171 n. 7, 180 n. 1, 183, 186 n. 7; abrogation of civil by canon law?, 96 n. 5; absolutism, 51 n. 1, 95 n. 1, 103; coronation of kings, 178 n. 2; exercise of rights, 156; inalienable sovereignty, 182; interpretation, 119 n. 2, 120 n. 5, 121 n. 2; natural law, 48 n. 2; origin of Empire, 164 n. 5; resistance to officials, 112 n. 2; transfer of property, 103
Baluzius, S., 9 n. 10, 174 n. 2
'Bannitus', 145
Barker, E., 30 n. 13, 48 n. 3, 163 n. 1, 168 n. 6
Bartholomaeus de Capua, xxxi, 8 n. 2, 10, 34, 73 n. 2, 93 n. 2, 173, 175 n. 2
'Bartolists', xvii, xxiii, xxxv, xxxvi
Bartolus, xiii, xiv, xvi, xxi, xxiv, xxxii, xxxvii, 12, 13, 17 n. 3, 49, 50 n. 6, 83 n. 6, 126 n. 4, 132 n. 6 and 7, 155, 163, 183, 189 n. 3, 195 n. 3, 196 n. 7; canon and civil law, 90–1, 96 n. 5, 132 n. 4; coronation of kings, 176, 179; delictal responsibility of corporations, 158; jurisdiction of secular and ecclesiastical judge, 89; papal superiority over Emperor, xxxi, 172; punishment, 148; reprisals, 197; rulership, 51 n. 5, 95 n. 1, 102 n. 4; swords, theory, 172–3; territorial sovereignty, xxiv, 90–1, 181; transfer of property, 103, 181; war and peace, xxxvi
—— and Lucas, 9, 23–4, 191; opposed by Lucas, xxxiii, 63, 78 n. 5, 79, 90, 127 n. 3, 145, 155, 172, 181, 197
Bassianus, xv, 127 n. 3
Beccaria, 143, 160
Benedict XII, 177
Benvenuto da Imola, 32 n. 1
Bernard, St., 32
Biblioteca Angelica, 10
Blasius de Murcone, 8, 9 n. 9, 11
Blesensis, Petrus, 32
Bodin, J., xvii, xxiii, xxiv, xxxiv, xxxvi, 11, 14, 50, 64 n. 2, 95 n. 1, 183
Body politic, theory, 39, 164–70, see also Government, Ruler.
Boer, N., 13
Boethius, 28
Bologna, law faculty, xv, 5, 96 n. 5, 130
Boniface VIII, xxi, xxx, 148 n. 2, 172 n. 5
Bracton, 5 n. 1, 46 n. 7, 50 n. 4, 52 n. 1, 92 n. 3, 152 n. 2, 188 n. 7
Buckland, W. W., 15 n. 2, 96 n. 1
Bulaeus, 9 n. 10, 175 n. 2
Bulgarus, xv. xvi, xxxiii, 187 n. 2
Butrigarius, Jacobus, 27 n. 1, 48, 91, 103, 117 n. 5, 118

C

Caccialupus, Joannes, 7 n. 4, 9. n. 10

Caillemer, E., xvii
Calasso, F., xiii, 7 n. 3, 8 n. 6, 9 n. 7, 10 n. 1 and 6
Calisse, C., xxxv, 20 n. 4
Canonists, xvii, xxi, xxv, 15, 27 n. 1, 96, 137, 142, 148, 172
Canon law, xvi, xvii, xxi, xxxvii, 4, 15, 21 n. 3, 27, 34, 37 n. 5, 69 n. 6, 71, 76, 132 n. 4, 137 n. 7, 138 n. 3, 144 n. 9, 145 n. 1, 146 n. 6, 149 n. 5, 155 n. 3, 156 n. 5, 170 n. 6, 171, 172, 176 n. 4, 187, 191 n. 3; abrogation of, by civil law, 96–9; application, 77–84; conflict with civil law, xxxii, 4, 77, 89–91.
Capilistius, Bartholomaeus, 7 n. 2
Carlyle, A. J., 35 n. 1, 37 n. 3, 40 n. 4, 42 n. 4, 43 n. 6, 47 n. 1, 49 n. 1, 50 n. 6, 89 n. 4, 93 n. 2, 104 n. 3, 170 n. 7, 171 n. 3, 177 n. 1, 183 n. 1 and 3, 188 n. 5, 201
Cassiodorus, 30
Castrensis, Paulus, xiii, 12, 104 n. 3, 130, 185 n. 3, 194 n. 1 and 2
Casus omissus, 43, 118–119
Charity, 41–2
Charles I (Anjou), 11 n. 2
Charles II, 7 n. 8, 11 n. 2, 88 n. 1, 189 n. 5
Chenon, E., xvii
Chiapelli, L., 34 n. 8
Children, legitimation, xxxii, 88, 91, 92; paternity, doubtful, 88–9, 97; punishment, 151, 155; witnesses, 123–4
Chrimes, S. B., 31 n. 5
Christian cosmology, xxi, xxv; role in legal theory, 1, 2–3, 19, 26, 31, 36
Chrysostom, St., 30, 36.
Church, 76, see Canon law, Ecclesiastical, and Judge; liberty, xxxii, 55, 84, 89, 185 n. 2, 193; property, 83–7; territory, 91
—— and State, xxi, xxix, 84–7, 166–7, 171, 193 n. 2
Cicero, xxv, xxvii, xxix, 29, 31, 36, 38 n. 1, 43 n. 6, 46 n. 3, 168 n. 5
Civic duties, 84–7, 166–7, 171, 193 n. 3
Civil law, xxi, xxxi, see Law and Roman law; abrogation of, by canon law?, 96–9; application, 77–84, 87–92; conflicting civil laws, 100; conflict with divine law, 103; with canon law, xxxii, 77–84, 89–91
Civitas, 100, 193, 197
Civitas Dei, 30, 39 n. 5, 46 n. 3, 108 n. 1, see also Augustine, St.
Citation, 131–2
Clarus, Julius, 13, 158 n. 6
Clerics, see Ecclesiastical.
Coke, 20 n. 4
' Concession theory ', see Corporation.
Confessions, criminal, 12, 133, 160
Conflict of laws, see Canon law, Civil law, Customary law.
Corneus, Philippus, 178 n. 1
Coronation of kings, xxxii, 175–80
Corporation, theory, xvii–xviii; delictal responsibility, 158
Corpus juris civilis, xii, 1, 2, 15, see also Roman law.
Coulton, G. G., 5 n. 1, 32 n. 5, 166 n. 3
Crime, theory, xxxvi, 40, 60, ch. vii; committed by soldiers, 152, 195
Crimen laesae majestatis, 182, 191, 192
Criminal, the, 47, 142, 144, 146–7, 149, 159; accessories, 157–8; persistent and habitual, 153; proceedings, 108, 123, 125, 130, 133, 138, 158–62
Crusades, 92
Cujas, xxiii, xxv, 20 n. 4
Customary law, xxxiii, ch. iv, *passim*.
Customs, xxii, 4, 62, 70, 81 n. 3
Cynus, xiii, xxiii, xxix, xxxii, xxxvii, 12, 24 n. 5, 34, 49, 111 n. 6, 132 n. 6, 134 n. 3, 148 n. 1, 182; abrogation of civil by canon law?, 96 n. 5; conscience of the judge, 127; coronation of kings, 177, 179; customary law, 63 n. 4, 69 n. 7; dualism of government, 171 n. 7, 174–5; interpretation, 119, 120 n. 5; justice and law, 40, 55 n. 6; law and ethics, 4; natural law, 48 n. 2, 81 n. 7; resistance to officials, 112; Roman curia, 138 n. 1; rulership, 53 n. 3, 102, 179; superior order, 150–1; territorial sovereignty, 91 n. 6; transfer of property, 102
—— and canonists, 132 n. 4
Cyprian, St., 30

D

Dahm, F., 142 n. 1, 145 n. 4
Dante, xv, xxx, 29 n. 18, 32 n. 2, 175 n. 2
Dawson, C., 2 n. 1, 31 n. 4, 39 n. 5, 46 n. 3
Debts, imprisonment for, 190–1
Decius, Philippus, 42 n. 3
Defence, 47, 132 n. 7, 192–3
Defensor Pacis, see Marsiglio.
Democracy, see People.
Demosthenes, 17 n. 3
d'Entréves, A. P., 52 n. 7, 54 n. 6, 61 n. 4, 94 n. 5, 163 n. 2, 188 n. 5
De Planctu Ecclesiae, xxxiv
De republica, xxxv, 14, see Bodin.
Desertion, 152
De Wulf, 2 n. 1, 165 n. 3, 169 n. 1, 184 n. 2
Dialectical method, xvi, xxvi, 1, 20, 21
Diplovatacius, 7
Diomedes Mariconda, 11 n. 5
Divine law, xix, xxvii, xxxiii, xxxv, 54, 57; conflict with civil law, 103; difference from human law, 48; essence, xxviii, 48; identified with natural law, xxviii, 46, 54, 58
Doneau, xxiii

Droit coutumier, xxiii
Drunkenness, 151
Duel, 103
Duff, P. W., 169 n. 3
Dulcetus, Augustinus, 13
Du Moulin, xxiii, xxiv
Dunning, A. W., xviii, xix, xxi, xxviii, xxxiv, 50 n. 2, 183 n. 3, 188 n. 4
Dynus, 24 n. 3, 40, 111, 117 n. 4, 182

E

Ecclesiastical, judge, 77–85, 133; persons, 69, 77, 84–7, 88; property, see Church.
Edward III, 154 n. 5.
Emperor, see Ruler.
Engelbert, abbot, 196 n. 6
Engelmann, W., 71 n. 1, 107 n. 9, 142 n. 1
Epieikeia, 41
Equality, before the law, 43, 133
Equity, xxviii, xxxiii, 41–3, 122, 169, 185
Esmein, A., xvii, xxiii, 158 n. 7
Ethics, 3, 28, 81 n. 4
Ethics and law, 3–4, 35, 36, 38, 45, 52, 54–5, 58–61
Euthanasia, 156
Evidence, court, 128, 130, 133; evaluation, 112, 122–30, 133
Exceptiones Legum Romanarum, 84 n. 4
Expropriation, 185, 187
Extenuating circumstances, 150–1

F

Fictions, 118
'Fiction theory', xvii, 158, see Corporation.
Figgis, J. N., 22 n. 6, 91 n. 5, 163 n. 1, 168 n. 6, 177 n. 2, 183 n. 3, 189 n. 3
Fines, 144
Fiscal policy, 183
Fitting, H., 40 n. 4
Fortescue, xx
Fragmentum Pragense, 42 n. 4
Frankish law, xxxi, 74
Frederick I, xxxiii, 187 n. 2
Frederick II, 6, 7, 72, 76, 77, 122 n. 3, 137 n. 1
French jurists, xvi, xvii, 90, see also Petrus de Bellapertica and Jacobus de Ravanis.
Fulgosius, Raphael, 119

G

Gandinus, Albertus, 144 n. 4, 155 n. 2
Gelasian principle, xxx, see also Ruler, Church and State.
Gentilis, Albericus, xxiii, xxiv, xxxvi, 101
Gerardus de Senis, 33
Germanic law, xvi, xix, xxii, xxxvii
Gierke, O., xiii, xx, xxx, xxxiii, 48 n. 3, 103 n. 4, 158 n. 6, 168 n. 6, 169 n. 3, 186 n. 7, 192, 201–2
Girard, P., 10 n. 2 and 6
Giustiniani, L., 8 n. 3, 9 n. 8, 10 n. 5, 11 n. 5, 34 n. 5
Glossa ordinaria, xv, xxxvii, 96 n. 5, 102, 117 n. 4, 121 n. 2
Glossators, xiv, xxv, 34, 37 n. 5, 66, 89 n. 4, 127 n. 3; difference from Post-Glossators, xvi, xvii, xxi, 1–2, 4, 35, 37 n. 2, 40, 42 n. 4, 184 n. 3
Golden Bull, 177 n. 4
Gomez, Antonio, 14
Government, principles, 185–6, see also Ruler, Monarchy; dualistic character of, xxix, xxxii, 80, 96, 99, 171
Gratian, xix, xxvii, xxviii n. 2, 86, 98 n. 2
Greenidge, A. H., 96 n. 1
Gregory, St., 31
Gregory XI, 10 n. 6
Grotius, xxviii, xxxvi
Guido de Baysio, 34, 100, 134 n. 3
Guillelmus de Cuneo, 123
Guillelmus de Pastrengo, 31 n. 5

H

Hadrian, 144
Hannibal, 75 n. 6
Haskins, C. H., 2 n. 1, 6 n. 1
Hazeltine, H. D., xvii, xxiii, 20 n. 4, 31 n. 5, 71 n. 1
Hearsay evidence, 123
Hefele, K. J., 9 n. 10
Hegesippus, 33
Henricus Acconzaiocus de Ravello, 9
Henricus de Cremona, 171 n. 3
Henry VIII, 154 n. 7
Hermes Trismegistus, 33
Herodotus, 33
Hinschius, P., 148 n. 2
Hippocrates, 33
Hobbes, xxxiv, 64 n. 2
Hohenstaufen, xxxiv
Holdsworth, W., xxiii, xxiv, 5 n. 1, 20 n. 4, 22 n. 6, 45 n. 6, 46 n. 7, 53 n. 3, 64 n. 2, 82 n. 3, 92 n. 2, 104 n. 1, 123 n. 6, 135 n. 5, 152 n. 2, 154 n. 5 and 7, 158 n. 6, 164 n. 1, 189 n. 4, 190 n. 2, 193 n. 1
Horace, 33
Hostiensis (Henricus de Segusia), 34, 66, 78 n. 5, 96 n. 5, 97, 100, 123
Hotman, F., 91 n. 5
Hugo, 34
Humanism, legal, xiv, xx, xxiv, xxxvi, 20 n. 4
Hundred Years War, 5 n. 1

I

Ignorance of law, 156–7

Imperium, see Ruler, State, Swords, Temporal.
Imprisonment, 189–91
Infamy, 96
Innocent I, 86
Innocent III, 85 n. 5, 176
Innocent IV, 27 n. 3, 34, 55 n. 6, 100, 123, 134 n. 3, 164 n. 5
International law, xxxvi, 193
Interpretation, 21, 24, 26, 43, 58, 107, 112–22; aim, 112, 115; analogical, 117–18; *casus omissus*, 43, 118–19; grammatical, 15; literal, 113; philological, 15; principles, 113–15; *ratio legis*, 112, 117–18, 119; types, 120–2;
—— and legislation, 112, 114, 115, 116, 118
Irnerius, xv, 37 n. 2, 40 n. 4, 47 n. 1, 49 n. 1
Isidore, St., 31

J

Jacob, E. F., 165 n. 3, 186 n. 2
Jacobus de Arena, 40, 132 n. 6, 177, 179
Jacobus de Belvisio, 24 n. 6, 148
Jacobus de Ravanis, xvi, xx, xxiv, xxxii, 90, 127 n. 3, 177 n. 1
Jason de Mayno, 104 n. 3
Jerome, St., 30, 75 n. 6, 109 n. 4, 115 n. 1, 167 n. 2
Jews, 93, 130, 176, 188 n. 1
Joannes de Laudo, 9 n. 4, 34
Joannes de Lignano, 34, 173
Joannes Teutonicus, 178 n. 2
Joecher, C., 8 n. 4
John VIII, 78 n. 2, 137
John XXII, 174 n. 2, 177
John of Jandun, xxx
John of Paris, 175 n. 2
John of Salisbury, xxv, xxvii, xxxii, 16, 17 n. 3, 18 n. 2, 21 n. 1, 31, 37 n. 5, 43 n. 6, 49 n. 3, 54 n. 1 and 5, 57 n. 3, 85 n. 1, 94, 115 n. 3, 140 n. 7, 165, 169, 170, 183 n. 5, 186 n. 2, 188, 196 n. 7
Jones, J. W., 20 n. 4, 58 n. 5, 183 n. 3
'Judex', 139–41
Judge, function, xxxi, 43, 65, 100, 105, 106–11, 112, 131–4; in criminal causes, 108, 123, 125, 156, 158–9, 161; conscience, 126–30; ecclesiastical and secular, xxxii, 4, 71, 77, 79, 82, 83, 88, 89, 90, 134, 136–8; independence of secular, 134, 136–8, 171; discretionary powers, 106, 108–9; impartiality, 108, 132; interpreter, 120–1, 135–6; objection to, 132; resistance to, 110, 111; miscarriage, 109, 111, 134–6
—— and law, 106, 108; and legislator, 105–6, 143
Judge-made law, 63 n. 5, cf. 120 n. 5
Judgements, 38, 105, 133–4, 139
Jurisdiction, secular and ecclesiastical, xxxi, 77, 82, 87–92, 134, 136–9, 171
Jus, concept, 43–4
Jus commune, 72, see also Roman law.
Jus gentium, 38 n. 2, 46, 47, 67
Jus naturale, see Natural law.
Justa causa principis, 53–4, 100–3, 185, 188
Justice, idea, xxxii, 2, 4, 35–41; source of law, xxviii, 4, 35, 37–9; basis of judgements, 105, 112; ethical virtue, 35–6, 76; implications, 38–9; miscarriage, 109, 134–6; natural, 42, 46, 47, 54, 113; principle of government, xxviii, 39, 167, 169, 188
—— and equity, 41–2.
Justinian, xiii, xix, xxxvi, 1, 2, 4, 71, 76, 120 n. 5, 178 n. 1; see Roman law.

K

Kaltenborn, H., xxviii
Kantorowicz, H., 15 n. 2, 27 n. 1, 37 n. 2, 40 n. 4, 42 n. 4, 142 n. 1, 144 n. 4, 155 n. 2
King, see Ruler.

L

Lactantius, 30, 36, 47 n. 7
Law, concept, 44; idea, 4, 17, 35, 38, 44, 66, 105; source, xxxiii, 16, 35, 39, 42–3, 48, 105; realized justice, 35, 39, 76, 105; nature, 17, 44–6, 54–7; creation, 48–55; framing, 57–8; abrogation, 66–8, 95–104; administration, 105–41; authority and binding force, 26, 38, 52, 54–5; invalid, 54–5, 77, 82; a moral and social force, 4, 16–17, 27, 45, 54, 55, 106, 108, 170, 188; customary, divine, natural, law, see under respective entries; human (positive), 4, 47, 58, 71, 78, 106, creation, xxxii, 48–58, conform with natural and divine law, xxviii, 54, 56, difference from divine, 48, *non obstante* clause, 104; feudal, 4, 27; judge made, 63 n. 5, cf. 120 n. 5; Lombard, xxvii, xxxi, 71–5, 103; penal, 57, 143; public and private, 58
—— and ethics, 3–4, 35, 38, 45, 163–4; and State, xix, 105; and morals, 61
Legal philosophy, 2, 4, 5, 15, 24, 62, see Philosophy and law.
Legal science, 3, 15–22, 24, 26; interpretative function, 112, 117, 121
Legislator, xxxii, xxxv, 48–58, 59, 60, 80–2, see also Ruler; as interpreter, 120; and interpreter, 112, 113, 115, 116, 118; and judge, 105–6
Legitimation, xxxii, 88, 91, 92
Lewis, E., 102 n. 2, 192 n. 8
Lex, concept, 43–4
Lex aeterna, xix

Lex naturalis, xix, see Natural law.
Lex Regia, 48–9, 179
Liberty, civil, xxxiii, 47, 100, 183–4, 189–92; of the Church, xxxii, 55, 84, 89, 185 n. 2, 193
Liszt, F., 142 n. 3, 159 n. 5
Livy, 33, 75 n. 6
Lombard law, xxvii, xxxi, 71–5, 103
Louis of Bavaria, 177
Lucas, life and studies, 7–9; glosses, 8, 11; commentaries, xxv, 10, value, 13, editions, 14; characterization, 15–16; influence and reputation, 11–15; independence of thought, xxvi, 21–4; knowledge of Greek?, 27; on gloss and authority, 21–4, 121; on juristic method, xxvi, 15, 20, 24, 26; on legal science, and teaching of law, 15–22, 24–6, 117; and contemporary scholarship, 23–4, 26, 137, 142, 145, 148, 164; and Bartolus, 9, 23–4, 191; against Bartolus, xxxiii, 63, 78 n. 5, 79, 91, 172, 197
Lunatics, 151
Lupold, Bishop of Bamberg, 175 n. 2

M

Macrobius, 29, 38 n. 1
Magna Carta, xxxiii
Maitland, F. W., xviii, xxii, xxiii, 48 n. 4, 82 n. 3, 92 n. 3, 103 n. 4, 123 n. 6, 168 n. 6, 186 n. 7, 201 n. 4
Malumbra, Richardus, 173–4
Maritain, J., 28 n. 8
Marsiglio of Padua, xxx, 61 n. 4, 175 n. 2
Martianus, 17 n. 3
Martinus, xv, xvi, xxxiii, 34, 127 n. 3, 132 n. 6, 187 n. 2
Martinus Sullimanus, 48
Matrimony, xxxii, 48 n. 2, 67, 79–82, 88, 96–9
McIlwain, C. H., xix, xxix, xxxiv, 14 n. 5, 20 n. 4, 102 n. 1, 103 n. 4, 165 n. 3, 171 n. 3, 177 n. 4, 186 n. 2, 189 n. 2
Medical and legal science, compared, 17–18
Menochius, Jacobus, 13
Merton, parliament, 92
Meyer, G., 103 n. 4
Meynial, E., 20 n. 4
Mezger, E., 146 n. 1
Miscarriage of justice, 109, 111, 134–6
Mistake in law, 156–7
Moeller, E., 14 n. 1
Monarchy, xxxii, 169–70
Monasteries, 166 n. 4
Montaigne, J., 14
Monti, G., 34 n. 8
Moroni, Nicolai, 12
Murder, 145

N

Naples, law school, xxv, 5–6, 7, 9, 11
Natural law, xix, xxvii, xxxii, xxxv, 46, 47, 100, 131; identified with divine law, xxviii, 46, 53, 58
Natural reason, xxviii, xxxiii, 16, 17, 41–2, 113
Natural rights, 47, 132
Necessity, 95, 153–4
Neoplatonism, 3, 29
Nicholas I, 171
Nicholas V (anti-pope), 174 n. 2
Non obstante clause, xxxv, 104
Nys, E., 194 n. 2 and 5

O

Odofredus, 24 n. 3, 40, 47 n. 1, 49 n. 2, 73 n. 1, 96 n. 5, 148 n. 4.
Officials, 70, 192; neglect of duty by, 143, 158; resistance to, 47, 55, 110, 111–12, 192
Oldradus de Ponte, 34, 158, 174, 178 n. 1, 188 n. 1
Organic theory of State, 165–6
Orleans, xvi
Orosius, 30, 51, 75, 147 n. 6
Outlawry, 145
Ovid, 33

P

Panziroli, G., 7
Papias, 15, 37 n. 2
Parents, rights to punish, 60, 155
Paris de Puteo, 9 n. 5, 11, 12, 31 n. 5, 188 n. 6
Paternity, doubtful, 88–9, 97
Peace, 195, 196–7
Pelagius, Pope, 78 n. 2
Penal laws, 57, 143
Penology, see Crime.
People, will of, xxxii, 48–50, 52, 63, 64, 65, 169
Perroy, E., 9 n. 10
Persona ficta, see Corporation.
Perusinus, Paulus, 10, 13
Petrarch, 6, 33
Petrus de Bellapertica, xiv, xvi, xx, xxiv, 24 n. 5, 49, 111, 134 n. 3, 151, 177 n. 1
Petrus Piccolus de Monteforte, 34
Philosophy and law, xxi, xxii, 2, 16, 26, 41
Placentinus, xvi, xxix, 34, 37 n. 2, 40, 43 n. 3, 49 n. 1, 127 n. 3
Plato, xxvii, 3, 28
Platonism, 31
Plautus, 33
Plenitudo potestatis, xxxiv, 10, 103, 171, 176, see also Ruler.
Pliny, 33
Plotinus, 28 n. 8
Plutarch, 29, 165 n. 2

Police, 143
Policraticus, see John of Salisbury.
Pollock, F., xxviii, xxx, xxxiv, 82 n. 3, 92 n. 3, 123 n. 6
Poole, R. L., 18 n. 2, 32 n. 3, 54 n. 3, 94 n. 1, 170 n. 7, 186 n. 2, 188 n. 4
Pope, 88, 101, see Church, Ecclesiastical.
—— and Ruler, 98, 99, 170–80
Positive law, xix, 4, 47, see Law, human.
Post-Glossators, xiii, xv, xvi, xx, xxxvi, 65, 67, 120, 148, 158 n. 7; achievements, xvii, 1–2, 50 n. 6, 142; influence, xxi, xxiii, xxiv, xxxvi; downfall, 12; political views, xxii, xxxv, xxxvii, 22 n. 6, 153; charges against, xxvi, 20, 21; writings similar to Year Books, 20 n. 4; and Glossators, xvi, xxi, 1–2, 4, 35, 37 n. 2, 40, 42 n. 4; and texts, 2, 4, 15, 35, 60 n. 2, 63 n. 2, 71, 184 n. 3
Pound, R., xix, xxviii, xxxvi, 20 n. 4
Powicke, F. M., 6 n. 1, 22 n. 6, 28 n. 8, 54 n. 6, 183 n. 4
'Praeses', 139
Precedents, legislative, 56; judicial, 120 n. 5.
Presumptions, 118, 123–4, 159
Previté-Orton, C. W., 85 n. 5, 166 n. 4, 196 n. 7, 201 n. 2
Princeps legibus solutus, xxxiii, 93–4, see Ruler.
Privileges, grant and revocation, 55, 179, 185–6
Proceedings, principles, 130–41; criminal, 108, 123, 125, 130, 133, 158–62; defence in, 132.
Propensities, criminal, 159
Property, distribution, 47; confiscation, 185; rights, 60; transfer, 100–3, 179; of the Church, 83–4
Provocation, 150
Public utility, xxxii, 84, 87, 133, 145, 161, 181, 185, 187, 192; promotion by Ruler, 39, 55, 185–6
Punishment, idea of, xxxvi, ch. vii *passim*

Q

Quaestio de Potestate Papae, 175 n. 2
Quaestiones de juris subtilitatibus, 40 n. 4
Quintilian, 30

R

Rashdall, H., 6 n. 1, 20 n. 4, 22 n. 6
Ratio legis, 112, 117–18, 119
Raymundus de Pennaforte, 92 n. 3
Raynaldus, Odoricus, 34 n. 2
Raynerius de Forlivio, 10, 24 n. 4
Reason, substance of law, 45, 46, 54–5, 65–6, 113; natural, xxviii, xxxiii, 16, 17, 41–2, 113
Rebuffus, Petrus, 14, 31 n. 5
Records in Court, 130–1
Renaissance, legal, xix, 2
Reprisals, 197–8
Resistance to officials, 47, 55, 110, 111–12, 192
Responsibility, criminal, 149–52, 153; of corporations, 158; individual and collective, 52–3
Rex Pacificus, 166 n. 3, 175 n. 2
Richardson, H. G., 92 n. 3
Right, idea of, 35, 38; the, 44, 45, 61; exercise of, 58–61, 105, 145, 155–6
Rights, natural, 47–8, 132
Robert, king of Naples, 7, 8, 10, 72, 98 n. 1
Rogerius, 40 n. 4, 49 n. 1
Rolandus a Valla, 10 n. 6, 13
Roman law, xv, xx, 1, 2, 15, 44, 48, 63, 71, 112, 120 n. 5, 132, 142, 145, 148, 163; the universal law, xxxi, 75–6, 77, 78, 80, 92; application, 77–82, 87–92; 'reception', xvii, xxiv
Romanus, Ludovicus, 119, 185 n. 3
Rome, 75, 138 n. 1, 196 n. 7
Ruler, universal overlord, xxxi, 76, 93, 99, 100, 163, 187; function, xxxii, xxxiv, 51, 55, 65, 94, 101, 165, 169–72, 176, 184–6, 187, 192; *legibus solutus*, xxxiii, 93–4; subject to higher laws, xxxii, 57, 132; derives his power from God, xxxvi, 50; is God's vice-gerent, xxxii, xxxv, 50, 54, 169, 176, 180; independent of Pope, xxx, 170–2; and responsible to God alone, xxxv, 51, 52–3, 101; superior to Pope in temporal matters, 96, 99, 171; as legislator, xxxii, 49–55, 57, 99, 100, 104, 179; limitations, 54–7, 132; *lex animata*, 53; personification of justice, 39; role in customary law, 63–5; will of, 53, 101, 104, 112; *justa causa*, 53–4, 100–3, 185, 187; sovereignty, 80, 88, 90, 91, 92, 102, 179; as judge, xxxiv, xxxv; transfer of property by, 100–1, 179, 180–2; expropriation by, 185, 187; privileges, grant and revocation, 55, 179, 185; fiscal policy, 183; taxation, 85, 180, 186–7; coronation, 175–80

S

Salicetus, Bartholomaeus, xiii, xxiii, 12, 94 n. 5, 173, 178 n. 1 and 2, 197
Sallust, 33
Sandys, J., 15 n. 2, 29 n. 18
Saracens, 92
Savigny, F., xiii, xvii, 7 n. 3, 8 n. 3, 20 n. 4
Scholastic method, xvi, xx, xxiv, 20
Schoolmen, xviii, 31
Schuldprinzip, 146

Schulz, F., 37 n. 5, 50 n. 4, 52 n. 1, 188 n. 7
Self-defence, 38 n. 2, 110, 154
Seneca, 29, 166 n. 2
Servin, 177 n. 2
Sicily (Naples), kingdom, xxv, xxvii, 72, 76, 78, 98 n. 1, 106, 120, 122 n. 3, 139-41, 160 n. 3, 172 n. 8, 173, 189 n. 5, 195 n. 1
Simon de Bursano, 9
Simoncelli, O., 13
Slavery, 47, 183
Social contract, 168-9
Sohm, R., 96 n. 1
Soldiers, 143, 152, 195
Solinus, 33
Sovereignty, legislative, xxxiv, 48-55, 57, 101-2; rights of, 51, 177-9; inalienable, 51, 179-83; territorial, xxiv, 90-1, 181.
Spiritual affairs, see Canon law, Church, Ecclesiastical, Judge.
State, idea of, xix, xxxiv, 39, 164-5, 166-70, 183; and law, xix, 105; and Church, xxi, xxix, 84-7; see also Ruler.
Statute and customary law, 66-8
Stoicism, 2, 31, 164, 166
Suetonius, 33
Summa Trecensis, 42 n. 4
Summum jus, summa injuria, 43, 114, 116, 117 n. 1
Superior order, 150-1
Swords, theory, xxix, 170-2

T

Taxation, 85, 180, 186-7, 189
Teaching of law, xxvi, 18
Teleology, 3, 17, 44
Temporal affairs, 77, 79, 80, 82, 84, 87, 89; see also Ruler, Civil law.
Terence, 33
Tertullian, 33
Texts, Roman, and Glossators, 1; and Post-Glossators, 2, 4, 15, 35, 60 n. 2, 63 n. 2, 71, 184 n. 3; interpretation, 113, 115-16, 119
Theology, xvi; and law, xix, 17, 20 n. 6
Thomas, St., xvi, xviii, xix, xxix, 3, 33, 37, 50 n. 6, 94 n. 5, 127, 188 n. 6
Tiraquellus, Andreas, 13, 14
Torture, 12, 126, 159-60
Toulouse, xvi, 7
Trevelyan, G. M., 5 n. 1, 166 n. 4
Trismegistus, 33
Turks, 92
Tyranny, xxxiii, 188-9

U

Ulpian, 37, 38, 48, 81 n. 7, 97
Ultramontani, 102, see also French jurists.
Unam Sanctam, xxx, 172 n. 8
Urban VI, 9 n. 10, 34 n. 2

V

Valerius Maximus, 30, 81 n. 2
Vargas, F., 14
Vinogradoff, P., xxxiii, 20 n. 4, 71 n. 1
Virgil, 33

W

Waddell, H., 32 n. 1
Wages, just, 47, 184
War, xxxvi, 87 n. 3, 131, 152, 193-8
Wenger, L., 96 n. 1
Witnesses, 122-5, 133
Woolf, C. N. S., vii, xvii, xxi, xxiii, xxxvi, 49 n. 2, 51 n. 5, 91 n. 2 and 6, 92 n. 4, 126 n. 4, 163 n. 1, 172 n. 4, 176 n. 5, 177 n. 1, 196 n. 6
Workman, H., 5 n. 1, 166 n. 3
Wronowski, M. M., vi, 7 n. 3, 10 n. 1
Wyclif, 5 n. 1, 166 n. 3

Z

Zasius, Ulrich, xxiii
Zulueta, F. de, xvi, xxiii, 20 n. 4, 71 n. 1

PRINTED IN GREAT BRITAIN BY RICHARD CLAY AND COMPANY, LTD., BUNGAY, SUFFOLK.